AF516162

Faith Movements and Social Transformation

Faith Movements and Social Transformation

Guru Charisma in Contemporary India

Samta P. Pandya

RAWAT PUBLICATIONS

Jaipur • New Delhi • Bangalore • Guwahati • Kolkata

ISBN 978-81-316-0906-4

© Author, 2017

No part of this book may be reproduced or transmitted in any form or by any means, electronic or mechanical, including photocopying, recording or by any information storage and retrieval system, without permission in writing from the publishers.

Published by
Prem Rawat for **Rawat Publications**
Satyam Apts, Sector 3, Jawahar Nagar, Jaipur 302 004 (India)
Phone: 0141 265 1748 / 7006 Fax: 0141 265 1748
E-mail: info@rawatbooks.com
Website: www.rawatbooks.com

New Delhi Office
4858/24, Ansari Road, Daryaganj, New Delhi 110 002
Phone: 011 2326 3290

Also at *Bangalore, Guwahati* and *Kolkata*

Typeset by Logiciels Info Solutions Pvt. Ltd, Chennai
Printed and bound in India

Contents

Preface vii

Acknowledgements xi

1 Introduction: Gurus, Sociality, Hegemony, and Social Transformation 1

2 Guru Agency: Combining Charisma, Teachings, and Proliferation 33

3 Faith Movements: Negotiating State, Market, and Civil Society 65

4 Faith Networks: Interplaying Social Issues, Action, and Service 93

5 Faith in Practice: Tangibility of Social Service 129

6 Faith Trappings: Shades of Hegemony and Hindu Nationalism 167

7 Transformational Actors: Private and Public Agendas 191

8 Actors in Social Transformation: Deliberating on a Model 235

References 253

Index 283

Preface

This book critically analyses a specific typology of faith movements broadly called the Hindu-Inspired Faith Movements (HIFMs) in contemporary India. HIFMs are guru-led and guru-charisma-governed. 'Hindu India' herein is presented as an embodiment of the divine, and the focus is on 'service' of the 'Hindu nation'. Historically, they provided an answer to challenges posed by colonialism by a re-invention of tradition. This book argues that HIFMs use sociality to craft citizenship, nationalism, and a modern civil society. Thus, the four pillars of HIFMs' contemporary presence are – gurus, sociality, hegemony, and social transformation.

Contemporary Indian sociopolitical and cultural fabric is neoliberal and postmodern, supporting the development of religion-oriented discourses in the public sphere. In this scenario, HIFMs realize themselves and make public assertions through sociality, *seva* governmentalities, and as actors in social transformation. This interest in sociality and social transformation is also a demonstration of HIFMs' practical mysticism. There is a commitment to 'looking out' to the wider community and testing faith through action. This impetus to engage is simultaneously politicised.

Gurus are *avatar* gurus, and the important element in their earthly mission is the setting up of institutional organizations. Gurus create a matrix of possible meanings (engaged cosmopolitanism) in their discourses which allows followers their own agency in picking up required ingredients for personal transformation. Sociality, the tangible part of which is social service, is essentially seen as a core strategy of proliferation/world affirmation across HIFMs. Sociality is orthodox, assimilative, or accommodative. The orthodox form is commune-oriented and retains sectarian/scriptural authority. The assimilative form is more expansive and inclusive in nature and demonstrates an apparent generosity towards occidental, syncretic, and secular tenets. The accommodative form takes the postmodern turn where Hindu-inspired movements aggressively use secular motifs and the language of spirituality to justify social service. This aspect is particularly prominent in the newer movements. These forms of sociality are not mutually exclusive but more complex where each HIFM expresses elements of all three (i.e. orthodox, assimilative and accommodative forms). There is a certain sense of Habermasian 'practical discourse' where HIFMs as actors are engaged in moral argumentations about the foundations of life thereby leading to a transformation of modes of social service. There is, thus, an upsurge of HIFM literature talking of their involvements in modern, secular, and developmental activities such as relief work after major disasters, the setting up of hospitals and colleges, and so on. The provision of free eye operation, check-up camps, and blood donation activities forms part of common repertoire of social service engagements undertaken by new guru-led organizations. One could say that such activities are at once emblematic of and enable a furtherance of the guru's multiple societal entanglements. Social ideals of HIFMs are developed through 'connections, appropriations, and influences' from traditional texts which are then viewed as 'living texts' espousing socially meaningful teachings. Service ideals, in turn, are shaped by worlds of patronage and brand creations – brands being popular meditative and spiritual techniques. Also in effect, there is 'guru governmentality' through this social service, where the state borrows from or harnesses the guru–devotee relationship in order to fulfil certain governmental ends.

Hegemony comes in because HIFMs' social service ominously foreshadows the Hindutva doctrine. Images of the 'national' are produced through their representational forms and religious authority. In a postcolonial nation-space, HIFMs weave communal/religious nationalism and cultural nationalism to define Hindutva. Service is directed towards building a society complying with Hindu nationalism's agenda of revolutionary nationhood. Hindu-inspired service is a *realpolitik,* which through the Hindu lens and neo-Vedanta ethos, treats social and cultural difference as illusory and therefore meaningless. Although there is a cosmopolitan feel, there is also the coexistence of the rhetoric of embracement and chauvinistic attitudes, which is perhaps suggestive of an inherent contradiction of globalizing Hinduism. Hence this kind of cosmopolitanism has considerable potential for ideological and technological creativity.

Social service in contemporary HIFMs can, thus, be called a fetishistic expression of the logic of Hindu ideology to the mediating logic that structures capitalist society. Historically, in response to the Morley–Minto reforms of 1909, faith representativeness in the colonial state impelled a Hindu unity – especially by the Hindu Sabhas. Contemporary HIFMs fuel the Hindutva effect in multilocal diaspora contexts culturally organized around the 'oneness' philosophy. Social service's secular garb feeds into this by an incipient identification with larger social causes and macro-social processes. The umbilical cord with the guru and his/her ideals remain. Social service is, in principle, a secular practice, but in the context of HIFMs it is infused with a religiosity which is transformative. The more important point here is that of guru-*seva* governmentality. This is re-tooled, which effectively means a re-purposing of an authoritarian aspect of the devotional relationship, in order to produce humanitarian or developmental effects. This service is not just an agency of devolved governance but a relationship consequent on radical asymmetrical exchange harnessed for governmental ends in an era of liberalization.

Service is qualified by memories of the guru or his/her expansive agency, which have been characterized as being beyond limiting categories. Guruship is akin to a floating signifier, lacking determination, in that it can participate in multiple domains while generating a sense of omnipotentiality. Remembrance of the guru is a catalyst for social action and demonstrates a preference for principles such as human rights, peace, and justice (which gurus are believed to embody). Oblivion or historical forgetting arises in the course of HIFMs' reflexive acts in redefining and refining their own positions in relation to the larger sociopolitical environ. Oblivion has been further enhanced by neoliberalization which has opened spaces for HIFMs to enter into the public realm in newer ways, as well as in mainstream 'secular' partnerships.

Based on field work with nine popular HIFMs, the focus of this book is to critically look at HIFMs' roles as actors in social transformation. One dominant epistemological strand in social transformation is that of theo-philosophy, which draws from the transformative epistemes of spirituality and faith. The attempt is to contribute to the sociology of faith through the HIFM lenses. A kind of mutuality between social transformation 'praxis' and 'altruistic pragmatism' of HIFMs is deliberated. For the larger civil society fabric, the relevance is in terms of enhancing the nuances of a category of institutional actors – HIFMs. They posit as leverages and fulcrum to generate faith-embedded social capital and play a quintessential role in the discourse on development, building into the 'hologram' (metaphor for institutional and interrelational multiplicity that is an existential reality) of civil society.

Acknowledgements

This book has been a fulfilling personal and professional journey. There has been a higher power which has guided me through this work. My parents supported and encouraged me to take my study forward and write a book. I am grateful to the Indian Council for Social Science Research (ICSSR), New Delhi, for initially providing the fellowship grant to undertake the study. I thank the office bearers of the institutions that I studied in, for giving me the access to their places and, more importantly, acknowledging the academic license to look at their work from a distance. To all the members of the order, followers, and beneficiaries who agreed to be the respondents of this study, a big thank you. Thanks are also due to the anonymous reviewers who gave important suggestions to improve the content. A sense of gratitude to Shri Pranit Rawat for giving impetus to this domain of work by agreeing to publish it under the banner of Rawat Publications. Finally to my well-wishers, many thanks for supporting my work.

Samta P. Pandya

1

Introduction: Gurus, Sociality, Hegemony, and Social Transformation

Faith, in general, and faith-based movements, in particular, play a quintessential role in contemporary civil society. Faith-based movements, through their ideological leanings, seek to stabilize an otherwise amorphous religious experience into a harmonious symbolic order – by lending it a tangible face. They present themselves as enterprises representing a collection of beliefs and practices associated with a particular faith or syncretic tenets. There is a tacit and explicit permeation of faith and associations based on faith into multiple aspects of human life. At one level it generates faith-embedded social capital. At another level, there is a crucial reinstatement of faith-based movements as important actors of civil society and as a dimension of statecraft (Johnston & Sampson, 1994).[1] A notable dimension here is that although the existence of faith-based movements is a historical phenomenon, they have not been studied frequently (Berger, 2003). However, there is a certain degree of visibility due to the Charitable Choice Reform in the US throughout Bush Junior's

1 Voluntary sector movements as crucial actors in the process of welfare and development are an important signature in civil society that needs cognisance. Faith-based movements in particular that represent a distinctive category through the institutional construction of faith (Sanctis, 1927) deem visibility.

regime recognizing the importance of faith-based movements and their contributions in civil society.

Among the distinctive typology of faith-based movements in the Indian context are those aligning and adhering to tenets of Indic faiths and syncretic tenets therein. Indic faiths are systematized faiths that have their origin in the Indian subcontinent and constitute the core subject matter of Indological studies (Madan, 2004). In terms of Indic faith-based movements, there is a further bifurcation – those aligning to Hindu tenets and the Indic pragmatists aligning to tenets of Jainism, Buddhism, and the multifarious sects and cults therein. Those aligning to and considerably drawing from Hindu tenets can collectively be called Hindu-Inspired Faith Movements (henceforth HIFMs).

HIFMs are headed by teachers or gurus and/or their disciples, their ideological leanings basically translating into the ideology, vision, or mission of the organizations. They have elaborate mechanics of institutional building – ethics of *seva* or service as crucial to the spirit of institution-building (Warrier, 2003). The origins of HIFMs can be traced to the Bhakti era and later to a series of reform movements in India during the eighteenth and nineteenth centuries that saw the rise of institutions such as the Brahmo Samaj and the Arya Samaj who drew inspiration from Christian missionaries, especially in fields such as education and medical welfare (Venugopal, 2004).

Historically, the first Hindu Sabha was set up in October 1909 and later became the Hindu Mahasabha in 1915. The setting up of the Rashtriya Swayamsevak Sangh (RSS) by K.B. Hedgewar in 1925 signified the early dynamic phase in the emergence of Hindu Nationalism. With time, the RSS set up a series of front organizations known as the Sangh Parivar. In the early part of the twentieth century, the Ramakrishna Mission along the lines of Swami Vivekananda's Practical Vedanta and Sri Aurobindo Ashram professing the integral vision of neo-Vedantic progressivism were set up (Beckerlegge, 2003). The establishment of Vishwa Hindu Parishad served as a clear marker of accelerated proliferation in the number of Hindu institutions. The Vishwa Hindu Parishad (or VHP as commonly known) was initially led by Shivram Shankar Apte (an RSS worker from Baroda) and Swami Chinmayananda from Kerala (a disciple of Swami Sivananda, the founder of the Divine Life Society). Hindu-derived renunciant consciousness and social service went hand in hand in these institutions.

Copley (2000) says that most of these movements are headed by teachers or gurus and/or their disciples, their ideological leanings basically translating into the ideology, vision, or mission of these institutions. Rustau (2003) has proposed that HIFMs are institutionalized religious structures which represent change of religion as a social institution and its role in civil society over time. They question hegemony and yet remain traditional in many ways, thereby characterizing a soft revolution (a clear sign of Hindu revivalism and drastic changes in the power dynamics between Hinduism and its hold over the civil society). They question hegemony and yet remain traditional in many ways, thereby characterizing a soft revolution (a clear sign of Hindu revivalism and drastic changes in the power dynamics between Hinduism and its hold over the civil society). Beckerlegge (2003) posits these movements as signifying a simplification of traditional tenets. 'Hindu India' is presented here as an embodiment of the divine and the focus is on 'service' of the 'Hindu nation'. Two elements that characterize these movements are spiritual universalism and cultural nationalism, that is, universality of the spiritual reality or Brahman and the cultural importance of one India (Heehs, 2003). O'Toole (2003) says:

> such movements made possible the imagining of a Hindu nation in a variety of ways – through the semitization of Hinduism (that is through the creation of a conceptually unified Hindu community with common doctrinal beliefs), the reform of anti-social practices (such as child marriage) and the posting of a past Hindu golden age with a vision of Hindu resurgence. (p. 76)

Warrier (2003) discusses that these movements are in many ways 'Hinduizing agents', popularizing the nationalist ideology of Hindutva proponents. However, the contemporary phenomenon is that of *avatar* gurus – important elements whose endeavour is the setting up of institutional movements. There are elaborate mechanics of institutional building; ethics of *seva* (or social service) as crucial to the spirit of institution building. Thus, *seva* is panegyric; that is, it constitutes an expression of the Hindu topography of the self where the prototypical act of worship is the glorification of the divine.

Social service is institutional action in the field of welfare and development. The activities in this area range from charitable work to service provision to radical action. Premised on the contention that 'faith works', there is a steady rise in global literature looking at faith-based social services (Cnaan, Boddie, & Danzig, 2005; Sangha & Sahoo, 2006). Development literature has evidenced three broad domains of studies with respect to faith-based organizations (FBOs): (a) organizational design elements of FBOs, (b) faith-based programme assessments, and (c) macro-level studies examining the stake of FBOs as civil society actors in the process of development. Studies in the cadre of organizational design elements are concerned with functional dynamics particularly concerned with secular funding, faith–secular partnerships, and state funding (Perlmutter, 1968; Chaves, 1993a, 1993b, 1994; Smith & Lipsky, 1993; Gronbjerg, 1993; Cnaan, 1997; Gronbjerg & Nelson, 1998; Wuthnow, 2000; Kennedy & Bielefield, 2002; Vanderwoerd, 2004; Harris et al., 2005; Dinham, 2008; Kvasmy & Lee, 2010). The two main criteria for analysis cutting across studies are as follows: (a) the degree to which 'faith' is central to the organization's identity, and (b) the extent to which 'faith' shapes and drives the practice of an organization. Studies in the genre of faith-based programme assessments have attempted to look at the effectiveness of programmes administered by FBOs. Primarily, the focus has been on clientele satisfaction as a parameter for efficacy (Ferguson et al., 2007) – the main settings here are criminology, health, and education. The focus of macro-level studies has been on critically viewing FBOs' roles in policymaking (Reese, 2004) and in addressing social issues either with or vis-à-vis the state. The propositions are that faith groups are important civil society participants in governance (Dinham & Lowndes, 2008) and that faith engagements are linked to policies of social inclusion and 'community cohesion'. The challenge is to strike a balance between the sense of openness and commitment to faith – the term then used to explain this relationship was 'religious civility', to emphasize that FBOs act in the service of democracy (Neiheisel et al., 2009).

There have been several critical and evaluative studies in the past decade that focused on the capabilities and effectiveness of FBOs in areas such as social work and social welfare (Campbell & Glunt, 2006; Chapman & Lowndes, 2008; Fridolfsson et al., 2009; Friedrichs & Klockner, 2009; Montagne-Villette et al., 2011). Particularly, FBOs work through habitus-mediated factors such as shared cultural forms (Bunn & Wood, 2012). Hence, despite several dynamics, FBOs have emerged as key players in the development scenario. Exclusivity and partnerships emerge therefore as a matter of convenience for FBOs. Exclusiveness is primarily ideological and partnerships between different FBOs manifest in their practical functioning when their functions overlap. The literature is dominated by Christian organizations, and comparatively fewer studies have looked at Muslim and Jewish organizations (Cloke, Williams, & Thomas, 2011; Göcmen, 2013). With respect to Hindu organizations, although the sentiment of *seva* is a historical one, its manifestation is particularly complex and only recently treaded by scholars, albeit with certain trepidations.

The attempt of this book is to critically look at HIFMs and their role as actors in social transformation. Social transformation can be driven by faith tenets. A kind of mutuality between social transformation 'praxis' and 'altruistic pragmatism' of HIFMs is deliberated upon. This book argues that HIFMs use sociality to craft citizenship, nationalism, and a modern civil society. Sociality refers to the interface with society through followers and their mandate of social service. In the contemporary Indian neoliberal and postmodern scenario, HIFMs make public assertions through this sociality manifesting dominantly through social service. Thus, the four pillars of HIFMs' contemporary presence are – gurus, sociality, hegemony, and social transformation. Gurus or teachers create a matrix of possible meanings (engaged cosmopolitanism) in their discourses which allows followers their agency in picking up required ingredients for transformation. Sociality, the tangible part of which is social service, is essentially seen as one core strategy of proliferation/world affirmation across HIFMs. Hegemony is an important feature because HIFMs' social service ominously foreshadows the Hindutva doctrine. Service is further qualified by memories of the guru or his/her expansive agency. Remembrance of the guru is a catalyst for social action and demonstrates a preference for principles such as human rights, peace, and justice (which gurus are believed to embody). Oblivion or historical forgetting arises in course of the HIFMs' reflexive acts in redefining and refining their own positions in relation to the larger sociopolitical environ.

The attempt is to contribute to the episteme of sociology of faith through HIFMs' lenses.

Dimensions of social service in HIFMs

Theological justifications and temple studies

Hindu scriptures have references to concepts which propel social service such as *dana*, *dharma*, and *seva*[2] (Divatia, 1993; Barlingay, 1998; Lysenko & Hulin, 2007). They also emphasize on a worldview specifying a divine cosmic consciousness in tune with theological tenets (Mastromattei & Rigopoulos, 1999). The theological justifications are two-fold – altruistic and social sentiments exist in scriptures; content analysis of texts by using key words can lead to the development of models about constructs such as peace, spirituality, *karma*, and *dharma* (Bhawuk, 2010).

Temples and the adjoining sacred complexes have been studied from the cultural anthropology perspective. Hindu temples have been perceived as significant institutions in the redistribution of ritual, symbolic, and economic benefits in society. The social functions of the temple flow from the many functions and ordered meanings that are associated with it (Appadurai & Breckenridge, 2004). Ethnographies have focused on two key aspects in relation to Hindu temples: (a) providing a mythical account of the temples and (b) temples' community-based welfare initiatives (Chaudhari, 1981; Clothey, 1983). Hindu temples have had a history of royal patronage. Particularly in the Gaudiya Vaishnavite temples of Bengal, historical events of charity by the Malla royalty were ways to enhance community support for the temples as well as for the empire (Pillai, 2007). They have also spearheaded social reform by becoming 'sites of movements' to address ritual traditions such as the *devadasi*[3] system (Trivedi, 1999; Royo, 2003; Meduri, 2005; Brown, 2007; Grau, 2007; O'Shea, 2007; Singh, 2007).

---

2 For a detailed enumeration of concepts linked to social service such as *seva*, morality, ethics, altruism, philanthropy, virtues, and compassion see Potter, K.H. (Ed.), (1995), *Encyclopaedia of Indian Philosophies*. 1 (II), pp. 902–1321. New Delhi: Motilal Banarasidass.

3 Devadasi women were dedicated to a temple as girls (and as such have been allocated a share in the temple land holdings) and trained in dance to perform at the temple ceremonies as well as household rituals of temple patrons. These patrons took care of the temple income and became sole sexual partners of the *devadasis* for the period of their patronage. During the late 19th and 20th centuries, Indian social reform campaigns sought to eradicate this system under the broader rubric of anti-nautch (Hodges, 2005).

Bhakti studies and emphasis on socioreligious reform

Bhakti studies emphasize that the Bhakti movement provided an anti-Brahminical and subaltern approach, which created a platform for affirmative social action and intervention. Formal education was an instrument with which the established socioreligious questioning inherent in Bhakti devotionalism was developed into a wider process of awareness of the exploitation within the Hindu society (Constable, 2000; Naregal, 2000). The critical tendencies of the Bhakti tradition, particularly its emphasis on vernacularization, led to the redistribution of cultural and political power – particularly an annihilation of the caste order. These sentiments have later been appropriated in what can be called Hindu-based transformative practice (Hardgrove, 2002; Jain, 2002; Chaubey, 2003; Brajranjan, 2005). This was particularly true for the *nirguna* tradition, which was subaltern, contestory, and lower caste vis-à-vis the *saguna*.[4] Studies have proposed that the movement produced cultural artefacts (prose, poetry) that provided historical evidence of human agency impelling society to look at change (Freitag, 2002; Upadhyay, 2002; Bhattacharya, 2003; Chakrabarti, 2004; Dutta, 2005; Ciotti, 2007; O'Hanlon, 2007; Narayan, 2008; Chandra, 2009). A kind of cultural capital was developed by creating new narratives and virtually inventing a new alternative history and language.[5] This also comprised of feminist expressions which challenged patriarchal diktats through forms of devotionalism (Ramaswamy, 1997). Women bhakti poets were iconoclastic creative women who engaged in a politics of resistance (Rajan, 2000).[6]

---

4 For almost a century now, scholars of medieval Indian bhakti devotionalism have relied upon the nirgun–sagun model (devotion to a form of deity–devotion to a formless God, respectively) to understand the theological and ideological differences between the sants and vaishnavas. More recently, some scholars have begun to question the idea of the existence of an impermeable divide between the two groups of bhakti devotees (Bahuguna, 2009).

5 These stories are about dissenting lower-caste characters glorified as Dalit heroes who fought against upper-caste oppression and injustice (Narayan, 2008).

6 The female sadhus (sadhvis) may be 'rebels' in their transgression of social norms and ideals, but they are not revolutionaries. Their use of sant bhakti paradigms thereby enables them to construct themselves as traditional and their asceticism as a gendered alternative to orthodox renunciation that coexists with dominant renouncer ideologies and practices. The sadhvis' lives, then, approximate those of the medieval female mystics. Their gendered strategies illustrate what anthropologist Judith Okely characterizes as the

HIFMs in development literature

The recent and dominant trends in Indian development literature are the discourses on marginalization, inclusion, justice, and equity. The language to negotiate these discourses is that of capabilities, entitlements, rights, and action (Baxi, 2006; Nussbaum, 2006). HIFM's spaces in development literature have emerged through the postmodern turn providing spaces for religion-oriented discourses in the public sphere (Robinson, 2004). The focus is on multi-epistemic aspects of sacred spaces, times, objects, persons, and arrangement (Saraswati, 2000). Along the lines of political theology, the view is that the relationship between Hindu thought and praxis is dialectical. HIFMs are looked at as institutions that make sociocultural freedom possible through the twin categories of tolerance and multidimensionality of truth (Chakrabarti, 1989).

Economic development literature also has empirical evidence of relating Hindu ideals to economic development (Singer, 1956; Mishra, 1962; Kapp, 1963; Dube, 1965). Prarthana Samaj, a religious society established in Bombay, India, in the 1860s attempted to reconcile Hinduism with the spirit of progress and to rationalize it. M.G. Ranade, one of its founders, preached values of Hindu Protestantism (Rao, 2004). Economic development might also be seen in relation to religious institutions, such as temples and monasteries that have been associated with the programmes of economic development. Taking the case of Tirupati temple in South India highlighting its development initiatives in the arena of agricultural investments and food security, Stein (1960) has illustrated the part played by religious institutions in economic development. HIFMs are thus seen as sharing a commitment of 'looking out' to the wider community and testing faith through action. While this is often expressed as charity, service provision, or interfaith dialogue, there is also the potential to politicize this impetus to engage (Jamoul & Wills, 2008). The fact remains that HIFMs do have a history of involvement in 'community cohesion' and 'regeneration' schemes.

Further in India, where HIFMs have largely originated, colonialism constructed the past of subjected culture in a manner that allowed the legitimation of the colonial rule. Several socioeconomic challenges were

---

'cracks of resistance' to normative traditions and institutions that enable the sadhvis to exert agency in the male-dominated tradition of *sanyas* (Khandelwal, 2004; Khandelwal, Hausner, & Gold, 2006; DeNapoli, 2010).

then posed to HIFMs in transgressing and challenging this legitimation. One such instance in history is that of the Sanatana Dharma Sabha (universal religion's council) movement's engagement with socioreligious charitable gifting practices or *dana* between 1915 and 1940. In late colonial India, elite donors used the language and forms of *dana* to rework relationships of patronage, reinforce power hierarchies, and transform the moral fibre of different 'publics'. Reformist orthodox Hindu socioreligious organizations affiliated to the Sanatana Dharma Sabha movement fostered and shaped *sanatana dharma* norms, precepts, and ritual practices through charitable gifting. Reforming *dana* was also a significant part of their project of revitalizing *sanatana dharma* to craft citizenship, nationalism, and a modern civil society. Sanatani organizations led public initiatives to prevent the misuse of monies by the managers of wealthy religious and charitable institutions and use this wealth to reinvigorate the Hindu society and religion. They also utilized the Religious and Charitable Endowments Acts as legal tools of reform to nurture a 'Hindu public' bound by caste and gender norms. This was a part of their ambitious project to revitalize and reconstitute religion in accordance with the socioreligious vision enunciated by *sanatana dharma*. By the twentieth century, Sanatanis, like other Hindu social reformers, also engaged with the intertwined issues of modernity and tradition to connect societal regeneration to the revival of a mythic, Hindu past (Kasturi, 2010).

Social service sentiment in HIFM literature

Several case studies have emphasized on the role of Hindu faith institutions in social spheres. The ashram of Chaitanya Mahaprabhu has been viewed as a potential site for socioreligious transformation (Kennedy, 1925). Arya Samaj's role in eradication of untouchability in Punjab has also been studied (Pimpley & Sharma, 1983).[7]

The Hare Krishna movement or ISKCON has invited the attention of several scholars due to its diasporic presence (Guerrlero, 2000; Madsen, 2000; Squarcini, 2000, 2002; Neubert, 2008; Crnic, 2009). Some scholars

7 The Arya Samaj found itself increasingly drawn into political action in defence of the Hindu community through its purification campaigns, anti-Muslim protests, and organizational developments such as the Arya Vir Dal, which placed the Samaj along the lines of the Hindu Mahasabha and the Indian National Congress (Jones, 1989).

have projected it as a movement with religious and social leanings. The social leanings came with their micro interventions in the area of education and health care and macro interventions in the arena of ecological consciousness and promoting an eco-friendly lifestyle among followers, including vegetarianism (Sullivan, 1985, 2000; Brooks, 1989). The other institution is Ramakrishna Mission, which echoes the correspondence between Vivekananda's practical Vedanta and nationalist discourses. From a historical-materialist perspective, Gupta (1973) talks of Ramakrishna Mission's transformation from an autology of renunciation characteristic of traditional Vedic tenets to a mission of faith-inspired altruistic service.

Babb's (1986) 'Redemptive Encounters' looks at three modern religious movements: Radhasoami, Brahmakumaris with its millenarian philosophy, and Sathya Sai Baba cult. Using deep continuities as the central theme, Babb establishes the fundamental unity in these three modern styles of Hinduism. Service to society and world affirmation/accommodation also emerges out of these deep continuities with the *dharma* of Hindu tradition. There are basic 'images' of Hindu religious culture, which are present in these three modern styles.

Adopting the historical-materialist approach and the historical method of investigation, Beckerlegge (1995) has analysed the Ramakrishna Mission with reference to its ideological leanings translating into the practice of '*seva*' – service to humanity; discussion being undertaken in the context of a historical tradition of continuity maintained with the tenets of social service in the faith. Developing upon the contentions further, Beckerlegge (1998, 2000a, 2000b) has also proposed that the mission's social service activities are a manifestation of the social stake of a religious organization within the purview of modern Hinduism. Extending the discussion in a comparative study adopting the historical and ethnographic method, Beckerlegge (2003) has presented the connection between the extensive promotion and practice of *seva* (service) within the contemporary RSS and the invocation of Vivekananda. The connection has been examined through the dialectical relationship between the first two leaders of RSS – Keshav Baliram Hedgewar and Madhav Sadashiv Golwalkar and the Ramakrishna Math and Mission.

Using the case study method, Warrier (2003) examined the mechanics of institution-building within the Mata Amritanandamayi Mission through the ethics of *seva* or selfless service propagated by the

Mata. There are means by which their *seva* effectively contributes towards the organizations' institutional expansion and growth. Srinivas's (2008) ethnography explores the relationship between Sathya Sai Baba and his internationally diverse, middle-class, city-dwelling devotees. She tells the story of the evolution of the global movement following Sathya Sai Baba, from the more Indo-centric religious pluralism developed by his predecessor Shirdi Sai Baba (*c.*1918) to a universalistic mission to re-establish love and service. Devotees negotiate their two identities as members of a worldwide community of faith who live in urban centres. Local community service (*seva*) is the site for the intersection of universal and local communities. Performing *seva* is a form of 'practical spirituality' (2008, p. 258), a way to enact Sathya Sai Baba's 'love all, serve all' doctrine. Devotees who practice *seva* take an active role in the betterment of their local communities. Their performance of *seva* demonstrates an alternative and non-nationalistic way to perform citizenship. *Seva* is a devotional practice in that serving others is viewed as serving Sai Baba, that is, 'feeding the divine in the body of the poor' (2008, p. 281). For the many devotees who will probably never make the pilgrimage to Puttaparthi in the erstwhile Andhra Pradesh, now Seemandhra, the new state (which is Sathya Sai's main centre in India), *seva* is an easily accessible pathway that connects a transglobal community to its religious teacher. Moreover, it is through *seva* that participation in the local life of one's city becomes a sacred activity through the alchemical mediation of the transglobal *avatar* Sathya Sai Baba. Social service is essentially seen as the core strategy of proliferation/world affirmation across HIFMs (Walliss, 2007; Locklin & Lauwers, 2009; Srinivas, 2010; Zavos, 2012).

Two important issues arise here – whether *seva* is pure or impure altruism[8] and how is it viewed in the context of the market. Since Hindu *seva* is as much to do with citizenship performance and obtaining a place in the devotee coterie or what can be called 'clubbiness', it is a manifestation of impure altruism. However, the purity comes with the delivery of philanthropy as a public good. More studies are required on how *seva* is actually performed and to what extent its activities steer clear of ulterior motives. The second issue is the positioning of *seva* in

8 See Bowman (2004) for a discussion on pure and impure altruism.

the context of the market. *Seva* performativity in the market parlance is the price paid for non-tangible benefits and transcendental commodities (such as guru's grace). This performance is a combination of mental engagement, symbolic participation, and actual service. This *seva* is also contingent upon state deregulation, which makes space for HIFMs in the social development sector. This partnership/plurality then propels acts of *seva* and participation in it.

Seva in HIFMs is essentially an evangelical import and hence there are aspects of 'mission-ization' (Gupta, 1973; Beckerlegge, 2000, 2010), such as spiritual rejuvenation, creation, and re-creation of communities – something that traditional Indian globalization literature has inadvertently skipped in its analysis. This beckons an analysis of the faith-related transnational flows – rootedness, cross-overs, conceptual bonds, and performance.

Forms of social service

Across sites of Hindu-inspired, faith-based social service, three dominant forms like Weberian ideal types can be seen – the orthodox, assimilative, and accommodative. These are not mutually exclusive with all contemporary HIFMs expressing aspects of one or more forms. Service is advocated through religious authority, and an institutional structure is built which is maintained over time. The orthodox form of social service is commune oriented and retains sectarian/scriptural authority seen often in the Swaminarayan movement (Knott, 1986; Burghart, 1987; Jackson & Nesbitt, 1993; Nye, 1995; Vertovec, 2000; Williams, 2001; Kim, 2008) and Chinmaya Mission (Locklin & Lauwers, 2009). The assimilative form is more expansive and bridging in nature and demonstrates an apparent generosity towards occidental, syncretic, and secular tenets frequently characteristic of the Ramakrishna mission, Vivekananda Kendra (Beckerlegge, 2010; Kanungo, 2012), Sai Baba movements (Warren, 2004; Bauman, 2012; McLain, 2012), Brahmakumaris[9] (Howell, 2005;

9 Walliss (2007) says that in the context of the Brahmakumaris, the assimilative stance can also be ambivalent as there are simultaneous aspects of transcendence-instrumentalism in processes through history. This dissonance is further intensified through the metaphor of consciousness. There is, according to Walliss (2007), an institutional use of spatialization that involves distinction between levels of consciousness: the realist

Walliss, 2007), and the older Brahmo and Sanatana Dharma movements. What is essentially seen is a combination of a monotheistic tradition and a utilitarian approach that advocates education and science for social change.

The accommodative form takes the 'postmodern' turn where Hindu-inspired movements aggressively use secular motifs and the language of spirituality to justify social service. This aspect is particularly prominent in the newer movements such as the Art of Living and Mata Amritanandamayi Mission. There is a certain sense of Habermasian 'practical discourse' wherein HIFMs as actors are engaged in moral argumentations about the foundations of life thereby leading to a transformation of modes of social service. Modernity in itself is negotiated and social service in the accommodative vein in the HIFMs is, in Appadurai's (1996) terms, 'emblematic of contestation' and 'constitutive of agency'. The outcome, in the cultural sense, may be a collage of transnational shared imaginations and transformed subjectivities (Warrier, 2006). There is, thus, an upsurge of literature focusing on HIFMs' involvements in modern, secular, and developmental activities such as relief work after major disasters, setting up of hospitals and colleges, and so on (Beckerlegge, 2006; Shah, 2006; Srinivas, 2008; Copeman, 2009). Indeed, the provision of free eye operation, check-up camps, and blood donation activities form part of common repertoire of social service engagements undertaken by new guru-led organizations (Warrier, 2003). One could say that such activities are at once emblematic and a furtherance of the guru's multiple societal entanglements. The aspect of asymmetrical engagement (McKean, 1996) comes with the scholarly suggestion that such organizations engage in *seva* activities at least in part as a means of divesting themselves of wealth for tax purposes (Warrier, 2003).

In all the three forms of service, the origins of social service sentiment and actual performance are either serendipitous or a priori streamlined. This dissipates the virgin alignment to faith and paves the way for to enter into the socioreligious playground. Where the orthodoxy retains exclusivities

distinction which proposes soul consciousness as true and body consciousness as false, and the two-world proposition wherein soul consciousness is true but it cannot be adequately explained in body consciousness terms. In tangible terms, this bifurcation and ambivalence has manifested in terms of shifts in world rejecting spiritual propositions to ethics of peace and nonviolence.

and assimilative groups portray diverse sensibilities, the accommodative ones claim to draw from diverse albeit legitimate spiritual-sacred realms to project their public roles based on minimum requirements of civic unity. The idea/mandate is to bring faith to the public realm in a visible way – beyond rituals, towards a community orientation.

Service ideals and strategies

HIFMs' service ideals talk of the ultimate goal of transcendence (Chakravarthi, 2001) and they provide alternatives to modern Western epistemology[10] (Paranjape, 2009). They oppose the dominance of rationality and invoke ideas of supra-rational such as the idea of the Supermind as proposed by Sri Aurobindo. There are 'connections, appropriations and influences'[11] (Valpey, 2010) from texts which are then viewed as 'living texts' espousing socially meaningful teachings (Sunderasan, 2000). Service ideals are shaped by worlds of patronage and brand creations (Saha, 2007) – brands being popular meditative and spiritual techniques. Furthermore, they encompass a central spiritual message and a less obvious political- and gender-shaped vision of the world (Bradley, 2011).[12] The quest is to arrive at a balance between the material and the spiritual (Hatcher, 2007).[13]

---

10 Paranjape (2009) has used terms such as 'Gnosis', 'gnoseology', and 'border thinking' to describe those knowledge systems that are on the margins of, or outside, the world colonized by Western modernity.

11 Valpey (2010) has proposed this in the context of the phenomenon of the translational and publicational presence of the Bhagwad Gita – particularly, the shifts in the text's use as some of its terms and concepts become known, appropriated by, and integrated into Western or 'globalized' cultural landscapes.

12 Bradley's (2011) discussions are based on a comparison and contrast of the religious discourses of three transnational movements – Ramakrishna Mission, Sadhu Vaswani Mission, and Mata Amritanandamayi Mission. Findings reveal how broad, open-ended religious concepts such as love and compassion are projected through and conflated with notions of women as mothers. Differences in the visions each Guru projects can be seen in the ways *dharma* is understood and talked about by them, which in turn determines their respective views on the role and responsibilities of women. In each case, education is an important dimension to their work which helps them to secure the next generation of devotees, raise money for their operations, and ensure their teachings continue to impact on how Hindus see the world. The desire to create a particular kind of society is politicized and each Guru is sure they offer the right and correct path through life.

13 Hatcher's (2007) observations are based on the exploration of the affinity between one early colonial version of Vedanta and the socioeconomic activities of its bourgeois promoters. Working from a rare set of Bengali discourses delivered at meetings of the

Service strategies entail the entire range from *dana* and charitable giving inspired by Hindu *dharma* (Kasturi, 2010) to sociopolitical engagements (Beckerlegge, 2007). Glorification of the guru and promoting his/her spiritual message is an important constitutive component of the service (Warrier, 2006). This is dependent more on the interior disposition of the performer and less on the inner transformation of the recipient (Srinivas, 2010). Hence, one aspect of the strategies is like a religious *sadhana* (penance and practice) which is a means to spiritual realization resembling historical forms of charitable action than objective service.

Doers and recipients of social service

The charismatic gurus occupy a familiar familial space which draws followers who do service into the HIFMs' fold (Mukta, 2000). For the doers of social service or *seva* in Mata Amritanandamayi Mission, it is seen as a component of spiritual development – a 'meritorious activity that wears down the egotism and selfishness of modernity' (Warrier, 2006, p. 186). This essentially placates their existential struggles and hence could have psychotherapeutic implications (Hoecke, 2006).[14] Gurus create a matrix of possible meanings (engaged cosmopolitanism) in their discourses which allows followers an agency in picking up required ingredients for personal transformation (Srinivas, 2010; Khandelwal, 2012). What motivates the doers of service in HIFMs is an impure altruism, as it entails consuming 'clubbiness' (communitas/network formation) as a private good along with philanthropy as a public good (Pandya, 2012).[15] For the devotees guru *seva* is *manav seva* (service

Tattvabodhini Sabha during its inaugural year (1839–1840), this essay demonstrates how a re-scripted Vedanta provided members with a worldview that legitimated both their spiritual concerns and their worldly activities.

14 Hoecke (2006) has described three paradigms in Indian psychotherapy: (a) the Bhagwad Gita paradigm, which guides the individual to larger macrocosmic domains instead of exploring the edges of individuality; (b) the guru-*shishya* (disciple) paradigm, which focuses on authority, context, and morality instead of normality; and (c) the abhyasa paradigm, which accentuates the interpersonal dimensions of the therapeutic relationship.

15 The extreme form of impure altruism is also disengagement or defection. In the context of the Hare Krishna movement Rochford (1989) has specified that disengagement can be at two levels: on an individual level there are fringe members, dissidents, and apostates; on a group level exist oppositional factions, schisms, and ex-member support groups.

to guru is service to humanity) and its corporeality persists in a newer domain of the medicalized gifts (health camps) such that we might begin to speak of a biopolitics of devotion (Copeman & Ikegame, 2012). There is in effect a kind of 'guru governmentality' through this social service, where the state borrows from or harnesses the guru–devotee relationship in order to fulfill certain governmental ends (Copeman & Ikegame, 2012).[16]

Service recipients resemble the general public welfare user in terms of financial/economic status. Furthermore, despite claims of the service doers that their services attract a cross-sectional clientele, the real leanings are towards Hindu preferences and hence there is a selective, exclusive bridging – cross-sectional in principle but parochial in actuality. Those who receive service generally perceive it as fulfilling their functional needs and enabling self-enhancement/actualization (Pandya, 2013a).

Situating this in the context of development literature on volunteerism,[17] it can be said that Hindu *seva* resembles the collective style of volunteerism (Hodgskinson & Weitzman, 1993). It is a practice of 'institutional kindness' (Wuthnow, 2000) and akin to faith-based volunteerism discussed in literature on non-profits and civil society organisations; there is a 'moral selving' (Allahyari, 2000) to the work of creating oneself as a more virtuous and often more spiritual person (p. 4) through volunteering. The range of work can be from charity to more progressive engagement which then affects the concept of *seva* in the HIFM context (which could be episodic or routine).

---

16 Gurus are treated increasingly as a kind of governmental shortcut well-suited to the present economic milieu. One instance in the Indian context is that of farmer suicides in Vidarbha, Maharashtra, in 2007 where breathing lessons by Sri Ravishankar and religious discourses by other assorted swamis were advocated (Gupta, 2009). Veerashaiva Maths in Karnataka and their involvement in welfare activities is another example of what Ikegame (2012a) called sacred public-private partnership. In a neoliberal era, this filling in for the state by guru-led organization is perceived as non-threatening – the renouncer's lack of kin creating an impression of incorruptibility.

17 The rich and ever-growing literature on volunteers crosses disciplinary boundaries, and there are complex and diverse models pertaining to why volunteers do what they do and how that relates to their performance (Grube & Piliavin, 2000). Today, volunteering is viewed as particularly critical (Govekar & Govekar, 2002). In the past fifteen years, studies specific to volunteerism in FBOs have begun to appear.

Politics of faith-based service delivery: nationalistic rhetoric, memories, and oblivion

HIFMs' social service ominously foreshadows the *Hindutva* (the political ideology drawing from Hinduism's proposed superiority) doctrine (Casolari, 2002; Mehta, 2008). This is in a doctrinally non-confrontational way camouflaged by what Zavos (2001) calls *sanatana dharma* as an unmediated reactionary force. Service is directed towards building a society complying with Hindu nationalism's agenda of revolutionary nationhood (Basu & Banerjee, 2006). Hindu-inspired service is a *realpolitik*, which through the Hindu lens and neo-Vedanta ethos treats social and cultural differences as illusory and therefore meaningless. Although there is a cosmopolitan feel, there is also the coexistence of a rhetoric of embracement and chauvinistic attitudes, which is perhaps suggestive of an inherent contradiction between globalized Hinduism in theory and how the practical real-time implications of Hindutva play out in the sociopolitical sphere (Copeman & Ikegame, 2012). Hence, this kind of cosmopolitanism as per van der Veer (2002) has a considerable potential for ideological and technological creativity.

Service is a fetishistic expression of the logic of Hindu ideology to the mediating logic that structures the capitalist society (Sartori, 2003). Historically, in response to the Morley–Minto reforms of 1909, faith representativeness in the colonial state was impelled Hindu unity – especially by the Hindu Sabhas. Contemporary HIFMs fuel the *Hindutva* effect in multi-local diasporic contexts (Zavos, 2010) culturally organized around the 'oneness' philosophy. Social service's secular garb feeds into this by an incipient identification with larger social causes and macro-social processes. The umbilical cord connecting the devotees (or service doers) with their guru and his/her ideals remain.

Social service is in principle a secular practice, but in the context of HIFMs it is infused with a religiosity, which is transformative. Ikegame (2012a) says that the more important point here is that of guru *seva* governmentality. This is re-tooled, which effectively means a repurposing of an authoritarian aspect of the devotional relationship in order to produce humanitarian or developmental effects.[18] Barrett (2008),

18 Ikegame (2012a) further says that 'insofar as a logic associated with one domain (bhakti) is transferred to another (governmental), with the production of potentially

Copeman (2009), and Cohen (2011) further say that this service is not just an agency of devolved governance but a relationship consequent on radical asymmetrical exchange harnessed for governmental ends in an era of liberalization. The humanitarian activities, from the devotee's perspective, are far from value neutral.[19]

Service is qualified by alive memories of the guru or his/her expansive agency, who has been characterized as being beyond limiting categories (Babb, 1986; Srinivas, 2010; Copeman & Ikegame, 2012). Guru-ship is akin to a floating signifier, lacking determination, in that it can participate in so many domains while generating a sense of omnipotentiality (Faubion, 2010, p. 93). Remembrance of the guru is a catalyst for social action and demonstrates a preference for principles such as human rights, peace, and justice. Oblivion or historical forgetting arises in course of the HIFMs' reflexive acts in redefining and refining their own positions in relation to the larger sociopolitical environ. Oblivion has been further enhanced by neoliberalization (Gupta, 2009; Ikegame, 2012a) which has opened spaces for HIFMs to enter into the public realm in newer ways as well as into mainstream 'secular' partnerships.

The general approach of social service in HIFMs is 'theistic existential', since faith assumes a dominant role in service delivery. The aspect that literature has not yet fully explored is the core intent (volitional/ulterior) that urges HIFMs and their associates to get into service. This makes a case for more ethnographic and psychoanalytical studies. Programmatic aspects of HIFMs' social service, such as policy, management, collaborations, partnerships, and funding dynamics, as well as who receives this service and their views on it, require more in-depth analysis. The economics of HIFMs' service, including philanthropy and non-rational forms of expenditure by associates, are interesting and

---

unanticipated results (e.g., life changing as well as lifesaving blood transfusions), we are provided here with a further striking example of the domaining effects of the guru.'

19 So, for instance, the leprosy medicine prescribed by Aghor ascetics (Aghories of Kasi) is *prashad* (like a divine gift), brimming with the guru's blessings (Barrett, 2008, pp. 94, 122); Sathya Sai Baba's biomedical hospitals rest on a spiritual vision and services are offered on the understanding that the day will surely come when the hospital will be superfluous since all will be healthy accepting the way of *sadhana* (Srinivas, 2008, p. 125); and certain Nirankari devotees donate their blood with the emphasis being as much on spiritually transforming 'transfusion recipients' as on saving them (Copeman, 2009, p. 78, ch. 4).

need a more nuanced understanding. Furthermore, how social service is managed translocally through the 'virtual' presence of HIFMs and their global followers is an area for critical scholarly exploration.

Seva in HIFMs in the context of the development discourse and particularly from the perspective of religion and development can also be studied from the faith-based programme theory approach. This comes from the emphasis on political capital rather than on social capital to understand religious institutions in civil society. That is, within the civic engagement debate, the focus is on redirecting thinking towards ways in which religion would strengthen citizen's involvement in society (Wagner, 2008).

The contextual prisms through which to examine this could include (a) faith-based programmes as implicitly and explicitly characteristic of religious beliefs and values of a faith tradition; (b) FBOs as using programmes, in whole or in part, to fulfill their religious mission; (c) faith being operationalized into explicit religious and social activities and anticipated outcomes for evaluation purposes; and (d) faith-based programmes having implicit theological assumptions and propositions for understanding, interpreting, and explaining phenomena (Weisbrod, 1998; Sider & Unruh, 2001). A scheme to explain this in Western literature comprises of the four ideal types – traditional, modern, charismatic, and enhancement (Harden, 2006). The traditional model emphasizes on the self-sufficiency and unencumbered nature of faith-based service; the modern model emphasizes on the secular and distinct (from faith) nature of social service; the charismatic model attributes primacy to faith; and the enhancement model prefers the exchange between the realms of faith and society. Situating *seva* in contemporary HIFMs within these contexts may throw further light on its exclusivity, partnerships, and peculiarities.

Gurus, sociality, hegemony, and social transformation: a priori contentions/ commencing propositions

Based on literature, some a priori contentions on HIFMs and their transformational visions are discussed as follows.

Gurus and HIFMs

Guru charisma is the core to HIFMs' origination (Copley, 2000; Ikegame, 2012), which is recreated and recast through hagiographies, social memory, and oral praxis (Srinivas, 1999). Hence in the classical Weberian sense (Swatos, 1981), there are varied elements of construction, consolidation, and performance in the charismatic play. The engagement then contributes to a giving, transfer, and fellowship development that formulates social-spiritual resource/capital (Percy, 2005; Rotberg, 2012). The charisma is then deified and venerated as an embodiment/incarnation with genealogical links to traditional scriptural authority (Locklin & Lauwers, 2009) to ensure legitimacy and continuation.

HIFMs' genesis can be attributed to charisma engagements, institutionalization (Rustau, 2003), and the Weberian concept of routinization (Stark, 1964). Furthermore, there are cause collaborators in the form of apostles, disciples, and followers – for whom the HIFMs were a welcome deviation and faith respite from the then existing socioreligious norms which were perceived as hegemonic.

Ideationally, HIFMs draw their core philosophical propositions from traditional tenets and there are modifications and syncretic trends to keep pace with temporal changes (Gupta, 1973). The scriptures/ texts are derived from the larger background of historical and oral accounts (Sunderasan, 2000). Stylization is through modifications and syncretisms, which personalize the philosophical repertoire as well as create a synthesis between tradition and modernity (Saran, 1969). Guru's teachings are in the form of epithets and signature pronouncements, which also have elements of social praxis embedded in them (Morearty, 1975). There are faith practices, which are sanitized and globalized (Van der Veer, 2007), thereby transporting the cultural capital of HIFMs to translocal terrains. They essentially direct the associates' world visions and place emphasis on transcendence and subjectivity experiences. These teachings are then performed by associates as practices suitably developed and transformed; they in turn shape the identity/selfhood perceptions of associates (Singleton, 2010).

Growth is at once culturally aligned, locally rooted, and translocal,[20] where HIFMs utilize multiple strategies to wade through realities, hyperrealities, micropolitics, and textualities. At one level there is a

20 Translocal growth has been explicated in studies by Guerrlero (2000), Madsen (2000), Zaidman (2000), Squarcini (2002), Howell (2005), Crnic (2009), and Williamson (2010) mentioned in the literature.

reified spatial growth, and at another, ideational proliferation creating cultural codes. Transnational growth is facilitated through religious tolerance/incorporation of recipient nations and HIFMs' plasticity (Kurien, 2006).

Sociality

Sociality includes the HIFMs' sociopolitical frame of reference; their visions for society and social stratification, social ethics, and consciousness; their positions on social issues, action, service, and work; and their repertoires of social service.

The sociopolitical frame of reference has nodal points of interface, such as state, global political economy, market, and civil society. With the establishment of international political economies, compliance, co-option, and consortium of nation-states have to be maintained to meet the aims of spatial-ideational outreach (Rodney & Parameswaran, 2008). As is the case with new age market theorizations (Redden, 2005), HIFMs too have marketable salvation goods, online presence, connections with the virtual followers' commune, and commodification and brand-building routines. However, non-market elements such as prospects for attaining transcendence also determine alignment (Percy, 2000). Civil society interface is hallmarked by revitalizing faith, transformation of the moral fibre of the follower/associate publics, and crafting citizenship that is agreeable to HIFM norms (Kasturi, 2010). The byproduct may be social capital and/or humanity–transcendence/divinity connections.

In terms of the establishment and global political economy, HIFMs' relationships are historical and nuanced. Akin to other social movements that stake a claim on social transformations, for example FBOs, HIFMs would also reckon with the imperatives for survival and market share vis-à-vis the state (Bellin, 2008). In state negotiations, agency, choice, and contingency, as opposed to structural determinism, shape outcomes. Vis-à-vis the global political economy there are aspects of contact zone interface, collaborations, and ideational internationalism. Essentially, a diasporic consciousness is cultivated (Vertovec, 1997) through which exclusivity is created and the spread is facilitated. There are ways in which they become visible sociopolitical players in non-home grounds (Blanke, 2004) through mission enhancement, spiritual rejuvenation, and commune creation (Mayaram, 2004). In a way they also create political capital[21] (Wagner, 2008), and a sort of commitment to 'looking out' to the wider community and testing faith through action (Jamoul & Wills, 2008).

Transcendence and consciousness discourses guide the HIFMs' visions on society and social consciousness. Stratification is sublimated in the transcendental quest but reified in practice (Hatcher, 2007). Ethics are HIFMs' moral positions on the 'social' (Crowe, 2011), which are a combination of de-ontological and teleological stances – aspects of 'moral considerability' of all subjects as part of the divine and hence to be included in social service schemes and 'moral weight' as appropriate Hindu-inspired adjudication in terms of deciding who is the most needy and deserving, both being included (Dalmiya, 2009).

Positions on social issues, action, service, and work are derived from and accompanied by the spiritual teachings package (Beckerlegge, 2007). Action is to dethrone colonial hierarchies (Marcos, 2009) and service inevitably stems from the *seva* epithet (Beckerlegge, 1998, 2000a, 2000b, 2003; Warrier, 2003; Srinivas, 2008). Action, service, and work have both transcendental goals – inner transformation – and practical goals – tangible 'social difference' making. In terms of positionalities on social issues, HIFMs would have their own distinctive positions stemming from

---

21 Wagner (2008) discussed how the concept of political capital rather than social capital is an appropriate metaphor to understand religious movements in the civil society. The attempt is to reframe the civic engagement debate by redirecting thinking about the ways in which religion may (or may not) strengthen citizens' involvement in society. The connections have been drawn to the works of Hannah Arendt's 'The Human Condition' (1958) and Habermasian thought. Arendt introduced the important distinction between 'social' and 'political', which is at the core of the argument. Arendt discussed that the secular legitimization of a deliberative democracy rests on two components: the equal political participation of all citizens in a political community, and the epistemic conditions for a democratic deliberation to produce rationally acceptable outcomes. Only based on this distinction can the role of religion and its relationship to civil society be properly understood. Habermas has formulated three epistemic rules for the use of religious arguments in the public sphere. First, members of religious communities must self-reflectively process the cognitive dissonances that result from the existence of other religious doctrines (respectively, the existence of other denominations of their belief) within a pluralistic society hitherto dominated by their own claims to truth. Second, communities of faith have to let their members reconcile religious doctrines with scientific knowledge about the state and origin of the world in a way that is not in conflict with their faith. Third, as citizens of a democratic polity, members of religious communities have to connect the egalitarian universalism and secular morality of the constitutional state with the premises of their own comprehensive doctrines.

their ideologies – elements of textuality entering and influencing how social issues are understood and constructed (Jayshree, 2006).

In HIFMs, social service is either initially serendipitous and later streamlined or systematically initiated as a part of the organizational ideology. The mandate is to bring faith back into the public realm (Isaac, 2003). The service ideology is mediated actively by religious-civil practices combining philanthropy and rituals (Vaidyanathan, Smith, & Hill, 2011). Norms of community organizing around the faith principle are created (Warren, 2009). Religiosity and ideological underpinnings of the HIFMs translate into service (Murray, 1980) and/or practices of *seva* thereby unveiling their social stake (Beckerlegge, 1995).

Among the HIFM associates there are volitional service tendencies, and also prescribed mandates and doctrines, akin to FBO trends (Kochuyt, 2009). Drawing from Hefferan (2007) it can be proposed that they provide spaces to negotiate realms not evident in strictly economic discourses such as good, evil, and morality and work directed towards higher purposes.

The entire complex of service – scope, mission, mandate, and management – reveals aspects of faith-based programme theorization where the faith component, personal spiritual growth, and beliefs development become the quintessence of service or *seva* (Weisbrod, 1998). The engagement in core service sectors entails a partnership in development goals in an essentially resource limited setting (see also Hester, 2002; Wills et al., 2009; Kline, 2010; Sutton & Parks, 2011). The mission is to respond to the faith calling and hence religious imagery accompanies the service mission to communicate faith-basedness in the 'public face' (see Ebaugh et al., 2003). Service mandate and management posits on the middle ground between the sacred and the secular: faith commune is primary (Cook, 1997), and this influences different aspects such as leadership, practical functioning, and finance policy. The overall understanding is to cultivate a faith-based context for service (Kaplan et al., 2006, 2009).

Multi-systemic HIFM relationships can be seen between different systems; for example, relationships between legal system, governance, economy, and civil society, including the followers–associates–beneficiaries complex. Amicability/compliance on the part of HIFMs characterizes their general relationship with the legal system and governance processes as their endeavour is to become crucial actors in the public domain (Pipes &

Ebaugh, 2002). A move beyond traditional market exchange characterizes HIFM's general relationship with the economic system, which somewhere down the line includes the questioning of the rational-choice market model (Stolz, 2006), mainly because philanthropy is the main source of funds and finance for HIFMs (Twombly, 2002). With the follower–associate–beneficiary subset, the core idea is to generate social capital (Lockhart, 2005).

The style of faith-based social initiatives of the HIFMs is characterized by dimensions such as political economy, memory, and oblivion. Political economy dynamics are determined by world perceptions and their translations into practice (Bradley, 2009). This would signify a collateral seepage of Hindu hegemony into the HIFMs' style and practice. Co-option and faith-coded biopolitics or governmentality reveal power dynamics between the HIFMs and the state and the civil society (Kennedy & Beilefield, 2006; Arif, 2008). Faith memories are created through cultural practices; there are elements of oblivion (or secularization) which in turn determine style of functioning. The style can be read through heuristic devices of ontology, episteme, ethics, and praxis.

Hegemony

Hegemony and Hindu nationalism are natural outcomes embedded in the HIFMs' perspectives. Hegemony is precipitated through Hindu theism and its attendant features, namely, caste, class, gender, and ethnicity. Hindu India is given credence (Beckerlegge, 2003) with re-imaginings of the Hindu nation/imagined commune in a variety of HIFMs' Hindu-inspired ways. The nationalist ideology of Hindutva proponents is popularized and valorized (Warrier, 2003). HIFMs design a political-religious discourse with an enduring set of practices, including ritual communication and pilgrimage (Pinney, 2002).

Ingrained within the HIFMs' ideology are aspects such as communalism, Hindu nationalism, secularization, and syncretic flavours. Communal nuances would imply modes and constructions of othering (Bharucha, 2003). Belongingness, or membership to the Hindu commune, which in turn would facilitate political engagements (Bacchetta, 1999; Basu, 1999; Reichley, 2001), defines constructions of nationhood. Using schematic images and mental frameworks of the ideal Hindu/HIFM ideology, social orders are constructed. However, in response to modernity's legitimation discourse, secularization-syncretism trends are also seen (Bratosin

& Ionescu, 2009). Probably it would not be the classical version of secularization based on the axiom of religious decline but a simultaneity in the sense of faith assertions alongside modern sensibilities and knowledge (Colpe, 1977; Carp, 2011). Syncretic trends are seen through different levels of mergers (Sears, 2009) and production of universal salvation goods.

Social transformation

Social transformation visions emerge from the main HIFM ideational stances and essentially reveal a 'sociology of hope' derived from faith: beckoning a divine fiat for change (Trompf, 2000). This is a sort of quest orientation (Reinert & Bloomingdale, 2000), wherein the self is an important component of discourse. Existential-social implications are about creation of not only structures and meaning systems (Heilman & Eliezer, 2000) but also a cultural habitus. Elements of social support, social learning through faith modelling, and faith–well-being links are proposed (Kohls, Walach, & Wirtz, 2009; Webb, Bopp, & Falon, 2011).

In terms of third sector/voluntary initiatives, HIFMs would provide institutional forms (Carp, 2011) and strategies of action (Clarke, 2006; Mihut, 2011). What would then emerge is a sort of metamorphosis and osmosis of newer genus and HIFMs ideals onto the third sector canvas. Genre re-creation would be in terms of insertion of the faith episteme into civic culture (Lam, 2006). Apart from the same, as per FBO literature, complementarity and demystification of superiority of secular services and collaboration could also be newer genus (Til & Ross, 2001). Osmosis is a sort of permeation of faith into the secular/profane fabric, which could be of the nature of faith-permeation, faith-centredness, faith-affiliation, faith-groundedness, and faith–secular partnerships. This is taking into consideration the tangible expressive ways in which faith manifests in action/programmes (Sider & Unruh, 2004).

Study design

Within the broadly qualitative paradigm, this work employs the multiple-unit case study design with a triangulation of methods.[22] For sampling,

22 The study also adapts Schrader-Frechette and McCoy's (1993) proposition of providing neo-Hegelian phenomenological and hermeneutic arguments in defending the method

the universe of HIFMs was charted. Keeping HIFMs' social engagements as the study's core criteria,[23] the sampling frame was determined from which nine HIFMs were selected at the first stage with the additional criteria of era of origin,[24] core ideological orientation as in the vision-mission (primarily faith-oriented and spiritual or primarily political), and size.[25] Six of the nine movements selected qualify as faith-based movements with a global spread and three have inter-country branches and a different kind of translocal presence entailing a 'virtual' export of the charisma.

Nine popular HIFMs have been looked at: Ramakrishna Mission, Bochasanwasi Shree Akshar Purushottam Swaminarayan Sanstha (BAPS), Shree Saibaba Sansthan Trust, Prajapita Brahmakumari Ishwariya Vishwavidyalaya (Brahmakumaris), Chinmaya Mission, Sri Aurobindo Society, Vivekananda Kendra, Mata Amirtanandamayi Mission, and Art of Living. Ramakrishna Mission, Saibaba Sansthan, and Vivekananda Kendra have branches and centres in India. The other movements have a global spread and followers in the diaspora. All the movements draw from Hindu tenets in varying degrees – some such as the Brahmakumaris claim that they profess another religion and are

of case study – of aiding investigation into differential consciousness through identifiable phenomena. Furthermore, there is also the Wittgenstein-Kuhnian justification for case study design where praxis reveals meanings.

23 They can be further classified in terms of whether undertaking social initiatives and type of initiative – developmental and rights-based work, conscientization work, spirituality and self-enhancing work, and philanthropy and charity – food services and food relief and education and health. This could be either in the affirmative or only at the ideational level primarily translating the faith mission or no specified social perspectives or initiatives.

24 The era of origin signifies medieval (1600–1850), early modern (1850–1900), modern (1901–1947/1950), late modern (1950–1980), and contemporary (1981 to present) movements. The medieval movements signify a Bhakti stronghold; early modern and modern movements signify colonial influences and socio-religious reform era, particularly syncretic cultures and little traditions; and the late modern and contemporary movements signify postcolonial assertions and postmodern developments.

25 Through my initial survey and search before beginning the study, I found nineteen organizations that qualified within the sampling universe. I selected nine HIFMs to cover all time periods of genesis, geographical spread, and involvements in social service projects covering the range of health, education, livelihood, and rural development initiatives, which are also the core sectors of interventions by voluntary organizations in contemporary India.

not Hindu.[26] The criteria for the selection of these HIFMs have been the extent to which they utilize traditional Hindu terms, norms, and motifs to justify their own stance, which warrants the inclusion of all the HIFMs under study. These HIFMs have founded sacred geographies through pilgrim and retreat centres thereby concretizing the charisma of the gurus.

Ramakrishna Mission (founded: 1897) is built around the ideals of Sri Ramakrishna Paramahansa and his disciples, particularly Swami Vivekananda, as his protégé. The Cossipore and Belur *maths* in West Bengal are the monastic headquarters. The Swaminarayan Sanstha or BAPS is the devotional coterie of Lord Swaminarayan and his successors. In the case of BAPS (founded: 1907), temple consecrations, the foundation and formation of Akshardham, and patronage among the local and diaspora commune (this branch of the Swaminarayan sect has a core patronage among the Kanbi Patidars, Rajputs, Kathis, and Thakkars both within the localized realms and across the globe) concretized the Swaminarayan charisma.

Saibaba Sansthan (founded: 1922) is the Hinduized institutional form of Sai Baba devotionalism built by his apostles.[27] The conversion of Shirdi

---

26 PBIV essentially operates on non-dualist and monist philosophical contentions – what emerges is a Saiva monistic trend with the concept of Bap Dada (the Incorporeal God Siva) and Brahma Baba (the corporeal form). Walliss (2007) proposed that PBIV is more a theodicy – a comprehensive meaning system (indicating a vindication of divine providence in view of the existence of evil – than pure theology. In terms of linkages to traditional tenets, the base is inevitably Hindu; that is, there are references to the Bhagwad Gita, Siva, Kalpa, and the practice of Yoga (PBIV, 2003, 2004, 2008). Modifications form the crux of PBIV: (a) there are interpretations in ontology and epistemology through the Raja Yoga propositions and metaphysical soul discourses; (b) in cosmology and historicity through the world tree (*kalpa vriksha*) concept and the world cycle; and (c) an eventual instrumentalism or instrumental knowledge for contemporary living and 'New Age-ification' in praxis (Pandya, 2013b).

27 In terms of his birth and parentage, it is said that Sai Baba was born in 1838 in a village named Pathri (Kher, 2001; Satpathy, 2001) in a Yajurvedi Deshastha Brahmin family bearing the surname Bhusari and was named as Hari (Kher, 2001). Two subsequent interpretations exist – one saying that he was placed under the tutelage of a spiritual guru called Venkusha during the period 1842–1854 (Satpathy, 2001) and the other that he left home at the age of eight in search of the Supreme owing to his natural spiritual leanings and submitted himself under the tutelage of a Sufi saint (Kher, 2001). It is also said that he was first seen in Shirdi in 1854 under a neem tree in meditation and later left the place in 1857 (Satpathy, 2001). Pertaining to his spiritual training and Sufi origins and leanings, Warren's (2004) study locates Sai Baba's birthplace Pathri in a socio-geographical context of the Nizam rule. The source of Sai Baba's Sufi origins for

into a pilgrim site and 'message' proclamation and epithet creation out of 'faith-patience' (shraddha-saburi) postulate are instrumental in building sacred geographies and concretizing/continuing the Sai charisma. Brahmakumari Ishwariya Vishwavidyalaya (also known as the World Spiritual University) was founded through the spiritual realizations of Dada Lekhraj, alias Brahma Baba, and his spiritual consort, Om Radhe. In the case of Brahmakumaris (founded: 1937), the sacralization of Mount Abu headquarters, Dada Lekhraj as Om Baba, subsequent women spiritual heads as Dadis through whom the murlis (divine proclamations) are perennially announced, ensured continuity of the guru charisma.

The Chinmaya Mission was formed by the disciples of Swami Chinamyananda alias Balakrishnan Menon, who wished to spread the spiritual message of Vedanta in society. Sri Aurobindo Society (Sri Aurobindo Society) was formed by Mirra Alfassa (later known as the Mother or the Divine Mother) to sustain and spread the integral vision and ideas on yoga of Sri Aurobindo Ghosh. In the case of Chinmaya Mission (founded: 1953) and Sri Aurobindo Society (founded: 1960), the continuity of the guru charisma is ensured through the Ashram (spiritual retreat) culture – a postcolonial orientalist form of the 'indigenous' and 'spiritual' cultural heritage. Continuity is further ensured through the transnational transfer of the allure through blessings and relics – creating imagined communes of charisma loyalists.

The Vivekananda Kendra was founded by Eknath Ranade (a member of the Rashtriya Swayamsevak Sangh, a right-wing Hindu militant organization) to build a cadre of workers for service based on the core notions of Swami Vivekananda of 'service to man as service to God.' Vivekananda Kendra (founded: 1972) signifies an institutional continuity of Swami Vivekananda's charisma: the sacralization of Kanyakumari and engraving the same in the public memory through the Vivekananda Rock Memorial being a prelude to the Swami Vivekananda charisma revival. Continuity is ensured through the glorification of the spiritual East vis-

---

this study has been the notebook of a devotee Abdul, the son of Sultan of Nanded, who lived with Sai Baba in Shirdi for a period of twenty-nine years and then till 1954, tending to Sai Baba's Dargah. This notebook called the Sai Baba Manuscript is a rare manuscript of Abdul's notes and jottings of the words and teachings he received from Sai Baba in Urdu.

à-vis the material West and the contention of spiritually oriented service (God realization and service to man as forms of worship).

Mata Amritanandamayi Mission is the organization founded to eulogize and spread the message of Mother Sudhamani aka Mata Amritanandamayi, who grew from being a local saint of her native village Parayakadavu (Alappad Panchayat, district of Kollam, Kerala) to the hugging saint now having disciples and devotees internationally. The Art of Living Foundation is the brainchild of the modern guru Sri Sri Ravishankar who initially obtained training under the Transcendental Meditation movement and later developed his own course on meditation popularly known now and patented as the Sudarshan Kriya. In the case of Amritanandamayi Mission (founded: 1981) and Art of Living (founded: 1982), Kollam and Udaypura signify the celebration of the orient-indigenous-sacral-culture in an essentially postmodern repertoire. The teacher charisma is 'located' and 'established' in the ashram/retreat premises as a virtual Archimedean standpoint – the fulcrum through which the levels of multinational operations of charisma transport and migration occur.

Field work

Data were gathered through organizational literature, interviews with key informants,[28] and non-participant observation. I did field work with each

28 Key informants included both members of the order or monastics and office bearers. In Ramakrishna Mission the monastics in ochre robes are also key office bearers. In the Swaminarayan Sanstha, the sadhus as ascetics and parshads as ascetics in training are the key personnel as well as householder followers who are office bearers. The Sai Baba Sansthan has office bearers appointed by the Maharashtra state government. Brahmakumaris have a trained cadre of committed men and women who have taken to the prescribed lifestyle and are called Brahmakumars (men) and Brahmakumaris (women). In the Chinmaya Mission there are men and women monastics known as Swamis and Swaminis. Those still in training and who have not completed their perpetual vows but are monasts are called Brahmacharis and Brahmacharinis. Apart from that there are also office bearers who voluntarily work for the Mission and devote resources and time to its activities. Sri Aurobindo Society has sadhaks (men and women) at the helm of affairs who have committed their lives to the Sri Aurobindo Ashram and its multifarious activities. The Vivekananda Kendra has *karyakartas* – who are lay persons and not ascetics, which is also the peculiarity of the Kendra. Mata Amritanandamayi Mission has a trained cadre of monastic members committed to Amma and the Mission. Apart from that there are also householder disciples as office bearers. Art of Living has a small coterie of monastic representatives and a large cadre of lay persons who have undergone vigorous training of the courses and teacher training modules to become qualified teachers of the Sudarshan

of the HIFMs between February and December 2011 as the first phase. Subsequently I did another phase of field work between April and June 2012. Initially I spent between a fortnight and twenty days in each of the places studying their organizational literature (in the forms of published literature, booklets, pamphlets, and collected works). This began at the respective centres in Mumbai city and later on at the organizational headquarters across the country. Starting at the first phase and moving on to the next, I interviewed key informants (comprising mostly of members of the order or key personnel in the HIFMs).[29] I visited the project sites of at least two social projects of each of the HIFMs as a non-participant. The content analysis of the organizational literature, discussions, and interviews with members of the order/office bearers and non-participant observations was done with the following *research questions* in focus:

- *What are the nuances of the gurus' charisma and teachings that proliferate the HIFMs' existence nationally and globally?*
- *How do HIFMs negotiate their existence vis-à-vis state, market, followers, and civil society?*
- *How does this negotiation pan into their understanding of social issues determining social action and designing the social service repertoire?*
- *What is the flavour of the actual social service done by HIFMs in terms of volition, doctrinaire propositions, memory, secular partnerships, and oblivion and style of faith-based social service?*
- *What are the shades of cultural hegemony and Hindu nationalism which accompany HIFMs' sociality and social service?*
- *How do HIFMs manifest as transformational actors for followers, the third sector, and civil society?*

Kriya technique. Hence, HIFMs' key personnel organization is a combination of order ministration of evangelical nature, loyal followers/disciples who assume responsibilities, and lay persons who are actively engaged in official capacities in pursuing the objectives of HIFMs.

29 In the case of Swaminarayan Sanstha or BAPS, I spoke to office bearers in the women's wing. To the male sadhus I wrote my questions and they answered in writing. Sadhus of BAPS are under perpetual vows of not looking at women and money. Thus, I maintained contact with them through the written word and to validate responses, I used e-mail communication. With all the other key informants comprising of members of the order and the office bearers I had face-to-face discussions and went back to them for revalidating the transcripts.

The study was geographically delimited to the HIFMs; headquarters and centres in Mumbai city. This was a limitation as the HIFMs had a translocal scale of outreach and operations. Second, projects selected for non-participant observation across HIFMs varied widely in their orientations and cultural parameters. Hence, this posed some challenges for comparison across the spectrum of different analysis criteria used in the study, making it difficult to set a level ground for assessment. Third, in the selection of key informants for in-depth interviews in the HIFMs, time–cost considerations were crucial in determining participants. However, maximum attempts were made to interview those informants who were closely associated with the social engagements of the HIFMs and data were validated by going back to them with transcripts for re-verification of interview transcripts of responses prior to commencing the analysis.

Book layout

The second chapter provides an overview of HIFMs. The third chapter discusses their sociopolitical frame of reference in terms of their relationships between the state, market, and civil society. The fourth chapter discusses the sociality of HIFMs. Sociality of HIFMs manifests in visions on society, social consciousness, ethics, and positions on social issues, action, and service. One important way sociality manifests in practice for HIFMs is social service. Chapter 5 looks at the tangible forms of social services in HIFMs and aspects such as volition, prescription, doctrinaire propositions, as well as aspects such as memory, oblivion, and style of social services of the HIFMs.

Chapter 6 is a critical discourse on the baggage of HIFMs and the accompanying prism which adds to their power dynamics with the state and society. This is studied through shades of cultural hegemony and Hindu nationalism. Chapter 7 is a discussion on HIFMs as actors in social transformation through their visions on social transformation, life course implications for followers, and understandings on social work, service, *seva*. Social transformation visions emerge from the main HIFM ideational stances, and, essentially, they beckon a divine fiat for change. Furthermore, how HIFMs re-create genres and osmosis and make assertions in the realms of the third sector has been discussed. What is then proposed is a model of Hindu-inspired social transformation – called the Hindu-Inspired Faith-Based Social Transformation (HIFBST) model.

From the earlier deliberations, Chapter 8 discusses the HIFBST model in terms of its ontology, episteme, praxis, ethics, and constitutive components. The substantive and practical questions which arise therefrom make a case for a new perspective/vision in social transformation discourses.

2

Guru Agency: Combining Charisma, Teachings, and Proliferation

The idea of a charismatic guru is the Archimedean standpoint of the HIFMs. Max Weber's classic stance on charisma is that of a specific revolutionary force in history, dependent upon social enchantment. Recognition of the power of charisma is the central aspect in the social and psychological dynamics of charismatic authority.[1] The cultural psychology interpretation of charisma is that it is a co-construction of intentional persons with transcendent attributes and the intentional worlds of individuals. Charisma for HIFMs can be understood as the experiential aesthetic that constructs and is constructed by engagement. Charismatic authority is the defining mark of nouveau faiths, which essentially rely on a process of charisma, charismatization, and charisma domination.[2] It is an active, conscious social process involving the confirmation of beliefs through non-cognitive methods of altering perceptions.

1 Furthermore, Schjoedt (2011) also proposes that there are cognitive mechanisms – sender's charismatic abilities affect recipients' neural response and subjective experience in interpersonal interaction.

2 Traditionalization is looked at as the nemesis of charisma, which as per Palmer (1988) is responded to by charismatic leaders through encouragement, acquiescence, displacement, and resistance. Two other aspects added by Roy Wallis are performance and responsibility to keep the enchantment alive.

Charismatic giving or transfer is oriented towards extending aspects of the 'inner' self of followers beyond cultural and physical boundaries.[3] This charismatic fellowship persists in being adaptive and continues to offer a viable spiritual resource within global revivalism that emphasizes on the importance of spiritual purpose and meaning. The female figures in the charisma repertoire, who are included in this work particularly – Sarada Devi, Mirra Alfassa, and Mata Amritanandamayi – can be viewed as offering a 'potent feminist theodicy and a post-patriarchal spirituality with the possibility to bring about social transformation' (Diesel, 2002, p.28).

Embodiment testimonies or testimonies of divine incarnation of the charismatic personas are the core to the proliferation of HIFMs. Specifically pertaining to the women in the charismatic repertoire , as proposed by Dalmiya (2000), is a reconstruction of femininity and a deconstruction of 'male master identity' as a spiritual goal. The acceptance of embodiment as a core dimension in HIFM development highlights Spivak's (2001) aspect of 'epistemo-affective specificity', which implies a 'structure of feeling' in thinking patterns as a presupposition. That is, in the realm of logic, 'emotive/feelings components' gain assertion and eventually become dominant. Through embodiment, what also occurs in the HIFM context is a reification of scriptural texts as ahistorical and using them to legitimize specific regimes of practices and beliefs. The embodied persona then is a divine being who virtually becomes 'super-sensible' (Grieve, 2003). This apparent symbolism of the divine allure is further intensified by apostles/ adherents who derive the non-material figuration through an enmeshed net of social practices. Thus, an ontological ultimacy (Kripal, 2004) of the charismatic persona is established who, in turn, is supposedly in deep communication with the follower coterie.

HIFMs can be actually said to challenge the critical voices of Nietzsche and Heidegger who discussed the progress of humanity following the decline of religion. Richard Rorty took this position to be the weakening or death of ontology in the postmodern age. The deconstructive notion of Being, which is proposed by the postmodern theorists (and Heidegger's

3 The notion of a 'charismatic gift' in the Weberian sense of a quality of authoritative inspiration is linked to a Maussian concept of the gift as breaking down distinctions between persons and between persons and objects (Coleman, 2004).

sardonic notion that it is no longer the other name of God in his opening pages of *Being and Time*), gets reconstructed in the charisma epithet of HIFMs. 'Being', then, is not, as Rivas (2008) proposes, a private and transcendental existence or an exercise in nihilism, but a reified expression as visualized in and through the charisma.

The genesis of HIFMs

The genesis of HIFMs entails a range of aspects: charismatic engagements, a commencing objective, collaborators to the cause, and a foundational hologram as well as social metaphor. Essentially there is an invisible hand of the charisma, or the foundation is overseen by the charismatic persona. Subsequently there is a formalization and consolidation by apostles, disciples, and adherents. Vivekananda Kendra is primarily built around lay leadership gaining inspiration from the Swami Vivekananda charisma. Faith-oriented spiritual proliferation is the core goal with a supporting 'social' stance. Eventually the HIFM-precipitated 'oriental spirituality' obtains a transnational support.

Charismatic engagements

For Ramakrishna Mission, Swami Vivekananda as the protégé, Sarada Devi (as the 'mother' incarnate and Sri Ramakrishna's spiritual-conjugal consort), and the monastic order packaged Sri Ramakrishna's spiritual practices, realizations, and revelations. The genesis of the Ramakrishna Math and Mission lies in the spiritual practices, realizations, and revelations of Sri Ramakrishna and the spiritual traditions of India as revived by him. Sri Ramakrishna used to say that his life demonstrated truth, that God realization and self-realization is the goal of life, that all activities of life should be so regulated by moral and spiritual principles that they may gravitate towards this goal (Sri Ramakrishna Math, 1942). Although Ramakrishna Mission was officially founded in 1897, the first Math had already been set up at Baranagore in 1886 in a rented house. On 11 December 1885, Sri Ramakrishna came to Cossipore House for treatment and there he trained his young disciples, especially Narendra, to live a monastic life. Although the process of uniting devotees gained momentum at Cossipore, it really started in Dakshineshwar. (The official history of the Ramakrishna Math and Mission also testifies to this fact.

Swami Gambhirananda has written that the Master united them at Dakshineshwar, Shyampukur, and Cossipore.) A householder disciple, Mahendranath Gupta, wrote Sri Sri Ramakrishna Kathamrita, which was later on translated into English as the Gospel of Sri Ramakrishna. The spirit of social service took shape with Sri Ramakrishna's exposition to two disaster situations, one at Deoghar and the other at Kalighata. This was further intensified through Swami Vivekananda's wanderings and his tryst with the various famines of colonial India. The Baranagore Math (monastery) thus became the fulcrum of the Ramakrishna order and later it was the Belur Math which is now the headquarters.

With respect to Swaminarayan Sanstha, deification of Lord Swaminarayan and the first spiritual successor Swami Gunatitanand, as well as corresponding temple consecrations, were the nuances of charismatic engagements. The Swaminarayan Sanstha was established by Yagnapurushdas aka Shastriji Maharaj in 1907 in Bochasan, Gujarat, with a temple consecration consisting of the twin idols of Lord Swaminarayan and his first spiritual successor Gunatitanand Swami. In terms of Saibaba Sansthan, the Sai Baba charisma was transferred and translated posthumously by apostles. Shree Saibaba Sansthan Trust (Saibaba Sansthan) was formed in 1922 after the passing away of Baba on October 15, 1918, by Hari Sitaram Dixit, a solicitor from Bombay to conduct the daily worship of Baba and carry on the day-to-day administration. It is popularly believed that Sai Baba gave an indication of his seemolanghan (passing to another stage) on the day of Vijayadashami, the Hindu festival after nine days of worship of feminine energy or Shakti. In terms of the Brahmakumaris, Dada Lekhraj was himself involved with the formation of spiritual congregations for individuals desirous of salvation and spiritual solace. The foundation of Brahmakumaris is through the Om Mandali whose history since its inception in 1936 and formalization in 1937 are crucial to the genesis. This Om Mandali comprised largely of women and girls who desired salvation and spiritual solace. During this time Lekhraj further proclaimed himself to be first as an incarnation of the traditional Hindu deity Krishna and later as Brahma Baba.

Chinmaya Mission story says that it was Swami Chinmayananda's intent to revive an understanding of the ancient philosophy of Vedanta and that it contained the basic and eternal truths underlying all religions and, therefore, was the heritage of all Indians. With the realizations obtained from interactions with Swami Sivananda and Tapovan Maharaj and the intent of propagation, Swami Chinmayananda pronounced his main mission as having the Bhagvad Gita and Upanishads accessible to every Indian. Hence, what commenced was a 'structured and systematic approach of the texts to revive an understanding of the ancient philosophy of Vedanta which contained the basic and eternal truths underlying all religions and therefore was the heritage of all Indians' (Thapan, 2005, p. 4). The first out of monastery lectures were delivered by Chinmayananda in his native place in Ernakulam in 1950 when he was called home for filial duties. This was, however, under the aegis of the Divine Life Society. From 1951 onwards, with the partial consent of his teacher Tapovan Maharaj (being a puritan ascetic he believed in the Ivory Tower philosophical speculations and hence was neither in favour of 'simplification' nor 'propagation'), he commenced the tradition of jnana yagnas or knowledge sacrifice sessions whence the high knowledge of Vedanta along with ritual accompaniments was passed on to the seekers. The first such session was held on 23 December 1951 in Pune in the residential premises of Sushila Mudaliar, followed by a 100-day discourse in English on Upanishads (between 31 December 1951 and 8 April 1952) in the Harihar Bhajana Samaj, Pune.

For Sri Aurobindo Society the Mother[4] translated Sri Aurobindo's[5] supramental and transcendental vision into an organizational form.

4 The Mother was born on 21 February 1878 in Paris as Mirra Alfassa to affluent parents. She is said to have had divine experiences since childhood and often went into a trance. In 1906, Mirra Alfassa formed a small group of seekers in Paris called the 'Idea'. Mirra Alfassa's first meeting with Sri Aurobindo was in 1914, when she accompanied her husband Paul Richards from France on business to Pondicherry. In 1920, she arrived back in Pondicherry to settle there permanently. From 1926 Mirra Alfassa, who had herself assumed discipleship of Sri Aurobindo, assumed more responsibility of the yogic guidance of the sadhaks. She began by collaborating with him in the publishing of Arya, which was the first point of many of Sri Aurobindo's important works, and later established the Sri Aurobindo International Centre for Education in 1952 and Auroville in 1968. In 1962, she went into solitude till her passing away in 1973.

5 Sri Aurobindo was born on 15 August 1872 in Kolkata and at the age of seven he was sent to England to study with his two older brothers. Later he joined the King's College, Cambridge, on a senior classical fellowship to study classics and literature as well as the curriculum of the Indian Civil Service. However, he did not graduate there but passed the Tripos in the second year. Furthermore, he did not qualify for the Civil Services as he did not attend the horseback riding exam. In 1893, on his return to India, he entered the State Service of Baroda and was employed in various administrative positions by

However, these were themselves preceded by Sri Aurobindo's engagements in secret societies and associations, and they jointly founded a secret association, L'Idee Nouvelle or the New Idea, prior to the formal establishment of the ashram and society. The genesis of Sri Aurobindo Society is traced to the Sri Aurobindo Ashram; however, the seeds of an institutional endeavour to realize the supramental and transcendental vision were visualized much earlier. A series of historical events took place to realize their vision. In 1905, Aurobindo Ghosh, then an academician and political analyst, had the idea of setting up a Bhavani Mandir in Calcutta as an army of men inspired by nationalism. In 1910, Mirra Alfassa set up in Paris a group called the Idea. In the same year, on his way to Pondicherry from Calcutta, Aurobindo Ghosh stayed for a few months with Motilal Roy at Chandernagore, who was a member of a secret political society there and in Chandernagore, and the first seed of starting centres in different parts of India dedicated to the practice of Yoga was sown. Furthermore, in 1913, in a letter to Motilal Roy, he wrote that an important part of his work was to first realize in himself the supreme and to establish a yogic sadhana which will not only liberate the soul but also prepare a perfect humanity. In 1914, when the First World War broke out, Aurobindo Ghosh and Mirra Alfassa founded a society with headquarters at Pondicherry and branch at Karaikkal. The name of the society was L'Idee Nouvelle or the New Idea, dedicated to the spiritual goal of development. In 1916, Aurobindo Ghosh wrote a series of articles under the monthly journal of the group, Arya, under the title 'Psychology of Social Development'. Since his arrival in Pondicherry in 1910 with the aim of developing yogic practices, a group of devotees or followers came along with him, and this led to the growth of the collective later on called

---

Maharaja Sayajirao Gaekwad. He studied Bengali and Sanskrit in Baroda and he says in his biography that his thirteen years in Baroda were those of self-culture, literary activity, as well as some silent political activity (Sri Aurobindo Ashram Trust, 2006). In 1906, he came to Kolkata as the Principal of the Bengal National College, but resigned soon after, and from 1906 to 1910, he was actively engaged in political activities. In February 1910 he withdrew to a secret retirement in Chandernagore and in the beginning of April sailed for Pondicherry in French India (Sri Aurobindo Ashram Trust, 2006). In the then French colony of Pondicherry, Sri Aurobindo began his spiritual work. His arrival there also marked an end of his active involvement in Indian politics and the Nationalist Movement. In 1914, after four years of silent yoga, he began the publication of the philosophical monthly Arya. Most of his more important works, especially those published since in book form, appeared serially in Arya (Sri Aurobindo Ashram Trust, 1972).

the ashram. From 1926 to 1960, Mirra Alfassa, then bestowed the title of the 'Mother' by Sri Aurobindo, undertook the work of spiritual and educational guidance of the followers. Furthermore, the administrative work of the Ashram and its proliferation was undertaken solely under her guidance. From 1940, several families were accepted in the ashram, and in 1952, a university centre was established. In 1960, the Mother founded Sri Aurobindo Society, with herself as its Executive President and Keshav Dev Poddar, a Mumbai-based businessman, who took the name Sri Navajata, as the first general secretary and treasurer of the society.

Vivekananda Kendra's genesis is attributed to the sanctification of the Vivekananda Rock Memorial at Kanyakumari, an idea floated by Ramakrishna Mission during his birth centenary year in 1963 and led by Eknath Ranade. For Amritanandamayi Mission, Sudhamani's aka Mata Amritanandamayi's divine visions and spiritual appeal were the core factors. Amritanandamayi Mission's genesis in 1981 paralleled Sudhamani's divine projections and also the sporadic arrivals of young educated men from the neighbouring villages wishing to devote their lives to spiritual activities. For Art of Living, Sri Sri's transcendental experiences and efforts towards institutionalization of spiritual training had an osmosis effect. Sri Sri's transcendental experiences emerged out of a ten-day quietude in Shimoga, and the first course on Sudarshan Kriya (SK) was started. Later, the Ved Vigyan Maha Vidya Peeth (VVMVP) started. Sri Sri initially used the tenets of Transcendental Meditation movement and worked informally from his ancestral house in Bangalore. The Art of Living Foundation was then formally established in 1982 as a 'non-profit, educational and charitable organization designed to enhance the quality of life' (TOI, 2006).

Cause collaborators

Organizational genesis of these HIFMs also accompanied certain cause collaborators who served as lynchpins for institutional establishment. The widest collaboration was with Ramakrishna Mission – with Swami Vivekenanda as protégé and founder, Sarada Devi as spiritual symbol, monasts and key householder disciples, and Westerners who supported Swami Vivekananda during his foreign voyages. He was the natural leader of the movement, and Swami Ramakrishnananda (1863–1911) was the central figure of the organization. The formal birth of

Ramakrishna Mission happened with Swami Vivekananda's return to India after a trip abroad, whence he called a meeting of his brother disciples. The meeting was held in Balaram Bose's house in Baghbazaar on 1 May 1897. There, Swamiji explained the aims and objectives of the organization, which were to preach Sri Ramakrishna's message of the divinity of mankind and also show by its work how divinity could be attained. Seven years after the passing away of Swami Vivekananda, this association came to be registered in May 1909 under the Act XXI of 1860 and its management was vested in a governing body consisting of the trustees of the Belur Math. Although functioning on the brass tacks of life, Ramakrishna Mission proposed to keep its vision fixed on the transcendental as typified by the significant monogram of the order. When Swami Vivekananda passed away on 4 July 1902, it was Swami Saradananda who was the secretary of the Math. Some of the Westerners who followed Swamiji also played a key role in the genesis of the Mission.[6]

Swaminarayan Sanstha's cause collaborators were the members of the monastic order as well as householder disciples – the Kanbi Patidars, Thakkars, Rajputs, and Kathis of Gujarat – and within the Diaspora commune. The first commencing point of the establishment of the sect was the schism emanating from differences about succession from Gunatitanand Swami (Pragji Bhagat, the main stakeholder and successor was of lower caste and, hence, not entirely accepted by the fraternity). The sect which followed Pragji Bhagat commenced its activities with five sadhus (monasts having taken perpetual vows) which then grew as a socioreligious organization against a colonial backdrop and was formally registered in 1947 as a trust due to the efforts of Shastriji Maharaj. It was

6 They were: George Hale, who was Swami Vivekananda's host in Chicago; Mrs. George Hale, who took into her house a stranded stranger from Chicago roadside and befriended him ever afterwards; Professor J. Henry Wright, who made possible Swamiji's entry into the Parliament of Religions as a delegate; Mrs. Ole Bull, Swamiji's host in Boston and a most loyal friend who supported his cause; Mrs. J. McLeod, a lifelong loyal American friend and a helper of his cause; Sister Christine, a dedicated American disciple who consecrated her life for serving Swamiji's cause in India; Captain J.H. Sevier, his English disciple who, along with his wife Mrs. H.H. Sevier, founded and nurtured the Advaita Ashrama in Mayawati at the insistence of Swami Vivekananda; J.J. Godwin, who took down in shorthand and transcribed many lectures of Swami Vivekananda now embodied in the Complete Works; and Sister Nivedita, who was his spiritual companion (Belur Math, 2009).

with the efforts of the next spiritual successor Yogiji Maharaj[7] that the organization commenced serious spiritual and social activities and work with families, children, and youth and subsequently had a transborder presence. Headquartered now at Shahibaug, Ahmedabad, the fifth spiritual head was Pramukh Swami Maharaj[8] who bequeathed his role to Mahant Swami in March 2013.

For Saibaba Sansthan, apart from the apostles, their progeny and followers/devotees, the original coterie comprised of the Dixit and Patil community groups of Maharashtra.[9] In Brahmakumaris, for Dada Lekhraj

---

7 The fourth successor Yogiji Maharaj was born in Dhari Saurashtra in 1892. Later he joined Shastriji Maharaj in Bochasan and was subsequently appointed to preach the Akshar Purushottam philosophy in villages. In 1953, he inspired three followers in London to start a weekly satsang, and in 1955 he visited Southern and East African countries with the objective of 'reviving Hindu dharma among Asian Indians'. He consecrated the first Swaminarayan Sanstha temple in Mombasa, Kenya, and later worked towards initiating many youth into the ascetic fold in India and overseas. It has been documented that in 1970, on his return from a visit to Nairobi, Kenya and Islington, North London, several youth returned with him to become ascetics. He passed away on 23 January 1971, bequeathing the charge to Shastriji Narayanswarupdas or Pramukh Swami as he is now popularly known. In simple kathiawadi language (a dialect of Gujarati) he was instrumental in 'spreading' the Swaminarayan message to youth and children worldwide, inspiring the key hagiographical work, 'Life and Philosophy of Shree Swaminarayan' by H.T. Dave and Harikalpataru, a Sanskrit text extolling Swaminarayan's divine episodes by Achintyanand Swami Brahmachari. He himself wrote the work 'Akshar Tirth', extolling the glory of the shrine Akshar Deri in Gondal. He also wrote a detailed letter to a devotee containing the essence of the work of Shastriji Maharaj titled 'Vachanamrut' which later came to be known as Yogi Gita owing to the superior quality of interpretation therein (Dave, 2000).

8 Pramukh Swami Maharaj or Shastri Narayanswarupdas was born in Chansad near Vadodara on 7 December 1921. He was named Shantilal by his parents who were themselves staunch disciples of Shastriji Maharaj. During childhood, he engaged in listening to folktales of deities in his village. In 1938, he received a message from Shastriji Maharaj, urging him to join the fellowship. Responding to this call he left home and in 1940 he was initiated as Narayanswarupdas Shastri in Akshar Deri in Gondal by Shastriji Maharaj. In 1948, he was appointed as the head of the Sarangpur temple, and in 1950 he was appointed as the administrative lead of the Swaminarayan Sanstha (the president) instructed to work under the guidance of the spiritual head Yogiji Mahraj, which he did until 1971, when Yogiji Maharaj passed away and he assumed the successorship (Sadhu Aksharvatsaldas, 2002).

9 To maintain the functioning of the Trust, an elected body was constituted in 1952 which functioned until 1960. Later it was caught up in litigation and a civil court in Bombay appointed a receiver to take over the administration of the Sansthan. The receiver functioned till August 1984 when the 22-member Board of Management was appointed by the Maharashtra Government to take over, with an executive officer in charge. Since then the functioning has been stabilized thus, with the headquarters at Shirdi and an office in Mumbai for liaison purposes with the State.

as the founder, Om Radhe served to be a spiritual consort and collaborator as also other spiritually inclined women committed to the trust. Owing to the initial societal rejection and persecution of these women who had assumed a monastic life (supposedly against their families wishes), Brahmakumaris adopted a stand of being world-rejecting millenarian organization characterized by a strong dualistic view in self-vision, image, and practice. Om Radhe was put at the helm of affairs and the trust comprised of eight women and all the moveable and immoveable properties of Dada Lekhraj were placed there. From 1937 to 1950, along with private spiritual pursuits, a residential school for imparting 'spiritual and regular education' to girls and women was started in Hyderabad (Sind) called Om Niwas under the direction of Dada Lekhraj. Furthermore, under the leadership of Om Radhe and other women committed to the trust, they simultaneously asserted the rights of women towards a monastic order and formulated their own philosophy that would form the core of Brahmakumaris ethos in future. Women monasts who were part of the trust went into trance-like states and claimed to be messengers of God (sandeshputris) and a formal structure, curriculum, and levels of classes for different levels of spiritual development were published. Rejection and persecution, however, continued and there was the formation of an Anti-Om Mandali comprising of influential business-class men (some of whose wives had joined the Om Mandali and were observing vows of celibacy and chastity and imperatives of group membership). This comprised of political opposition, vilification, court trials for restoration of conjugal rights, and a fact-finding tribunal by the Allah Baksh ministry propelled by the Anti-Party insistence[10] (Walliss, 2007). This also corroborates the

10 This is a group made up of predominantly ex-members of Brahmakumaris and is highly critical of what they allege to be the increasing worldliness and corruptness of the university hierarchy. On their website they have declared that Brahmakumaris has become a 'Ravan Rajya' – demoniac world, where pomp, show, and grandeur are given preference over godly knowledge. A number of prophetic failures, the prominent one being that of world destruction, were instrumental in Brahmakumaris shift in world orientation and the Advance Party schism in the 1970s. Effectively, the outcome has been that the Advance Party has re-interpreted the millenarianism. While accepting the importance of Dada Lekhraj, the Advance Party claims that he was only one chariot or earthly manifestation of God. Rather, his business partner Sevak Ram was the one who was the corporeal medium of Siva. The story of Adhyatmik Ishwariya Vishwa Vidyalaya (AIVV) or the Advance Party is narrated thus: Sevak Ram helped in setting up the Om Mandali along with a certain Geeta Mata. He eventually left because of certain differences with Lekhraj and died in 1942. From 1942 to 1969, the deity Siva continued to speak to

proposition made by Roy Wallis (1984) that for the Brahmakumaris, the paranoia exacerbated by actual or perceived external prosecution found creative outlet in theodical elaboration and delineation of the elect from the forsaken. Its members underwent 'death in life' to find place in the divine world; to further attest to this, Hindu mythology was drawn upon. Post 1947 partition, Karachi and Hyderabad (Sind) became a part of the Islamic state of Pakistan; the then low-key Om Mandali renamed itself Ishwariya Yagna and stayed on in Karachi for three years. By 1950, most of Dada Lekhraj's original fortune had run out and hence they accepted anonymous donations and dowry amounts from the family members of those women residents who had committed themselves to the organization and were not likely to return to 'conjugal life' . The group then came to Abu in Rajasthan to settle and establish their headquarters.

Chinmaya Mission's collaborators were the middle-class urban-dwelling followers of Chinmayananda who were inspired by the discourses also called jnana yagnas[11] (knowledge portals of sacrifice for transcendence). This spearheaded the tradition of similar discourses at several places with the pronounced motto of 'converting Hindus to Hinduism and thereby ushering a cultural, spiritual, and social renaissance in a country newly awakened to nationhood' (Thapan, 2005, p. 8). In 1953, a group of enthusiasts in Madras, inspired by the first jnana yagna, formed a society in 1953 and planned a programme of activity to sustain what they had gained from Swami Chinmayananda's teachings. The society, as it was registered, was

---

the world through Dada Lekhraj. In 1969, when Dada Lekhraj died, the Advance Party claimed that Siva manifested through one Virendra Dev Dikshit and not through Sister Gulzar as claimed by Brahmakumaris – as Siva could not technically mount a virgin. Dixit, on the other hand, is said to have become aware of his role as the corporeal medium of Siva after he became disenchanted by Brahmakumaris and in his in-depth study of the 'murlis' he is claimed to have revealed that their Raja Yoga understanding was not complete. Debarred from Brahmakumaris, he then settled in his native village Kampil in UP from 1982 onwards and therein began to promulgate his spiritual insights. The party has effectively created their own version of the millenarianism.

11 A typical jnana yagna lasted for seven days and focused on two texts – one of the shorter Upanishads or a section of an Upanishad covered in one-hour lectures in the early morning and one chapter of the Gita over one-and-a-half hours every evening. The first jnana yagna was held in Pune in 1951 and lasted for about a hundred days. Gradually as the number of devotees increased, the centres multiplied and the demands on the Guru grew in proportion, the number of days of the yagna were reduced and eventually fixed to a standard one week. This continues to be the tradition of Chinmaya Mission even today.

named Chinmaya Mission, and subsequently Chinmayananda was approached for its recognition and ratification. Later the Mission had the Central Chinmaya Mission Trust as the central governing body located at Sandeepany Sadhanalaya, Powai, Mumbai – a retreat-like structure created through a land donated by Tara Swarup, a Mumbai-based devotee and philanthropist, in 1962.

With respect to Sri Aurobindo Society, the Mother was the chief spiritual collaborator as also the sadhaks drawn to the integral spirituality of Sri Aurobindo and associated with the ashram. In terms of Vivekananda Kendra, Eknath Ranade harnessed the Indian government's support through the Vivekananda Rock Memorial, transgressing initial oppositions[12] to realize Ramakrishna Mission's vision of commemorating the birth centenary of Swami Vivekananda and RSS's nationalist agenda. Hence, the committee approached Guruji Golwalkar of RSS. The task was handed over to his aide Eknath Ranade, who assumed the post of the organizing secretary of the Vivekananda Rock Memorial Committee. He then used his convincing powers and political astuteness to convince the then Nehru government at the Centre, as also two-thirds of the Members of the Parliament, appealing to the Swami Vivekananda charisma and his 'noble' vision of nation building by capitalizing on the heritage and spirituality of India. Simultaneously he also managed a nationwide fundraising drive, labelling the Rock Memorial initiative as the first step in the task of national reconstruction (Parameswaran, 2007). On the eve of the inauguration of the Rock Memorial, Eknath Ranade brought out a commemorative volume of 800 pages titled 'India's Contribution to World Thought and Culture'. The proceeds from this book became the seed capital for the formation of Vivekananda Kendra as a spiritually oriented service mission inaugurated in Kanyakumari on 7 January 1972 (Bhide, 2003). Through this organization Eknath Ranade perceived the concretization of the vision of Swami Vivekananda, and he viewed

12 The story of the rock memorial construction has several episodes of opposition. The Catholic fisher community wanted the installation of St. Xavier's cross there and the Kanyakumari temple Devaswom Board claimed that the rock was its property because of the footprints of the temple deity perceived on it. The local governance of Ramnad district wanted the statue of Raja Sethupathi alongside Vivekananda as the king had helped Swami Vivekananda during his travails abroad. Bhaktavatsalam, the then chief minister of Tamil Nadu and Humayun Kabir, the Union Cultural Affairs Minister, were also not in complete favour of the rock memorial (Parameswaran, 2000).

the RSS and Ramakrishna Mission as the mother organizations of the Kendra.

For Amritanandamayi Mission the cause collaborators included an initial group of educated young men from villages close to Idamannel and Vallickavu villages (native villages of Mata Amritanandamayi or Amma as she is popularly called) who renounced family life to practice spirituality. The snowballing effect further garnered international followers through the Ramana Maharshi ashram as lynchpin. The first in that order was a young man of twenty named Unni Krishnan (later re-named Swami Turiyatmananda) who came to Idamannel to stay with Sudhamani, who had by then acquired the title of the Mother. By 1978, the nucleus of the spontaneous ashram grew when a group of educated young men belonging to nearby villages renounced family life to practice spirituality. Most of them were from the town of Haripad, about 20 kilometres north of Vallickavu (village on the mainland opposite the backwaters near the Idamannel family property) and came from upper-class families. In the same year, Mother Sudhamani directed her disciple Balu to go to the Ramana Maharshi abode at Tiruvannamalai and meditate there for 41 days (Amritaswarupananda, Puri, 1988). There he is said to have met Gayatri, Madhusudana, and Nealu (from Australia, Reunion Island, and the US, respectively) and he is said to have convinced them to come to Vallickavu to meet Mother Sudhamani. This was also the hallmark of the informal commencement of the ashram with international leanings and three years later, on 6 May 1981, with a view to preserving and propagating the teachings of Mother Sudhamani alias Amma aka Mata Amritanandamayi,[13] the Mata Amritanandamayi Math and Mission Trust was founded and registered under the Travancore-Cochin State Literary and Charitable Act of 1955 at Kollam, Kerala, India. Art of Living cause collaborators constituted Sri Sri's consanguine relations (his sister Bhanudi and other relatives) initially and later Sudarshan Kriya and Pranayama (SK&P) supporters and followers who aligned with the inner-engineering norms.[14]

---

13 From this time she adopted the name Mata Amritanandamayi given to her by her brahmachari (monastic) sons.

14 Consequently began the development of an ashram on a rocky wasteland on the outskirts of Bangalore in Udaypura, which is now the international headquarters of the organization.

Hologram and social metaphor

Foundational hologram and the social metaphor[15] accompanied the genesis of HIFMs. Certain logos became synonyms and metaphors for these institutions' social-spiritual presence. Ramakrishna Mission proposed that God-centred life is necessarily a life of love and sacrifice to others. The ideal of working for the welfare of the world actually means *'jagat seva'* or *'siva jnane jiva seva'* – serving all beings looking upon them as God. This was the 1884 realization of Sri Ramakrishna, of the difference between compassion and service as also the proposition of divinity of humankind. The foundational hologram of Swaminarayan Sanstha was drawing and then branching out from the Swaminarayan sect, which was a modified version of traditional Vaishnavism. It was proposed that the sect would be developed by the Akshars or spiritual successors of Lord Swaminarayan. The social metaphor is unveiled in the motto of social and spiritual care. The twin message epithets in terms of Saibaba Sansthan are shraddha (faith) and saburi (patience). Social metaphor is reflected in the contention of 'benevolent syncretism'. This is mirrored in the belief in social mobility, exchange, and annihilation of social negatives through a spirit of syncretism and accommodation drawing from devotion to Saibaba. Brahmakumaris' social metaphor is characterized by a shift in world orientation from world rejection, and isolation to active proselytization and world service with 'Om Shanti' (the chant for universal peace) as the epithet.[16] For Chinmaya Mission, the core entails transformation of society achieved by individuals who are spiritually awakened. This awakening, which combined the social external and spiritual internal, was to be realized through a 'revival of timeless values embodied in the Hindu scriptures' (Thapan, 2005, p.2). In terms of Sri Aurobindo Society, the established motto was:

---

15 Social metaphor is defined as the symbolic insertion by the HIFMs of the social mandate into the largely faith repertoire which characterizes their vision and mission. This then translates into the actual work of social service and action which they undertake.

16 The year 1950 was a turning point in the organizational history for the following reasons: the group decided to come to India, and they did so as a group of 400 who travelled from Karachi to Okha port in a steamer and from Okha to Mount Abu by train; renamed themselves as members of the Prajapita Brahmakumari Ishwariya Vishwavidyalaya (Brahmakumaris) or Brahmakumari World Spiritual University while still retaining trust status; and shift in world orientation from world rejection and isolation to active proselytization and world service.

'to know is good, to live is better, to be that is perfect' (Sri Aurobindo Society, 2010). The declared objectives of the society revealed the social face, which included: integral growth and perfection of the individual, social transformation; a new India offering its best to the world; and realization of human unity in a rich and organized diversity (Sri Aurobindo Society, 2010). With foundational claims to the 'rousing call to the Hindu nation' ideal of Swami Vivekananda, the two main thoughts propagated were: each soul is potentially divine, and they alone live who live for others.

In terms of Amritanandamayi Mission, the knowledge path (*jnana marga*) was considered to be the precursor to all other spiritual and social service activities. So as to facilitate this knowledge path, Nealu, the disciple from the US brought his collection of 2000 books from his earlier place Ramanasrama at Tiruvannamalai. Furthermore, on 27 August 1982 the Vedanta Vidyalaya was started in order to impart the traditional Vedantic and Sanskritic knowledge to ashram residents alongside rigorous and prolonged meditation rituals. Art of Living's social trajectory is unveiled in the five-fold foundational vision: promoting human values, fostering interfaith harmony, building communal unity, encouraging social responsibility, and spearheading humanitarian causes.

Weberian 'routinization of charisma' is basic to HIFMs' genesis and institutional development. Further in terms of proliferation, there are dimensions of 'cosmopolitanism,' which entails investment in organizational management and harnessing international growth potential. The genesis of HIFMs has internal properties such as memberships of apostles and adherents, and a strong relational conception, which refers to the lack of alignment to extant and dominant sociocultural patterns. Hence, the penchants for the new and alternate[17] are core aspects to the genesis of HIFMs and their subsequent development. The transnational export of the 'oriental spirituality' of HIFMs can be viewed as parallel to Hejduk's (2010) category of the 'social sacred' – a spatial category which entails that space, time, persona, architecture, and urbanism coalesce to define and embellish the notion of the sacred.

17 Ashcraft (2005) has also proposed that the 'new' has elements of anticult behaviour which needs further exploration.

Philosophy and teachings

The philosophical core of the HIFMs, drawing from Chakravarthi's (2001) study on Indian theories of consciousness, can be said to be the ultimate goal of transcendence. The design arguments promote theism,[18] and it can also be proposed that they provide alternatives to modern/Western epistemology.[19] They oppose the dominance of rationality and invoke ideas of the supra-rational, such as the idea of the Supermind proposed by Sri Aurobindo. The core further promotes a symbolism of sorts (as given by Mircea Eliade), with an a priori understanding of the sacred as the constituent factor of human consciousness.

In terms of linkages to traditional tenets, there are as Valpey (2010) puts it, 'connections, appropriations and influences' that provide momentum to both the text (i.e., the traditional Hindu texts) and the HIFM context. These texts are then viewed as 'living texts' derived against the larger background of recorded history and other available oral accounts. Every text is effectively discussed, debated, and discoursed in its original form prior to its integration/merger into the HIFM philosophical core. The canonical literature is then looked at as 'true discourse', premised on the understanding that truth is constructed and constituted by the commune of sages who have authored the text. Furthermore, deriving from Taylor's (2008) analysis, there are five dimensions to this: the authoritative voice in which the text is enunciated, their universalization, level of adherence to canons, degree of intertextuality, and its subsequent naturalization in the contemporary context. In the doctrinally open and polyphonic scheme of things with respect to Hindu faith, traditions have competed for orthodoxy, acceptance, and resources, that is, religious capital, and this competition is manifest in the text traditions. These texts have been created in contested discursive spaces and were then adapted by HIFMs to only further intensify the complexities through their own spiritual-spatial dynamics. This process of valorizing an established sacral authority has

18 See Brown (2010) for a commentary on three classical Hindu thinkers Sankara, Udayana, and Ramanuja – belonging to two juxtaposed philosophical schools for a discussion on design arguments, that is, the question of design in the universe and its implications for theism.

19 Paranjape (2009) has used terms such as 'Gnosis', 'gnoseology', and 'border thinking' to describe those knowledge systems that are on the margins of or outside the world colonized by Western modernity.

also been used by HIFMs as a legitimizing trope. The texts utilized by HIFMs tell the audiences how to live and see the world. They are words of God or sages in divine locations; hence, there are creators and narrators of the texts which are 'performed' in divine settings and have 'power claims', that is, benefits, both spiritual and worldly. Modifications are like stylistic factors, which simultaneously perpetuate and preserve tradition, and this in effect has a positive value akin to the tactic of 'transcendent conversion'. This epistemological mutation then builds into the HIFM cultural corpus.

Core teachings

The teachings of the HIFM teachers elucidate, explicate, and rearticulate the raison d'être of Hindu thought duly modified. Faith practices come across as praxis – the modus operandi of living the teachings. Developments and continuity of teachings are ensured through personas, practices, and propositions.

In terms of signature pronouncements and the essence of teachings, the distinctive facets of HIFMs are elucidated here onwards. In Ramakrishna Mission, the core teachings of Sri Ramakrishna can be placed in an octagonal frame, with its eight core domains being: (a) equal divinity of the relative and absolute, (b) immanence of God in creation, (c) fusion of the rhetoric of oneness and devotion, (d) motherhood of God, (e) divinity of human beings, (f) religion as an experience and harmony of all religions, (g) synthesis of the personal and impersonal God, and (h) purity and renunciation as quintessential to God attainment. The domain of equal divinity of the relative and the absolute, the relative consciousness or 'bhavamukha', enabled Sri Ramakrishna to fuse apparently contradictory aspects of this worldliness and renunciation into a singular frame. The second domain of the immanence of God in creation has three main implications: man's real nature is divine, divinization of human relationships, and spiritualizing of his entire outlook on life. The third aspect is the fusion of the rhetoric of oneness and devotion; the nondualism of Advaita and the dualism of Bhakti fuse to form a qualified nondualism. This means that the dualism of devotion merges with the nondualism of oneness to form a theologically hybrid vision of competent oneness. In competent oneness, the being experiences a higher stage of being-ness than earlier by revering the Higher Being – a form and yet formless (Raghavachar, 1986). The fourth aspect is the motherhood of God – the currency and centrality given to Kali and, subsequently, the Holy Mother (alias Sri Sarada Devi) as a personification of supernatural being (Roy, 2006). The fifth domain is the recognition of divinity of human beings – God himself becomes phenomenal universe along with all the beings in it. There is a recognition of God in all, and adoration to him takes place through the worshipful service of all (Walters, 2006). The sixth domain is that of religion as an experience and the harmony of all religions. To rise above rationalism to direct experience and realization and this growth of man from the sensate to the super-sensual dimension is the crux of religion (Ranganathananda, 2006). The seventh domain is the synthesis of the personal and impersonal God, which is also popularly comprehended in terms of reconciliation of the idea of Bhakti and Vedanta. Ramakrishna realized the fundamental unity of the God of the jnani and the bhakta and the complementary character of the two paths of affirmation and negation (Ramakrishnan, 2006). The eighth domain is that of purity and renunciation as quintessential to God attainment (Bhuteshananda, 2006) – that being the sole purpose of existence (Tathagatananda, 2010).

For Swaminarayan Sanstha, there are three core components to the teachings[20]: philosophical, religious, and moral. The philosophical renditions discuss soul–Absolute being discourses and establish Swaminarayan as the Godhead with sublime attributes and further creations as his manifestations of gross and subtle nature. Cosmic evolution is also described from the Swaminarayan Sanstha lens – Swaminarayan as occupying a key position in the evolutionary schema (akin to ecclesiastical thought). Religious teachings establish the sectarian presence of the sampradaya[21] – scriptural hermeneutics prevail. Moral teachings are in the form of prescriptions for ascetics, householders, royalty, married women, and widows, covering aspects of nonviolence,

20 The teachings of Swaminarayan and the subsequent teachers – Gunatitanand Swami, Pragji Bhagat, Shastriji Maharaj, Yogiji Maharaj, and Pramukh Swami form the syllabi of the Satsang examinations held by Swaminarayan Sanstha. Hence, the text corpus encompassing the teachings is very well defined. Some of the main texts are Shikshapatri, Vachanamrutam, Vedras, Swamini Vato, Shri Harililakalpataru, Satsangajivan, Bhaktachintamani, Nishkulanand Kavya, and Shri Harililamrut.

21 Although the term *sampradaya* has many connotations, in the context of BAPS it is used interchangeably with the meaning of sect.

conduct, vegetarianism, practical spirituality, and business ethics. Swaminarayan Sanstha teachings have also visualized a journey through historicity: from prescribed injunctions for monastic and householder disciples as laid down in the Shikshapatri and Vachanamrutam to life skills orientation with essays and preachings on happiness, self-improvement, peace, and finally to packaged messages for the Diaspora commune of followers striving to attain the fine and delicate balance between the material and the spiritual.

Saibaba Sansthan's teachings repertoire is complicated. The main messages are shraddha, implying faith and saburi, implying patience – which has assumed the form of trademark for the Saibaba imagery. The base of the teachings is available in the hagiography Sai Satcharitra and is a syncretic combination of Vedantic terminologies and approach, as well as Sufi tenets. To quote a senior official:

> In fact, for most of Saibaba's life he acted as a spiritual master, or pir, to a floating population of itinerant Sufis wandering around Maharashtra in the second half of the 19th century. But the final decade or so of his life saw the influx of many Bombay Brahmans who discovered him through the kirtans of Das Ganu or the eminent Nana Chandorkar, a devotee who held senior positions in government at that time. At this juncture Saibaba had to change and accommodate his Islamic language and tailor his advice to suit the understanding and sensibilities of the new Hindu audience. (Mumbai, February 2011)

Warren (2004) says that Saibaba had to accommodate himself in two ways. The first one was for his murids or Sufi aspirants who were already committed to the spiritual path with the accepted goal of God realization. The other way was for the Hindu householder devotees, who viewed him as a miracle person. Hence he changed his nature of advice and method from Sufi dhikr (repetition of the name of God) to namasmaran. He would often use *bhakti* and *Sufi* terms interchangeably, some examples being guru/pir, sadhana/tariqa and saksatkara/baraka. With the core of oneness as 'Allah Malik' or 'Sabka Malik Ek', he proposed several sayings as outlined in the Satcharitra with regard to orthopraxy, individual and social ethics, as well as the function of karma (action) and the way it operates.

Teachings of Brahmakumaris have the following connotations: (a) metaphysical soul discourses, (b) the Raja Yoga technique, (c) the world tree and the world cycle chronicles, and (d) instrumental knowledge for contemporary living of the order of spirituality-oriented life skills. Metaphysical soul discourses commence with Shiv Baba as the incorporeal mother-father of all souls and beings as soul and not body (as body consciousness is understood as the root of all vices). Raja yoga technique's core is the inculcation of spiritual consciousness, communication between the self and the supreme, and mental link or union of mind with the supreme consciousness. Its difference from the traditional Patanjali yoga is emphasized – physical postures and breath control are not incorporated. The fundamental proposition is that with the mental union/connection, as also through abstinence, withdrawal, concentration, contemplation, and absorption, consciousness is attained. Furthermore, Raja Yoga is seen to provide a synergetic effect – by connecting the change of individual consciousness to change in societal consciousness – for the better (Hassija, 1996, 2006).

World tree and the world cycle chronicles talk about the impending apocalypse and Brahmakumaris herculean efforts to accommodate all aboard on the vehicle of soul immortality on which they have already occupied their places owing to the efforts of the original soul – Brahma Baba. Those who are 'fortunate' to align to the corporeal being (Dada Lekhraj in this case; the salvation army comprises of the Brahmakumaris), it is prophesized that they would emerge victorious at the end of the catastrophe. In a distinctively millenarian sense, exact details of the apocalypse and the number of survivors eventually which would hallmark the beginning of the 'New Age' is also specified. Those who have already commenced the sojourn are said to survive in the purushottama sangamayuga or the age of confluence. The kalpa tree is a metaphor of the systematic progression through its growth, proliferation through its branches, and eventual decay. It further symbolizes the root-to-branch logic of declining 'purity'. The decay is then redesigned as a new growth with Brahma Baba (the Adam of the new race) and his spiritual consort Om Radhe (Eve). The current Brahmakumaris army is the reservoir of progenitors required for the formation of the New Age. Instrumental knowledge for contemporary living comprises of components of values discussed and deliberated – peace, spiritual love of love for the Absolute (akin to Agape), knowledge of God, forbearance, and patience.

In Chinmaya Mission, the teachings of Swami Chinmayananda and other acharyas, that is, members of the order and the current spiritual head, Swami Tejomayananda, are available through commentaries and independent works drawn from the traditional texts. The content matter of teachings can be enveloped under the following heads: (a) puritan Vedantic metaphysical tenets; (b) the Body–Mind–Intellect (BMI) chart as a hermeneutic modification and scientific representation of transcendental gnosis; (c) the praxis face of Vedanta, wherein the malleability/ductility of metaphysics is visualized in arenas ranging from emotions, life skills, corporate ethics and social responsibility, and political morals, desiderata, and utopia; and (d) the Chinmaya Mission version of evolutionism, religion, and Hinduism in particular. Puritan Vedantic metaphysical tenets encompass soul discourses, karmic exegesis, and totalitarian vision. To quote a member of the order:

> The life of harmony can be lived by rising above our mere egocentric view of things and happenings and expanding our mind to accommodate a constant awareness of the totality of the world, the entirety of the mind and vastness and wholeness of the universe and its manifestations. (Mumbai, March 2011)

The BMI chart discusses the 'self' through concepts such as sheaths that envelop the soul packaged in the gross-subtle-causal bodies. Swami Tejomayananda (1995) proposes that what the BMI chart essentially posits is that the essence of knowledge lies in transcending the bliss sheath which is writ with negativities. Through reason and logic it rectifies the basic fallacies that we have about the cause of multiplicity in this world, our identification with the body, our attachment to the objects in this world in pursuit of pleasure, our feeling of doership, what binds the souls, and how to attain liberation. Furthermore, Tejomayananda (1998) also says that it tackles the subject of the mind and its purification. The simultaneous attempt through the BMI chart and its subsequent formulations is the infiltration of the paradigm of scientism in an essentially metaphysical repertoire; in other words, it is the use of arguments emanating from logic, diagrammatic representations of the intangible and abstract, imposed layering and gradations to demonstrate sections, compartments, and subsequent interlinkages to translate an essentially nonfigurative formulation into analytical tractability – the very characteristic of science.

The praxis face of Vedanta is unveiled through its oneness contention that endows a vision and a worldview, which finds applications in emotions, life skills and self-enhancement (CCMT, 1990a; Tejomayananda, 1997), collective and corporate ethics, and political utopia and desiderata of Hindu socialism (Ishwarananda, 2004). In terms of the Chinmaya Mission version of evolutionism, in religion and Hinduism in particular, what gets emphasized is as follows: the history of evolution passes through four stages or ages of perception, observation and superstition, scientific inquiry, and contemplation. The last stage of contemplation is the final stage of intellectual development to which philosophy and religion relate and which is far ahead of scientific knowledge known to humankind. Science is juxtaposed and placed epistemologically on a lower rung of the ladder than religion, which is considered a perfect blend of philosophy and ritualism. Religion is the art of focusing the attention on the spiritual core, which is the real nature of beings, and when the infinite dimension of the being is understood, one develops, in the experience of supreme bliss, a total dispassion of anything that the material world can offer. Effectively it is the applied science of life (Chinmayananda Swami, 1976, 1990a). Hinduism is then the perfect package offering all of the above – epistemology and metaphysics, ritual, mores and codes, and a way of life – all available through the Prasthanatraya including the Gita, Upanishads, and Brahma Sutra, particularly the Adi Sankaracharya[22] version.

22 Adi Sankaracharya, to whom is attributed the formation and establishment of the 'math' traditions that continue till date (and which prove to be the repositories of ancient Vedic knowledge in its pure pristine form), was born in Kalady, Kerala, to Aryamba and Sivaguru in 786 AD. As the legend goes, he was spiritually inclined since childhood and underwent training in philosophy under the teacher Govindapada Acharya in village Omkarnath. His forte was the nondualist proposition, the Advaita thought, which he developed and established through debates and discourses with scholars of the dualist, monist, and qualified monist schools during his sojourns or intellectual pilgrimages. Eventually, from the geographical landmark of Kashi he initiated disciples and established six 'maths' (monasteries) across the country to propagate nondualist philosophy. Sankaracharya is essentially responsible for the development of the Nirguna Bhakti trend.

In terms of Sri Aurobindo Society, the teachings are encapsulated in the main works of Sri Aurobindo[23] and transcribed conversations of the Mother. The main works elucidate and elaborate on certain core teachings which can be abstracted thus: (a) the supramental manifestation upon earth commences with the perfection of the body as the first step towards supermind attainment; (b) the stages of evolution are matter, life, mind, and supermind; (c) mysticism is the core source determining operations in the cosmos; (d) integral yoga is the science of consciousness (Dalal, 2001); (e) the path then involves a combination of aspiration and supreme grace with the personal effort as the triple labour of aspiration, rejection, and surrender; and (f) the last stage is complete identification with the Mother as the embodiment of the divine being. Furthermore, there are tenets such as (a) all life is yoga; (b) love, knowledge, power, and beauty are the four attributes of truth; (c) the infinite multiplicity of the 'One' and the eternal unity of the 'Many' as reality on which manifestation is founded (also entailing a repackaging of the traditional Advaita principle); (d) work, knowledge, and devotion as main pathways; and (e) the importance of grace as the instrumentality towards order maintenance in the cosmos. Therefore, the main teaching of integral yoga entails not a departure from the world but an existential change. This change or transformation also has threefold connotations: (a) the opening of the occult inner mind, inner vital, and inner physical, so that one becomes aware of all that lies behind the surface mind, life, and body; (b) the opening of the psychic being or soul by which it comes forward and governs the mind, life, body, turning them all to the divine; and (c) the opening of the whole lower being to the spiritual truth – this last may be called the psycho-spiritual part of the change. This is also called supramental yoga – the simultaneous ascent of God and the descent of Godhead into embodied nature.

Teachings propagated by Vivekananada Kendra are: (a) tenets of fourfold Yoga – Karma, Jnana, Bhakti, and Raja; (b) Vedanta as delivered through Swami Vivekananda's lectures in the 1890s; (c) the scientific

---

23 As a prolific writer and mystic philosopher, Sri Aurobindo penned several works, including letters, poems, diary writings, and philosophical renditions. His main works are *The Life Divine* and *Savitri* (the epic poem). Others important works include: *The Synthesis of Yoga, Letters on Yoga, Records on Yoga, Essays on the Gita, The Human Cycle-Human Unity-War and Self-Determination* among others.

interpretation of Vedanta; and (d) service and Eknath Ranade's version of 'Hindu' spirituality and its links with national regeneration. Swami Vivekananda, as the cultural translator of India for the occident, perceived Yoga as a way of life, which ensured a vision of reality through which man perceives truth in its entirety along with existence, knowledge, and transcendental bliss. Furthermore, with the contention of the potential divinity of the soul the goal is to manifest divinity within by controlling internal and external nature, which is possible through Yoga. In terms of Vedanta, Swami Vivekananda viewed it as a mode of 'man' making; an all-inclusive contention in three progressive stages of duality, qualified monism, and nondualism. In a lecture delivered by Swami Vivekananda on 25 March 1896 at the Graduate Philosophical Society of Harvard University, Swami Vivekananda proposed that just as Spinozism is the beginning of the understanding of the manifold, Vedanta hallmarked the beginning of the understanding of oneness. Vedanta orientalism and occidental rationalism and scientism are amalgamated in Swami Vivekananda's repertoire to make the Vedanta as a salvation good palatable to international audiences. The contention is that science investigates part of the universe, the physical universe, which is external to and excluding the investigating human personality. Hence, it is empirical and material in its orientation. Vedanta, on the other hand, is understood to maintain the scientific and the rational approach but focussing on the full philosophy of reality, life, and existence as also a support to morality, ethics, aesthetics, and religion. Thus, what Swami Vivekananda proposed is akin to a Vedantic rationalism (Mukhyananda, 1988). Service renditions equate the seva contention to worship (Swami Vivekananda, 1985, 26e). In his lectures from Colombo to Almora (15 January 1897–31 March 1901) Swami Vivekananda further distinguished between discriminate versus indiscriminate charity; Vedanta inspired service and real worship entailed in discriminate charity (Advaita Ashrama, 1997a, 17e). Eknath Ranade's version of Hindu spirituality drawn from Vedanta and Yoga repertoire views it as a singular national idea with the Hindus, which has innate nation-building capacities. Furthermore, Ramakrishna is posited as the nation's ideal (Advaita Ashrama, 1998b, 13e) with his rhetorical revivalism of Advaita Vedanta and soul discourses – characteristically annihilating all (read Christian, Buddhist, Mohammedans, and Agnostics) from soul struggling.

Teachings of Amritanandamayi Mission's Amma can be classified in four-fold ways: (a) renditions on the self and self-transcendence; (b) modus operandi, desiderata, and raison d'etre of this worldly existence; (c) the quintessentiality of love and service from the standpoint of faith; and (d) universality, harmony, and peace from the fulcrum of oneness. In terms of renditions on the self and self-transcendence there is a focus on (a) detachment, or rather attachment with a detached attitude; (b) awakening and developing the spiritual potential through meditation and paths of devotion; (c) action and knowledge; (d) performance of duty, and purification of mind through sacrifice, charity, and penance; and (e) gratitude to the universe, Absolute, and the guru or teacher who is supposed to specify the path (Swami Ramakrishnananda Puri, 2003). In terms of self, there is a focus on four-fold qualifications – discrimination, dispassion, quest for liberation, and the six-fold disciplines beginning with mind control. In the words of a monast at Amritapuri:

> In terms of self-enhancement and transcendence, Amma tells us to observe seven vows for a week – diminishing anger, adding a smile, formal spiritual practices, doing away with bad habits, abstinence in terms of food, helpful attitude, and silence. Amma also talks of discretion, detachment, the quest for self-transcendence, patience, equanimity, forbearance, faith, and contentment. These are known as qualifications because self-knowledge will take root only in a mind in which these qualities have been properly developed. If we are deficient in any of these, it means that we need to put in more effort to develop them, but it is not that we are unqualified for spiritual life. (Kollam, April 2011)

The modus operandi, desiderata, and raison d'etre of this worldly existence according to Amma is to realize the truth – which can happen primarily through spiritual practice; service to others not in terms of material charity but actual work and tithing practices; and surrender to God as the Absolute being. To quote a senior office bearer:

> Amma says that the main purpose of this worldly existence is to realize the truth – and that can happen through the guidance

> of a teacher who helps in interpreting scriptures as per the age and culture of birth. For that there is a need to cultivate divine qualities of patience, innocence, humility, alertness, and compassion. Jivanmukti (liberation) is not something to be attained after death, nor is it to be experienced or bestowed upon you in another world. It is a state of perfect awareness and equanimity, which can be experienced here and now in this world, while living in this body. Having come to experience the highest truth of oneness with the self, such blessed souls do not have to be born again. They merge with the infinite consciousness. For that Amma has prescribed the IAM (Integrated Amrita Meditation) technique. (Mumbai, February 2011)

On love and service, the main contention is to see the divine in all beings; hence, the love prophesized is an unconditional parallel to practical love, Platonic love, and theologians' agape. From the fulcrum of oneness there is a discussion on universality, harmony, and peace; this aspect is discussed from the lens of harmonious integration, the core of which is Sanatana Dharma, based on the all-encompassing Vedanta.

Art of Living teachings are filled with the following designs: spirit of inquiry, love, mind, life, relationships, knowledge, and emotions. The range is from the material to the spiritual, and the practical to the ethereal. The commencing point of the 'spirit of inquiry' is the universal question of 'who am I' – the positing of the abstract as the locus classicus of inquiry. The journey of this knowledge of the self undergoes stages and ultimately the knowledge of God or the absolute being is attained (as knowledge of self is considered synonymous to the knowledge of the divine; Vyakti Vikas Kendra, 2005b). On love is the much celebrated discourse on divine love – viewing love not as an emotion but in the ecclesiastical sense as the very base of existence (Sri Sri Publications Trust, 2006). The mind has been viewed to have three compositions: intellectual, experiential, and existential. The endeavour through spirituality is to transcend the mind (Sri Sri Publications Trust, 2007b). On life, the discussion is centred on the goal of life, which is essentially that of perfection in action or work, in speech, feelings, and intention, and its essential impermanence (Vyakti Vikas Kendra, 2005a). With relationships the movement is towards the ethical domain with extolling of virtues pertaining to viewing divinity in all, service and compassion; the true impression of relationships being revealed through silence or soul to soul communication (Sri Sri Publications Trust, 2005). Knowledge, then, is the pathway to attain the Absolute and not an end in itself; both knowledge and emotions need to be geared towards the sublime quality of love from wherein emerge qualities of service and meditation (Sri Sri Publications Trust, 2010b).

Teachings of HIFM gurus, thus, reveal the aesthetic side of pragmatism – a kind of 'art of life' emphasis. HIFM guru teachings can be said to be further shaped by the world of episteme, patronage, and brand creations[24] (such as Raja Yoga, Integral Yoga, SK&P, and Integrated Amrita Meditation techniques) – highlighting considerations that do not always revolve around an unblemished transcendental quest. Apart from a central spiritual message, teachings also reveal a less obvious political- and gender-shaped vision of the world. HIFM guru teachings are socially constructed – by authoritative traditions, mysticism, and reification. Cross-cultural validity is ensured through claims to direct access to God through epithets, meeting spiritualized expectations of universalism/ universalization, and 'postmodern' mysticism juxtaposed with scientism (such as Chinmaya Mission, Vivekananda Kendra, Sri Aurobindo Society, and Art of Living). The teachings make claims of an epistemologically extraordinary experience (direct/transcendental experiences) to validate the guru/clan authority to substantiate the traditional theological/ theoretical deficit. The idea is to create an agency not bound by traditional faith/theism definitions through new modes of philosophical enquiry, lending credence to subjective, religious experience and appropriate a space within the faith/spiritual schemata. The simultaneous utilization and subversion of traditionalist expectations is eventually to create the HIFM as an active and authoritative agent in designing a nouveau faith tradition with a translocal appeal.

---

24 Brands are identification marks, and for institutions they are like signature statements – literal and symbolic. HIFMs deploy meditative and spiritual techniques and modify them with their own signatures as a point of connect with society as well-being is the premium gained by the recipients. These meditative and spiritual techniques are marketed (spiritual marketing) as brands, which become representational icons of the HIFMs. Brand creation is a mark of proliferation.

It can be said that HIFM faith practices act as sites of both reproduction of and resistance to traditional images of Sanskritic Hinduism. These practices diminish the boundaries between the spiritual seeking subject and the HIFM as the subjective realm. Developments and continuity of teachings and faith practices are as per the 'social and spiritual capacities' (Appleton, 2011) of followers[25] and monastics. There is a simultaneous focus on evangelization, modernization, and orientalization – moving beyond historical binaries of reform and revival towards 'postmodern' textuality. Performative dimensions, including teachings and praxis, authorize both, the teacher and the nouveau tradition/cultural potpourri. Disciples, adherents, protégé, and apostles add elements of multivocality. Furthermore, these developments are in hermeneutical spirals – faith materializes as beliefs shape perceptions and vice versa.

Proliferation and growth of HIFMs

The proliferation and growth trajectories of the HIFMs include (a) retrospective 'phase identification' and ideational trajectories; (b) transnational outreach and spread; (c) contemporary local and global spread; and (d) branching operations including evolution of sister concerns. Drawing from Lucas's (2004) postmodern critique of new religious movements and their developments, it can be said that the characteristics of the HIFMs' growth entail a 'hyperpluralism' (HIFMs modify their strategies/practices depending on local/translocal cultures) and a 'domination of simulation'. Domination of simulation refers to

25 Most followers of HIFMs in India are from the middle class, generally middle-aged and older adults in the working sphere, residing in urban areas. The proportion of women adherents is slightly higher, and there is a large majority of Hindu adherents. In general, the education levels are high and followers belong to privileged social class. The class superiority, and also the generational peculiarities of IFBO adherents, finds certain parallels to "New Age" adherents/aligners (Pandya, 2012). With respect to gender in particular, HIFMs function as enclave communities where women are able to reproduce faith norms. Higher proportion of women alignment is also due to their historical conformism with Indic eschatology, ritualizations, and interdictions—which now take the form of contemporary yet traditionally rooted spiritual alignments. However, a more in-depth analysis of the gender lens is required to understand the feelings of belonging, the real respect of women for the HIFM obligations, and the ensuing creations of subjective/objective identities vis-à-vis their male counterparts (ibid., 2012). Beneficiary profiles of HIFMs social services resemble those of general public welfare user profile in terms of financial/economic status (Pandya, 2012).

the fact that the followers' experiences are mediated by the synthetic images of divinity produced and disseminated by the HIFMs. Growth demonstrates an affinity to New Age activism and cultural renaissance. HIFM growth dimensions also demonstrate a metapraxis of sorts, evolving new circumstances to legitimate religious practices both implicitly and explicitly. The developments are hallmarked by a tension and complementarity between the 'material world' and the 'symbolic devotional world'. As the material world grows and changes, the concrete place helps to shape the ontological objectives of the followers. As the symbolic devotional world grows, it helps to situate the sacred place of HIFMs' origin and give it significance by recasting the central axis between agency and structure.[26]

Ramakrishna Mission and Vivekananda Kendra use iconographic images of Sri Ramakrishna–Sri Sarada Devi–Swami Vivekananda triune for organizational growth through seva activities.[27] Swaminarayan Sanstha sadhus, through renunciation and service, have become institutionalized agents for maintaining unity across cultures where the sect has a presence. The early history demonstrated a heightened sensitivity of Swaminarayan Sanstha order to the public sensibilities while introducing Swaminarayan devotionalism. In its transnational sites such as the US, Canada, and the UK, the discursive and sociological dynamics of 'religion' and their intersection with Swaminarayan devotionalism is crucial.[28] Contemporary ones such as Amritanandamayi

---

26 Based on a study of Puttaparthi as the sacred city of Sathya Sai, Srinivas (2010) further draws on sociologist Daniele Herview-Leger's contention that globalization of religio-cultural groups is linked to the problem of identity construction as it leads to 'novel forms of religious sociability'. The harnessing of spatial imagination towards increased devotion rests on the Taylorean concept of the social imaginary where large groups of people imagine 'how they fit together with others, how things go on between them and their fellows, the expectations that are normally met, and the deeper normative notions and images that underlie these expectations'.

27 Beckerlegge (2004) further proposes that these iconographic representations reveal an unresolved tension between symbolism designed to inculcate social activism and constant allusions to an ideal of renunciation pre-eminently associated with the role of the ascetic.

28 Kim's (2010) paper essentially looks at how a non-Western tradition responds to its framing within 'religion', beginning from the premise that the category religion is constitutive of a Western episteme and that this in turn supports discursive formations and teleologies which are often assumed to be universal. Through ethnographic encounters it has been highlighted how discourses on religion have been mediated by

Mission and Art of Living combine, using Wilson's (2008) proposition, perspectival complexity with creativity to meet the adaptive challenges of the contemporary world. It is also seen that the non-urban origin of the charisma of HIFMs is, in the later years, associated with suburban and urban sites. In the growth process, the religious imagination of the HIFMs recreates a behavioural, communicational, and spatial model that develops particular kinds of topological domains in different historical and social milieus. Through certain 'root paradigms', newer cultural codes of adherence are created.[29]

International expansion of the HIFMs can be understood by borrowing Orye's (2004) proposition that there is a conceptual link between religion and social theory while looking at globalization. The focus is on a metatheoretical reflexivity in placing the reconfigurations of faith. Transnational growth of HIFMs has generally been triggered by two core factors: (a) policies pertaining to religious incorporation and toleration of the recipient nations and (b) the HIFMs' ability to present tenets which are compatible to a foreign terrain. HIFMs replicate imported cultural patterns as well as serve to be arenas in which resistance and assimilation to the new host culture is measured and moderated. In the US in particular, multiculturalism after 1965 brought in an appreciation of hybrid forms of religiosities.[30] In the growth trajectories of HIFMs

---

specific Swaminarayan practices such as temple building. Swaminarayan temples have been emphasized as multivalent structures responding to both public expectations and personal devotional desires. The temple, or mandir, defines the ways in which its publics—that is, its followers, visitors, guests, and even critics—will inhabit its spaces. And, yet, the mandir is also physically and figuratively grounded in multiple histories and epistemologies and supported by its own normative ideals, categories, power relations, and discourses. In other words, the Swaminarayan Mandir, in spite of its structural solidity, is an evolving and flexible structure, separable neither from its devotional moorings nor the historical and political contexts in which it is embedded.

29 Srinivas's (1999) thesis is based on the cult of Shirdi Sai Baba, the holy mendicant/saint (fakir/sant): a paradigm which was associated historically with non-urban locations; in later years, the incarnation (avatar) is to be found associated with suburban and urban sites. The urban topos of Bangalore is studied through the root paradigms of the Saibaba cult. The guru is seen to have an elective affinity with the constructs of the metropolis and its citizens.

30 Huffer (2010) says that rationalist neo-Vedantic theism of this-worldly worship dominated Hindu religiosity (and American ideas about Hindu religiosity) between 1820 and 1965. The advent of multiculturalism after 1965 encouraged immigrants to adopt and valorize their native cultures and religiosities, creating hybrid or hyphenated identities. The relaxed immigration policies of 1965 had a massive effect on the nature

transnationally the metaphor of concentric circles can be utilized. The inner circle could be the traditional practices and the outer as the newer practices introduced culturally.[31]

---

of Hinduism in the United States, effectively transforming it from a narrow neo-Vedantic masculinized interpretation to a more diversified interpretation that integrates the feminine. The integration of the feminine (in terms of ordinary women, goddesses, and female avatar-gurus) transformed what was initially a distinct form of American Hinduism into an Indianized cosmopolitan Hinduism that much more closely resembles its Indian counterpart. The influx of Indian Hindus after 1965 diminished America's reliance on Hindu texts, missionary accounts, and the neo-Vedantic interpretations of the initial waves of Hindu gurus; it created a dialogue between Western interpretations and 'authentic' Indian ones. While often a site of contentious debate, this dialogue ultimately serves to increase discourse and fuel the continuous reinterpretation and vivification of Hindu beliefs and practices in the American religious landscape.

31 This metaphor has been used by Zaidman (1997), based on his study of an American ISKCON temple. Kocsis (2004) has looked at the ISKCON presence in Hungary to understand similar contentions.

3

Faith Movements: Negotiating State, Market, and Civil Society

The sociopolitical frame of HIFMs is defined by their relationship with global political economy, the nuances of exchange between HIFMs and the State, HIFMs' relationships with the market, and their interfacing with the civil society. HIFMs have associations with the primary, secondary, and tertiary spheres of the social compass (i.e., the civil society, market, and national-global political economy). The norms and forms of interface range from collaboration to consortium and from mild opposition to general compliance. With the market there are elements of brand building, commodification, and routinization; in the civil society the focus is on generating social capital. Particularly with the global political economy and the state, HIFMs have evolved strategies of negotiation of their identities to gain legitimate spaces in transnational and national arenas. Their interface with the state and global political economy can be inferred as being actively imbricated in the domains of symbolic production – juxtaposed between the state–establishment alignment and adherence to Hindu norms.

HIFMs and the global political economy

In terms of their relationship with global political economy, Ramakrishna Mission's stance is that of multilateralism and exchange. With a policy of co-subsistence, toleration, pluralism, and secularization in the global scene with respect to religion, there is a certain penetration of sanctified 'Hindu' norms in the universal sphere. Resistances and antagonisms are suitably mitigated through dialogue, discourse, and dressing Ramakrishna Mission's work with a pluralistic-syncretic-secularist overcoat.

Swaminarayan Sanstha posits as a religious institution practicing and developing its own ideals 'internally', where state religions exist and in a 'propagation mode' where secularization and pluralism permit. The growth of international centres has been also in terms of the places of settlement of the Diaspora Gujarati community – the Kanbi Patidars, Thakkars, and Kathis. Hence, where the sociopolitical climate permits such as in the US and the UK, the range of work has extended beyond immediate followers. In Gulf countries, developments have been more inward; the purpose of Swaminarayan Sanstha centres being that of maintaining tradition among the followers.

For Swaminarayan Sanstha, aspects of symbolic and real social-spiritual exchange with the global polity have thus been: establishment of centres, temple consecration, and satsang (spiritual propagation) tours of the spiritual heads to build a spiritual habitus amidst the Diaspora community. The culture of the translocal spread by positing Swaminarayan Sanstha as an organization shielding the religio-spiritual Hindu dharma heirloom has facilitated a two-fold relationship of the Sanstha with global establishments. First, Swaminarayan Sanstha agency is seen as a vanguard of Hindu epistemology making communicative assertions in the global horizons (especially in countries where state religion is dominant and overarching). Second, Swaminarayan Sanstha is seen as a transcendent version of traditional Vaishnavism (a neo-qualified dualism) offering integrative-assimilative prescriptions not only for the Diaspora commune but also for the social compass in general (particularly in countries where state has a pluralist/secular tone).

Shree Saibaba Sansthan Trust's local orientation proposes an abstract connection with the global economy primarily through the Sai charisma. Brahmakumaris' relationship with the global polity economy is that of assimilation, exchange, and assertion. Assimilation is visualized in terms of adaption of transcultural ideals in global branches and the willingness to translate the core message in languages of other faith. For instance, parallels are drawn to ecclesiastical theology, Judaism and Buddhism, in interpreting the divine message or 'murlis', which are periodically believed to be revealed and read out. This naturally translates into exchange relations of a bilateral nature wherein Brahmakumaris and local country cultures and norms give and take from each other. Multilateral exchange relationships are seen where Brahmakumaris, local country culture and polity, and other organizations collide to provide a spirituality package – as in the case of Indonesia.[1] With its UN involvements there is a definite assertion of the spirituality agenda – millenarianism and spirituality are considered as essentials and designed as non-negotiables for universal values of peace and harmony. At one level there is a development and reinterpretation of Raja Yoga to suit a world-affirming cultic milieu. This is viewed in the elaboration of the original world-rejecting theodicy through aspects of globalization discourses, new-age-ification, and emphasis on self-reflexivity of followers and its accompanying instrumentalism. At the second level, there are formal techniques to negotiate the world ambivalence by distinguishing between 'front stage' and 'backstage' areas (Walliss, 2007) – the front stage being about universal values of equality, justice, peace, and harmony; the backstage being the inner world of the soul. With this interface what happens alongside is an ongoing re-creation of tradition – what is sacrificed at the altar of world renewal (exclusivity and narcissism of sorts) is re-enforced in a new garb. The transformational episteme has 'universal Raja Yoga as true Godly knowledge' and 'world tree' thesis modified to appease the global palette. To quote a Brahmakumar:

---

1 The Brahmakumaris and the Anand Ashram, whose meditation courses have featured prominently in lifestyle magazine articles on health and stress management since the 1990s, have also helped to introduce urban publics to a de-confessionalized and partly scientized notion of 'spirituality' (using the English borrowing or Indonesian cognates such as spiritualitas) as an attractive alternative to devalorized but conceptually overlapping concepts such as kebatinan (literally 'inwardness', but more broadly 'spirituality' or 'mysticism'). This usage keys into the international growth movement and New Age literature that is now well represented in major bookshops in Indonesia and variously puffed or critiqued in local publications. The term 'New Age' is used also by journalists and critics to refer to local spiritual groups and activities that do not conform to high modern conceptions of proper religiosity but have a certain cachet derived from their similarities to international New Age activities. In major cities of Indonesia Brahmakumaris and Anand Ashram meditation courses are now part of a broad array of loosely 'spiritual' training programs alongside Reiki, Celestine Prophecy, Spiritual Quotient, Satori, Parent Effectiveness Training, AsiaWorks, and numerous domestic versions of spiritualized stress relief and leadership and management training (see Howell, 2005).

> When we connect with the world both at the national and global level, Brahmakumaris' spirituality stands in sharp contrast to the degradation of world ethos. Through this the urgency of change is felt and this justifies everything – the early world rejection of Brahmakumaris because they knew of the impending sarvanaash (apocalypse), and the later world embrace because of Brahmakumaris' own generosity and willingness to share the true Godly knowledge with the outside world. That way probably the catastrophe can be minimized or even adopted. When the world will turn towards the universal message of Raja Yoga, then together everybody will be able to prepare in the limited time for the golden age and the new cycle. All persecution and doubts will then end. All the souls who have aligned to Brahmakumari globally – either as adherents or as beneficiaries of our training programmes and health services will be able to remember their true nature and then live a regal existence in the coming age. (Abu, March 2011)

Chinmaya Mission's position with the global political economy is as an ambassador of Indology, Vedanta, and Indic cultural capital. The nuances of its global interfaces can be elaborated thus. Appealing to the medieval hagiographies of Adi Shankaracharya as the inspiration for his work as the founder of Chinmaya Mission, what Chinmayananda and his collaborators engaged in was a creative retelling of the life story of the eighth-century saint to authorize their twentieth-century movement (Locklin & Lauwers, 2009). They charted what Tweed (2006) has described as 'translocative' identity from and for the Advaita tradition – effectively rationalizing its emergence as a global religion while also re-rooting in Indian culture. According to the Chinmaya Mission vision, the universal message of Advaita comes to full expression in a dynamic, ongoing historical movement with its unique fulcrum and privileged disclosure in Shankara's Dig-Vijaya or victory tour which traditionally conquered the four 'quarters' of the Indian mainland. Swami Chinmayananda translated this ancient trope into yet another idiom and new social context to set an agenda for the Chinmaya Mission and to rationalize the emergence of Advaita Vedanta as a global movement. The distinction of Chinmayananda and his disciples lay in the employment of the 'Dig-Vijaya' theme. According to Chinmaya Mission and Chinmayananda, just as Shankara revived, unified, and defended the Advaita tradition in his conquest tour, so should members of Chinmaya Mission in the contemporary era. What Chinmaya Mission, as a Hindu faith-based movement, has also done is to add to the complexity of the two typical and juxtaposed responses to the diffusion of Hindus and Hinduism across national borders. At one level is India-centred bio-piety and geo-piety in the RSS–VHP context of religious nationalism and at another there is a more expansive Hindu universalism (of the Vivekananda–Ramakrishna genre). Swami Chinmayananda has described the ideational content of Chinmaya Mission as 'science of reality' similar to natural sciences but distinguished by its inward focus (Locklin & Lauwers, 2009). However, one of the important points of departure of Chinmayananda's missionary programme was the revival of the Indian nation. Western adherents were certainly included in the movement from very early on, and some of them have become prominent as both lay teachers and renunciant Acharyas at major Chinmaya Mission centres. The primary focus nevertheless remains on the formation of a committed network of educated Hindus in India and the Indian community living abroad.

In terms of Sri Aurobindo Society, development of branches globally has meant a correspondence and compliance with global mandates. For Vivekananda Kendra, the interface with the global political economy is virtual, the Kendra not having physical presence per se. However, some gains of 'brand building' and 'image creation' are accrued through the translocal export of Swami Vivekananda's image through history (1893 to present) and some concrete connections through Ramakrishna Mission (Ramakrishna–Vivekananda Vedanta centres have a worldwide presence). Furthermore, Vivekananda Kendra International designed to promote a 'civilizational dialogue' from the Swami Vivekananda vantage point is one assertion in the international arena, currently at the nascent stage. The intent is to promote Swami Vivekananda's ideas of Hinduized nationalism and spiritually inspired social service, which Vivekananda Kendra stands for on a global platform.

With respect to Mata Amritanandamayi Mission there are elements of congruity and collaboration – Amritanandamayi Mission positing itself as a civil society organ, the quintessential third domain. Hence,

Amritanandamayi Mission in India, and Embrace the World (ETW, the name by which Amma's charities are known worldwide) globally, collaborate on issues of poverty and disasters with a clear subscription to the establishment/state diktats. Spiritual norms and Amma's messages (of love and service) are added to the intervention strategy. For Art of Living, the nuance of collaboration with the global polity is through Sudarshan Kriya and Pranayama (SK&P) meditation and breathing technique which forms the locus classicus. This is done through using the vision and mandate of peace and interfaith harmony and the position that self-transcendence and breath control leads to personal transformation which in turn may provide social transformation possibilities.

Thus, with respect to Ramakrishna Mission, Sri Aurobindo Society and Art of Living owing to their international spread are 'contact zones' with international systems and structures. In the spirit of communicative rationality,[2] what is created is a lifeworld of service and action within the organizational mandate, thereby ensuring a global outreach. For Swaminarayan Sanstha, collaboration and cooperation have characterized their relationships with global political economy for several years. In Saibaba Sansthan, there is a spontaneous Sai charisma transportation. For Brahmakumaris, the real tryst commenced with its internationalization drive in the 1970s and UN association in the 1980s. It is primarily with the UN association that the traditionalist stance of the Hindu-origin Raja Yoga metaphor had a linguistic and epistemological transformation. The new version that developed was of the technique as instrumental in promoting 'world values' of peace and harmony. With its active participation in programmes such as the 'Million Minutes of Peace Appeal' and the rhetoric of world family, peace, and harmony at the global platform, Brahmakumaris assumed the form of an epitome of 'universal brotherhood'. Chinmaya Mission's image at the global political economy levels is that of a Hindu vanguard and missionary since history. In Vivekananda Kendra, the revivalist discourse is appropriated on behalf of the postmodernists to pave the way for Swami Vivekananda's version of Hinduism to become global. With respect to Amritanandamayi Mission,

2 Jurgen Habermas's communicative rationality says that meanings are constructed in shared lifeworlds and in processes of interaction and rational action (Ashenden & Owen, 1999).

cordiality and collaboration are core characteristics of the interface with translocal establishments through historicity.

In general in working with the global systems, although aligning/ collaborating is the key modicum, it certainly does not always capture the ambivalence that characterizes the nature of global differentials in attitudes to faith-based movements. Hence, interventions of HIFMs, whose overarching focus is spiritualizing action, try to collate two different positions – one, the collaborative, and the other, subtly persuasive. Within the collaborative regime, two key modes emerge as paradigms – spiritualized rationalism and spiritualized structuralism. The spiritualized rationalist mode approaches issues in a global context from a logical, real, and scientific angle, positing harmony and equality as the sole and inevitable outcome of deliberations and actions, with region-specific systems made to move towards the same. The spiritualized structuralist mode approaches issues with an application for 'agency and ideational modifications' to ensure faith-based assertions – a sensitization in the cognitive domain towards HIFMs' goals and objectives in its mission of global spread. This is viewed in terms of the principles and practices of Ramakrishna Mission, Sri Aurobindo Society, and Art of Living.

In terms of the global political economy, drawing from Vertovec (1997), HIFMs can be said to cultivate a 'Diaspora consciousness' among the communes of reference. This does two things: (a) creates exclusivity and (b) facilitates the spread so as to gain grounds in foreign lands. It is about developing trajectories of memories, roots, and traditions on newer grounds. Aspects of cosmopolitanism are inevitable as there are encounters-mergers with non-native cultures, which may fracture the puritan realms and replace/recast mixed identities/discourses. Away from the homeland, the reified notions of boundary and homogeneous culture of HIFMs undergo some transformations – contextual aspects of pluralism and cross-cultural consciousness enter. As transnational presence is the goal, such metamorphosis is easily adapted, with specialized HIFM markers (such as Vedanta, Raja Yoga, Integral Yoga, Sudarshan Kriya) becoming instruments of proliferation. The other peculiarity is that cultural aspects such as family ideals and food habits (particularly vegetarianism) assume quasi-religious forms (David Pocock in Vertovec, 1997), and the disembedding process is not always smooth across cultures, creating thereby some contradictions. Probably in cases where multiple HIFMs coexist in a foreign locale, boundaries may need to be redefined and epithets/symbols may be manipulated and subsumed under the singular garb of the 'oriental' or to the lowest common denominator of Hindu faith. This is only a preliminary contention and requires further cross-cultural investigation. In particular, how HIFMs manage politics of heritage and nostalgia in transnational context, simultaneously catering to market economics and retaining their own exclusivities vis-à-vis their immediate others (i.e., other HIFMs) and significant others (e.g., transnational civil society organizations) is a matter for further exploration.

The fact remains that HIFMs are visible sociopolitical players in non-home grounds too.[3] The styles are oriented towards 'mission'-ization, spiritual rejuvenation, and creation and re-creation of communities – something that traditional globalization literature has inadvertently skipped in the analysis. This beckons an analysis of faith-related transnational flows – rootedness, cross-overs, conceptual bonds, and performance. What is undisputed is that these HIFMs compel us to think post-nationally while keeping alive oriental nationalisms, (nation) state, and sovereignty. They speak from 'within' even though their voices may be fractured and disjoint – they believe themselves to be refraining from making the premature mistake of superseding the traditional/orient/ Hindu universal.

State/establishment exchange nuances

Most HIFMs comply with state/establishment norms, prescriptions, and ascriptions. Since the colonial period, the Ramakrishna Mission has had a collaborative and congruent attitude towards the state. The state is viewed as an overarching superstructure – an edifice on which Ramakrishna Mission's social outreach endeavours can be constructed. In terms of the state and

3 Blanke (2004) looked at how in the 1970s religious organizations became active participants in public policy debates on Latin America in Washington, DC, by moving as visible foreign policy players into the public sphere. Having been directly in touch with the social and political conflict in El Salvador, faith-based groups presented their concerns regarding the human rights situation in El Salvador to the US and Salvadoran governments. Even though they could not stop the flow of US aid to El Salvador or lobby for a better distribution of that aid, their awareness campaign and 'power of information' was decisive for attracting the attention of a small but important group of policymakers in Washington, DC.

establishment in the national context, Swaminarayan Sanstha has historically posited itself as a sectarian institution with 'social' and 'accommodative' leanings maintaining the tone of harmony, exchange, prescription, and ascription. Historically, as per BAPS literature, the original founder Lord Swaminarayan also had patronage relationships with the Kathi royalty and with the British government. In particular what is highlighted is his meeting with Governor John Malcolm of Bombay in 1830 in Rajkot where the latter sought his audience as he had heard of his spiritual prowess. The points of discussion in that meeting were the support to the colonial mandate of sati abolition and prevention of female infanticide. Swaminarayan is also said to have proposed to Governor Malcolm to look into issues of cow protection. The scripture Shiksha Patri penned by Swaminarayan was presented to the governor, which is now preserved in the Bodleian Library in Oxford. Subsequently, in 1930, Shastriji Maharaj, the founder of Swaminarayan Sanstha, showed solidarity to Gandhi in his freedom agenda whence the latter met him enroute the salt march to Dandi (Ishwarchandradas, 1979). Currently its social and spiritual work is done within the state prescriptions and rules, with Swaminarayan Sanstha seeking professional assistance to maintain the decorum. To quote a woman office bearer:

> Since history our spiritual heads have always been revered sources for the royalty and political figures. As they are epitomes of dispassion and detachment, interested in pursuing only higher spiritual goals and spreading that message and grace which is beneficial to all, they have always been welcome. Swaminarayan Sanstha has always been a peace loving sampradaya interested in its own religio-spiritual work. Even when centres are established abroad, the main objective is satsang and providing socio-cultural arenas for the Diaspora community where they can feel at home and connected with their roots. As we have the material means and value base, we also do social service. That is done mainly in keeping with mind the larger agendas of the state and establishment. We are always pro-state as we believe that they know their jobs well. When we collaborate on social service projects it is mainly to supplement their efforts and provide the necessary spiritual touch which is very beneficial. (Ahmedabad, June 2011)

Saibaba Sansthan's relationship with the state is that of exchange, prescription, and ascription; the Maharashtra state government played a historical role in streamlining trust management and its various activities. Furthermore, with Shirdi as a core pilgrim centre contributing to the state economy, official representations do oversee shrine modalities as well as its social service activities. Hence, what commenced as reverence to a 'fakir' with transcendental powers has now become a hub of faith-motivated philanthropic activities and tax-exempted donations regulated under the overarching memorandum laid down by the state government.[4]

Brahmakumaris have historically been proto establishment since even in the early stage when the group faced societal persecution; the differences were more with the anti-party than with the Karachi government. As per Brahmakumari literature, Dada Lekhraj was in written correspondence with most political leaders like Jinnah and Liaquat Ali Khan from 1947 to 1950 and is said to have offered perspectives on issues of freedom 'revealed' to him (PBIV, no date). The only anti-state document available with Brahmakumaris is the pamphlet 'Is this Justice?,' published by Om Radhe and contemporaries as an answer to the prosecution tribunal which was interrupted by the 1947 partition. This proto-establishment stance continues with the Rajasthan government as also with the central government. Brahmakumaris have largely posited themselves as a

4 To maintain the functioning of the Trust, an elected body was constituted in 1952 which functioned until 1960. Later it was caught up in litigation, and a civil court in Bombay appointed a receiver to take over the administration of the Sansthan. The receiver functioned till August 1984 when the twenty-two-member Board of Management was appointed by the Maharashtra Government to take over, with an executive officer in charge. Since then, the functioning has been stabilized with the headquarters at Shirdi and an office in Mumbai for liaison purposes with the state. The fifteen-member committee which oversees the trust management is appointed by the state. This aspect has accompanying political controversies owing to the political connections of members. In a recent PIL (public interest litigations) filed by two Shirdi residents, Rajendra Gondkar and Sandip Kulkarni, which said that the committee had carried on way beyond its legal tenure, Justice Naresh Patil and Justice T.V. Nalawade of the Aurangabad bench of the high court directed the state government to appoint a new committee, failing which it said that a three-member panel would be given the reins of temple administration. The three-member committee which is in place of a new committee comprises of the collector of Ahmednagar, the additional district judge of Kopargaon, and the CEO of Saibaba Sansthan. The original tenure of the committee was three years, which ended in August 2007, but it has continued for over seven years. As per the Shree Saibaba Sansthan Trust (Shirdi) Act, 2004, the term is for three years and the existing committee could continue on an ad hoc basis until a new committee was formed. The move was accepted by the CEO (Thomas & Jaisinghani, 2012).

spiritual educational centre 'beyond' party politics and 'partisan' stances. Its millenarianism is in that sense an aid to project a 'looking above' image. Its sister concerns Raja Yoga Educational and Research Centre and Academy for a Better World have sections looking at business, social service, and politics which design courses exhorting for a spiritual/Raja Yogic perspective for overall transcendence.

In terms of Chinmaya Mission's relationship with the state and establishment two aspects are visualized: at the level of its own growth, expansion, and service projects, there is a compliance in the sense of abiding by the establishment norms, prescriptions, and ascriptions. The second component is the collaboration on the Hinduizing/Indianizing missions of the state and polity (Swami Chinmayananda was historically a patron sympathizer of RSS and Hinduized state leanings, and Chinmaya Mission also participated in the birth centenary celebration of Guruji Golwalker, the founder of RSS) and the Hindutva/Indian cultural heritage revival agenda. Sri Aurobindo Society's relationship is that of prescription and ascription for all its projects. Although, historically Sri Aurobindo advocated an initially violent and later a doctrine of passive resistance against the British empire,[5] currently Sri Aurobindo Society

5 In 1906, Aurobindo Ghosh came to Kolkata as the Principal of Bengal National College but resigned soon after. From 1906 to 1910, he was actively engaged in political activities. He commenced with writing revolutionary articles (from 1902 onwards he had started writing some political articles in *Indu Prakash*) and formation of secret societies that would eventually realize the goal of swarajya or freedom. The opportunity to enter politics was further propelled by the 1905 outbreak of the agitation against the partition of Bengal. Initially, he co-founded one significant radical group, the Anushilan Samiti, and participated in the revolutionary movement that developed in association with the radical movement, Jugantar. Later agitation in Bengal furnished an opening for public initiation to move forward and direct political action, as opposed to the moderate reformism which had been the creed of the Indian National Congress. Hence, in 1906 he joined an extremist New Party which had the vague ideal of non-cooperation.At first Sri Aurobindo took part in Congress politics only from behind the scenes as he had not yet decided to leave the Baroda service, but he took a long leave without pay in which, besides carrying on personally the secret revolutionary work, he attended the Barisal conference broken up by the police and toured East Bengal along with Bipin Chandra Pal and associated himself closely with the forward group in the Congress. It was during this period that he joined Bipin Pal in the editing of the *Bande Mataram*, founded a new political party in Bengal, and attended the Congress session at Calcutta at which the extremists, though still a minority, succeeded under the leadership of Tilak in imposing part of their political program on the Congress. The *Bande Mataram* agenda was that of swaraj, swadeshi, boycott, and national education. After the *Bande Mataram* case, he became a leader of Nationalism in Bengal. He also took up a charge of a Bengal daily, *Nava Shakti*,

has a congruent and parallel relationship with the establishment systems and the structure.

In terms of the state and establishment, Vivekaṇanda Kendra in all its service activities and faith-oriented work posits as a right-wing Hindu nationalist spiritual service mission. As per a *karyakarta*:

> Just as Swami Vivekananda spoke about rejuvenating the youth with Hindu cultural and spiritual ideas and creating an army of young men and women dedicated to the task of nation building, Vivekananda Kendra's vision on the national platform as founded by Eknathji is to do exactly that. To translate the invaluable knowledge available in our scriptures towards the noble mission of service to the poor by visualizing God in them and engaging in national reconstruction. We are not a political organisation, but our approach is to offer the ideological view, the point of view offered by Swami Vivekananda to the task of national development. (Kanyakumari, April 2012)

Vivekananda Kendra adopts the Tocquevillian mode of spiritualizing religion (Basu, 2002): neo-Hinduism positing as a self-limiting religion through a corporatist construction of Hinduism. This revivalist discourse is thus appropriated to pave the way for Swami Vivekananda's version of Hinduism to become national.

Amritanandamayi Mission largely complies with state norms for its basket of faith-oriented initiatives in terms of consecrating temples, ashram centres, and conducting meditation camps and congregational

---

and moved from his rented house in Scott Lane, where he had been living with his wife and sister, to the office premises of the newspaper. He was arrested from there and sent to Alipore Jail in 1908 and was acquitted after a year. Later on, this proved to be a fruitful year, for during this period he had intense spiritual experiences, which set him definitely on the path of his future work. After detention for one year as an undertrial prisoner in Alipore Jail, he came out in May 1909 to find the party organization broken. For a year he strove for its upkeep and hence he published *Karmayogin* in English and *Dharma* in Bengali propagating the spiritual-political views of the party. In February 1910, he withdrew to a secret retirement in Chandernagore and in the beginning of April sailed for Pondicherry in French India. Two other charges were levied against him – one for the doings of a revolutionary group founded by his brother Barindra where he was acquitted, and the second while he left for Pondicherry. The third prosecution was launched against him for a signed article in *Karmayogin*, but the conviction was squashed under appeal to the Calcutta High Court (Sri Aurobindo Ashram Trust, 2006).

prayer and social initiatives in arenas of education, health, livelihood and social entrepreneurship promotion, disaster relief and rehab operations, and ecological conservation. In that sense it functions typically as a law-complying non-profit enterprise and in the Gramscian sense it is a civil society institution which protects state interests operating on the assumption of the overarching concept of welfare state. For Art of Living, the establishment is the source of prescription and ascription initiatives by granting sanctions, attestations, and providing the mainstream framework of operations (particularly with reference to educational initiatives). Even though the entry point for Art of Living in its sociopolitical initiatives is the SK&P programme of various levels, there is an eventual compliance with state/establishment-prescribed objectives, albeit with the 'Art of Living touch' of programme packages catered to the group under reference. Hence, in education, health, ecological initiatives, women empowerment, rural development, prison programs, substance abuse prevention, and disaster interventions, the main thing is the spiritual curriculum, which posits as a hologram – built on which are other endeavours in line with superstructural directives.

Vis-à-vis the state/establishment, HIFMs reckon with organizational imperatives for survival and market share like other organizations. Agency, choice, and contingency shape faith-based outcomes for HIFMs, as opposed to structural determinism. Agency, choice, and contingency are seen in HIFMs' faith retention in negotiations with the state, in their prerogative in degrees of 'letting go' and communal asserting, and other cost-benefit dynamics (Bellin, 2008). In forging political alliances, HIFMs rationally calculate their organizational interests, pragmatically sacrificing their ideological purity when costs of purity outweigh benefits. This can be said to be the prima facie norm, just as state compliance and congruence is the general trend in HIFMs. However, a more minute project-related examination is warranted for discerning finer nuances of the dynamics of HIFMs' political-economic behaviours. The important question would be whether HIFMs prioritize organizational concerns and firm-like behaviour over fidelity to ideological components in their relationships with the state/establishment. This may throw light on faith-behaviour and to what extent rational choice influences it, for even though there are elements of selfless motives/seva HIFMs too operate in a world of scarce resources and hence need to factor in the cost-benefit dynamic in their outreach.

State/establishment in turn accommodates HIFMs, which probably speaks of their collective efficacy, resource, and political strengths. Two other things can be derived: first, the Indian state's historical commitment to multi-faith, secular, harmonious integration shapes the likelihood of their accommodation of HIFMs. Second, in an overarching scheme of glorification of the orient/spiritual, the state and HIFMs have a legacy of institutional-ideological compatibility (cases of Ramakrishna Mission, Swaminarayan Sanstha, Vivekananda Kendra, as well as Art of Living and the Amritanandamayi Mission): the Indian state willy-nilly draws on the spiritual wealth of which HIFMs are vanguards – which also feeds into the nationalist discourse. In a way HIFMs create a realm of the public sphere to influence the state,[6] which is incidentally not singular but multiple, as all HIFMs are not necessarily on the same page.

Whether it is state/establishment or global political economy, for all HIFMs under study politics is in parentheses – the focus is first on associates and the institution, which may over time exert a lasting political influence. Actually that is precisely how the local gets reconfigured through historical processes in the translocal and transnational. Faith has a 'double function' – as apology and legitimation of the status quo and as a means of change and liberation. The linear assumptions of secularization theories are challenged – faith becomes a vital expression in exchange relations with state mechanisms and global polity.

Relationship with the market economy

All HIFMs' narratives say that their general relationship with the market has been that of brand building, commodification, and routinization of spiritual capital and charisma. In terms of the Ramakrishna Mission, the nuances are somewhat as follows. In the league of social service, their work entails a certain credibility building and brand creation of a spiritually inspired social service work. Commodification, for the Mission, is visualized in terms of marketing of salvation goods for facilitating

---

6 Pedziwiatr (2007) analysed the critical engagement in public debates of the Muslim Council of Britain (MCB), an organization formed by second-generation immigrants. They created a public sphere and influenced state policies, positing British Muslim interests vis-à-vis the government.

the spiritual goal of transcendence – the meditative panel photo of the triune 'Ramakrishna-Sarada Devi-Vivekananda' as the locus of overt and covert spiritual practices; the organizational logo (which comes in varied shapes and sizes) symbolizing the core contentions/teachings; the calendar art with images of embodiment and a virtual rewriting of history; and range of multilingual modestly priced publications extolling virtues and emphasizing the teachings/gospel of Ramakrishna-Sarada Devi-Vivekananda. Further translations and textual interpretations done by the monastic order and the householder disciples also constitute the literary repertoire. Virtually, a legendary genus of Ramakrishna narrative is fashioned through the renditions – with every aspect of the lives of the trinity examined and re-testified. Routinization is visualized in the institutionalization of ideas about the normative-ideational frame of the organization as the appropriate path and the way forward – done primarily through individual and group study endeavours.

For Swaminarayan Sanstha a certain brand building takes place with the maintenance of BAPS (a sister concern having global volunteer and patron base), an organization that looks into 'social and spiritual care' (particularly since the time of Yogiji Maharaj and Pramukh Swami), with the launch of charities under the BAPS label a more recent example of what, as an organization, it aspires to project itself at both domestic and global fronts. Commodification is viewed in its range of salvation goods – publications in Gujarati, English, and Hindi; the audio-visual material of devotional renditions; and diaries and calendars which contribute widely to the turnover of Swaminarayan Aksharpith[7] (the publications unit of Swaminarayan Sanstha). The Swaminarayan Sanstha website which was developed in 1999 is like a global connection point of followers worldwide with regular postings from the scriptures as daily thoughts and aphorisms, the itinerary of Pramukh Swami and other prominent sadhus, satsang examinations, BAPS charities updates, Swaminarayan Sanstha social projects updates and details of youth, children, and women groups worldwide; sale of ritual worship material along with the trademark Swaminarayan emblem (U shaped in sandal paste with a large

7 Diaries and calendars also contribute to recreating history from the Swaminarayan Sanstha lens with anniversaries of the spiritual founder and subsequent successors as also temple consecration dates locally and globally along with dates of commencement of projects and sister concerns highlighted.

vermillion dot within adorned by all men Swaminarayan adherents); and miniature icons of Lord Swaminarayan and Gunatitanand Swami that can be installed in households.

Routinization is a necessary outcome of sectarianism – Swaminarayan followers are staunch in their belief system of the Swaminarayan Sanstha's modified version of Vaishnavism. This loyalty permeates onto all realms of existence, including material exchange; most of Swaminarayan Sanstha's staunch followers are the Kanbi Patidars, Thakkars, and Kathis, who are traditional business and/or agribusiness communities (the Kathis are especially involved in agribusiness); their business ethics and dealings are also governed by Swaminarayan Sanstha norms historically emerging from the scriptures Shiksha Patri and Vachanamrutam. Tithe practices, philanthropy, and norms of sharing profits with kith and kin are derived from these texts. These sect dialectics (most adherents call themselves followers of Swaminarayan dharma or satsangis) then prove to be the locus classicus of capital emergence, development, and enhancement – both material and human.

For Saibaba Sansthan, the market has an influence in fourfold terms: brand building, commodification, routinization, and syncretic metaphysical ritualization within the Hindu hegemony fold. Brand building is seen in the construction of a 'society of Sai images'; Sai as a metaphor of the Godhead who is benevolent, assimilative, and accommodating. What is constructed through this is a simulated society where aspects of imagery or representation of Saibaba dominate the social fabric – Sai being a symbol of austerity, penance, and direct communion with the Godhead from a Bhakti–Sufi lens. Commodification is visualized in terms of marketing of salvation goods for facilitating the spiritual goal of transcendence. The organizational diary symbolizes the core contentions/teachings. The calendar art has images of Saibaba as the embodiment; thus, there is a virtual rewriting of history by marking significant events around Saibaba's life. Further traces of commodification are also seen in the sacred ash 'udi' which is given with each donation made, symbolizing regeneration and life, and in the Sai Satcharitra, the holy book extolling Saibaba, published in several languages and ritually read and studied by devotees in a span of eight days at a stretch either in the parayan (prayer) hall or in a sanctum of devotional worship. Routinization is witnessed in the institutionalization of ideas about the normative-ideational frame of the organization. 'Shraddha' (faith) and 'saburi' (patience) are considered as the appropriate path and the way forward. Furthermore, there is a syncretic metaphysical ritualization – dominant images are that Saibaba was a saint who propagated the idea of 'syncretism'.[8] Hence, he called his place of stay *dwarkamai masjid* – Dwarka as the birthplace of Krishna, the Hindu deity, and masjid as symbolizing the mosque. The eminent point of this projection is nevertheless 'Hindu' – assimilating generously Islamic and Sufi ideals.

For Brahmakumaris, Raja Yoga assumes the form of a salvation good in the Weberian sense, packaged as per perceived levels of capacity, attainments, and entitlements. This market is intensified and expanded further through the historical paradigm shift from asceticism and world rejection to instrumentalism and world affirmation. Particularly, this is significant in terms of development of tailor-made courses, shift in emphasis from solely abstract soul discourses to life skills enhancement (Brahmakumaris now also conduct course on 'how to be effective and successful', 'how to lead a stress free life', 'how to develop and maintain effective relationships' among others). Commodification is particularly

8 The Hindu interpretation of Saibaba gained momentum since his death in 1918. His burial in the Dixit Wada and the subsequent predominance of the Patil clan in propagating Hinduized versions of his teachings were responsible for the same. Furthermore, the major biographies of Saibaba were written after his death. Dabholkar's *Satcharitra* was begun in 1910, but only two of the fifty-three chapters had been written till 1918 and the biography was not completed and published until 1929. Research for Narasimha Swami's four volumes on the *Life of Saibaba* did not begin until 1936 and was completed only in 1955–1956 (Warren, 2004). The source of Saibaba's Sufi origins as per Warren's (2004) study has been the notebook of a devotee Abdul, the son of Sultan of Nanded who lived with Saibaba in Shirdi for a period of 29 years and then till 1954, tending to Saibaba's Dargah. This notebook called the Saibaba Manuscript is a rare manuscript, being Abdul's notes and jottings of the words and teachings he received from Saibaba in Urdu. The study has proposed that it displayed Saibaba's familiarity with Islamic history, starting from the family of Prophet Mohammed, the companions of the Prophet, the early developments of Islam, the Khalifas or the line of succession of the early Islamic dynasties, early Shi'ism, and the later esoteric teachings of the Isma'ilis in India. Sufism in India is also presented with the lists of its organization into various orders with their silsilas or chain of succession. Furthermore, Shah Waris Ali, a Sufi saint, was also Saibaba's teacher according to the study and is subsequently said to have explained to Abdul the four aspects of Islam – shariat (the law), tariqat (the way and mystical practices), haqiqat (the reality of God as the only truth), and marifat (gnosis). Although he did not align himself formally to any established Sufi orders, he had a number of features common with the Chisti order and due to his moods; he was like a majzub – meaning one who is attracted to God.

visualized in terms of market development, maintenance, and promotion of multilingual publications of Brahmakumaris, the periodic and serial publications of the 'murlis' (the extant and continual revelations), pictures iconography and calendar art, audio-visual material covering the seven-day Raja Yoga course content, picture images of the world cycle and world tree as original, and specific revelations and most significantly the 'meditation lamp', which is believed to constitute the supreme soul. Furthermore, in the market scenario there is a brand building by Brahmakumaris comprising the twin components of soul discourses and spiritual universality. Hence, in exchange terms – the answer to the ontological question of 'who am I' leads to an epistemological universalism ('I am the peaceful soul') stemming from which are practical, teleological ethics of peace and harmony. The brand image thus built by Brahmakumaris comprises this very connect and exchange.

For Chinmaya Mission the following aspects are visualized: there is the transborder capitalization of the Shankaracharya brand of Advaita Vedanta with exalted messages of oneness and soul discourses as prominent. What is then catered to is a sophisticated repackaging of salvation goods as 'ancient spiritual wealth' serving the core purpose of revenue generation for the Mission through a supply of transcendental benefits for the followers/devotees. Commodification is then visualized through the multilingual publications, audio-visual material, calendar art, and iconography and periodicals. Routinization is regularized through the archives – preserving norms and forms of Chinmaya Mission through historicity as well as in continuity as a part of genealogical continuity of the Vedanta Shankara Bhashya epithet.

In Sri Aurobindo Society there is a fourfold translation: the building of integral yogic brand imagery – integral yoga as characteristic of the ideational norms of Sri Aurobindo Society and distinct from other yogic forms such as Raja Yoga and Bhakti Yoga. The second aspect is the definition of yoga as a translocal commodity with Sri Aurobindo as the spiritual ambassador and the Mother as the transcendental executing authority. This yoga is defined and packaged as the way of life – a way forward in the existential scheme of things. Furthermore, this is operationalized through the routinization of the Mother as the embodiment of the Divine Grace, the quintessential Shakti, and Sri Aurobindo as the agent of the Absolute belonging to the genre of the Yoga Literati – his divine realizations and the claims of him emanating white light during and after his physical lifetime attesting the same. Eventually this assumes the nature of commodity manifestations – through symbols, photo imagery, and calendars; and salvation goods of incense and art, which are ephemeral mores of the ethereal existence. Apart from salvation goods, there is also the component of recreating histories with the ashram and society observing days of specific importance of the charismatic personas as the congregational worship days; the Sri Aurobindo Society's routine is organized around that rather than the conventional almanac.

Vivekananda Kendra insists on a brand creation as vanguard of Hindu youth cultural habitus. Terms of exchange are determined through Swami Vivekananda as a nationalist figure through history, which in effect guides, to some extent, the nature and quantum of commodification of spiritual-salvation goods as core revenue source for Vivekananda Kendra. There are multilingual publications in the form of periodicals and *Complete Works of Swami Vivekananda* (in eight volumes) marketed as an Indological treatise on national reconstruction and oriental exegesis. Other goods marketed include calendars and diaries with Sri Ramakrishna–Sri Sarada Devi–Swami Vivekananda iconography, a systematic endeavour to demonstrate a historical continuity for Vivekananda Kendra as well as its overlap and allegiance to the Ramakrishna imagery.

For Amritanandamayi Mission there is the translocalization of the Integrated Amrita Meditation (IAM) technique as a salvation good, commodification, and routinization. Initially commencing as a short breathing and relaxation procedure then known as the 'Ma-Om' meditation technique, which was re-franchised in the year 2003 (which was the 50th birth year of Amma) as an event for world peace and harmony, and this was also a watershed year for Amritanandamayi Mission that ensured an international platform, funding, and network. It was soon re-fashioned as IAM. This technique was then inserted in the league of Yoga techniques – an assertion of 'New Age spirituality' launched worldwide as Amritanandamayi Mission's trademark. Despite being a salvation good, it is essentially non-priced (IAM technique is taught free of cost in India and abroad by either Amma herself or her monastic disciples who accompany her on a rotational basis, on world tours undertaken in two rounds in a calendar year covering different parts of the globe). In view of the growing intensity of its demand among Amma followers, it has assumed the form of a necessary spiritual good for the coterie. Commodification is visualized in terms of the sale of multilingual publications of Amma's teachings written by her disciples or audio-visual products, including transcribed conversations of Amma with her devotees; calendar and diary art containing Amma iconography as well as a virtual rewriting of dates and pictures of the 'embrace' which has become the raison d'être of the iconic Amma. Furthermore, spirituality for Amritanandamayi Mission also has a cyber face – an active presence on Facebook, a website regularly updated with Amma's teachings selected periodically by the electronic data processing department of the Amritapuri Ashram, Twitter revelations of world tours of Amma and certain senior monastic disciples, and also an electronic bulletin board with posts from projects, services, centres, and branches worldwide. There is also a detailed hospitality management plan for desiring national and international visitors – the initiated and the uninitiated. Routinization manifests in twofold terms – institutionalization of Amritanandamayi Mission ideals as the desirous universal way forward towards absolute values of peace and harmony and the secularization and syncretization of an essentially Hindu stance by the claim of having a beneficiary outreach 'irrespective of caste, creed, sex, nationality, and ethnicity' (Mata Amritanandamayi Mission Trust, 2010).

For Art of Living, commodification is visualized through sales of multilingual transcribed talks of Sri Sri in printed form and disks and also compilations of the much-celebrated knowledge sheets; calendar art, fabric art, and trivia with images of charismatic Sri Sri or virtues extolled by him such as 'peace', 'silence', and 'Aum' (the three syllable word which is the core of Indic thought); and systematic marketing of salvation goods taking the material form of devotional music, meditation CDs, incense, Ayurveda, and organic products, all with the hologram of Sri Sri. Routinization is unearthed through the moral packaging of Art of Living norms and forms and in particular SK&P as the 'personal', 'social', and 'political' way forward. The other element of market relationships is the creation of a virtual community with cyber connectivities. The grandiosity in Art of Living lies in its virtual face – Sri connects with the worldwide adherent base through regular uploads of knowledge sheets, Facebook, Twitter, and various blogs. The site in interactive and is regularly updated along with sites of sister concerns. Updates are of a nature of ideological discourse, Sri Sri's positions on a range of contemporary sociopolitical issues, course updates, centre details (most Art of Living courses of various levels boast of a strong faculty base as also accessibility for all), and the global and local travel itinerary of Sri. The virtual sense of a Guru who is available to all at any given time and provides a practical philosophy of life is therefore created. With the carefully designed course curriculum, faculty, course materials, and the global reach, Art of Living creates a translocal brand image of 'Indian spirituality' remodelled and repackaged in the form of SK&P and Sri Yoga.

With respect to HIFMs' interfaces with the market, several parallels can be sought with general economics of faith-based organisations' (FBO) literature and New Age market theorizations. In general, there is the market model logic of Peter Berger that is applicable.[9] Percy (2000) proposed that there are certain non-market elements in alignment to FBOs such as transcendence experiences of followers/devotees and the realm of the inexplicable. HIFMs also comply with the New Age perspective wherein the various spiritual traditions are public property and not the private preserve of religious elites.[10] Salvation goods and their exchange

---

9 Peter Berger's market model proposes that in a situation of free market, New Age religions and FBOs compete with each other on economic and non-economic terms. Furthermore, rational-choice theorists of religion have assumed that Adam Smith's Wealth of Nations advocates a free market of religion, which they argue leads to increased religious vitality. Peterson (2009), however, proposed that while Smith opposed direct government subsidies for religion and argued that a free market was the first-best solution, as a second-best policy he advocated religious regulation, including state-appointed clergy and the reduction of clergy income. Smith's rational-choice approach to religion, which springs from his understanding of public goods, externalities and the need for civil peace, and government stability, does not always support a policy of religious free markets (Redden, 2005; Das & Datta Ray, 2008).

10 New Age perspective further includes the following theological notions: the scheme in which HIFMs fit in. The first contention is that human beings are essentially Gods in themselves. Each individual is believed to contain a 'God-spark', a central infusion of divinity. At one's deepest level, one participates in and identifies with the Godhead. A second generally held idea is that human beings undergo successive reincarnations as part of an evolutionary process, which returns them to full God-realization. Third, a prominent New Age doctrine is that the human individual is responsible for creating his/her own reality. The last relates to the concomitant conviction in the power of positive thinking to mould and shape our own destinies. It is balanced, but not necessarily defeated by the understanding that our behaviour is in part influenced by our actions in previous lives. Finally, however, New Age places the entire evolutionary quest and desire to transmute ignorance and negative *karma* into its comprehension of the universe as a single interconnected field. This ultimately holistic notion provides the New Age spiritual orientation with its guiding transcendent value. It is the very context

form another characteristic of market materialism of the HIFMs.[11] HIFMs align to a notion of a 'global spiritual marketplace'[12] wherein salvation goods are determined by values attributed to cultural products.[13]

The active use of media by HIFMs posits a mediatization of religion (Loveheim, 2011) where they have an agency of religious actors who take part in the shaping of media and society. In particular, the 'virtual' space presence of HIFMs as a package of expansion leads to a cyber diasporic politics of Hinduism (Lal, 1999). The Hindu diaspora is rewritten through the techno-informational lines of the web pages in which one can visualize subaltern counterspheres as cross-hatched by contradictions: the heterogeneous strands of secularism and faith which coexist in an eclectic fashion. The 'online presence' of HIFMs creates a 'glocalization' of sorts – headquarters as local sites retain their exclusivity while simultaneously permitting access to adherents worldwide.[14] These online

---

which also provides the New Age with its justifying rationale for attempts to spiritualize commodification and commercial exchange (York, 2001).

11 As Zaidman (2003) discussed, traditional consumers and New Agers differ in their perspectives about commercialization of religious goods. The New Age subculture endorses a spiritualized counterpart of capitalism – one that seeks ever-extended markets and new sources of marketable goods. In traditional religion, more importance is given to the movement of meaning from the cultural world to the object. In the New Age subculture, the individual is the main source of meaning attribution, and the authority rests in the individual as a consumer. Pace (2006), on the other hand, theorized as follows: salvation goods are governed not only by the exchange economy but also by the gift economy. They have less to do with the logic of social action aimed at profitable returns and more to do with the non-utilitarian aspects of behaviour. The salvation goods have features that cast serious doubts on the hypothesis that they are basically governed by market forces.

12 Zaidman (2007) said that key among the factors that affect the market of New Age goods is the value societies attribute to their cultural products. He argued that New Age is an open system that manifests differently in different contexts. Contextual influences prioritize the acceptance of particular notions that are part of the New Age network, and these priorities in turn shape the market of New Age goods in each country.

13 In the context of New Age conceptualization Muir (2007) further maintained that cultural appropriation and commodification is predicated on the assumption that transformation of cultural goods into commodities is essentially a process of alienation from tradition and that salvation goods in themselves have greater agency than what is recognized.

14 Scheifinger (2009) studied the online darshan facility at the Jagannath Temple in Puri, Orissa, India. The study challenges those globalization theorists who claim that local sites decline in importance as a result of advanced communications technologies and instead supports Roland Robertson's theory of 'glocalization'. Online darshan is an important development for devotees of Jagannath because it allows access to the deity which may previously have been difficult or even impossible for most of the year. In his

practices of HIFMs essentially signify the remediation[15] of new media conceptualizations of digitality, network capital flows, hypertextuality, and virtuality.[16] HIFMs are repurposing 'older' media forms such as photographs of deities, calendar art, the analogue sacred texts and books, and audio tapes of religious discourse through their textual and discursive practice of representing online postings. Likewise, aspects of digital media such as hypertextual connectivity, virtual forms of dis/embodiment and im/materiality (of the charisma), and mobile flows of capital and culture are deployed to pay service to place-centric, embodied, and material practices shaping HIFM faith cultures. In this 'remediation', both HIFMs and new media as cultural forms can be said to be reinvented as 'desktop spiritual cultures'.

Interface with civil society

Interface with civil society through followers, devotees, and the general public forms another core of the sociopolitical frame of reference of HIFMs. The nuances of interface for each of the HIFMs are, however, distinct. For Ramakrishna Mission, the market image of branding is then catapulted onto civil society with the twin strategies of impressionism and religio-spiritual capital creation. Specifically, the locus lies with the monastic

---

study on photographs of Vivekananda taken in the US and the UK, Beckerlegge (2008) said that instead of glocalization imported localism explicates the situation better. In his appearance, Vivekananda embodied (in and for the 'West') a tailored presentation of Hindu and Indian culture (the 'East') as a form of universal religion. His vigorous rejection of the exclusivist claims of institutional Christianity was proclaimed in the 'Chicago Pose', which was originally produced for an American audience. The 'Contemplative Pose', on the other hand, symbolized more positively what his message appeared to offer to the spiritual seekers drawn to Vedanta Societies. Neither of these representations, as Beckerlegge (2008) says, would have summoned more traditional associations with the figure of the sanyas in Hindu India. Yet, when seeking to understand early Vedanta in the US and the UK, due recognition also needs to be given to the level of importance attached by some American and British followers to the specifically Indian and Hindu dimensions of Vivekananda's mission, an 'imported localism' that rather runs contrary to the process of 'glocalization'.

15 Remediation in Bolter and Grusin's (1999) influential theorization of new media is a refashioning characterized by a 'double logic' whereby new media 'remediate and are remediated by their predecessors'.

16 Mallapragada (2010) has articulated these to be the ideas of the Hindu image, embodied ritual practice, and the temporal and spatial logic of the temple as sacred place.

order that form, at once, the inner sphere as also a crucial link with the outer hemisphere. As commenced traditionally by Sri Ramakrishna, the spiritual ministration still continues with the training of members of the order and initiation of householder disciple or the followers into the 'religion of Ramakrishna'. The beneficiaries are generally viewed as people in 'need of service', and, apart from expecting an expressed interest in Ramakrishna–Vivekananda ideals and the Mission mandate of translating Ramakrishna vision into practice, they claim no discrimination in service delivery.

For Swaminarayan Sanstha, the civil society realms for interface are fourfold: (a) parshads and sadhus as ascetics in training and renunciants having received permanent vows respectively; (b) householder adherents with a history of patronage relationship with the spiritual heads (the syllabi books of the satsang examinations, particularly the three volumes of satsang readers have the biographies of such devotees and disciples, families of whom continue the veneration and adherent traditions); (b) member adherents who are part of the yuva mandals (youth groups), bal mandals (children groups), and kishore/kishori (adolescents) groups along with mahila mandals and volunteer groups; and (d) beneficiary groups consisting of adherents and the general groups. As Swaminarayan Sanstha has a history of connection with rural Saurashtra and central Gujarat and tribal groups therein, several beneficiaries are also adherents.

In Saibaba Sansthan, the group comprises of direct member adherents who visit Shirdi regularly and subscribe to *Saileela* – the monthly organ of Saibaba Sansthan – and followers and devotees who believe in the powers of Saibaba and have been instrumental in organizing local communes of Sai worshippers and their own organizational entities, adherents of the proposed Sai incarnations such as the Sathya Sai cult, and beneficiaries of Saibaba Sansthan projects. Essentially they converge to form the Saibaba following, cutting across geographies, parent faith orientations, and categorical imperatives of caste and class, thereby building Sai-oriented social capital under the aegis of Saibaba Sansthan.

With respect to the civil society, Brahmakumari Ishwariya Vishwavidyalaya has an abstract connection with the larger realm through very concrete links with the monastics – the Brahmakumars and the Brahmakumaris (as spiritual progeny of the charismatic gurus Brahma Baba and Jagdamba Saraswati) – who have committed to the institution as members of the salvation army and occupants of the Noah's Ark as created by Brahma Baba, the golden and fortunate souls to survive the inevitable catastrophe of the present Iron age. Other concrete links subsequently developed when Brahmakumaris shunned its world-rejecting defences to transfer to a world-accommodating stance by introducing Raja Yoga courses for lay adherents/householders/beneficiaries. Three types of courses exist: (a) an open-to-all beginners' seven-day course held at various centres across the country conducted by Brahmakumaris; (b) graduate courses (local and central) comprising early morning sessions on 'murli' readings (open to those who have undertaken the preliminary course and wish to delve deeper – the local course entry determined by Brahmakumaris expressed satisfaction over the 'spiritual progress' of the individual); and (c) tailor-made course for different levels of professionals. Hence, there are 'instrumental adherents' in search of self-enhancement techniques, and 'seekers'[17] who wish to search deeper within and align more closely to Brahmakumaris and adapt to lifestyle modifications as suggested by them – chastity, spiritual lessons and study, vegetarianism, and abstinence.

In Chinmaya Mission, there are the acharyas and monasts who have undergone the Vedanta training course and are willing to dedicate their lives to the mission, with whom there is the element of tradition perpetuation and continuity as well as cadre development. In terms of followers, the patron varieties exchange material collaterals for the spiritual advantage obtained from Chinmaya Mission.[18] With member adherents at large, what is formed is a devotee service capital. With beneficiaries of service projects such as education, rural development, home for elderly, and health there are the twin elements of goodwill accumulation and garnering of cultural loyalists in the Vedantic heritage preservation mission. In Sri Aurobindo Society, there are the member adherents who, apart from the sadhaks who are devoted to the ashram life, are householder devotees who imbibe, internalize, and follow the

17 See Walliss (2007) for more details on types of followers of the Brahmakumaris.

18 Land donations, cash donations, and material donations are recurrent common features among Chinmaya Mission devotees; Chinmaya Mission, on the other hand, has a well-chalked-out policy for grant/donation receipts with several subordinate trusts formed under which donations are remitted – all under the umbrella of CCMT.

teachings of the Mother and Sri Aurobindo. Member adherents are viewed as a core part of the divine sadhana or spiritual practice, recipients of the grace of the Mother and Sri Aurobindo, and, more importantly, 'vehicles of supramental realization', or the descent of the supermind and the divine life on the earth. According to a sadhak:

> Our members are those who are in quest of realizing the divine. Their spiritual urge brings them here. Through Sri Aurobindo's teachings they realize the importance and meaning of the evolution of the mind to the supermind through this world and the true meaning of the divine life upon the earth. (Pondicherry, August 2011)

Vivekananda Kendra's connections with civil society are with volunteer cadres (lifetime workers, service workers, senior citizens, and student volunteers) as well as some non-cadre member adherent patrons who contribute to the service cause (these amount to around 5 percent of revenue generated) and beneficiaries who are then viewed as potential candidates for volunteering. Amritanandamayi Mission has an indirect link through its international and local monastic disciples and householder adherents. With the program/project beneficiaries, however, the link is more concrete. Hence, vis-à-vis civil society, Amritanandamayi Mission's role is that of a liberal stabilization of societal institutions such as family and meso-level institutional systems of education and health on the basis of faith. It comprises a spiritual realm including the edifice of Amma's teachings drawing from scriptures; her pronounced eclectic vision with the rhetoric of peace, universality, and harmony; subsequently developed branches, ,centres and 'Amrita family' groups; and spaces created for 'outsiders' (uninitiated into Amma's lifeworld) to whom moral choices are demonstrated.[19] In Art of Living the connections are with civic bodies and associations, member adherents, and volunteers and beneficiaries. Whereas coalition and collaboration characterize the former, for the latter its agenda is social capital formation.

With civil society, in the HIFM realm, the quest for socioreligious capital generation is akin to what Tilson and Venkateswaran (2006)

19 Householder disciples and monastic disciples persistently strive to discuss Amma's teachings with any lay person who enters the Amritanandamayi Mission setup and also show the balance struck between transcendental goals and humanitarian activities – translating the faith mandate into the universal and secular directive of social service.

maintain as a covenantal model of public relations[20] vis-à-vis contractual. These relationships between transcendence, divinity, and humanity enable a reframing of what it means to be spiritually aligned in the context of HIFM cultures and subcultures. From the lens of theological anthropology, it locates followers in the context of a web of relationships with the ethereal and transcendental, which then extend to realms of spiritual-material culture. There is a certain link that is then established for the followers between the material and the metaphysical: the quest for transcendence and its eventual attainment by devotees-followers through HIFM association being the last link in the chain.

20 The covenantal model of public relations refers to a model that is based on an agreement held to be the basis of a relationship of commitment with God.

4

Faith Networks: Interplaying Social Issues, Action, and Service

The 'social' dimension in faith repertoires comes with HIFMs' visions of society, social stratification, social ethics, and social consciousness. This further lends into HIFMs' positions on social issues, action, service, and work. Perspectives on social issues include linear, systemic, structural, theistic, and evolutionary perspectives. They are understood from the functional, structural, and post-structural lenses. Further diminished religiosity and psychosocial pathologies are also understood as causes. The pivot of this understanding, which is transferred to the social realm, is generally derived from the ideational core of HIFMs. Illustrations are the Ramakrishna–Vivekananda gospel, Swaminarayan religiosity and filial propensities, Sai-inspired faith–service link, pure idealism, practical Vedanta, and Integral Yoga. In terms of range, there are qualifying positions on certain social sectors which define the distinctiveness of HIFM interventions. Peculiar positions are available on health, education, inequalities, poverty, development, gender, class, ecology, and natural disasters. There are emancipation, restoration, and resurrection stances on action which are spearheaded by metaphysical/spiritual contentions. The service–work notions have largely evolved through HIFM ideological peculiarities superimposed on pure Hindu tenets. Essentially, it can be said that the equation or connection between the 'self-other self-Absolute self-universal social consciousness' is prevalent in consecrating the 'service' and the 'social'.

Visions of society

HIFMs' visions of society stem from the doctrine of 'belonging'; the real practical world belongs to the Absolute and the ethereal. HIFMs innovatively reconfigure the social space – discursively shaping community notions coalesced around sets of faith-oriented lenses and resonating differentially in a complex network of 'public spheres'.[1] Some philosophical derivatives of the various HIFMs' visions on society can be stated as follows.

For Ramakrishna Mission, society is generally viewed as a macrocosm, a larger existential and tangible yet ephemeral reality on which the divine play or *lila prasangas* are undertaken. Human beings are actors and larger administration rests with the higher power. In the binary scheme of things, the society comprises the material world 'out there' vis-à-vis the spiritual world within. For Swaminarayan Sanstha, society is essentially the material world. In the parlance of Saibaba Sansthan, the individual is the microcosm and the society is the macrocosm – a material field of activity and operations. Furthermore, there is a perceived link between the external phenomenal world and the world of spirit internal to us – the external world being a reflection of the inner being. Brahmakumaris' vision on society is that it is the subtle and in the physical realm of existence. For Chinmaya Mission, from the Vedanta lens, society is the material realm of praxis, action, and existence. With respect to Sri Aurobindo Society, society is essentially a manifestation of the divinity upon the earth with human beings as components of the Absolute God. In Sri Aurobindo's social philosophy, 'both individual and the community are like humanity and the whole universe, living powers of the eternal reality in its cosmic manifestation; they are the individual self and the collective self of the one universal Being – hence an organic relationship exists between the individual and society' (Ghosh, 1962, p. 34).

Society for Vivekananda Kendra is the microcosm of the macrocosmic universe – the material, tangible, and real world which holds the propensity

1 See Reddy and Zavos (2010).

for transcendence. For Amritanandamayi Mission, society is a playground of human activity – a platform to operationalize the agenda of faith-inspired service. It is then conceived in terms of epistemology in favour of metaphysics, and there is a dichotomy between subject (knowers of reality as in Amritanandamayi Mission followers) and object (the larger society out there or the field of praxis). In a more critical sense, there is a combination of the intransitive (the real world including processes and events) and the transitive (the Amritanandamayi Mission followers' purposes, motives, and intentions). With respect to Art of Living, society is viewed as the basic existential domain – a composite of beings that are supposed to be in quest of the Absolute. Society in Art of Living terms is effectively matter – the reality which is attainable, knowable, and which should eventually be on the path of transcendence.

On social stratification

On stratification there is a bourgeois balance in HIFMs, that is, between the material and spiritual[2] – stratification is reified in practice but sublimated in the transcendental quest. For Ramakrishna Mission, stratification is a part of natural laws of society, a functional prerequisite for systemic operations. There is however a certain kind of ambivalence about the nuances of core categories of stratification such as gender, caste, class, and ethnicity – since everything gets subsumed under the powerful message of nondualism, oneness, and unity.

Swaminarayan Sanstha has historically either maintained traditional caste hierarchy or actively engaged in 'swaminarayanization' of patrons ranging from tribal groups to Patidars, Thakkars, and Rajputs. The entire focus is on *sampradaya* development, and stratification assumes a new form. Within the *sampradaya* moving away from bourgeois caste hierarchies and overarching stratification patterns, there is a different cultural politics

2 See Hatcher (2007). Hatcher's (2007) observations are based on the exploration of the affinity between one early colonial version of Vedanta and the socioeconomic activities of its bourgeois promoters. Working from a rare set of Bengali discourses delivered at meetings of the Tattvabodhini Sabha during its inaugural year (1839–1840), this essay demonstrates how a re-scripted Vedanta provided members with a worldview that legitimated both their spiritual concerns and their worldly activities.

of sorts.[3] There is a prevalent conception of the BAPS spiritual-cultural industry and the penetration of sect and sectarian norms into realms of imagination and psyche. Traditional Vaishnavism is parodied – all emergent signs, representations, constructs, and realities are modified as per Swaminarayan norms. In that sense, the spatiality of the Swaminarayan text permits a subjective dislocation of traditional dictums only to replace them by newer ones. In a very neo-Marxian sense, Swaminarayan Sanstha culture is a social category – engineering micropolitics and revisiting the traditional class–caste logic. What emerged as a mild form of schisms from mainstream Vaishnavism in nineteenth-century Gujarat has assumed a philistine form – Swaminarayan Sanstha having consecrated its own deities and conceptions of transcendence. Gender is negotiated within the overarching 'swaminarayanism' through (a) privileged segregation; (b) benevolent separation; (c) accommodation; (d) widows endowed with the status of samkhyayoginis; and (e) the opportunity of salvation erstwhile unavailable and being only a male prerogative is made available also to women.[4]

---

3 With Lord Swaminarayan as the core and his version of Vaishnavism defined by *ekantik dharma*, and his pedigree devotee coterie comprising Khachar and Khuman tribes and Kanbi Patidars, Thakkars, and Kathis, institutionalized forms of hierarchy spearheaded by Brahminical supremacy are challenged. These identity narratives, Lord Swaminarayan as the core reference point along with his Paramahamsas (the core disciple group including Gunatitanand Swami and others), and the tailor-caste householder Mahant Pragji Bhagat's prominence have redefined ideological and structural forces of caste and class. New centre margin hierarchies are created in terms of degrees of proximity to Swaminarayan's patronage. Hence, the traditional caste 'totality' is questioned, the sect having laid down its own norms of transcendence, realization, and levels of attainment – Swaminarayan being the established Godhead and the subsequent Paramahamsas and successors (irrespective of their ascribed origins) at the apex. This apex positioning subsequently leads to a 'brahminization' as Paramahamsas and sadhus assume priestly duties in the consecrated temples at various centres. In keeping with the historical trends, however, the patron–client profiles are socially reproduced through historicity, the bourgeois householder adherents forming the next level of hierarchy. Bourgeois attributes include a historical family allegiance (families aligned to head successors of Swaminarayan Sanstha through various temples across Saurashtra), Kanbi–Patidar and Thakkar lineage, which is the flourishing trade community of Gujarat, and diaspora presence (families who have residents in countries where Swaminarayan Sanstha has a presence). Hence, this rejection of traditional caste hierarchies has a strategic position of power in the Swaminarayan Sanstha social fabric – class and duration and source of sect adherence are new sources of status formations.

4 Privileged segregation implies that men and women have designated areas of operation in the social and spatial geographies of Swaminarayan Sanstha. Benevolent separation refers to a spatiality that then assumes the form of a speciality – places of exchange for

For Saibaba Sansthan, there is a naturalization of stratification by viewing it as a constituent component of larger society. Within the Hinduized frame of reference caste hierarchies with the purity pollution schemata prevail in ritual worship of Saibaba – which is a marked departure from Saibaba's original stance of inclusiveness, his exhortation of the Bhakti saints and the syncretic leanings of Kabir, Nanak, Eknath, and Chokhamela. Class hierarchies are evident in terms of donor, patron, and ordinary devotee categorizations – further concretized in terms of pilgrim categories on the basis of affordability of residential services offered and availed of. Gender stratification is also an innate reality with renditions on different *puruhsa* (man) *dharmas* and *sthree* (woman) *dharmas*.

Brahmakumaris' take on social stratification comprises 'pure' and 'impure' souls (Brahmakumaris, 1996b, 1998), which is the essence of its stratification logic. This is called 'soul samskara' – the soul culture logic whereby the 'pure' ones are the soul-conscious Raja Yogis or Brahmakumaris and the 'impure' ones are those believed to be wallowing in the morass of 'body consciousness'. This 'purity' and 'impurity' is ascertained by 'past life actions or karma' – the access and attainment of 'purity' and its levels determined by the nature of actions performed by the souls in the past physical life. Hence, what is emphasized is a qualitative distinction between the inner and outer worlds and between body and soul. Within the Brahmakumaris' Raja Yoga repertoire, as per Walliss (2007), the inner life is seen to represent all that is true, eternal, and good, whereas the outer represents all that is false, evil, and transient. This distinction is further intensified with reference to lifestyle recommended for Raja Yogis – vegetarian diet, celibacy, spiritual study, and spiritual associations – the set of guidelines for practically delineating themselves from 'polluting others' while maintaining their own spiritual exclusivity and ontological superiority.

In Chinmaya Mission, caste hierarchy and Brahminical patriarchy is well internalized and accepted, along with an addendum on gradations – based on levels of Agape (divine and universal love; CCMT, 1991b) and intellectual convictions of oneness and unity. There are no particular

women are special and remote from renunciants. Accommodation means that women are permitted to study and teach scriptures. Widows are endowed with the affirmative status of samkhyayoginis implying that they can serve the Lord and the fellowship in specially developed spaces, ritually segregated, yet together mystically.

commentaries on stratification in Sri Aurobindo Society – the traditional explanations being accepted and Sri Aurobindo Society philosophy also talking of an equality and non-discrimination paradigm. In Vivekananda Kendra, social stratification attests hierarchy of both caste and gender developed and consolidated by Eknath Ranade and further connections with RSS and right-wing political groups. Furthermore, it takes on Swami Vivekananda's 'ideal state' notion as one in which the knowledge of the priests, the culture of the military, the distributive tendencies of the commercial/business classes, and the ideal of equality can all be kept minus their evils. In a lecture delivered at Shakespeare Club House, Pasadena, California, on 18 January 1900 (Collected Works, Volume 8), Vivekananda had proposed that caste is the basis of Indian social order, and hierarchical interdependence between caste groups is one of the main features of the caste system. The interrelation is hierarchical and metonymical – based on religious values of purity and pollution, with purity at the top and pollution at the bottom. Religion is superior and encompasses politics and economics in a metonymic way; that is, the political and economic spheres are seen as subordinate to, but part and parcel of and directed by, Hindu religion. Marriage relations and norms of commensality are also seen in the light of these religious values. Furthermore, this understanding is ossified in gender hierarchies – there is a glorification of motherhood; feminine roles and parallel gender constructions are accepted and internalized. Gender is further intertwined with caste – lower-caste women are perceived as having fewer opportunities than their higher-caste counterparts.[5]

For Amritanandamayi Mission, stratification is viewed as systems formed by customs and the unconscious structures underlying institutions

5 As per Vivekananda's analysis, in a Hindu society this differential is also visualized in terms of remarriage opportunities (the Brahmo culture at that time had focused a great deal on widow remarriage as a tool for women's emancipation; Vivekananda built on this along with his understanding of caste and transported this to the West as a gender concoction of the Indian scenario). Vivekananda proposed that fewer women in the higher castes lent lesser opportunities of women to remarry vis-à-vis in the lower castes if the situation was reversed. However, for higher-caste women, celibacy as sanctioned and preferred by Hindu religion worked to women's advantage; more women opting for celibacy post-widowhood. Hence, a cultural 'othering' of women encapsulated in institutions of caste is role-defining – women's 'happiness' as perceived in either institutions of marriage and motherhood or self-imposed celibacy post-widowhood was seen as a hallmark of high culture.

and social relations and is the basis from which the models that constitute the social structure are built. This is responsible for unequal scenarios of poverty and discrimination, as binary oppositions are at the core of these unconscious structures. Social distance and social space define stratification – and this heterogeneity and inequality constitutes social dynamics which need to be addressed. Art of Living contends that as society is a composite of beings, there is an inherent understanding that there is equity for all and, hence, there is no space for social stratification or rather there is a denial of division based on any other categorical imperative other than quest for spiritual perfection. There is a recognition that there are levels of spiritual attainment and stratification of beings is based on that. The very essence of social stratification based on caste or class is rejected. Nevertheless, the essence of stratification is not discarded, only the modicum is different – a paradigm shift from social categorical imperatives to spiritual categorical imperatives: levels of transcendence/ spiritual attainment being the criteria under consideration.

Social ethics

The deontological dimensions of HIFM ethics are moral religious sentiments containing notions of divine nature and their attributes. The teleological dimensions of HIFM ethics are perceptions, that is, ways of taking the world and differential theological sentiments as expressions of reflective/reflexive acts on the part of the faith commune.

For Ramakrishna Mission, the social ethics of praxis are both absolute and relative, which is a combination of deontological and teleological positions. As per a Swami at Belur Math,

> Ramakrishna Mission believes in certain absolute ethical principles prescribed by Sri Ramakrishna – they take the following prescription – through *shraddha* (faith), *sadhana* (discipline and austerity), and *brahmacharya* (celibacy) one attains *sakshatkara* (realization), and this is the base of the main ethical stance of the mission – *viswaprema* (universal love). Our non-negotiation with respect to ethics is the fact that there is God in all – all beings are one – and there is the manifestation of the higher being. (Belur Math, October 2011)

Hence, the positionality of love becomes an absolutist ideal – the ethical edifice on which the relative or teleological positions are built. This love, or universal love, is parallel to 'agape' or divine love stemming from the basic apophthegm of 'siva jnane jiva seva' (service recognizing divinity in beings). These epistemic claims of equity manifest in terms of teleological ethical reasonings that deliberate on inclusivity, equality, and nondualism. Ethics of praxis dominate, with 'actions' (which are within the ambit of morality) being the core to governing existence.

Swaminarayan Sanstha's social ethics comprise of altruism within and beyond boundaries defined by the sect and patriarchal norms. Where ascetics extend spiritual altruism to householders in general, tangible *seva*, philanthropy, and altruism are qualities of a householder in the Swaminarayan Sanstha fold. This extends to the less endowed within the Swaminarayan fold and also to the lumpen proletariat[6] outside. Ascetics prescribe norms of service in writing to the women's wing, who in turn carry out their activities within the prescribed spatial and territorial limits.

Saibaba Sansthan social ethics of praxis are prescribed in the Satcharitra as drawn from the Gurucharitra.[7] Some of the key ones include self-rectitude, frugality, faith, truth, self-control, love, and propensity for service. In its 'exclusivist paradigm', Brahmakumaris propose a set of 'deontological' codes including the strict adherence to the Raja Yoga regimen and the stoic belief in the 'world tree' theory wherein the Brahmakumar/i (BK) souls alone are the embodiment of 'truth' and 'light'. There is a calculated 'othering' of non-BK souls or beings – an erasure of their very existence, mentally first, and then believed to be physically inevitable in the apocalyptic premonition. In its 'assimilative and world affirmative' paradigm, Brahmakumaris' repertoire is instrumental, both at the level of epistemology and praxis. The epistemological instrumentalism emerges from its shift in focus and teachings from pure metaphysical soul discourses to the ethnography of everyday living. Apart from the regular course and advanced meditation course for those spiritually enlightened

6 Lumpen proletariat is a Marxist terminology (term originally used by Marx in 1920s) to refer to the apolitical lower orders of society uninterested in revolutionary advancement (Kolakowski, 1978).

7 Gurucharitra is a sixteenth-century text of the Dattatreya cult penned by Saraswati Gangadhar extolling the lives of Sripada Srivallabha and Narasimha Saraswati – two seminal figures of the Marathi Datta sampradaya.

and ready to receive, Brahmakumaris also conduct tailor-made courses in areas of 'material success' and 'worldly relationships' – all garnished with the Raja Yoga apotheosis. The praxis instrumentalism then emerges in the shaping of the metaphysical Raja Yoga to a tailored form – non-Brahmakumari souls not being apocryphal but perceived by Brahmakumari souls as in need of an anchor, which they supposedly provide.

For Chinmaya Mission, ethics entail the Chinmaya Mission version of Hindu ethnocentrism – operating wherefrom is the tripartite social connectivity of 'love, harmony, and service' (Tejomayananda, Swami, 2001b). The social and teleological ethics are attributed to the 'action' component of Vedanta, to which are attributed the twin aspects: (a) a dynamic vision of life and worldview which is totalitarian and (b) this worldly spirituality through work sans attachment to fruits of labour (CCMT, 1989b) – a spiritual alienation of sorts that would accumulate transcendental benefits for the individual and synergetically for society at large. Hence, in certain ways a Hindu utilitarian ethical vision prevails – Hindu ideals of oneness, equity, harmony, service, and spiritual attitude in work (Chinmayananda, Swami, 1980; Emir, 1994) ensuring the greatest good for the greatest number.

In Sri Aurobindo Society, the backdrop of social ethics is the whole notion of political liberation and the evolutionary destiny of man. The eventual goal is spiritual liberation which is believed to be not individual oriented, albeit collective – the establishment of the divine life on earth (*ihaiva*; Mukherjee, 1990). As described by a sadhak,

> Our position of ethics is also spiritual. Integral spiritual sadhana has for its goal not merely the spiritual liberation of some isolated individuals from the shackles of phenomenal Ignorance – *avidya* – but the establishment of divine life upon earth – *ihaiva*. But, since matter is the foundation of all evolutionary efflorescence of life here upon the terrestrial plane, our physical body assumes a supreme importance in the total scheme of our spiritual achievement. A divine transformation even of our physical sheath, *annamaya kosa*, is an indispensable concomitant of a truly divine living in the world. But in the actually realized status of consciousness of man the mental being, this transformation can by no means

> be achieved, nor even initiated on the plane of the material body. What is actually envisaged is the control and conquest of the prevailing determinism of our bodily system by the higher determinism of the supernatural grades and powers of our consciousness. And when the supermind, the divine gnosis, takes charge of evolution, nothing is impossible. (Pondicherry, August 2011)

For Vivekananda Kendra, social ethics are Vedanta endowed – Swami Vivekananda construed and compartmentalized in 'oriental' straitjackets; the Hindu view of society with its baggage of hierarchy and hegemony accepted as appropriate. In Amritanandamayi Mission, social ethics stem from the traditional core of social justice and human rights. Some of the ideas on social justice and rights which appear in the literature on humanitarian activities include (a) social justice as a system of distribution and retribution that is governed by valid moral principles; (b) equality of treatment as a prima facie requirement of justice; (c) transcending differences and aspiring towards a common good – the utilitarian greatest good; and (d) striking of a balance between liberal thinking and equality – the equal basic liberty and difference principle, that is, providing for those who do not have. As per a monast at Amritapuri,

> At Amritanandamayi Mission we believe that even if there are differences in the distribution of resources, these differences must be to the greatest benefit of the least advantaged and accessible to all under conditions of fair equality of opportunity. That is the only 'difference' that is acceptable to us – to provide for those who do not have a little more in comparison to those who do so that equality and balance is restored. (Amritapuri, December 2011)

The Art of Living discourse on social ethics says that it is an advanced version of personal ethics, divided into *yama* (social ethics) and *niyama* (personal ethics), being levels of ethical discursivity. Both feed into the statute of Yoga – a core pillar of Sri Sri's teachings. For *yama*, there are five rules to living peacefully in society and the environment: *ahimsa* (nonviolence), *satyam* (truth), *astheya* (not missing what you don't have at the moment), *brahmacharya* (celibacy), and *aparigraha* (meaning not taking what is not yours). For *niyama* again there are five rules for one's inner development: *shaucha* (cleanliness), *santosha* (contentment), *tapas* (prayer), *swadhyaya* (self-study undertaken for pure knowledge), and *ishwara pranidhana* (surrender to the divine). Hence, the entire repertoire is deontological in nature – ethics are absolute and governed by pure reason.

Thus, as Dalmiya (2009) makes a comparison of Swami Vivekananda's concept of ethical love and feminist care ethics, HIFMs can be said to address 'framework questions' and, to some extent, 'application questions' in ethical realms. Examining social ethics or ethical subjectivity not from the point of the moral agents but from the point of view of the objects/persons who are recipients of the ethical concern of HIFMs reveals two dimensions: moral considerability (which is the framework question demanding a criterion of having standing in the ethical domain) and moral weight (or the application question of adjudication or judgement as to who should obtain the benefits most). HIFMs' stance on social ethics proposes that all 'beings' as part of the Infinite are worthy of moral consideration. This is an ethically expansive move as it invites all socially ostracized groups squarely back to the moral table. On the application question, HIFMs' stance is that of universal care, which is, however, not devoid of the politics of power and privileges that willy-nilly enter the discourse.[8] Basically, what comes to the foreground with respect to HIFMs' social ethics is the duty of beneficence – notions of moral/social duty and a generalized ethical subjectivity.

Social consciousness

On social consciousness, it can be said that HIFMs have managed a collated Hindu theistic stance in three stages: (a) objectification of faith

8 HIFMs' stance on moral weight may not necessarily include all the aspects of feminist care ethics, particularly the notion of a relational self that is central to care ethical ideas of a moral agent. It says that bonds of love and care that we have with some others give us a self-identity 'in-relation' to them and enable us to take their point of view into consideration in our decision-making. In case of larger social reform, appeals to the relational self become inadequate. What is then introduced is a (re)construction of the self-in-relation to new Others – to people whom one does not consider the self to be 'in relation' with. Such reformulation of self-identity presupposes a prior motivation of wanting to connect and constitute a self-in-relation to the hitherto excluded others.

as a distinctive aspect of social life; (b) its individualization in terms of making it an individual's psychophysical potential and the transcendence embedded within it; and (c) the universalization of faith as an episteme and worldview.

With respect to Ramakrishna Mission, social consciousness is derived directly from their ethical positions. As discussed by Tyagananda (2006), the divine social consciousness of Sri Ramakrishna is about seeing the living God within and without; the ideal of seeing everyone as an embodiment of God. Ramakrishna Mission's position on social consciousness is a symbolic transaction of the social, the divine, and God realization. With the social as the subset of the divine, social consciousness assumes the role of a core pendulum oscillating between the existential social and the transcendent God. To run a streak of divinity from the existential to the extra-terrestrial is the essence of the divine and, hence, of social consciousness.

Swaminarayan Sanstha social consciousness is built by the sociocultural rhythm of the sect and its overarching philosophy – the prominent dictum being 'in the joy of others lies our own' (BAPS Sadhus, 2003). For Saibaba Sansthan, social consciousness is a simultaneous affirmation of divinity of existence and benevolence to all. This is believed to be attained by spiritual contemplation on Saibaba. The practical means of attaining this realization is moral conduct, philanthropy in the name of Saibaba, and spiritual discipline (SSST, 2011). Oscillating between the 'exclusivist' and 'assimilative and world affirmative' paradigms, Brahmakumaris assume an ambivalent stance on social consciousness – hegemonic in its exclusivist form and patronizing and vicariously ameliorative in its affirmative form. With respect to Chinmaya Mission, social consciousness operates on Hinduism as the lowest common denominator – on the edifice of which is built the greatest common vision of oneness. Hence, Hinduism operates as the base for human values (CCMT, 2003) and Hindu culture a virtual measuring rod of civilization, with social ethics and consciousness referring to the bounden duty of each Chinmaya Mission associate to unearth the sacred message of Hindu scriptures and highlight their philosophy for the rest of the mankind to follow.

In Sri Aurobindo Society, there are two levels of understanding social consciousness – one is in favour of religious nationalist leanings as propelled by the writings of Sri Aurobindo on Bankim, Tilak, and

Dayananda, and the other is more towards a spiritual consciousness drawing from the basis of integral yoga. The second level is the movement of upward evolutionary progress; this concept of progress is teleological, implying a purposive development directed towards a goal or an ideal towards perfection. Here, Sri Aurobindo was influenced by Karl Lamprecht, who was the first social thinker in pre-war Germany to put forth a psychological theory of history and social development – a departure from the materialist historical conception of history and social development which dominated the sociohistorical thought in Europe till the first decade of the twentieth century. As proposed by Sri Aurobindo, 'the first essential sign of the readiness of the common human mind for the advent of the spiritual age must be the growth of the subjective idea of life, the idea of the soul, the inner being' (Gandhi, 1965, p. 46).

For Vivekananda Kendra, social consciousness implies the soul tweaking that is required to arithmetically subtract the 'evils' of the Hindu totality, the absence of which ensures an appropriate social formula for social statics and mechanics (Advaita Ashrama, 2000). Amritanandamayi Mission's stance is that of a moral philosophy for society, the twin components of which are equality and moral autonomy of human beings. The moral principles of altruism, equity orientation, love and compassion for all, unconditional love, and detached attachment are all considered to be universal and within the bounds of rationality so as to ensure common good (MAM Trust, 2010). There is clearly a moral universalism positing the existence of rationally identifiable transcultural and transhistorical moral truth which further pleads the case for the need and existence of a moral community in the form of Amritanandamayi Mission followers building bridges with others in civil society.

For Art of Living, in terms of social consciousness, apart from the aspect of Oneness, two prophetic claims have been made: one is the garment of social consciousness as interwoven by spirituality and communism which mutually comply and collide, and the other is the contention of Vasudhaiva Kutumbakam (the world is one family). To cite an excerpt from the discourse by Sri Sri:

> Spirituality is the technology of the consciousness and the whole world is the play and display of consciousness. The consciousness should be governed by communism as the basis

> of both spirituality and communism are caring and sharing. In a society plagued by domestic and societal violence we need to globalize wisdom. Though we have advanced technologically, we have cared very little for the emotional and spiritual needs of the people. A sense of belongingness to the whole world is the need of the hour. We need to celebrate diversity by honouring all cultures and religious traditions rather than letting it become the cause of strife or violence – concept of one world family. (Sri Sri Publications Trust, 2007)

Social issues

The sociological imagination of Ramakrishna Mission posits the understanding of social issues in a linear, positivist, structural-functional frame wherein problems are believed to be an outcome of dysfucntionalities in systems, structures, and processes (Adiswarananda, 2006). In a traditional sense, Swaminarayan Sanstha has a structural position on social issues – poverty, inequality, and diminished access to resources considered to be outcomes of current structural arrangements (Swayamprakashdas, 2008). Saibaba Sansthan possesses an evolutionary logic to social issues; that is, in the cosmic evolution there is a disruption caused by maleficent elements which give impulsion to social pathology. Societal predicaments quintessentially have this pathological origin. To quote one of its office bearers,

> Saibaba believed and told his devotees that all social problems are due to inherent evils in society. They need to be countered so that peace can prevail. (Shirdi, January 2011)

For Brahmakumaris, social problems are inevitably due to decline in human values and the subordinate binary of 'body consciousness' (Hassija, 2006). In Chinmaya Mission, there is a consciousness and transpersonal approach towards social issues: the ephemeral 'ego' at multisystemic levels is believed to prevent harmony and peace. This is further intensified by materialistic worldviews as juxtaposed with spiritualism and ethics in Vedanta (Chinmayananda, 1991; CCMT, 1991b).

Based on an essentially evolutionary philosophical schema, social issues are viewed by Sri Aurobindo Society as a problematic offshoot of lower planes of existence and evolution. The present evolutionary crisis is believed to be a result of reason and dogmatic religion (Saint-Hilaire, 1963). The utopian quest of divine life upon the earth would negate and annihilate issues that concern a materialist conception of social development. For Vivekananda Kendra, social issues are owing to deep-rooted materialism which forms the edifice of the problematic (Parameswaran, 2004), gradationally affecting individual ego and, subsequently, societal malfeasance. The stance of Amritanandamayi Mission is that issues are the combined outcome of systemic malfunctioning. Societal systems are in turn understood as comprehensive systems of reciprocally accessible communicative actions. To quote a monastic member based at Amritapuri,

> Social problems are because our systems do not function at their optimum level. We need to strive to work towards making systems such as the economic, political, and legal systems amenable to change and good functioning. Then, social problems will gradually vanish. (Amritapuri, December 2011)

The sociocultural imagination of the Art of Living foundation also rests on a nonlinear and structural formulation of social issues. To quote an AOL teacher:

> There is not one single cause. Society is very complex and the contemporary world particularly so. Domination happens not at one level, but at several levels and in several domains. That is the cause of oppression and human suffering. To alleviate that we need to counter things at many levels and bring changes in all structures and systems. (Mumbai, May 2012)

Origins and forms of social issues in the HIFM language

Social issues as per Ramakrishna Mission have structural-functional origins – dysfunctionalities in the social realm such as poverty, resource inadequacy, unequal distribution of resources, and the social stratification are believed to precipitate the same. The twin dimensions of heterogeneity and inequality are said to prevail, which are in turn determined by consolidation and intersection of parameters which constitute social dynamics. The pivot is the Ramakrishna–Vivekananda gospel of this world being a microcosm of the macrocosmic universe or the Absolute being. This Absolute being is perfect and has infinite attributes. As the source is perfect, the imperfections lie in its manifestations and these dysfunctionalities need to be rectified through systematic interventions (Ramakrishnan, 2006). Educational inequalities are believed to be due to lack of structural and institutional capacities. Similarly, health issues are primarily owing to deficit in quality care and hence there is the need for specialized and dedicated services. Rural and tribal development efforts are primarily geared towards a holistic social development, the crucial declaration being that of integrated development for which the Ramakrishna Mission mandate is to provide the 'enabling' and 'empowering' paraphernalia. The members of the monastic order, engaged in rural and tribal development efforts, are guided by the overarching ideals of Ramakrishna-Vivekananda of 'jagat hitaya' or universal welfare. The conception of development is generally linear and positivist; however, the emic lens and context specificity wherein development is to be done keeping in mind indigenous cultural realms remain. Hence, there is a certain element of intersubjectivity in the development renditions. As a part of the indigenous development discourse of Ramakrishna Mission, disasters are considered impediments to development (as they are considered to have an impact on morbidity, mortality, and livelihoods) and they need to be tackled through efforts of relief, rehabilitation, and reconstruction (Lokeswarananda et al., 2006).

In Swaminarayan Sanstha, diminished religiosity, excessive self-orientednesss, and a decline in 'family values' that deepen the material divide and lead to the 'materialist denial' for the poor (BAPS Sadhus, 2003) are considered to be the core reasons for social issues/problems. Although the micro-macro link for Swaminarayan Sanstha in terms of conceptions of social problems is the said connection, 'ontological decadence–filial value depreciation–social mores/codes imbalance–global imbalance', there is a clear line of 'structure' argument which flows. The rectification is seen through Swaminarayan religiosity and improved filial ties.

With respect to Swaminarayan Sanstha, some defining positions are on class antagonisms, caste inequalities, gender issues, and multisystemic violence. Class antagonisms are due to 'access-attainment denial' for the plebeians. This denial is due to consumerism, capitalist orientations, and nonalignment to 'family' codes and mores. Similarly, multisystemic violence is due to a distortion in social consciousness caused by materialist ways. On caste inequalities, Swaminarayan Sanstha posits that in the 'higher realm', there is an inherent equity among beings as they are all equal in the eyes of Lord Swaminarayan. However, sect-based hierarchies based on heredity are unequivocally accepted as the principles of sectarian organization. About gender, there is an inherent antagonism in the Swaminarayan Sanstha frame of reference – its claim to 'liberalize' and 'emancipate' women (separate worship areas, women's wing for social and spiritual activities, claimed right of women to salvation traditionally denied in mainstream Vaishnavism, and reengagement of widows in spiritual social service) being in sharp contrast to the 'real' and the 'actual' status of women and the prevalent patriarchal ethos. Within the overarching hegemony of 'Brahminical patriarchy', the dominant practices include (a) ascetic abstinence of women (equated to material resource/wealth) leading to their spiritual distancing and simultaneous objectification; (b) Swaminarayan Sanstha text prescriptions for women and widows that specify 'values', 'morals', and 'desirable' codes of conduct for being a good 'wife, mother, life partner', and 'chaste widow' with a life dedicated to the service of the Lord; (c) social geographies of distance (separate benediction spaces, specified limits to entry – Swaminarayan Sanstha has very clear demarcated areas in their constructions and spaces where women are strictly prohibited entry); and (d) rigid sexual binaries and gender constructions virtually 'closing doors' to any alternate forms of sexual orientations. In the Swaminarayan Sanstha patriarchal repertoire some 'natural' discourses are anatomy as destiny, sexual division of labour, preserving 'purity' and 'chastity' of widows by urging lifetime commitment to spiritual service (thereby preserving patriarchal family and private property), and control over women's sexuality and labour power.[9]

---

9 There are specifications in the Shikshapatri about the wifely duties being sexual satisfaction of the spouse and ensuring progeny; giving away her own material resources, if required even *sthreedhan* for the progress of her husband. Domestic work and child rearing are declared exclusive responsibilities of women, and even in the diaspora face of women, where increasingly women work outside the homes, the Shikshapatri mandate remains unchanged (in fact, what is projected is the benevolent face of the *sampradaya* which 'permits' its women to take up paid work outside). Hence, although

For Saibaba Sansthan, social issues have pathological origins – a dysfunctionality in the cosmological rhythm. The hinge is the teachings of the charismatic guru of the Saibaba Sansthan – particularly emanating from the core positions of faith and service. Saibaba Sansthan's defined positions are available on health issues, education and poverty, and resource inadequacy. Health issues are looked at as having karmic origins. Educational inequalities are believed to be due to a divinely ordained classificatory system which naturally endows access to some and withholds access for others. The rectification is then benevolently ensuring access and attainment for all through 'free' education initiatives, thereby reproducing the spiritual capital of Saibaba Sansthan. Pertaining to chronic issues of poverty and resource inadequacy, the contention is that discrepancies in the accounting systems of individual lives lead to cosmological disturbances and, through that, class inequalities and poverty (Kher, 2001).

In Brahmakumaris, the sole position on social issues is that 'body consciousness' is the main cause of social issues and problems. In particular, Brahmakumaris posit that particular entities within the world of experience are not real and the universals are not sense objects but products of thoughts, 'thought objects', and ideas. There is a view of history of human society as a dialectical movement of ideas marching towards the realization of its essence – ideas are assigned independent existence and held as a reality. The 'Absolute Idea' or Shiv Baba is considered as the subject and the material world is placed in the position of the predicate – the real world is seen as the external, phenomenal form of the Idea (PBIV, no date). Only the soul consciousness or the propensity for transcendence can alleviate and ameliorate problems and issues.

their work participation is liberating to one extent, it is only partial; for 'true adherents' of the sect domestic chores and raising children are still relegated to women – at times manifesting as double workload. What emerges then is, for Delphy (1970), two modes of production: industrial and domestic – the first giving rise to capitalist exploitation and the other to patriarchal exploitation. In the Swaminarayan Sanstha sect social structure, women's identities are further intertwined by caste and class realities – although patriarchal subordination prevails, its manifestation across the haves and have-nots in the Swaminarayan Sanstha social realm differs. For instance, the Kanbi Patidar women's constructions of patriarchal exchange and negotiations differ remarkably from that of a Kathi woman. Further through the Balika, Kishori, and Yuvati mandals, femininity is inscribed (Chowdrow, 1978), thereby leaving very little to conscious choice and much to the realm of the unconscious or psyche.

The 'body consciousness' – a metaphysical metaphor for the material, tangible, and real – is responsible for decadence. It is also a symbolic for 'negativities' and 'narrow-ness' vis-à-vis soul consciousness which gives 'positivity' and 'generosity of mind' (Hassija, 2006).

Chinmaya Mission has a distinctively psychoanalytical view: 'ego' being the root of all issues – particularly violence, discord, and wars. Theistic humanism is the underlying tenet with a twin focus on people and theology. Hence, there is a thrust on recognition of human beings as executors of ethical, political, and moral judgements derived from Vedantic thought. The focus is therefore on behaviour modification of the individual through Vedantic tenets and adaptation to the Chinmaya Mission Hindu religio-cultural environment as concrete goals. In a phenomenological sense, the central assumption is that of intentionality, which presents Chinmaya Mission adherents as active interpreters of their experiences in the Chinmaya Mission world rather than passive reactors. At the same time there is a kind of recognition of the world or society with certain structural complexities, which Vedanta alone is believed to have the potency to address. The desideratum is a carving of lifeworlds and realms of intersubjectivity within which 'community of Chinmaya Mission attitudes' are shared. The 'stock knowledge' of Vedanta is a paramount reality leading, then, to the designing of perspectives, typifications, and presumptions to address social issues. Furthermore, in the interactionist sense, there are deliberations on mind, self, and other aspects that aid adjustment, relationship formation, and maintenance and adaptability to the environment – all answers to which are available in practical Vedanta (Ishwarananda, 2004).

In Chinmaya Mission, with respect to structural issues such as lack of education and healthcare access as well as development deficits/ uneven nature of development (CORD programmes pertaining to rural development address developmental issues as per their mission statement), the understanding is structural-psychoanalytical: social inequity, deficits, and binaries which perpetuate regimes of patronage and exploitation are due to the 'ego' of the material bourgeois who fail to take cognisance of residual and institutional welfare. At a slightly more advanced level, family values and socialization are also assumed to play a key role in determining problematics in the social fabric as per the Chinmaya Mission stance. Value/moral deterioration of this perceived 'core' social unit of society is the source of issues pertaining to abuse, isolation, and neglect at the familial level and that catapults onto societal-level violence and disharmony (Chimnayananda, 1990).

For Sri Aurobindo Society, social issues have their origins in evolutionary antagonisms and contradictions (Sri Aurobindo Society, 1997), which would eventually get resolved in the quest for the divine. The pivot is the evolutionary, transformative, and transcendental stance. In Sri Aurobindo Society pronounced positions are available on education, health issues, gender, ecology, and social development. The positionality on education is idealistic (vis-à-vis materialist and social reproductive) which problematizes only curriculum-based education in favour of an amalgam of physical, vital, psychic, and spiritual education (Sri Aurobindo Ashram, 1956). Furthermore, in the experiment there are aspects of participative learning and learner-oriented pedagogy as the ultimate orientation is towards a change in consciousness (Joshi & Artaud, 1974). That is the core of spiritual education, which then aims for inner transformation and development leading to the union with the divine presence (Dowsett & Jayaswal, 1975). The conceptions on health issues are that their source is the imbalance of the human body with the environment and primal substances – the commencing point for rectification and rejuvenation being the physical body and its discipline.[10] Gender conceptualizations quintessentially depict the notions of the divine feminine (as the Absolute is considered synonymous in Sri Aurobindo's repertoire to the Divine Mother). The notions of masculinity and femininity are considered akin to the Indic binaries of *puruhsa* and *prakriti*; however, this difference is considered to be more at the level of the psychic than physical and, hence, the need to go beyond biological determinism is emphasized (Sri Aurobindo Society, 1978). Motherhood is considered nonnegotiable in the realm of gender discourses; however, for women engaged in spiritual sadhana the way to conquer sexual desire, which is an imperative, is believed to be that of yoga and divine love (Sri Aurobindo Society, 1978).

10 Sri Aurobindo Society actively promotes indigenous forms of medicine and natural healing. It brings out a periodical called NAMAH – New Approaches to Medicine and Health, which discusses various aspects of this healing through current and ongoing research.

Spiritual and ecotheological notions dominate discourses on ecology for Sri Aurobindo Society (Vijay, 1981; Sri Aurobindo Society, 1999a). The underlying proposition for ecological consciousness is that there is the Absolute Being (Godhead) in every atom. Being one with that inner Godhead is instrumental in establishing the contact (harmonious coexistence) of all 'beings'. Yoga enmeshed with Vedanta is considered to be the base of ecological consciousness. Divinization of nature is instrumental in promoting ecological consciousness where the teleology implies that "living beings are the reality and the whole cosmos is the Ultimate Reality" (Sri Aurobindo Society, 1999).

On social development and transformation, the core argument is that of divine life on earth – the governance of earth by the absolute 'Truth', which is believed to descend from the Godhead (Bhavani & Elia, 1999). In one of the regular discourses on the works of Sri Aurobindo, a *sadhak* explicated:

> A transformation of human nature can only be achieved when the substance of the being is so steeped in the spiritual principle that all its movements are a spontaneous dynamism and a harmonious process of the spirit. But even when the higher powers and their intensities enter into the substance of the Inconscience, they are met by this blind opposing necessity and are subjected to this circumscribing and diminishing law of the nescient substance. A supramental change of the whole substance of the being and therefore necessarily of all its characters, powers, and movements takes place when the involved Supermind in Nature emerges to meet and join with the supramental light and power descending from supernature. Mind and mental humanity would remain as one step in the spiritual evolution, but other degrees above it would be there, formed and accessible by which the embodied mental being, as it became ready, could climb into the Gnosis and change into an embodied supramental and spiritual being. On the basis of this the principle of a divine life in a terrestrial nature would be manifested; even the world of ignorance and inconscience might discover its own submerged secret and being to realize in each lower degree its divine significance. (Pondicherry, August 2011)

Vivekananda Kendra's austere adherence to structuralist contentions to social issues derives from Swami Vivekananda's constant deployment of binaries throughout his writings and speeches: traditional-modern; East-West; orient-occident, and others. However, contrary to traditional hegemonies, Swami Vivekananda deemed the former superior: reversing the tables on Western scientism and using the agency of religion and spirituality as a heritage of India and the East (Advaita, Ashram, 2000a). Vivekananda Kendra positions are historically defined in terms of caste hierarchy, race and gender issues, and ecology. For extant social practices, religion was viewed by Swami Vivekananda as a rationalizing medium subtracting the dogma which was believed to perpetuate evil. On caste, Swami Vivekananda proposed it as a universal character of societies – equivalent to the pure, affected, and impure (*sattva*, *rajas*, and *tamas*) components. Justification for caste hierarchy was derived from the doctrine of qualitative difference as central to the concept of natural rights. Hence, trait as a divisive authority (rather than birth status) and a larger acceptance of caste, Sanskritization and Brahminization are proposed. On race, Swami Vivekananda imported the concept of Aryanism (the most comprehensive discussion on the subject was taken in his lecture 'The Future of India' delivered during his course of travels from Colombo to Almora in 1897 post his return from the first trip to the US), deploying it as a creolization notion and thereby providing an innovative critique of the conventional myth of the racial purity of the Aryans. This demystification of Aryan race superiority established by Western scholars through the use of creolization as an explanatory category served two purposes: explaining caste complexities in simplified race terms (Aryan-Dravidian) to suit Western mentalities, and catapulting of caste issues in the Indian context to an international platform by drawing parallels to Apartheid. For Vivekananda Kendra, Hinduism is then an answer to transcend the 'evils' of caste and race (the existence of issues is not questioned) – as it represents the 'general will' of people; abstract and overarching norms where transcending dynamics created by differences and hierarchies, statics is derived and stability is maintained.

On gender, commencing from the Swami Vivekananda heritage, there are binaries of masculine and feminine: dominant ideas associated by women are ideals of purity, refinement, intellect, and strength. Images of women subsumed under Brahminical patriarchy are in saffron terms, representatives of enlightened India (Vivekananda Kendra Prakashan, 1992). Feminine chastity is translated to national pride; women's issues arising solely due to lack of access which religion-based education can bridge. There is a sexless image of the ideal woman, which Swami Vivekananda borrowed from Ramakrishna's depiction of Sarada Devi, which is used to successively bridge the gap between two opposing ideas of progressive reform for women as advocated by the Brahmo Samaj against the ideals of restraint and divinity that is contained in the proposals of the conservative Hindu reformers' views on the role of women in the private sphere. With the RSS twist and Eknathji's pioneering role, Vivekananda Kendra further stresses on the 'power of celibacy' – which is viewed as awakening the 'totality of manhood'; setting youth on the diverse paths to freedom through work, renunciation, and sacrifice. The woman question here is entwined with negating sexualities, both in the personal and social realms. The spirit of renunciation and ascetic lifestyle that are essential to the practice of brahmacharya (celibacy) are seen as power-enhancing functions for ideal social and political conduct. To that extent the positions on women's issues in the Vivekananda Kendra setup are a juxtaposed admixture of RSS and Gandhian theories, the common thread being that of ethical restraint, celibacy being of particular advantage for women in public life as well as promoting notions of chastity, and freedom from distractions for the transcendent goal of service to society. There is an inimitable link between self-control and sociopolitical potency and sociospiritual emancipation. In the Brahminical spirit, women in Vivekananda Kendra can achieve those by either committing to monogamous marriage, refraining from remarriage, and/or lifetime celibacy (Advaita Ashrama, 1998a, 1999c, 2000a). In terms of ecology and developmental issues, the problem is seen in the hegemonic paradigm of Western scientism and technocentrism (Kulkarni, 1998; Vasudeo, 1998). The sole mode of rectification is to adopt the sacredness of natural contention and organic worldviews as expressed in Vedanta thought and Swami Vivekananda's Yogic propositions. What is offered is then a framework for eco-consciousness from an indigenous standpoint and alternative technologies as reification of the rhetoric of nonduality as a form of eco-theology.

Amritanandamayi Mission posits that 'colonization of lifeworlds' are triggered by acute materialism and cause social problems

(Amritaswarupananda, 2008). There is a recognition in Amritanandamayi Mission of the capillary form of existence of power and its exercising through multitude of interactions at the micro level of society called micropolitics – operating in different localities, contexts, and situations. For Amritanandamayi Mission, the pivot is metaphysics – Amma's spiritual vision as the pathway to transformation (MAM Trust, 2010). The range encompasses positions on health, education, livelihood, ecology, and disasters as also levels of vulnerability requiring institutional and material care. For all the core social sectors, the lone stance is the materialistic tendencies of the world which cause imbalances and need to be addressed. On macro political issues such as war and conflict between nations, the explanation is metaphysical; that is, ego is believed to be the cause of all misery and should be tackled. To quote a member of the order,

> All social problems, whether they have to do with our country or with other nations, are due to ego. Ego is the root cause and that should be tackled. When individuals change and recognize the importance of love and service, societies will change. (Amritapuri, December 2011)

The sociological imagination of Art of Living provides a structural interpretation of social issues, viewing the multisystemic frame of reference. Heterogeneity and inequality coupled with intersections of parameters that constitute social dynamics form the origin point of social issues. The sociological imagination of Art of Living, stemming from Sri Sri's social face, posits as the axis guiding further operations.

The Art of Living range encompasses positions on women's issues, poverty, ecology, education, and politics. On women's issues the stance is liberal and socialist with the rhetoric of equality and empowerment, as well as acknowledging their roles in production and reproduction. The cause of poverty has been understood as the unequal distribution of resources and the structural nemesis which causes the economic advantage to tilt to the side of a few. Sri Sri's position on ecology is cosmological and ecotheological, which governs all ecological initiatives ranging from organic farming to Ayurveda (Sri Sri Publications Trust, 2010a). Particularly, what is opined on ecology is the sacredness dimension of nature, reverence for life principle, and seeking evidences for God in the phenomena of nature. In the discourses of Sri Sri, 'nature is the perfect being or a reflection of the perfect being – the Absolute' (Sri Sri Publications Trust, 2008a), which supports the resacralization of nature thesis as well as Sri Sri's celebrated soul–cosmos relationship, and an organic or emanationist model of the God–world relationship – the Absolute God as the author of nature, the world, and the universe.

Sri Sri has posited education as an a priori necessity as well as a lifelong venture. Taking a structural-functional stance on educational issues, the focus is more towards emphasizing the twin requirements of formal and non-formal modes and also building an 'imagined community' of indigenous 'traditional roots' oriented cadre of graduates (particularly through the Sanskrit schools that were commenced initially). On politics, Sri Sri has opined that there is a clear need to 'spiritualize politics' as 'politics is primarily for the welfare of the people'. Furthermore, there is a nationalist leaning and orientation towards political issues.

HIFMs' understandings on social issues demonstrate a colonial-nativist continuum; there is at once a fascination towards individual and indigenous explanations and the macro sociological imagination. Hence, there are elements of textuality and there are different ways in which social issues are understood and constructed. There are also performative elements[11] as social issues are shaped through the ways HIFMs perform them. The central tenet is unarguably the faith narrative – HIFMs' core yarn to spin. Through that, conceptions on social issues are structured, maintained, and debated. The faith pivot may oscillate between being liberatory and restrictive for the laity audience, but for the order members the core thread in the social storyline remains intact.[12] Positioning the

11 Jayashree (2006) has provided account of the services of the Church of England Zenana Mission Society in Trivandrum during the period 1864–1964 based on two documents, The Land of the Conch Shell by Augusta M. Blandford, the founder of the mission at Trivandrum, and an unpublished document prepared by another missionary, D. Taylor, who joined the mission in 1964. The two narratives tell the story of a school, built brick by brick, and together form a corpus that gives valuable insights into the making of colonial modernity in a small principality in the south of India. Aspects such as micro history and Judith Butler's performative acts in gender and social construction have been used for the analysis.

12 Cojocaru, Cojocaru, and Sandu (2011) have examined the phenomenon of social services in post-1989 Romania and have emphasized the role of faith or the religious factor in the establishment and operation of nongovernmental organizations active in the area of family and child protection/child welfare. However, it was also found that during

stances on core social sectors does twin tasks for the HIFMs – determines the range of interventions and the social spread. These stances are governed by God conceptions, HIFMs' historiographies, and spiritual metaphors as well as public acceptability and mainstream/establishment alignments/legitimations. Where 'margins' are accepted in the social jargon, a certain fine-tuning of the vocabulary of defining it takes place through the HIFM lens. For instance, whereas social inequalities are recognized, at the juncture of explicating it, HIFMs' core stances (such as body consciousness, lack of spiritual appetite, diminished religiosity, and familism) make a wildcard entry. This also probably explains the peculiarities of certain explanations/conceptions on social issues and problems.

Social action

HIFMs' stance on action emerges from a distinctively indigenous cosmo-vision and cosmology. The quest for social justice is effectively a de-colonial effort in which the mantle of Hindu-derived spirituality-philosophy is utilized by HIFMs to dethrone colonial hegemonies. The mandate operates within a field determined by colonial and postcolonial formations of meaning: HIFMs signify a cultural production of sorts in which the sphere of the socioreligious is rearticulated.

Ramakrishna Mission posits itself as a crucial religio-spiritual actor responsible for emancipation. Action essentially transcends self – the motto of selfless action and the aphorism of selfless action prevail. According to Bhajananda (2006) and Smarananda (2006), there are four broad types of action, or what is called in Indic literature, karma yoga, existing in the Ramakrishna Mission – *nishkama karma* or work without motive; *bhagawat pritikarma* karma or work done with the desire of pleasing the Lord; *prapatti* or total self-surrender to the Lord; and work as participation in divine *lila* (acts of divine).

For Swaminarayan Sanstha, the Swaminarayan religion is viewed as an emancipation mechanism from this structural entrapment – it

implementation there were aspects of dilution, secularization, and fragmentation in response to secular donors. Secular donors, on the other hand, focused on the building-restoring of faith establishments rather that exclusively towards the social programs.

accommodates all who believe in their tenets and eventually lead to swaminarayanization (equivalent to brahminization and sanskritization). This is done through two modes – one is the material advantage through Swaminarayan Sanstha affiliation (through their educational and health services), and the second is an alleviated religiosity through the family rites and rituals prescribed. Adaptation to them leads to incorporation at one level and symbolic initiation into a 'higher' realm of existence on another (Amrutvijaydas, 2007).

For Saibaba Sansthan, the Sai incarnation in itself is a gospel of action. Hence, there is the view that divine interventions resurrect social dysfunctionalities. Furthermore, for action the vital precept is that of it being sans desire and detachment (SSST, 2011); that is, action minus expectation for rewards is the *summum bonum*. All activity in relation to external objects creates complications; hence, there is the need to perform action with perfect detachment. For Brahmakumaris, the sole 'action' component is the proselytizing propagation of Raja Yoga as a 'moral renewal for complete purity, peace, and prosperity' (Hassija, 2006, p. 34). Chinmaya Mission's notions of action and righteous action, in particular, are drawn from the metaphysical contentions and categorical imperatives of Vedanta (Tejomayananda, 1995). For Sri Aurobindo Society, action is to be directed towards divine aspirations and truth (Vijay, 1978), the contention being that altruism and duty to family, country, and humanity become prisons of the soul when they are not the instrument of divine realization (Vijay, 1984). Action for Vivekananda Kendra is emancipation for which the antidote is spiritualism and, even further, associated with attributes of dispassion, detachment, oneness of the other, and service (Parameswaran, 2004) as the modus operandi. The Amritanandamayi Mission stance towards action is universalistic, involving tackling multiple systems geared towards the clientele. Art of Living action has the following qualifications: spiritualized, dialogic, devotional, and dispassionate. The concept that is given for action is 'Ishwarapranidhana', that is, recognition of the divine in all and subsequent devotion. *Tapa* (penance), *swadhyaya* (self-study undertaken for pure knowledge), and *ishwarapranidhana* (seeing the divine in all) are all called kriya yoga or the yoga of action (Sri Sri Publications Trust, 2007a).

Social service and work

On service and social work, Sri Ramakrishna has emphasized the importance of selfless action – Ramakrishna's gospel of service is based on the spirit of practical Vedanta. The summum bonum here is to work simultaneously for one's own liberation and for the good of the world (Adiswarananda, 2006; Dhar, 2006). As per a senior member of the monastic order,

> Liberation of Vedanta calls for self-knowledge which requires self-purification through selfless action. The gospel of service is the expression of dynamic self-knowledge which is radically different from the sterile self-realization of old Vedanta. Meditation and action are interconnected. The gospel of service is the gospel of divine love in action; love of God begins by loving all as God's children. *Moksha* or *mukti* of practical Vedanta comes in the wake of self-knowledge. This self-knowledge is not merely a freedom from delusion, limitations, attachments, and aversions, but also rising to the level of Universal Consciousness where one sees one's self in all and all in one's self, and dedicates oneself to the welfare of all. Being good and doing good must complement each other. (Belur Math, May 2011)

Three forms of understanding service and social work emerge: the 'normative' through the dictum 'siva jnane jiva seva' (i.e., serving beings as manifestations of Godhead); the 'ideational' through the adage 'atmano mokshartham jagat hitaya cha' (meaning for one's own liberation and good of the world); and the 'epistemological', where there is a theistic notion of service; a theistic existential appropriation of social work is undertaken. Theistic existential appropriation basically implies the given-ness of this worldly existence; sufferings as a natural outcome of existence; the imperative of transcendence; the existence and proof of God and Divine being posited later as the Divine Mother; and Ramakrishna Mission's endeavours as that crucial organ to alleviate this-worldliness to divinity by accepting divinity of beings. The modus operandi of those endeavours is the theistic existential appropriation of service.

Swaminarayan Sanstha has certain norms for service and work laid down for its own members. Largely, they are in keeping with the altruism tenets of the Hindu scriptures (Jnaneshwardas & Mukundcharandas 2001). For instance, on donations for social causes, three purposes are laid down – one as a purificatory ritual for the donor, the second as a moral duty, and the third as pathway to divinity for the donor. As per an office bearer at the women's wing,

> Swaminarayan Sanstha believes that for those who give and serve, the foremost sentiment should be that one is fortunate to be able to do so. Pramukh Swami also says that it should be kept a secret; that is, not too much noise should be made about it and one should have no expectations in return of the service and giving. Also, it is important to exercise discretion in terms of to whom one should donate. Swaminarayan Sanstha has a systematic social service wing and several departments to look into its various projects such as health, residential institutions, educational institutions, ecological projects, and disaster interventions. They can provide a need assessment database which can be a determinant for directing giving and volunteering there. The main aspect should be the sentiment that everything belongs to the Almighty and one should work and give with that spirit. (Ahmedabad, March 2011)

The purport of service and work for Swaminarayan Sanstha is to comprehend the meaning of life (Paramananddas, 1998), to comprehend the path to the divine (Aksharjivandas, 1997), and to restore peace in society with balance and divinity in family values as the fulcrum (Amrutvijaydas, 1998). One of the distinctive aspects in this service/work mandate is the practice among BAPS family fraternity to 'offer' one child of the family/household towards congregational service of Swaminarayan Sanstha for participation in its religio-spiritual and social activities. This has an ecumenical feel, the idea being twofold: one to obtain human power to ensure continuity and propagation of the fellowship, and second, which is peculiar to Swaminarayan Sanstha, to have a firm patron base from families of those who have taken initiation and perpetual vows.

There is a systematic emphasis on philanthropy and service placed in Saibaba Sansthan – philanthropy as an existential categorical imperative operationalized as 'daan' (Warren, 2004) – collected under the heads of education, medical, and food donations. In the words of an office bearer,

> Just as Saibaba lived a life of frugality and altruism – doing good to others at all times, so does the Sansthan continue that tradition. All our charitable activities are done with that spirit. That leads to liberation for all – for those who serve and for those who receive – all get Baba's grace. (Shirdi, November 2011)

Service in Saibaba Sansthan is visualized as the core of human existence. This emphasis on service as a categorical imperative is endowed with a two-fold meaning: first, as instrumental in manifesting the divinity quiescent in the individual, and second, as a coalesce of the moral path and illumination. The twin endeavours of service and philanthropy amalgamate to provide the formula for salvation.

Service for Brahmakumaris assumes the form of a 'divine trait' (Hassija, 2006). Furthermore, 'renunciation' and 'service' are 'companion divine traits' (PBIV, 1999). Through the emergence of the 'service' dictum, Brahmakumaris' original world-rejecting/transcending stance has assumed the 'exchange, interaction, affirmation' stance. There is a recognition of the 'other' beyond the conventional 'hegemonized souls' – an emphasis is placed on the 'balance' of 'knowing and being' (which is the original soul discourse and consciousness characteristic of Brahmakumaris) to 'becoming' and 'giving'. The 'giving' of Brahmakumaris is the 'instrumental' version of the 'transcendental being'; that is, Brahmakumari souls who have reached the spiritual zenith enable other souls to attain those prescribed heights – initially by 'tangible and material' assistance and later by 'spiritual guidance' through Raja Yoga. In the words of a senior member of the order,

> Dada (Lekhraj) has told us that there are two types of traits that beings and souls can have – divine and demoniac. If the soul is a true form of Godhead – a real attribute of the incorporeal Shiv Baba, then it would build on the divine traits. Renunciation and service are a part of the divine traits. Service for us means spiritual efforts directed towards humankind as well as discipline. Renunciation and service go together. When

> you withdraw from the material world and practice austerities, the propensity to serve others automatically comes. Service can be of various kinds in this world. But the highest service is to turn a person from the evil path and set him on the right path. Raja Yoga has all the answers about the right path. Even in our service, there are two steps. The first step is catering to the needs of the souls or beings, understanding their realities and instrumentalities (*nimitta*). The second is then elevating them to the consciousness of Raja Yoga, that is, moving away from body consciousness, which is the root of all miseries, to soul consciousness of Raja Yoga, which is sublime and supreme. (Abu, February 2012)

For Chinmaya Mission, there is a mandate of conscious living with dictums of 'share and care' (Ishwarananda, 2002) and abiding by the ethics in Vedanta which prescribe 'virtues' or 'standards of inspired living' for Chinmaya Mission adherents such as selfless service (*nishkama karma*), spirit of holy sacrifice (*yagna*), honesty (*satyam*), non-violence (*ahimsa*), charity (*dana*), fortitude (*dhriti*), and harmony (*ekabhava*). Furthermore, there are also steps for living these values, such as spiritual development, faith and prayer, detachment, contemplation, and love (CCMT, 1991b). Particularly with respect to service, some of the principles of 'working for others' are: learning to give, generosity, and universal caring. Metaphysical contentions signify a sense of oneness that connotes love and service for all (Tejomayananda, 2003); devotion to people as devotion to the supreme Self; the notions of existential totality and ensuing experience of oneness (CCMT, 1991a); gross happiness as contingent on dissolution of the individual ego (Chinmayananda, 1991).

On service and work, Sri Aurobindo Society has a firm conception, that all life is yoga and the efforts are to be directed towards alleviating all moral acts to the spiritual level. Service and work then is also to be directed towards spiritual growth – that being the main and most natural source of rendering help and contributing to the growth of humanity.[13] To quote a sadhak,

13 According to Srinivasan (2010), moral altruism does not dissolve the ego but only shifts it to a moral plane. In altruism, serving others becomes a means of self-satisfaction of

> Even Sri Aurobindo has specified in his letters on Yoga that the greatest service to humanity, the surest foundation for its true progress, happiness, and perfection, is to prepare or find the way by which the individual and the collective mankind can transcend the ego and live in its true self, no longer bound to ignorance, incapacity, disharmony, and sorrow. It is by pursuit of the eternal and not by living bound in the slow collective evolution of Nature that we can best assure that evolutionary, collective, altruistic aim of our modern thought and idealism has set before us. The steps for this are renunciation of fruits and rewards, perception of unity, offering our activities to the divine, and constant and vigilant self-observation to detect and reject the self-seeking ego in every level of our being – physical, vital, emotional, mental, and moral . . . sometimes also spiritual ego. (Pondicherry, August 2011)

Vivekananda Kendra's core contentions on action, service, and work are (a) service to other as manifestations of Godhead; (b) confluence of *yogas* (*bhakti*, *jnana*, *karma*, and *raja*) endowing the requisite attitude; (c) renunciation and service as twin ideals; (d) ethics as base of service propositions; and (e) Eknath Ranade's linking of service to austerity with the larger ideal of 'lokasamagraha'. Hence, as a continuity of the Ramakrishna aphorism this tenet of service has been forwarded. Furthermore, the confluence of the *yogas* (*bhakti*, *jnana*, *karma*, and *raja*) is believed to endow the requisite attitude for service. The twin ideals of renunciation and service (Advaita Ashrama, 1996) are derived from Swami Vivekananda's monastic leanings and his firm contention that the

---

the moral ego and this moral satisfaction has great danger for the spiritual seeker as it extinguishes the spiritual aspiration. The main focus of the spiritual seeker is his own spiritual development, which leads to the discovery of his true self. To concentrate on one's spiritual growth and experience is the first necessity of the sadhak – and to grow in spirit is the greatest help one can give to others, for then something flows out naturally to those around that help them. This applies not only to individual development but also to the growth of the collectivity. When we look deeply into the root cause of all conflicts, misery, and violence among human individual and collectivities, we will find at the bottom the human ego and its greed, ambition, and attachments, so the greatest good we can do to human evolution and progress is to facilitate the spiritual evolution of the individual and the collective from its confinement within the ego to the egoless and limitless unity consciousness of the spirit.

ideational stance required for service, which meant diluting the self–other difference, could be acquired only through the qualities accompanying the renunciant. There are some parallels drawn by Ranganathananda (2007) to Kantian ethics as the base of Vivekananda Kendra's service propositions such as the link between poverty and charity.[14] Building on the above, Eknath Ranade linked service to austerity with the ideal of 'lokasamagraha' or general welfare (Lakshmi Kumari, 1991a) – the utilitarian greater common good[15] which the Kendra carries forward.

Amritanandamayi Mission's social work is ecological, geared towards addressing social systems, and restoring their functioning. To quote a member of the order:

> MAM believes that in terms of its social work, the main thing is to address systems and make them work in a proper manner. This is done through assisting systems, as sometimes lack of functioning is due to lack of resources at disposal. Hence, mostly through our volunteer forces, we assist systems. (Mumbai, February 2011)

The Art of Living foundation has an elaborate rendition on service and social work subsumed under the syntax of 'seva' – a crucial and essential milestone in their spiritual practice. As discussed by Sri Sri in

14 This link has been made in Kantian Lectures on Ethics (Infield, 1963), the central themes expressed within his moral philosophy include the ideas of equality and the moral autonomy of rational human beings, faith as teleological ethico-theology encompassing theological and ethical dimensions within it, and a rational theology which along with proof of existence of God is also the course of morals and ethics. God as the entity ultimately distinguishes between 'good' and 'evil' – with the purport of establishing/ founding the kingdom of God on earth (Greene & Hudson, 1960). Thereby, moral imperatives emerge as categorical imperatives – psychosocial evolution then imply the spiritual growth in man. The development of a spiritual-social character is then in this religio-social-centred will – householder then spiritually grows into the citizen. Finally, this creatively feeds into national integration – nation-building through man-making through devotionalism as the foci.

15 Commencing with the base of life's values and purpose, the eventual movement is towards the transcendental quest – or searches for the eternal, which all individuals as deemed to possess as per the self-actualization proposition. Service is then an outcome of this journey – self-reconstruction (i.e., orientation towards higher concerns) leading to self-realization (inwardness along with a sense of oneness with the Absolute and the other) and eventually tangible service for national reconstruction.

his discourses under the rubric 'Celebrating Love' (Sri Sri Publications Trust, 2005):

> There are essentially five types of *seva* – first type is done when one does not even know that one is doing it, it becomes one's very nature; second type of *seva* is done when it is needed for the situation; the third type is done as it gives joy; the fourth type is done when it gives merit; and the fifth type is for exhibitionism. The endeavour is to undertake selfless *seva* – by seeing divinity in all and loving all. (Mumbai, May 2012)

Essentially, the premise of *seva* for Art of Living is seeing the divine in all beings and universal love owing to the quintessential equity and oneness of all beings. Service or *seva* then becomes an essential qualification for a seeker. The other domain of discussion on *seva* is oriented towards consciousness and the self – *seva* for expansion of individual consciousness to universal consciousness. One of the knowledge sheets as compiled in the Intimate Notes to a Sincere Seeker (Sri Sri Publications Trust, 2010c) propound the following contentions of Sri Sri on *seva* for individual consciousness enhancement – individual being a microcosm of the macrocosmic universe.

HIFMs' stances on service and work also reinforce the link between community development and spirituality. Spiritual teachings of HIFMs are generally placed at the top of the hierarchy of service (to body, mind, and soul) (Beckerlegge, 2007) with variations on political engagement policies. Furthermore, one peculiarity of HIFMs' stance on service/work is that the general delivery of *seva* is dependent more on the interior disposition of the performer and less on the inner transformation of the recipient. Service position is more as a 'religious sadhana', a means to spiritual realization which resembles historical religious forms of charitable action rather than featuring objective service. In some way, the derivation and appeal to traditional Hindu stances to support the service rhetoric also makes HIFMs the prisoners of the past – history, historiography, and hagiography determining what service should be and how it is defined.

The core of service/work proclaims more of ultimate goals – transformation, recognition of divinity in beings, supramental manifestation – and less of proximate goals such as inequality and poverty alleviation. However, it is more a matter of degree – the focus not being exclusively on consciousness raising. In contrast to the secular service sector where philosophies draw from different sources and epistemes, in the HIFMs' contexts the philosophy of service/action/work is derived solely from its core faith-oriented ideational stances. The service/work positions of HIFMs eventually resemble an 'experiential realism' – where although secular and faith-based approaches deal with the same reality, faith inserts the divine mandate in the service. It challenges the secular to acknowledge the transcendent frame of reference and moral accountability. The secularist insight and presence on the other hand challenges the faith orientation to reconceptualize general assumptions on God, creation, and eschatology so as to integrate secularist ingredient in service. The appeal to an inner transformation of recipients of service of HIFMs bears resemblance to Martin Luther's emphasis on the communication of attributes (*communicatio idiomatum*).[16] At one level, the divine is bestowed on the human by considering human beings as manifestations of the same. At another level, the human issues and suffering in particular are divinized and attributed a dignified place in God's reality. This exchange results in a simultaneous ascendance of the human to divine and descent of the divine into human as a cosmological desiderate.

16 Penumakka (2006) compares Luther's communication of attributes to Sankara's pure Advaita. Where Advaita oneness entails shedding of historical and personal attributes resulting in dubbing suffering as unreal, Luther's communication idiomatum gives place for a healthy soteriology – as here the 'human suffering' is dignified by receiving a place in God's reality.

5

Faith in Practice: The Tangibility of Social Service

Faith manifests in practice in HIFMs through tangible social service. The genesis of social service for the HIFMs has been initially serendipitous and later systematized or a priori streamlined for translation of charisma and faith. There is a certain evolved calculus and scheme for justifying/ratifying the service mandate through the faith lens. The initiation and streamlining of social services in HIFMs has been through a coalition of charisma power and devotees' and followers' interest in perpetuation, which was also to gain a social standing. This actually dissipated, for most, the virgin alignment to the faith/religiosity rhetoric and entered the arena of the socioreligious or the social face of faith. There is, as derived from Sen's (2010) 'reading' of the Vedanta temple of San Francisco, in the origination story a need to create a world of shared meanings and practices through the haptic domain of tangible service. The social service genesis within HIFMs has also meant a paradigm shift from the traditional 'privatized' role of faith, with a focus on the spiritual-sacred, towards the 'public' role, which embodies multidimensional social capital.

The idea/mandate is to bring faith to the public realm in a visible way – beyond rituals towards a community orientation. The mandate also entails a kind of 're-authoring', the HIFM being the navigator of the process; the reconfiguration is derived from HIFM faith and spiritual knowledge.[1] The derivative is a formation of dense active social capital connections. Ideologically, faith is essentially seen as providing a moral base on which to rebuild a de-territorialized global culture, transcending economics and essentially dealing with the essence of humanity and what is right. The portrayed governing idea of HIFMs is to serve the cause of social integration by re-creating bonds of solidarity in an imagined commune. The question nevertheless remains in terms of whose commune and what nature of integration. The service ideology of HIFMs is not of the nature of armchair prophecy but mediated actively by religious and civil practices – philanthropic giving, collective prayer, and rituals. Habitual practices of *seva*, *sadhana*, and yoga within the HIFM context, rather than simple espousal of beliefs, have been responsible for the service repertoire. Within this practice-driven ideational account there is a relationship between faith, affiliations to HIFMs, and philanthropic engagements of concerned stakeholders. Faith discerns certain meaning systems of self–other exchange within which the tradition of service as well as the norms of community organizing around the faith principle are created.

The scope encompasses the core social sectors of development such as education, health, and livelihood as well as certain customized programmes. The mission is inevitably 'social' through the prism of faith. The mandate is 'service' through which to eventually realize twin transcendental ideals of spiritual-material upliftment and proliferate the 'message'. Both these are derivatives of the mission – the HIFMs mission-ideals then seep into the social canvass through the projects either in an a priori, parallel, and/or retrospective manner. The management of these institutionalized efforts have a 'missionary consciousness' – there is an order ministration of evangelical nature.

1 Ramsay et al. (2010) have explored how the members of the Brahmakumaris World Spiritual University (BrahmakumariWSU) based in centres in New York applied spiritual knowledge to understand the destruction of the Twin Towers of the World Trade Center in New York on 11 September 2001. Drawing on primary BrahmakumariWSU texts and ethnographic data from field research conducted in 2007, they have illustrated how the spiritual knowledge and practices of its members (Brahmakumaris) uniquely shaped their perspective on catastrophic events.

Genesis stories, scope of social services, and the nature of systemic interfaces

Ramakrishna Mission's genesis of the social service mission in an organized way was started on 15 May 1897. It was organized by Swami Akhandananda in Murshidabad with a capital of Rs.150 sent by Swami Vivekananda, and the assistance of Swami Nityananda and Brahmachari Suren. This relief work was named the Mahabodhi famine relief work. On 17 July 1897 the Alambazaar Famine Fund was found. Furthermore, Swami Akhandananda initiated institutional relief activities through the founding of an orphanage at Sargachi in Murshidabad District of West Bengal.[2] Some of the journals documented early philanthropic activities. *Brahmavadin* made an appearance in Madras on Saturday 14 September 1895 as a religious and philosophical journal printed by Thompson and Co. The main objective of the journal was to propagate the Vedanta religion of India (Ghosh, 2006). In Volume 5, 1899 issue of the journal the term *Vedanta Missionary work* has been used.[3]

---

2 Swami Akhandananda (1864–1937) became the third president of the Ramakrishna Mission in 1934. He initiated a number of people after assuming office, including Madhav Sadashiv Golwalkar, the second sarsanghachalak of the Rashtriya Swayamsevak Sangh. He was the first monk of the Ramakrishna order, who gave shape to the cherished desire of Swami Vivekananda to begin rural development work, even before the Mission was established. In 1894, Akhandananda began his campaign against poverty. The idea of working for the poor was conceived while he stayed in Jamnagar with an Ayurvedic physician. While in Khetri, Rajasthan, in 1894, he worked for the cause of education of tribal groups. He first came in contact with widespread famine during his travel in the Murshidabad District of Bengal. On 15 May 1897 Swami Akhandananda opened a relief centre in Murshidabad to save people from an all-devouring famine. Swami Akhandananda started an orphanage in Mahula, Bengal, on 31 August 1897 and then established the first Rural Branch Centre of the Ramakrishna Math and Ramakrishna Mission in Mahula. In 1899, he opened an ashram in Shivnagar near Sargachi which continued for 14 years. In 1899, he opened a free school there to deal with the problem of illiteracy in the locality. Carpentry and weaving section also were added to revive those perishing village industries and made boys self-reliant. Cotton cultivation was taught to the rural women to enhance their family income. In 1913, the present ashram was founded on 13 acres of land in March 1913. He also led in relief activities in the Bhagalpur District of Bihar and during the Munger earthquake in Bihar (Adiswarananda, 2006).

3 The Mission's work received its definite shape, both in its form and function, after Narendranath emerged as a world figure under the name of Swami Vivekananda from the World Parliament of Religions held in Chicago in 1893. He further emphasized that 'service implies the dedication of one's capacities and energies to the order conceiving it as a symbol of the Master. Spiritual talents are therefore more important than worldly abilities, but by the very nature and object of the order a harmonious combination of

For Swaminarayan Sanstha, history has instances of serendipitous involvements of the founders in service activities. Later systematized initiatives commenced in 1971 under the guidance of the erstwhile spiritual head Pramukh Swami. There are instances of Swaminarayan's voluntary participation in the 1813 Kathiawad famine relief work and promotion of ecological/environmental awareness. Systematic activities of social service commenced in 1971.[4]

---

both is ideal' (Tapsyananda, 1995). Although it is recognized that the important struggle is to know transcendent reality, the work or service is the means to that knowledge. Through devoted service the Mission believes it is possible to be disillusioned from false notions of the ego and body consciousness and move to selflessness and universal consciousness (Mumukshananda, 1997).

4 In the four decades of work thus far, several aspects have been covered. From 1974 to 1979, Swaminarayan Sanstha volunteers served during three disasters: 1974–1975 famines in Gujarat and Maharashtra, Andhra Pradesh typhoon in 1977, and the 1979 Morbi dam disaster. In 1982–1983, Swaminarayan Sanstha volunteers served during the Saurashtra floods and in 1987 during the drought and famine in Gujarat. In 1987, Swaminarayan Sanstha Gunatit Vidyamandir, an educational institution, was established in Gunatitnagar, Bhadra. In 1991, the Swaminarayan Sanstha Swaminarayan Chhatralaya, Nadiad, was established followed by three developments in the following year. First, Pramukh Swami Health Services, a division of Swaminarayan Sanstha, undertook the administration of TMV hospital in Botad. Second, the Swaminarayan Day School was started in London, and third, Swaminarayan Sanstha volunteers served during the Jamnagar famine. In 1993, services were provided during the Latur earthquake, and in the following year the Swaminarayan Sanstha students' hostel at Mehsana was established. In 1995, the Mumbai Pramukh Swami Eye Hospital was inaugurated followed by the Pramukh Swami Health Care and Research Centre in the following year. In 1996, Swaminarayan Sanstha volunteer efforts were also dedicated to cyclone rehab operations in Andhra Pradesh and subsequently during Gujarat floods. Two institutional developments took place in the following year: the Swaminarayan school was established in Nagpur and the Akshardham Centre for Applied Research into Social Harmony was set up in Gandhinagar. In 1998, Swaminarayan students' hostel was set up in Dhuliya, and in the following year Swaminarayan Sanstha mobile dispensaries were launched for tribal populace of Khedbrahma, Pavi Jetpur, and Dharampur. In the same year, relief and rehab operations were undertaken after the Orissa supercyclone (Amrutvijaydas, 2007). The decade from 2000 onwards saw several developments as well. In the first year, there were de-addiction campaigns by Swaminarayan Sanstha children; inauguration of the Pramukh Swami Hospital in Dabhoi; mobile dispensaries in Rajpipla, Dang, Vansda, and Devgadhbharia; the Pramukh Swami Prathamik Aarogya Kendra at Chansad; and the Swaminarayan School for Girls in Karamsad, Saurashtra. One of the most significant and elaborate projects include the Earthquake relief operations in 2001 which involved immediate relief, reassurance, rehabilitation, and reconstruction, including infrastructure development. In the same year, Pramukh Swami Hospital and Research Centre was started at Atladra near Vadodara, and the Orissa flood relief operations at Jagatsingpur and Krishnapada were undertaken. In 2002, mobile dispensaries were set up for Sankari, Vijaynagar, and Dharampur villages of Kathiawad, and the Pramukh Swami Vidya Mandir and Swaminarayan Sanstha Swaminarayan Chhatralaya, Sarangpur

For Saibaba Sansthan, social service paralleled the genesis of the organization, and the scope encompassed education[5] and health initiatives.[6] In terms of the genesis of Brahmakumaris' social service, the commencement is parallel to its international expansion in the 1970s, and more so with its UN associations in the 1980s. With this external outlook and world accommodation stance 'large scale influence of Raja Yoga spirituality' (Hassija, 2006) was perceived. Raja Yoga being an essential ingredient, the apodictic universal values of 'peace' and 'harmony' are then viewed in that light.[7]

---

were set up. Schools were also set up in Mount Abu and Silvassa, Atladra, Valsad, and Bakrol. Relief operations were carried our post-2004 tsunami, Hurricane Katrina and Surat floods. Another Pramukh Swami hospital was set up in Surat in 2005 followed by de-addiction campaigns in 2007 (Swayamprakashdas, 2008).

5 In terms of educational initiatives, in 1984 an industrial training centre was established for students around Shirdi with the approval of the State Government for employment training and livelihood skill development at subsidized rates. In 1990, the Saibaba English medium school was established for students around rural areas in the Rahata District, and subsequently a girls' school, Shree Saibaba (Marathi) Kanya Vidya Mandir, was established in 1993. In 2000, a junior college was also established.

6 In terms of health, in 1964 the Sainath Hospital was established to provide medical services at low cost for patients below the poverty line. Later in 1980, the Shri Saibaba Hospital with super-specialty facilities was established, which provided services such as concessions for heart operations for patients of lower-income groups and a blood bank was also set up. Furthermore, Saibaba Sansthan also provided financial aid termed 'Sai Prasad' to low-income patients who needed expensive medical treatments. An upcoming project of Saibaba Sansthan is the Development of Integrated Socioeconomic, Health, Education, and Essential facilities approved by the National Committee for Promotion of Social and Economic Welfare, New Delhi, under Section 35 AC vide Notification No. S.O. 1473 (E) dated 17 June 2008. Under this project beneficiaries belonging to economically weaker sections of society whose income is below Rs.18000/- per annum receive freeship.

7 In 1988, Brahmakumaris launched a 'Million Minutes of Peace Appeal' project which collided with the UN year of peace, and 1 billion minutes of peace in the form of prayer, meditation, and positive thoughts were gathered through members in 88 countries. In the same year, the project 'Global Co-operation for a Better World' was launched so as to seek an increased cooperation between nations, individuals, and communities, gathering the hopes and visions for a better world of people in 129 countries. These were then synthesized in 'The Global Vision Statement', which forms the heart of the UN Peace Messenger and the UNESCO-supported publication 'Vision of a Better world'. In 1991, the J. Watumull Global Hospital and Research Centre was established in Mount Abu with the objective of offering spiritually oriented holistic healthcare services which subsequently developed branches and outreach programmes for vulnerable groups. In 1994, the project 'Sharing Our Values for a Better World' was launched, which adopted as its central focus the tenet in the preamble of the UN charter, that is, 'to re-affirm the faith in the fundamental rights, dignity, and worth of human persons'. The project

Social service activities in Chinmaya Mission have emanated through two sources: the vision of the spiritual heads, and the service propensity of individuals committed to the Chinmayananda ideals. The 'secular' service projects have been equated to the historic 'jnana yagnas' of Chinmayananda – as activities of nation-building with the understanding of Hindu religion/dharma as embracing every aspect of life[8].

---

essentially aimed to raise awareness of core spiritual values and their development at both, individual and collective levels. Subsequently, sister concerns developed, such as Raja Yoga Meditation and Research Foundation, Academy for a Better World, and World Renewal Spiritual Trust.

8 The first such service project was the Chinmaya education movement which was launched in 1967 as a small nursery in Kollengode, Kerala, contemporarily taking the form of eighty Chinmaya Vidyalayas (including one in Trinidad affiliated to CBSE or local boards), eight Chinmaya Institutes of Higher Learning, School of Inspired Leadership, and one Chinmaya International Residential School, Coimbatore. Apart from these, there are also Hari Har schools in villages as a component of the rural development package to provide zero-cost academic and vocational training. The essential ingredient of this educational endeavour apart from ensuring equitable access, attainment, and equitable schooling opportunities is the Chinmaya Vision Programme – a 'value-based programme incorporated in the schools and colleges of Chinmaya Mission'. The specified core components of the programme are integrated development, Indian (read Hindu) culture, patriotism, and universal outlook. The second aspect in the service arena is the Chinmaya Organization for Rural Development (CORD), which began its activities in 1982–1983 at the behest of a GOI-issued directive for selection of NGOs for family planning services and maternal healthcare. Although that proposal did not come through, with the help of USAID, in 1985, a rural primary healthcare and training centre was formed under the aegis of Chinmaya Tapovan Trust (the local trust to look after the admin affairs of Sidhbari Sandeepany), Sidhbari, Himachal Pradesh. In 2003, it was registered as the Chinmaya Organization for Rural Development (CORD) with multiple programme components. The CORD model has been replicated in Orissa and Tamil Nadu – in Orissa CORD Lathikata in District Sundergarh, CORD Deuladiha in Keonjhar District; and in Tamil Nadu, CORD Tamaraipakkam in Thiruvallur District and CORD Siruvani in Coimbatore District. Apart from the above there are heath initiatives and residential institutions for vulnerable groups. Health initiatives include the Chinmaya Mission Hospital in Bangalore and the Aarogya Seva Project in villages of Maharashtra and Gujarat. In terms of residential institutions, in 1982, in Ellayapalle, Kerala, the Chinmayaranyam Ellayapalle Ashram in Kerala was formed for underprivileged girls to provide them with formal education along with other welfare activities. Earlier, in the 1970s the idea of having a senior citizen's wing was floated to Swami Chinmayananda by elderly devotees; hence, the Central Chinmaya Vanaprastha Sansthan (CCVS) was started as the senior citizen's wing of Chinmaya Mission with headquarters in Allahabad. The entire connection was visualized between aging and spiritual pursuits along with looking into issues of health, finance, and legalities. Currently, there are 200 sub-centres in the country; one advocacy initiative has been the participation in the formation of the National Policy for Older Persons. Eight residential institutions run under the aegis of CCVS called Pitamaha Sadans. The focus is on providing elderly care and viewing spirituality as a tool for effective aging. Furthermore, in terms of institutional

In Sri Aurobindo Society, the genesis of all projects, including the social service endeavours, commenced in congruence with the development of society post 1960; within a decade the foundations of most social projects were laid. Institutionalized endeavours of Sri Aurobindo Society are in the arenas of education[9], health[10], and rural development and an Auroville[11], as a model township demonstrating the praxis spirituality of Sri Aurobindo and the Mother. The Sri Aurobindo Rural and Village Action and Movement (SARVAM) is geared towards developing models of village development based on the integral ideals of Sri Aurobindo Society which are sustainable, scalable, and replicable.[12]

---

developments, in 2007, the Chinmaya Vijaya orphanage for girls was founded in Kaza near Vijaywada in Andhra Pradesh.

9 Sri Aurobindo International Centre for Education (SAICE) was founded in 1952 to realize the goals of spiritual education of the Mother and Sri Aurobindo. The components that build into this spiritual education are the aspects of physical education, education of the vital, and psychic and mental education. The system is liberal and permits learning at one's pace and any combination in terms of choice of subjects of study (Sri Aurobindo Society, 1979). There is an annihilation of the banking concept of education in favour of a pedagogy which is interactive.

10 Sri Aurobindo International Institute for Integral Health and Research (SAIIIHR) aims to study and understand 'Health' in all its dimensions, with a new and total awareness of the human being, help individuals to become aware and to develop the healing powers within for prevention and cure of illness, synthesize various modern and traditional systems of medicine, and promote a new approach to health based on yogic psychology and the spiritual dimension of health.

11 What catapults Sri Aurobindo Society onto a global philosophico-spiritual platform is the project Auroville – an international township based on the ideals of Sri Aurobindo and the Mother's vision of divine life upon the earth operationalized through human unity and harmony. Participation in the collective experiment post its foundation laid by Mirra Alfassa, alias the Mother (the then Executive President of Sri Aurobindo Society), is based on certain spiritual and material conditions (Alain, 2000). Inner discovery, freedom, disinterestedness, sense of commune, and forfeiting the proprietary sense of possession, work as the key modicum and instrument which connects matter to the inner consciousness, consecration towards the divine Mother, and thus paving the way for a transformation and supramental realization, are the main elements. Although the funding is a combination of indigenous and international, the management is by the members under the Auroville Foundation Act (propelled by certain developments in 1980 when the management of Auroville assets and undertakings was taken over by GOI temporarily and later vested in an autonomous institution – the Auroville Foundation). Most of the activities are self-driven by residents who arrive voluntarily and be a part of the Auroville endeavour which projects collective, harmonious, and sustainable living (Alan and Tim, 1998).

12 The community of reference for SARVAM comprises of 1376 families belonging to scheduled caste and Vanniar (MBC) communities in two villages in Villupuram District of Tamil Nadu – Poothurai and Perembai. The approach is that of adopting the village

As Vivekananda Kendra commenced as a spiritually oriented service mission post the establishment of the Rock Memorial, the service component was embedded in its initial design. Swami Vivekananda's message as drawn from Sri Ramakrishna – 'naraseva narayanseva' (service to man is service to God) – was drawn on explicitly by Eknath Ranade. Perpetuation of the Vivekananda memory and translating into action his ideals of 'man making [*sic*] and nation building' served to be the vantage point. The scope of institutionalized endeavours of Vivekananda Kendra includes education as a pioneering service activity, including Vivekananda Kendra residential/non-residential schools and balwadis particularly in North Eastern states; rural development programmes, NARDEP, or natural resource development programme including Gramodaya as a model initiative[13]; and training/mainstreaming initiatives in Arunachal Pradesh, Nasik , and Orissa.[14]

---

and engaging in multifaceted development in aspects of education, health, economic development, vocational training, organic farming, water harvesting, and other components of ecological sustainability.

13 NARDEP is a natural resource development programme based on the ideal of spiritual ecology, eco theology (Vivekananda Kendra, 1995; Yoga Prakashan, 1997; Kulkarni, 1998; Vasudeo, 1998), and Gandhian tenets to address the issue of environmental degradation in a paradigm of development writ by Western scientism and technology. Hence, the focus is to promote eco-friendly cost-effective technology which has moved into areas of biogas plant construction (NARDEP, 1996b; 1997b; Sathyamoorthy, 1999) and tapping of renewable energy resources (NARDEP, 1997a); cost-effective house construction technology (developed by Laurie Baker from Thiruvananthapuram with an emphasis on use of local material for construction purposes); water management; organic farming (including dissemination of technologies of farm yard manure, NARDEP compost, biogas slurry and vermin compost along with propagation of azolla and blue green algae as bio fertilizers and bio pesticides; NARDEP, 1993, 1996c, 1998); and alternative medicinal therapies such as Siddha and Ayurveda (NARDEP, 2000). NARDEP collaborates across state bodies, semi-government organizations, autonomous organizations, and funding organizations. With a grant from CAPART, a Technology Resource Centre as a training centre has been established at Kalluvilai about 5 km from Kanyakumari town. The Gramodaya model has been created to demonstrate the indigenous, cosmological, and inclusive posited vis-à-vis the Western, Cartesian, and exclusive. Furthermore, feminine values of *sneha, prema, daya,* and *bhakti* (affection, Agape, compassion, and devotion) are viewed as integral for ecological conservation along with roles of family and traditional *jatis* which are instrumental in maintaining the ecological balance (Vivekananda Kendra, 2004).

14 Education is one of the main service activities of the Kendra with objectives of access, attainment and cultural infiltration, and cadre generation. There are twenty-five formal education schools across the country abiding by the Central Board curriculum, including schools in Tinsukia, Dibrugarh, Golaghta, and Bokuloni in Assam; Port Blair, Rangat, and Hutbay in Andaman; and Valliyur and Kanyakumari in Tamil Nadu. They are a

In Amritanandamayi Mission, the genesis of social leanings is seen from the sporadic and spontaneous acts of helping of Mother Sudhamani (aka Mata Amritanandamayi) in the Parayakadavu village wherein, as per her biography, 'she would step in almost anywhere to help people in poverty and need' (Amritaswarupananda, 1988, p. 17). Furthermore, as the narrative goes, she proclaimed having a divine rendezvous where she heard a voice tell her that she was not in this world to merely meditate in isolation but to go out and serve and spread the feelings of love and compassion for all fellow human beings. With that individual episteme, and with the formal setting up of Amritanandamayi Mission in 1981, the base for spiritual-social endeavours was set. The first formal initiative, however, was undertaken in 1987 when with the corpus created from individual donations and also from the paternal family property of Amma, the first school for Sanskrit teaching, which was free of cost, and an accompanying branch ashram were opened in Kodungallur, Kerala. Subsequently, from 1989, formal setting up of institutions and training centres under the aegis of Amritanandamayi Mission was undertaken in and around Kollam District of Kerala. The scope and range for Amritanandamayi Mission encompass educational services,[15] residential

combination of residential and nonresidential initiatives along with several *balwadis* as pre-schools attached. Rural development initiatives include self-help groups and livelihood efforts including training in alternative technologies and farm technologies as well as educational initiatives in the form of formal schools, pre-schools, or non-formal education centres. The specified objective is cultural infiltration along with livelihood and self-sustenance. Currently, rural development efforts afoot in select villages of Kanyakumari, Tirunelveli, Tuticorin, Virudhunagar, and Ramanathapuram in Tamil Nadu are also now extended up to Thiruvananthapuram in Kerala and Chandil in Bihar. The project Arunjyoti in Arunachal Pradesh has multifarious activities including education, rural development, and natural resources development, aiming at retaining the Arunchalee people in the mainstream. The Vivekananda Kendra Pratishthan Va Seva Prakalp, Nasik, runs a hostel for tribal and rural children and engages in rural development work. The Utkal Seva Prakalp project in Orissa was started in January 2007. It contains 24 *Anandalayas*, that is, non-formal education centres run by 18 *shiksha vratis* or youth workers in Utkal, Deoband, and Devagiri blocks of Keonjhar District. The non-formal education package comprises of hymns, patriotic songs, and play activities in a two-hour session attended by approximately 840 local youth across.

15 In terms of educational services, the first school and branch ashram was opened in 1987 in Kodungallur, Kerala, followed by an industrial and vocational training centre in 1989, and the School of Applied Sciences in 1990, initially named Amma Institute of Computer Technology, was started in Kollam, Kerala. In 1995, teachers were sent to remote tribal villages in Northern Kerala by Amritanandamayi Mission and a School of Engineering was started in Coimbatore. Later, in 1996, the School of Business was started in the

institutions for vulnerable groups,[16] hospice and healthcare services,[17] disaster relief and rehab operations,[18] food services,[19] environmental initiatives and ecological conservation,[20] and livelihood development.[21]

---

same campus, and in the Kochi Ashram premises the College of Pharmaceutical Sciences was started. In 1997, the School of Hearing and Speech Improvement was established in Thrissur. In 2003, the School of Engineering was started in Bangalore and Kollam. Later in the same year, the School of Science and Management in Mysore and School of Journalism in Coimbatore were started. In 2005, the teacher's training college in Mysore was inaugurated.

16 In terms of residential institutions for vulnerable groups, the first orphanage was taken over by Amritanandamayi Mission in 1989, which is now called Amrita Niketan. At present, it houses 500 mostly from tribal communities. They attend the Amrita Sanskrit Higher Secondary School close by, and the records also say that more than 35 per cent go on to pursue higher education, and all of these are fully sponsored by Amritanandamayi Mission. Apart from formal schooling, they are also taught traditional art forms, and during the holidays most of them stay back at the Amritapuri Ashram. In 1996, the project Amrita Kuteeram that aimed at building free houses for the poor was launched. In 1998, care home for the elderly, Anbu Illam, was opened in Sivakasi, Tamil Nadu. In 2003, the Amrita Kripa AIDS care home was started in Trivandrum. In 2005, two care homes for the elderly were started in Karnataka. In 2007, the Amrita Nilayam Working Women's Hostel was established. In 2009, during Amma's visit to Kenya, the Watato Boma Children's Home was inaugurated. Managed by Amma devotees (the orphanage is on the banks of Athi river and has an occupancy of 108 children).

17 In terms of hospice and healthcare services in 1995, the first hospice for cancer patients, Amrita Hospice, was started in Mumbai. In 1998, Amrita Institute for Medical Sciences (AIMS), a multi-speciality hospital was inaugurated. In 2003, colleges of medicine, dentistry, and nursing were opened at AIMS, Kochi. In 2004, the Amrita Kripa Hospital was started in Wayanad, Kerala, and the Amritapuri Campus at Kollam got a biomedical research centre. In the same year, an Ayurvedic medical college, hospital, and research centre was inaugurated at Amritapuri, Kollam. In 2007, the Amrita Kripa Hospital in Mysore was inaugurated.

18 In terms of disaster relief and rehabilitation operations, initiatives were undertaken in Gujarat, Chennai, Bihar, and Tsunami-affected regions, Kashmir–Pakistan border areas, and international disasters such as Hurricane Katrina.

19 In terms of food services Annadanam services are available at headquarters and most centres. Similar initiatives have also been launched in the US and Spain. In the US it is called Mother's kitchen where volunteers provide 73,000 meals per year for the homeless in 47 cities throughout North America. The Mother's kitchen also supports social service groups in the US using their in house kitchen facilities.

20 In terms of environmental initiatives and ecological conservation, Amritanandamayi Mission is engaged in promoting local participation in conservation efforts worldwide in its centres and branches, now called the Green Initiative. Furthermore, the Amritha Bharatam programme has been launched as a campaign for clean-green Indian cities and villages.

21 In terms of livelihood development in the year 2006 the Amrita SREE – Self Reliance, Empowerment, and Education programme was launched. In the same year, the Amrita Nidhi pension project for physically and mentally disabled persons was also

Genesis of social service of Art of Living can be traced to the early 1980s, colliding with the genesis of the Foundation. In early 1985, the Care for Children programme geared towards the educational development of children in the surrounding rural areas of the Udayapura ashram and the VISTA India programme geared towards women empowerment were launched. Commencing as a figment of Sri Sri or a follower's imagination (with the sanction and permission of Sri Sri) these social initiatives have been launched. Art of Living social initiatives' scope encompasses education,[22] health[23] and substance abuse interventions, livelihood and empowerment through rural development efforts,[24] women's empowerment,[25] prison

---

launched. Amrita SREE is a livelihood project of Amritanandamayi Mission, which focuses on aiding women through the development of self-help groups, operating on the premise that empowering women with equal economic opportunities is one of the most effective ways to reduce poverty. This is done by providing vocational education, start-up capital, marketing assistance, and access to microcredit loans from small-scale banks. Self-help groups are based on the formulas established by RBI and NABARD. Volunteer programme coordinators first identify each targeted community's particular needs and existing skills and resources before launching a phase of vocational training. Courses are selected from the proposals that emerge from the targeted communities and offered at reputed vocational institutions. Finally, self-help groups are formed according to geographical proximity, each consisting of approximately twenty women. Men who are family members are also eligible to receive vocational training. Self-help groups operate autonomously, and Amritanandamayi Mission helps each group in coming up with a viable business plan and assists in packaging and marketing retail products. For economic and capital enhancement, each group is encouraged to open a bank account.

22 Education encompasses five aspects – information, concepts, attitude, imagination, and freedom. There exists a combination of formal and informal endeavours – the first one being that of the commencement of the Sanskrit school, and later on Ved Vigyan Maha Vidya Peeth as a rural school in 1981. A local volunteer was appointed to look after the children and give them basic lessons in hygiene, teach them educational games, and serve them healthy food for lunch. This became a big attraction for children and their parents and continues till date. As the school has progressed, a formal educational structure has been established and the number of teachers and students has increased. Today the school has become a model for ninety-two similar free schools in rural and tribal areas with students being first-generation learners.

23 Apart from proliferation of Sri Sri Ayurveda as a sustainable system of medicine, the SK&P programme is also considered as a viable alternative for lifestyle diseases prevention and cure.

24 The 5H programme is generally employed in terms of rural development – health, hygiene, homes, human values, and harmony in diversity. A model village – Punarjani – was created at Pathiyoor District of Tamil Nadu to demonstrate the rural sustainable development mandate.

25 Women's empowerment is generally geared towards economic empowerment and leadership training, some examples being the VISTA, India, and the peanut butter

programmes,[26] sustainable development,[27] disaster and trauma relief, and peace initiatives of political and communal nature. For disasters there is a threefold plan: immediate medical aid and service, near-term trauma relief, and long-term rehabilitation. According to a senior faculty in the AOL foundation:

> The goal in disaster management is to help people rebuild the human spirit along with infrastructure in the affected areas.

Peace initiatives are projected to have a metamorphosis from conflict to communion. On interventions in the Naxal violence-prone regions, a teacher says:

> There were no retaliatory massacres after the recent Jehanabad killings even after Ranbir Sena openly vowed to avenge the killings of its cadres. Instead the warring groups came for a satsang of Sri Sri in the Ekwari village, the nerve centre of Naxal violence in Bihar. Similar references are made to Sri Sri's sessions in various other conflict-prone regions such as Iraq and Kashmir. Through his initiatives and addresses Sri Sri has consistently emphasized the need for reinforcing human values and recognizing humanity as our highest identity. Fostering interfaith harmony and calling for multicultural education as the remedy for fanaticism are significant parts of his efforts to achieve sustainable peace on our planet. He gives a message of a one world family – inner and outer peace are possible through that. A stress-free, violence-free society can be created through

---

project, Murewa, Zimbabwe.

26 Prison programmes include the SK&P training sessions with the prison inmates for stress relief, mitigating negativities, and contribution to rehab and corrections.

27 Sustainable development initiatives encompass organic farming, the Sri Sri Mobile Agricultural Institute which brings agriculture-related knowledge right to the farmers' doorstep, service projects for tree plantation (Bahrain, Haiti, and Sydney), indigenous species protection, and water conservation. One project of water conservation is the Meri Delhi Meri Yamuna (MDMY) project. Deepening Roots was created in 2005 by volunteers from the AOL headquarters to offer youth a unique, experience-based approach to sustainable agriculture and leadership. The five pedagogic elements of deepening roots are meditation, health and wellness, sustainable agriculture, empowerment, and community.

> service, and a reawakening of human values and Sudarshan Kriya. (Mumbai, May 2012)

The engagement of HIFMs in core sectors of development such as education, health, and livelihoods describes the scope of social service of HIFMs at one level. At another it also projects the HIFMs' assertion/partnership in development goals in a resource-limited setting by simultaneously factoring in culture. The mission is to respond to a religious calling and cultivate a faith-informed vision of care using faith resources. All the HIFMs use some form of religious imagery in their mission statements to communicate their faith-basedness in the 'public face'. In fact, for HIFMs, the service as a part of the mission is also considered as a practice of faith not too distinct from other expressions of faith. Discourse is an important tool by which HIFMs' missions are highlighted, through which the HIFMs' stance is projected as a lived religion comprising social practices and the construction of meanings and identities. Mission statements of HIFMs with their 'social' and 'faith' amalgam are culturally patterned for determining relevance for its public. In realizing the service mandate through the social initiatives, HIFMs establish a middle ground between the secular and sacred – focusing on the faith community efforts in influencing/effecting change.

In terms of practicalities of management, HIFMs' public face is characterized by religious phraseology in their mission statements and religious symbolism in their logo. Headed by the charismatic guru, the members of the order are in charge and the adherent base forms a volitional second line supported by paid staff with a fair degree of formalization in recruitment. 'Faith' nevertheless remains the overarching raison d'être for engagement at all levels. Finance generation is through modes of exchange beyond market logics – philanthropy being one core source. In terms of social service goods delivered, HIFMs provide flexible services involving relational programmes, faith-oriented services also being a part of the package. The organizational culture is imbued with 'faith' as the overarching and underlying tenet. There is a certain kind of reliance on secular expertise but not sans the spiritual veto power in information-processing and decision-making. Hence, the secular/profane is not discounted in managerial aspects; faith is an important and unnegotiable add-on.

In the management of HIFMs' projects there is an engagement of leadership, use of HIFMs' structures and resources, and practical amendments in HIFMs' functional policies to aid intervention. There is an inbuilt understanding in the management of the importance of providing a faith-based context for service. The HIFMs' financial status and the orientation of the monastic order also influence the policy and management issues of social projects. Management entails an involved mediation process – with media, environments, and networks through which symbols and expressions of faith are circulated and coalitions/ partnerships built. Certain programmatic and systemic effects result from the infusion of HIFM players, having consequences for the profile of services and who gets served. This, in effect, influences the transferability of HIFM interventions across religious and secular applications in order to satisfy constitutional issues of equity and public choice.

Furthermore, the affirmative relationship of HIFMs with the legal system is an exercise in practiced legitimacy, a way to consolidate their stand as reasonable social actors. HIFMs' amicability with political and local governance is also a result of the state policy to view HIFMs as 'communities of character' that can generate social capital that contributes to social change and development. Somewhere, this falls in the realm of post-Enlightenment ethics discourse that dominates contemporary public policy discussions; HIFMs are becoming crucial actors in local/translocal politics. Essentially, they have demonstrated a potential in service outreach, partnering or assisting the state welfare agenda and rights mandate. This relationship of HIFM with the state also signifies a policy shift from government to governance, with emphasis put on the way in which discourses and traditions shape service delivery simultaneously drawing attention to beliefs and worldviews that shape public choice (see Biebricher, 2011; Ikegame, 2012a). The amicability is most defined in state policies of externalization wherein HIFMs have managed to circumvent state-imposed restrictions through the faith rhetoric and emerge as dominant transnational actors.

The compliance with state mechanisms is almost wholehearted, sometimes even complementing government welfare efforts. The add-on, however, is the HIFM ideology, with the signature teachings of the gurus actually becoming the principal rhetoric supporting service. Drawing from Hula et al.'s (2007) theoretical framework for looking at faith-based initiatives as alternatives to conventional governance structures, it can be said that HIFMs have certain 'unique resources' to fit the bill. To suit the coalition requirement, HIFMs demonstrate a leaning towards the notion of macro virtue ethics and public good drawing from their respective ideologies. Not satisfied with simply delivering the goods, they also add the faith and morality ingredients into the basket. In this respect they maintain continuity through myriad shifts. Even though state alliance/compliance may be a political act, for HIFMs it is an act of applying faith to 'this world' and connecting to the roots. Sometimes, they also ensure catering to clientele that fall through public service safety nets because of their relatively lenient sifting-sieving criteria – the 're-inventing government' argument.

With the economic system there are relationships beyond market exchange as HIFMs essentially deal with religious goods that are acquired or received through charisma and/or transcendental forces. Charisma and/or transcendental forces provide charismatic gifts[28] in the form of meditation and spiritual and life skills techniques, which become signature goods of HIFMs. Even though these goods involve certain rational actions in terms of demand and supply, the market model does not adequately describe the tactics. Funding options are essentially the state, individual, and institutional philanthropy[29] and self-sustenance.[30] Philanthropy is, however, the main source and HIFMs essentially enjoy strong fiscal health.

With the follower groups in civil society, HIFMs tap the intrinsic-extrinsic religiosity-spirituality and tamper with the religio-spiritual orientations to then affect notions of self and cognitions of associates. HIFMs' beneficiaries are viewed as an imagined community of would be followers, with HIFMs' utilizing their faith capital along with social service

---

28 Coleman, S. (2004). The Charismatic Gift. *Journal of the Royal Anthropological Society, 10*(1), 421–442. Simon Coleman has talked about charismatic gifting and its significance for the sense of premium gained and well-being for followers of religious movements.

29 Institutional philanthropy is like what Eikenberry (2007) has called 'giving circles' – groups that entail individuals pooling resources and then giving them away. They highlight the trade-off between grassroots independence and non-coercive collaborative action that enables a contribution to democratic governance and public good.

30 Self-sustenance can be seen as having two connotations – income-generating activities at one level and the estimate of monetary value of social service activities provided (Stritt, 2008) at another level.

to reach out. They also extend, using Wilson's (2011) term, an ethics of hospitality towards potent service seekers, especially in situations where alternatives are limited. That way a combination of bonding-bridging social capital is generated.

How sociality is cultivated and sustained: Volition, prescriptivism, and doctrinarism

Volition entails innate faith tendencies and service propositions stemming from virgin faith leanings. Prescriptivism is the streamlining and straitjacketing of volition through HIFM schooling. Doctrinaire propositions alleviate the prescriptions to the level of instrumental directive.

The volitional component of Ramakrishna Mission's initiatives commences with the component of God realization. On the highway to God realization is the critical juncture of service which is seen as a naturalistic component of the aspiration. For Swaminarayan Sanstha, volition is the inner belief in the Swaminarayan philosophy, accepting Swaminarayan as God and Pramukh Swami as his manifest abode. Service then flows out of this contention. To quote an office bearer,

> Seva originates from our firm belief in Pramukh Swami. His ideals guide us – we are part of the Swaminarayan faith because we want to be, the rest of it – whether it is temple consecration, donation, or participating in social service activities, it just flows from there. (Ahmedabad, March 2011)

Volitional slant in the realm of Saibaba Sansthan is derived from faith in Saibaba and the penchant to follow his Sufi austerities – poverty and renunciation being the core. From renunciation comes the will to give and that will is operationalized through philanthropy. The Hinduized version of this is 'dana' accepted by Saibaba Sansthan under the heads of health, education, and rural development.

Brahmakumaris' volitional stance comes with the 'quest for spirituality' which is looked at as the individual soul's starting point from where flow the 'social' and 'service' leanings. With the recognition of soul consciousness, the individual's consciousness is expanded from narrow confines to the larger universe. So, the 'service' lens is inserted in terms of souls who have arrived in terms of divine realization and proximity to the absolute being, who then enables those who are still beginners on the journey. To quote a Brahmakumar,

> For us the essential requirement for anything, including social service, is the quest for spirituality and the willingness to understand the concept of soul consciousness and imbibe it. If that condition is fulfilled then the remaining part is taken care of. This is because we believe that the true and highest form of social service is raising the consciousness of all individuals – raising them from lower states of existence and body consciousness to a higher level and God consciousness. (Abu, July 2011)

For Chinmaya Mission, with respect to both householders and monastic disciples, the quintessential requisite is the 'thirst for knowledge' of Vedanta in Chinmaya Mission's packaged form. Realizing and recognizing Chinmaya Mission as the paragon of Hinduized metaphysical, philosophical, and practical view of life and the willingness to fit into that kaleidoscope is the primary component. That, in Chinmaya Mission terms, cannot be cultivated or infiltrated, but has to be inborn. In the words of a senior Swami,

> The main thing for everyone who come in contact with CM in whatever capacity is to be interested in Hindu philosophy and thought processes. The real thirst for that true knowledge must be there. (Mumbai, February 2011)

For Sri Aurobindo Society, social inclinations naturally arise from a penchant for spiritual attainment – that is, enlarging the consciousness to wider goals of society and the cosmos rather than the limited individual. Hence, a volitional spiritual tendency is congruent with social transformation leanings. A simple moralistic altruism is viewed as narrow in favour of a larger encompassing stance which is supposed to be spiritual and, therefore, consciousness oriented. To quote a sadhak,

> We can also say that even if the starting point is spiritual selfishness, the eventual outcome is naturally selfless and philanthropic as the domain of spirituality and consciousness is so wide that there is no scope for puny things within that. When one decides to grow spiritually, automatically the consciousness widens and when that happens we see universality in beings and beings as manifestations of the Godhead. The dictum of divine love then penetrates all beings and one is naturally able to enlarge one's consciousness to the wider world. (Pondicherry, August 2011)

In Vivekananda Kendra terms, volition is the urge for spirituality and propensity to engage in 'ideationally inspired religiosity incumbent' nation-building ventures. Service for Amritanandamayi Mission is an integral part of harnessing the 'spiritual DNA' (Ramakrishnanda Puri, 2006), and, hence, the volition is a natural outcome of spiritual quests. The preliminary translation of the social service mandate of Art of Living happens at the level of the individual member adherents and Art of Living volunteers and teachers. In the Art of Living genre, volition and prescriptivism collide as *seva* (service) has been laid down as an essential component of *sadhana* (or spiritual practice). Spirituality, as per Sri Sri, is the 'technology of the consciousness and the whole world is the play and display of consciousness' (Vyakti Vikas Kendra, 2005a). *Seva*, then, is construed as seeing God in the next person ('when we serve, we are able to go deep within, the deeper you go the more you are able to serve – they complement each other', Sri Sri Publications Trust, 2005). The self–world connections are inevitably established as *seva*, which is considered a crucial pathway to *mumukshatva* (desire for total freedom and enlightenment). *Seva* assumes multiple forms – the hermeneutics are broad enough to encompass a range of fields, from scientific research to disaster interventions to empowerment efforts and charitable giving. To quote a teacher,

> It all depends on the individual who wishes to do *seva*. For some it may be donations, for some service, and for some aspects of documentation and even research. It is the spirit with which you work and that is *seva*. (Kanyakumari, April 2011)

Prescriptions or prescriptivism for various HIFM are as follows. In terms of Ramakrishna Mission, as the spiritual ministration comprises of both monastic order and the householder devotees, the prescribed notions for both stakeholders differ. For the monastic order the twin goals of renunciation-service need to coexist; for the householder devotees, the spiritual propensities are to be enlivened through this-worldly endeavours. The underlying assumption is that it is the spiritual self of the individual that needs to be addressed and all transactions are within the reference system of that self. All other aspects of existence converge into, or diverge from, that spiritual self. In that sense, there is a systematic vertical-horizontal, self-other-context-spiritual, and a holistic mode to the spirituality prescribed for householder devotees.[31]

For Swaminarayan Sanstha, there are differentials in terms of requirements for ascetics, householders, and women. For ascetics, abiding by 'norms and forms' of *sampradaya* functioning is mandatory. These are laid down at the time of initiation into the *parshad* fold and re-enforced at the time of perpetual vows. Alignment constituting the twin mandate of social and spiritual care is a mandatory dictum. The other aspect is the concept of 'village vicharan' to be undertaken by the ascetics, which refers to travelling to villages to speak to people about the *sampradaya*, conducting discourses, understanding needs, and suggesting newer social initiatives on the basis of felt and perceived needs. For householders, on the other hand, there are suggestive prescriptions. For instance the verse 147 of the *Shikshapatri* (which is a bible for the sect) prescribes that 'Householder devotees should donate one-tenth of their income or of their agricultural products to the sanstha. Those who are not so well off could donate one-twentieth part. Such donations purify one's wealth. Profits and products which are not shared in such a manner may corrupt the possessor and his virtues are diminished." Similarly, of the 212 verses there are also mentions of *seva* as a desiderate for householders and for women being

31 In the vertical-horizontal approach, the vertical dimension has to do with relationship with God and horizontal dimension has to do with relationship with self, others, and environment. The self–other–context–spiritual (SOCS) circle contains a presentation of four life realities – self, other, context, and spiritual. The holistic model of spirituality considers spirituality as the centre of the person surrounded by psychological, spiritual, biological, and sociological aspects of the individual. The outer circle is synergetically the wholeness of the spirituality of the person in relation with all domains of existence (see Carroll, 2001).

a compatriot in householder initiatives of *seva* and *dana* is the foremost. Seva is supposed to give 'inner peace' and facilitate the attainment of 'akshardham' (heaven as defined in Swaminarayan parlance).

With respect to Saibaba Sansthan, prescriptivism has a Brahminical proforma – there is a prescribed *upasanakrama* and through the Saibaba-inspired historical culture of 'giving' (Rigopoulos, 1993), *dakshina* has emerged as a means of tangible solidarity. Hence, 'dana' does not remain in a traditional Brahminical sense but assumes a new meaning where 'philanthropic offerings' are made as *dakshina* at the altar of Saibaba as the guru or teacher. For Brahmakumaris, prescriptivism emerges with the basic one-week course as mandatory requirement for all followers, and certain components of this course are redesigned for beneficiary groups (for instance, at the health and prison settings). Hence, this redesigned course essentially comprises a reinterpretation of the message to suit the larger audience. It serves to introduce the basic concepts of Raja Yoga and a spiritually based life while simultaneously satisfying varied instrumental desires – subliminal quest for seekers, stress relief, and life skills for searchers, and perhaps centring and solace for vulnerable groups. In the tailor-made courses the overtly spiritual language is replaced with psychological language and spiritual goals are represented as instrumental ones. The instrumental courses provide both an experiential and a philosophical basis to the original world-rejecting theodicy. In these instrumental courses any overt spiritual ideas such as soul, purity, and karma are replaced with more psychological-cum-New Age terminology, such as the self and higher self. To quote a Brahmakumari:

> Brahmakumari Vishwavidyalaya has prescribed a unique thing for all its members – the entire knowledge of the universe is packed in a span of seven days. Those who obtain the fortune of doing that course are truly blessed. For our members we have the seven day package – but there are certain sections of society for whom fulfilling basic needs or other concerns are more important. Then, PBIV looks into that first – for instance in our prison programme, we do not at once introduce the seven-day programme – we do it step by step, first by just talking to them, understanding them, and then going into other discussions. (Abu, July 2011)

For Chinmaya Mission, prescriptivism and doctrinarism assume twofold forms: (a) the metaphysical-philosophical spread, and (b) the praxis–service propagation ensemble. The metaphysical-philosophical spread comprises of levels or gradations of courses on the ideational core of Shankaracharya's version of Vedanta – the forms for householder adherents being *jnana yagnas* (as per the historical method of Chinmayananda referring to austerities and sacrifice to attain 'true' knowledge), spiritual camps, study groups, lesson course (a correspondence course on the fundamentals of Vedanta), the three-month residential *dharma sevak* course, and the two-and-a-half-year residential course in Vedanta for aspiring ascetics who wish to join and perpetuate the monastic order of the mission. The praxis–service propagation ensemble comprises of casting the Chinmaya Mission propagation in the mould of service-outreach-work for others and the nation through the practical philosophies embedded in and drawn from Vedanta itself – the categorical imperatives being oneness, karma yoga, and *nishkama karma* (work as austerity and unattached work), and *seva* as *sadhana* (service as a form of penance ensuring other-worldly transcendental benefits). To quote a Swami,

> At the Mission we impress the ideal that service is a form of *sadhana*. The main thing is to expose the ego which otherwise takes the support and shelter from anything and everything and thus remains elusive. All *sadhana*, by enabling action to reduce the ego becomes methods of self-purification, which in turn enables self-discovery. (Mumbai, February 2012)

Prescriptivism for Sri Aurobindo Society is the mandate of spiritual *sadhana* and the practice of integral yoga[32] – all efforts being directed

32 Integral yoga is compared to Advaita Yoga of the Gita and Vaishnava Bhakti to discern differences. It aims not at a departure out of the world and life into heaven or nirvana, but at a change of life and existence, not as something subordinate or incidental but as a distinct and central object. The object sought after is not an individual achievement or a divine realization for the sake of the individual, but something gained for the earth consciousness here, a cosmic, not solely a supracosmic achievement. The thing to be gained here also is the bringing in of a power of consciousness – the supramental – not yet organized or active directly in earth's nature. The method is total and integral change of nature also called triple transformation – psychic, spiritual, supramental

towards integration with the divine. For householder aspirants, the sufficient condition is engagement with the ideational component of Sri Aurobindo Society in terms of reading the literature and collective meditation. For the order called the *sadhkas* or ashramites, the a priori condition is the decision to dedicate life to the divine realization. In the words of a sadhak,

> But to be true to his/her resolution s/he must be sincere, faithful, modest, and grateful in his/her consecration because these qualities are indispensable in all progress. And progress, a steady rapid progress is necessary to follow the pace of nature's evolutionary advance. (Pondicherry, August 2012)

Prescriptivism for those engaged with Vivekananda Kendra is the training for workers and volunteers (*seva vratis, jeevan vratis, vanaprasthis,* and *shiksharthis*) as per the prescribed training package and the acceptance of 'postings' in areas (even remote and in the interiors) where Vivekananda Kendra service projects are operational. In Amritanandamayi Mission, what are prescribed are the spiritual- and service-oriented regulations for monastic and householder disciples. To quote a member of the order,

> Amma has specified for us that apart from spiritual activities and mastering of scriptures, we must also engage in social service – there are a host of projects and either we may choose or we are assigned to work with any one or more of them. According to Amma, no spiritual exercise is complete if compassion for fellow human beings and concern for those in poverty and need is not accomplished. Further, the Mission branches in India and abroad have aligned to them what we call

(Sri Aurobindo Ashram Archives and Research Library, 1993). Sri Aurobindo was further influenced in his Integral Yoga by Krishna Chandra Bhattacharya – one of the contemporaries who was influenced by Kant and the Advaita Vedanta school. He was interested in Indian idealism and wrote extensively on Advaita Vedanta and the Samkhya Yoga philosophy. He emphasized four grades of thought – empirical; pure objective or contemplative; spiritual and subjective; and transcendental. From Brojendranath Seal he derived the ideals of relate art with morality, particularly a fusion of mysticism with rationality (Sanyal & Roy, 2007).

> 'Amrita families' – they are householder groups, the *grihasthas*, who have other occupations in life, but are still ardent devotees of Amma and wish to associate themselves with the Mission. So apart from meditation and devotional music, we also tell them that they must participate in the social service activities of the branch ashram. Most of the centres have some projects like hospice, *annadanam* services, etc., and they are encouraged to participate in them. (Amritapuri, December 2011)

On the postulate of doctrinarism, the varied facets of the HIFMs can be explicated thus. With respect to Ramakrishna Mission, the doctrinaire propositions are twofold: inherent equity and transcendence. This entails shifting from theological/communion with God notions, to more surreal and transcendental notions of spirituality, simultaneously constructing personal meanings of spirituality through service; moving from duality-oriented beliefs to non-duality orientations; and reinstating unconditional love and altruism.

For Swaminarayan Sanstha, the doctrinaire turn comes with certain mandatory elements for householders and ascetics. For householders, the Swaminarayan Sanstha group participation (*bal* and *balika mandals* for children, *kishore* and *kishori mandals* for adolescents, *yuvak* and *yuvati mandals* for youth, *mahila mandal* for women, and *vadil mandal* for men above the age of 45) is an unspoken mandate for participating in the mission and its multifarious activities. These groups are coordinated by monastics or senior devotees dedicated to the Sanstha and have gone through the rites of passage; in this case, having been members of such groups/weekly assemblies earlier is enough. The Swaminarayan Sanstha has departments to centrally coordinate such groups worldwide, and they regularly produce guidance literature, manuals, activity sets, and programme flyers for regulating the group functioning. The second aspect of doctrinaire propositions for householders is the *satsang* examinations consisting of a nine-grade/level course. Most of the serious adherents undertake a few levels of examinations and those who complete all the levels have the option of joining the renunciant fold.

In Saibaba Sansthan, the doctrinaire turn is asserted through organized charity. The social dimensions of Saibaba's core teachings form the base of charity. Regularization of this charity is further propelled through the state sanctions, as all donations made to Saibaba Sansthan are tax-exempted,[33] enabling the movement of welfare beyond laissez faire and volitional domains towards more rational and scientific legitimized operations. Charity conceptualizations are thus influenced by reason and rationality – a conception of welfare that emerges from notion of public good and totalitarian ethics. The idea is to float a moral philosophy with ideas of equality and moral autonomy of rational human beings.

Strict doctrinaire practices characterize Brahmakumaris, and in that sense it is a total institution (Brahmakumaris as main stakeholders, sincere seekers following suit, and joining the spiritual mission as householders). This also translates into the service version – 'spatialization' (Walliss, 2007) as the core characteristic of the same. This spatialization or spatial distribution is maintained in all service activities as a distance from the outside world on claims of transcendence competence (Brahmakumari souls vis-à-vis other souls) and internally (the celibate Brahmakumaris and the householder adherents).

In Sri Aurobindo Society, flowing from prescribed propositions, the doctrinaire postulates integral sadhana – an aspiration of a life based on spiritual realization for self as well as the 'not' self: oneness being the

---

33 Saibaba Sansthan has a systematic modus operandi of accepting funds under various heads for faith-based and social service activities. With lakhs of pilgrims visiting every day and the number almost doubling during festivals (the calendar of which has been reconstructed by Saibaba Sansthan as per Saibaba's life history), Saibaba Sansthan receives donations in crores of rupees and probably is only next in line with the Tirumala Tirupati Devasthanam and the Padmanabha Swamy temple. In fact, the localization of Saibaba Sansthan has transformed Shirdi into a cauldron of devotees arriving from all parts of the country – with a Mecca-like status being endowed on it. Apart from anonymous donations which are put in the Hundi as per Saibaba Sansthan's guidelines, which in themselves amount to lakhs per month, faith-based donations which are not tax-exempted and yet serve to be salvation mechanisms are the *abhishek* fund (holy bath as per the Hindu ritual), *naivedya* fund (holy meal), festival fund, *kothi – dhoop deep* fund (incense fund), and the Shri Sai Satyavrat–Satyanarayan fund (a Hindu prayer ritual attributed to the Lord Satyanarayana, a puranic deity and reconfigured in Shirdi as the Sai Satyanarayana Vrata Pooja). In terms of social service activities, the donations are tax-exempted under Section 80G of the Income Tax Act, 1961, and received under the heads of charitable/developmental donation, general fund, building fund, medical fund, *Annadaan* fund (food donation), education fund, and *Nitya Prasadalaya Annadaan* scheme. This sacred ash is believed to have curative properties and is made out of the ash produced from the fire lit in Dwarkamai Masjid, the residence of Saibaba for several decades. This is packed and sent to all devotees who make donations. Two chapters of the Sai Satcharitra (Chapters 33 and 34) have been devoted exclusively to extolling the virtues of Udi through anecdotal references.

epistemological underpinning. This lends an element of catholicity as the emphasis is on a collective aspiration for the descent of divinity. To quote a sadhak,

> The stress here is on change of consciousness and nature, with a view of preparing the individual and society for the next higher stage in evolution. All activities are centred on this faith or truth. Each member chooses the work most congenial to his or her nature and carries it out in a spirit of selfless service and dedication, keeping always in view the aim of integral transformation. (Pondicherry, August 2011)

With respect to Vivekananda Kendra, the doctrinaire twist arrives with the acceptance of the Vedanta as having transcultural and transnational implications, viewing nationalism as an overarching norm inspired by the historical 'man making [*sic*] and nation building' temper of Swami Vivekananda and also as the spiritual nationalism of Guruji Golwalker. The language for Vedanta in the public domain is a moral universalism based on compassion for, and connectivity with, society. The ethics of Vedanta coupled with nationalism are then embodied in acts of yoga practice, vegetarianism, camaraderie with fellow volunteer workers, and righteous norms of conduct derived from practical Vedanta (all sincere Vivekananda Kendra members undertake Vedanta study, yoga, and service) translatable across a range of sociopolitical sites. Hence, what is crucial in shaping the doctrinaire forms of Vivekananda Kendra are sites of sociality in the form of follower/volunteer training and social service projects, Vedanta, and the non-discursive realm of nation-building. Vivekananda Kendra also promotes as a doctrine Vivekananda's conception of Vedanta socialism (as distinct from Marxian socialism, with spirituality as the underlying principle) as an abiding tenet of political organization[34] (this is evident through a detailed rendition on

34 Whereas Marxian socialism has a materialistic substratum, Vivekananda's socialism has Advaita Vedanta as its base – realization of the man as essentially divine and manifestation of that divinity as a way to overcome alienation. Vedantic socialism proposes a climate of change through an arousal of spirituality and the practical interpretation endowed to the 'Hindu' concept of Vedanta. Traditional socialism according to Swami Vivekananda would retain the proletarianization of the masses – Vedantic socialism would naturally alleviate (Parameswaran, 1987).

Vivekananda's thought as well as Eknath Ranade's mission in every programme organized at Vivekananda Kendra and its branches). What is proposed is Vivekananda as having historically shown the spiritual-socio-political path, temporally transported by Ranade and transposed in Vivekananda Kendra. The genealogy of Vivekananda leadership has, as per Vivekananda Kendra, served the purpose of reinstating moral values that enable engagement in transcendental tasks of nation-building. The doctrinaire propositions are introduced for the Vivekananda Kendra followers heuristically, commencing with inwardness of self-discovery through yoga, then catapulted onto a meaningful outwardness of service at the vital level, and finally nation-building at the surreal level. To quote a *karyakarta*,

> For the Kendra, the first thing is to be interested in spirituality, then the willingness to see Vedanta as a universal religion and adopt to it. Further, for all *karyakartas* training is essential – in this training there is a twin focus on self-development and society orientation just as how Swami Vivekananda and Eknathji emphasized on man-making and nation-building. (Kanyakumari, April 2011)

In Amritanandamayi Mission, the doctrinairism comes with the consolidation of faith–service link taking the forms of service groups and tithing practices. To quote a Swami,

> Now it has become almost mandatory for Amma's followers to be a part of the service groups. Also, people are encouraged to donate a part of their income to Amritanandamayi Mission which is utilized solely for service activities of the mission. (Amritapuri, December 2011)

Doctrinarism for Art of Living is the mandatory allegiance to the Art of Living courses as the inevitable way forward. The courses are of basic and advanced levels, along with Sahaj Samadhi Meditation, Divya Samaj ka Nirman (DSN; meaning creation of a divine society), an All Round Training in Excellence (ART-Excel) course for children, Youth Empowerment Seminars, corporate programmes, and Sri Sri Yoga.

The volitional tendencies are, drawing from Sapp (2011),[35] representative of imago dei, incarnational theology, and a faith active in love. The imago dei concept holds that all people are created in the image of God, which has inherent self-giving implications. Incarnational theology focuses on the image of the Absolute Being and the HIFM guru/charismatic teacher, in solidarity with the oppressed. Hence, what is justified and glorified is the sacrificial/renunciant act of the guru flowing then to the associates' sympathetic participation with humanity. Volition for associates arises precisely from this knowledge of human suffering which needs to be annihilated – engagement is to have and build enduring relationships vis-à-vis just an episodic involvement with society. Faith active in love is the inherent tendency of faith to reach out, symbolically signifying beyond self and cognitive-virtual-real alliance with the other self.[36]

Through prescriptivisms, HIFMs actually construct the selfhood of adherents/associates as a deeply moral endeavour. From the theoretical insights of Pierre Bourdieu[37] it can also be said that embodied faith practices of ritual prayer, dietary restrictions, and *seva* form within the associates a moral disposition or habitus. Faith practices have morally constitutive properties, serving as key elements in the process of developing and solidifying moral dispositions of significant associates over time. Prescriptivisms are also social mechanisms by which communities of faith are built – akin to Marcel Mauss' analysis of religious gift giving

---

35 Sapp (2011) has analysed President Obama's interfaith service challenge to US students to commit to year-long interfaith service projects that engage constituencies across campus, across faith traditions, and across the wider local community. While they were included in pre-challenge planning, university chaplains, and religious life staff were omitted from the list of partners. This omission challenged college chaplains and campus ministers to articulate a theology of interfaith service that represented their enduring priorities to engagement across faith lines and in service to others.

36 Faith active in love is also a concept explicated by Martin Luther who has discussed, in the context of Christianity, that love is the litmus test of faith. Love does not create faith, but love is an instrument of faith, and this instrument speaks the language of service.

37 For French theorist Pierre Bourdieu, microstructural processes are socio-structural elements that configure individual embodied practices called the habitus. The concept of 'habitus' has its roots in the works of Durkheim and Weber. Bourdieu conceptualizes habitus as a durable, but not entirely inflexible system, of learned attitudes, perceptions, and behaviours. Habitus is acquired through socialization within families and groups and integrating past experiences. Viewed in the context of religious systems, it serves to link structure and agency (Flanagan, 2008, p. 237).

and reciprocity, there are elements of 'giving' by associates, 'accepting' by beneficiaries, and a divine protagonist who suggests 'reciprocity or spheres of spiritual-material exchange'.

HIFMs' prescriptions and doctrinaire propositions also complement the contemporary theoretical work on 'lived religion' (Winchester, 2008). HIFM traditions not only supply relevant doctrines, narratives, and belief systems but also embodied 'technologies' through which the moral subjectivities of associates can be transformed. Akin to Pierre Bourdieu's concepts of practice and habitus, the HIFM doctrines play a key role in shaping the moral and faith-oriented selves of associates. Taken together they provide space in which to negotiate and contest realms not evident in strictly economic discourse on development such as good, evil, and morality. These categories along with the notion for social justice are expressed while working towards a 'higher purpose' – a kind of holism wherein the goal is not solely spiritual enhancement of self but of the commune and a lifestyle orientalism of sorts, meaning living life in the manner prescribed by Hindu faith tenets and providing examples for nonbelievers.

Memory, oblivion, and styles: HIFMs' sociality in practice

Memory is the political economy of faith assertions, organizational memory transferring onto public memory creation and recreating ideational stances. Oblivion is the non-transference of organizational memory to public memory. The service style is characterized by the antagonisms and contradictions derived through the correspondence between memory and oblivion.

The postulate of memory is an important component feeding into the service style, the differential HIFM domains of which can be elucidated thus. In Ramakrishna Mission, a public and social memory is created of the 'Ramakrishna Religion' and the Ramakrishna–Vivekananda ideals as lived by the order. The monastic order then presents itself to civil society as a lived metaphor of reconciliation of juxtaposed notions of renunciation-service. Against this backdrop of faith practices and discourses, in Swaminarayan Sanstha there are recurrent memories of Swaminarayan religion and Pramukh Swami (and now Mahant Swami) as the epitome of giving and service, and sectarian ethics are dominant. The 'Swaminarayan' presence is overarching, propelling a way of thinking and being which is sect-specific – householder adherents and volunteers in particular, comply with the sect structure, hierarchies, visibility/invisibility politics (particularly with respect to gender), and endogamous preferences. Largely, apart from the ascetics, the administrative staff and workers within the social initiatives are also 'Swaminarayanis'.[38] This vertical-horizontal Swaminarayan social calculus is preserved, maintained, and perpetuated very smoothly, pervading all its operations, whether social or spiritual.

In Saibaba Sansthan, the organizational memory of faith derived from teachings gets translated onto a sort of a public memory of Saibaba through service, encapsulating the ideational stance. The interplay of 'memory' and 'oblivion' in Brahmakumaris service delivery intensifies Walliss's (2007) 'world ambivalence' thesis. Memory is strongly evident and recapitulated in the construction of universal memories of Brahma Baba, the Absolute soul, and Raja Yoga as the desirable way forward. This is further intensified through the 'avyakta murlis' revealing periodically the affirmation of the divine, and Godly knowledge emerging from the 'Incorporeal God' himself. Apart from deep metaphysical renditions, 'murlis' also contain interpretations of contemporary world events from the Brahmakumari (Brahmakumari) lens and fitted into the Brahmakumaris' world-tree and world-cycle scheme of things. Hence, the 'iron age' and its associated 'deformities' (like corruption) are elaborated and explained, and the 'Brahmakumaris as the apostles of change' is emphasized. Through the 'murlis' who are supposed to be 'soul discourse' from the Absolute, the socio-political stance of Brahmakumaris is also anyhow conveyed to the Brahmakumari corporeal kith and kin along with member adherents at centres worldwide. So, the 'metaphysical memory' of Dada Lekhraj is transferred from the 'real' 'Dadi Gulzar' to the 'murli' archives consisting of positions on a range of socio-political issues, the predictions on the apocalypse, and the subsequent emergence on the New Age. The lateral

38 The sect has its own practices of bottom-up inclusion and swaminarayanization – a Swaminarayan variant of sanskritization where the 'class' distance is covered by providing for the basic needs of the lesser-endowed among its members. The 'traditional caste' distance has a nouveau package to say that all have the grace of Pramukh Swami. Differentials are solely on the basis of historical involvement. Generations of engagement with Swaminarayan faith automatically elevates the status within the sect, even if class–tradition caste–ethnicity gaps persist.

transfer of 'traditional' wisdom is then done towards 'New Age' thought, with 'rejuvenation', 'rebirth', and 'resurrection' being the keys.

In Chinmaya Mission, what remains perpetually alive is the memory of Gurudev-Guruji (Swami Chinmayananda-Swami Tejomayananda) as heralders-sustainers of Hindu revivalism and 'Indian' cultural heritage. In Sri Aurobindo Society the organizational memory of faith derived from teachings gets translated onto a sort of a public memory of Sri Aurobindo and the Mother through service encapsulating the ideational stance. This transference is subtle: symbols of integral yoga, divine life on the earth, supramental manifestation, and the triple modes of aspiration of the divine, rejection of materialist controls, and surrender to the divine Mother are entrenched in the public memory. Through service endeavours, the public memory of Vivekananda Kendra is characterized by two aspects: images of Vivekananda perpetuated through Eknathji taking the form of Vivekananda Kendra as a vanguard of national re-construing/nationalist reconstruction on the Indian/Hindu cultural edifice and a 'back to the indigenous sacral roots' sentiment.

With respect to Amritanandamayi Mission, twin memories are created: Amma as the divine feminine personification of the love–compassion epigraph and of the characteristic embrace and unconditional-love apophthegm. In Art of Living, the strong 'memory' of faith is permeated with the projection of Sri Sri as a brand ambassador of 'ancient' philosophy sophisticatedly repackaged into the contemporary. He becomes an epitome of spiritual tradition-continuity-change within a postmodern-postcolonial epoch.

What accompanies the postulate of memory is the shadow effect of oblivion or historical forgetting, a mirroring of secular and profane in the faith repertoire. With respect to Ramakrishna Mission service delivery, oblivion prevails through the metaphorical effects of the secular and profane during actual service delivery, since most of the initiatives and projects display a programmatic focus and claim a universal outreach. In Swaminarayan Sanstha, sectarian ethics permit a limited oblivion. However, in Saibaba Sansthan, the transference is subtle, with the routine operations, the historical Hinduization, and subsequent sophisticated 'Saidharma-oriented dana' and Sanskritization endeavours giving a sense of oblivion. Although Hinduization has been a historical phenomenon, what has emerged subsequently is philanthropy in the name of Sai religion or Saidharma and *dana*. The sophistication arises from the transition of this traditional Sai-inspired collective style of volunteerism to a more reflexive style, b- with more emphasis on fiscal benefits than Sai devotionalism. This is typically suggestive of the concept of asymmetrical engagement (McKean 1996), supporting the scholarly suggestion that such organizations engage in *seva* activities, at least in part, as a means of divesting themselves of wealth for tax purposes (Warrier, 2003).

In Brahmakumaris' drive towards world affirmation, accommodation, and assimilation, which also reflects in its current clientele (covering castes, class, race, and nationality through the international centres) there is a sense of oblivion of the 'traditionalist' message, its intensity being evaporated in 'new-ageification'. The move, then, is to project the 'spiritual-secular-assimilative' as an acceptable stance vis-à-vis 'spiritual-traditional-Raja Yoga.' For instance, some of the recent booklets on stress management, healthy lifestyle and relationships have a 'simple' version of Raja Yoga explained, contrary to the seven lessons course which has the teachings in-depth.

In Chinmaya Mission, temporary amnesia and oblivion occurs in routine managerial activities which bring two components – a sense of corporatism, and a mirage of de-sacralization-secularism. Similarly, in Sri Aurobindo Society, a focus on work and routine operations makes the transcendental memoirs evasive. In Vivekananda Kendra, routine and market transactions, as well as collaboration/partnerships, betray a neutralist image or a sense of oblivion. Oblivion for Amritanandamayi Mission is not complete in the sense of making memories evasive. Rather, what is visualized is a sense of fuzziness in routine business and collaborations with national bodies such as the RBI and NABARD (for instance, for the Amrita SREE self-help groups) - from here the projection of Amritanandamayi Mission being a non-profit with humanitarian concerns (albeit guided by the charisma of Amma who has 'secular and inclusive' leanings) is born. The Art of Living service omnibus, with its routine, fades the faith stance. At another level, the continuous emphasis on the interfaith harmony position, as well as soirees with other faith groups, tends to make the stance almost rhetorically secularized.

The confluence of memory and oblivion projects the service style of the HIFMs. The varied facets and manifestations of style are as follows. The Ramakrishna Mission style is a synchronized version of: (a) theistic existential appropriation of service, (b) Hinduized versions of ecclesiastical notions of missionary work, and (c) a rapprochement of Ramakrishna-Vivekananda ideals, as well as sophisticated and abstract notions of faith-oriented service delivery. The style of Swaminarayan Sanstha in terms of faith based service delivery has the following characteristics: (a) there is an interplay of sect based social ethics, (b) the 'bijana sukhma aapnu sukh' (i.e., one's own happiness lies in the happiness of others) apophthegm, (c) positioning of renunciants on the social change/development mission, and (d) portrayal of the 'Akshar Purushottam'[39] epigraph. Sect based social ethics are derived from the text, practices, and material endowments which practically permit the altruism. The apophthegm of Pramukh Swami signifies the 'self–other' merger and 'othering' of vulnerabilities/needs which have to be addressed, automatically translating into an almost apostolic positioning of the sadhus-parshads on a social development mission. The mission of social-spiritual care is then perpetually coloured by a rhetorical portrayal of the 'Akshar Purushottam' epigraph. The grace of the Lord and his continuing corporeal manifestations (Pramukh Swami and Mahant Swami) are considered as the source, origin, and continuation of the social and spiritual care.

Saibaba Sansthan style is characterized by (a) faith in the Sai imagery and (b) secularized autopoiesis; that is, there is a self-reproduction and self-regulation of secular tenets in routine operations. The style of Brahmakumaris' service delivery is an interplay of (a) soul consciousness, (b) body consciousness as the depreciated binary and root of all problematics, (c) Raja Yoga apophthegm and Brahmakumaris as Promethean interventionists, and (d) finally, in its ambivalent form, spirituality–service interface. The spirituality–service interface refers to the perceived 'natural' flow of spiritual tendencies and quests into service inclinations and interventions.

The Chinmaya Mission style has tenets of (a) Hindu theism and faith-inspired sadhana–service link, (b) Vedanta epithet containing the normative-ideational-praxis norms, and (c) a very uninhibited flow of

39 The Akshar Purushottam theodicy reads as follows: Lord Swaminarayan is the sole doer (karta), has a form (sakar), and is the transcendental, supreme entity (sarvopari) who is ever present on earth (pragat). Gunatitanand Swami, who is Aksharbrahman personified, is the divine abode of Shriji Maharaj (another name for Lord Swaminarayan), and the Satpurush is the gateway to Akshardham.

'Hindu' hologram in the service agenda. Sri Aurobindo Society's style is characteristic of the following: (a) an overarching realm of consciousness beyond human cognition and its perpetual significance and (b) a collective and natural representation of something 'above' – a 'higher-up' positioning in all the endeavours. Effectively, the style of service delivery portrays a representation of Sri Aurobindo as the epitome of the Yoga of Works consecrated to the Divine Mother[40] – as the paragon of the virtue of supramental realization. Owing to the strong Hindu-origin base and Vivekananda as a historical and cultural translator of oriental thought, the Vivekananda Kendra's style is hallmarked by an animated Vivekananda imagery. There is an ideational broadcast through claims of philosophical universalism of home tenets – Vedanta. On the subtle edifice of fascistic Hindu norms, the pronounced service objects that typify the style are mission attainment, spiritual infiltration, provision of tangible needs, steadfast social capital generation, and embodying a perceived matter-of-fact answer to Christian proselytization.

The Amritanandamayi Mission's style is an interplay of two dimensions: (a) the Amma persona as the hologram and metaphor of grace, unconditional love, and service as underpinnings and (b) translocal collaborations and routinization that facilitate the secularization epigram camouflaging the subtle penetrations of micropolitics of Brahminical leanings. The style of Art of Living's social service delivery is an interplay of (a) SK&P and SSY in an orientalist imagery and (b) manufacturing of practical spirituality, that is, salvation through service norms by transcending faith at one level (by spiritualizing it) and catapulting it at another (by the edifice of Vedic tenets under the garb of ancient wisdom). This continuum of 'seva sadhana' functions like an aphorism, an apophthegm that eventually latches onto a spiritualized and yet secular position. Hence, what emerges in terms of a service stance of Art of Living is a complex interplay of faith memory, its simultaneous oblivion, and a spiritualized assertion; writings of 'faith' and erasures of 'secularized spirituality' coexist.

40 The Mother according to Sri Aurobindo is the embodiment of divine Sakti – she has a fourfold form – Mahakali, Mahalakshmi, Maheshwari, and Mahasaraswati. There were analogies drawn between her and the female goddesses in the Hindu pantheon. The entire spiritual sadhana was eventually consecrated towards her – Sri Aurobindo saw in her a form of a divine consort, and more so a compatriot towards the mission of integral yoga.

The style of service of HIFMs has dominant discourses of Hindu hegemony making a backdoor entry. In Ramakrishna Mission, hegemony seeps in as there is an emphasis on imbibing teachings and a systematic emphasis on comprehending the onomasiology of Vedanta as the desirable way of good living. To quote a senior member of the monastic order,

> We serve all people equally – as Sri Ramakrishna has emphasized on the harmony of religions. But for those who are inclined, we tell them to study Ramakrishna literature and Vedanta works as they provide complete and comprehensive ideals for living life well. (Belur Math, May 2011)

In Swaminarayan Sanstha the Swaminarayan dharma is posited as a transcendent version of Vaishnavism first and the universal Hindu *Sanatana Dharma* later. As per an office bearer,

> Once newcomers are initiated into the Swaminarayan lifestyle and philosophy, we explain to them higher things such as the subtle differences of Swaminarayan dharma and Vaishnavism, the uniqueness of Swaminarayan thought, particularly in the fact that God is already present for this dharma, and finally that it is actually an advanced version of Hindu *Sanatana Dharma* having universal ethics. (Ahmedabad, March 2011)

In Saibaba Sansthan, along with the teachings enters the dominant discourse of Hindu hegemony into the praxis mode; claims to equity get coloured by stratification mechanisms and micropolitics of power in the operational field. For instance, in technically concessional services, subtle preferences permeate in terms of 'giving' – beneficiaries with a possible clout/connection may tend to jump the queue. In Brahmakumaris, there are two ways: the first proposition is that the initiated/co-opted individuals are perceived by Brahmakumaris to be on the privileged plane of existence, that is, those who have already embarked upon the original religion of existence proclaimed as 'Adi Sanatana Devi Devata Dharma'. The second way in which the dominant Hindu discourse percolates into the larger social fabric as also the beneficiary fold is the 'simplified' version of 'traditional wisdom' which is presented for universal comprehension. In the words of a Brahmakumari,

Whoever comes in contact with Brahmakumaris, either through our courses or services, is fortunate. They are reaping the fruits of good actions in their past lives and are a part of the godly kingdom of Brahma Baba which he named as Adi Sanatana Devi Devata Dharma. The level and extent of contact and connections then determines to what extent they develop. Whoever comes in contact with Brahmakumaris is told about its spiritual heritage. Things are explained to different people differently as per their levels of comprehension. (Abu, July 2011)

In Chinmaya Mission, the apparent myth and camouflage of 'secular', 'all encompassing', and 'universal' are systematically erased and demystified through the continued emphasis on 'Hindu' philosophy and Vedanta as the distinctive way forward. The rewriting is therefore 'revivalist Hindu' – a syndicated package comprising oriental and postcolonial answers to Enlightenment rationality, occidental ethnocentrism, and modernist scientism – Vedanta being the historical 'Hindu scientific' paradigm. With respect to Sri Aurobindo Society, the teachings of integral yoga and supramental manifestation form the metaphors of all development. This in turn creates subtle hierarchies between those who comprehend the complex philosophical repertoire by their attained language and cognitive proficiency vis-à-vis those who have not. As for Vivekananda Kendra, there is an austere emphasis on comprehending Vedanta universalism and the Ramakrishna–Vivekananda version of Hindu philosophy – a mode through which the discourse of the Hindu enters praxis. In Amritanandamayi Mission, it occurs with the emphasis on 'ancient Indian heritage'. In Art of Living, the hegemony seeps in inconspicuously as the core position is that 'wisdom' lies in the Vedas primarily. With other tenets such as Buddhist and ecclesiastical, there is the whole element of seeking congruity – the vantage point of comparison being the Vedic repertoire.

HIFM memory is, thus, like a spiritual-rationality wherein there is a shared inherent purpose to experience connectedness with the transcendental vision demonstrated by HIFMs. The rationality element validates this-worldly action – shared higher-level purposes being connectedness with the Absolute and others. Essentially, social conditions influence how memory acquires meaning through faith and related practices. Faith informs social practices of HIFMs and remembrance of the charismatic guru lineage is a catalyst for social action. This memory then demonstrates a preference for principles of human rights, peace, solidarity, and 'signs of the times' are considered as the basis for social analysis across. Memory also very strongly shapes social imaginations – placing on the charismatic guru and teachings a kind of doctrinal responsibility to feed into the pragmatics and contextualities of social justice. HIFM memory is culturally loaded – they ensure a cultural continuity by preserving the 'knowledge' through mnemonics (practical Vedanta, Raja Yoga, Integral Yoga, BMI chart, IAM technique, and SK&P and SSY techniques being illustrations), rendering it possible for followers to reconstruct their cultural identities. Mnemonics interplay with social action through image creation of the charismatic guru as a 'socially aligned' figure, ceremonial practices that combine ritual prayer with service, narrative building of the embeddedness of service in the HIFM historiography and genealogy, and inscriptions in its publics.

For HIFMs the oblivion dynamics arise in the course of HIFMs' reflexive acts in redefining and refining their own positions in relation to the larger sociopolitical environ. Oblivion has been further enhanced by neoliberalization, which has opened spaces for HIFMs to enter into the public realm in newer ways and probably also enter into mainstream 'secular' partnerships such as those of Vivekananda Kendra and Swaminarayan Sanstha projects.

HIFM's style of service/action goes beyond simple instilling/extolling of virtues; rather it portrays itself as vanguard of fulfilling social obligations. The operational ontology of HIFMs contains communitarian notions of social citizenship.[41] Essentially the immanence of the soul is emphasized. Other aspects are that of integrality of the human experience, commune as predominant, and social justice notions as fertilizing/impregnating virgin aspects of charity/philanthropy. There is a stylized form of faith-based social logic[42] and the 'public good' factor in HIFMs' ideals is the utopia towards which sociality is geared.

41 Communitarian notions of social citizenship are in contrast with a privatized, economic, and individualistic 'civil society' (McMillin, 2011).

42 See Huff (2010). Huff (2010) has looked at how one faith-based nonprofit organization and its various Pentecostal and evangelical church partners in El Salvador are creating associational contexts within which local community development projects are identified

Faith and a collateral seepage of Hindu hegemony through service is the general political economy for HIFMs. This is manifested through service religiosity, staff religiosity, and in general organizational faith. There is an institutional coupling of service with the resources, authorities, and culture of HIFM ideas. Two analytical frames, to draw from Bradley (2009), define the political economy dynamics: one is the way faith shapes their perceptions of the world and their actions in development and the other is the way this translates into practice. HIFMs are particularly inclined towards engaging in services that promote well-being and are in line with their faith-based outlook. Contrary to being unblemished 'armies of compassion' (Kennedy & Beilefield, 2006), HIFMs have their mandate of initiation/co-option spelt out in their mandate. This initiation/co-option is either a direct derivative of faith and/or truncated from the teachings–praxis calculus of the HIFMs, the latter being more prominent. Faith-based services enumerate vulnerable populations and circumscribe their continued survival within bounded spatial realities. This process of 'emplacing', to use Arif's (2008) concept, suggests a faith-coded biopolitics of HIFMs, that is, a practice of governmentality that puts agents other than state, and thus the HIFMs themselves, in a position from where they exert power over continued social life.

---

and implemented. Corresponding analysis of interview data portrays how these same actors relied on diverse social logics – which are both religious and practical in nature – to make sense of and assess some of the key assumptions of a particular form of faith-based development.

6

Faith Trappings: Shades of Hegemony and Hindu Nationalism

HIFMs and their social leanings and efforts reveal aspects of hegemony and dimensions of Hindu nationalism. There are subtle hegemonies within an overarching syncretic, assimilative, and accommodative frame. The Hindu episteme, as also terminologies derived from them, are adapted and valorised. The same are then catapulted onto the national domain.

Shades of hegemony

Essentially, the hegemony of HIFMs is derived from their theistic propositions and the Hindu metamorphosis. These factors interface with the materialist domains of caste, class, gender, and ethnicity, and the logic of hierarchy in them prevails in subtle and covert modes. A structuralist reading of the texts unveils the micropolitics of this interface. Amritanandamayi Mission is spearheaded by a charismatic woman, Sri Aurobindo Society was continued by a woman's charisma, women occupy a centre stage in Brahmakumaris, and Ramakrishna Mission has specific stands on the gender question. However, the gender equity norm is not a universal given but is invented, created, resisted, and subverted at the fulcrum of multiple identities. At one level, there are agential trajectories such as endowing women access to the world of spiritual action and faith-inspired public life, and at another level, the 'chastity of women' rhetoric defies equity norms.[1]

The Ramakrishna Mission is systematically rooted in Hindu ideals, commencing with the locus classicus of Vedanta. Shades of hegemony are visualized in a threefold manner: (a) ontological hierarchies and subtle binaries of this world and other worlds (as Self and higher Self are distinct entities and the salvation epithet posits a distinctive difference between tangible world and higher planes of existence), (b) essentially Hindu theism with an incorporation of pluralism and syncretic thoughts (the prominent thoughts being Advaita translated and transferred translocally), and (c) the divine feminine as biological determinism (the bestowing of divinity on women does not transcend, but enlivens, the nature–culture debate).

For Swaminarayan Sansthan, shades of hegemony are visualized through (a) sectarian sentiments and cultural and social reproductions within (there is a certain degree of staunchness in Swaminarayan Sansthan belief systems and positions characteristic of all sects), (b) perspectival-ritual modelling and referential-snowballing dynamics (members actively engage in propagation, recruiting newer believers and promoting their own beliefs that eventually define identities), (c) a new grammar of sect-based stratification and spatialization, (d) institutionalized performative acts of Brahminical patriarchy constituting norms and forms of gender discourse, and (e) an 'othering' of vulnerabilities wherein Swaminarayan Sansthan adherents place themselves on the superior binary of 'giving' and 'serving'.

In Saibaba Sansthan, 'unity', 'equality', and 'notions of oneness' which pervade the Sai hagiographies reveal hegemony – the references to 'man' betray a predominantly masculine theology and theism. The first level is the Hinduization of the Saibaba phenomenon (Warren, 2004) from its essentially Sufi and syncretic leanings. There is a dichotomy of 'purusha dharma' and 'sthree dharma' (the man's moral conduct vs. the woman's

1 The entire oeuvre of practice, both discursive and material – the imagery of Bharat Mata, the valiant historical figures, and subservient mythical wives – all allow women to become avenging angels in moments of crisis. When these moments ebb away, they return to the mode of nurturing mothers and obedient wives (see Sethi, 2002).

moral conduct) – 'shadowness', 'invisibility', and 'boundaried existence' considered as womanly virtues (Ranade, 1953). The second level of attestation of the stratification logic is the purity–pollution schemata as acceptable and internalized; birth order-related ascribed status believed to facilitate the maintenance of social balance. Most of the writings in the apostolic genre such as the Stavanmanjari and the Sai Ramayana have been written in a high tide of Brahminism, thereby subtly demonstrating the alterity of the subaltern as replicated in culture.

Despite the oneness endeavours, indiscreet Sanskritization endeavours are evident with mass participation in Hinduized rituals presided by priests. In that sense there is a revivalist and reformist liberalism. With an inability to imagine the non-Brahmin 'other', there was historically a Hindu theistic existential usurpation of the Saibaba phenomenon by the Bombay Brahmans who set up the Saibaba Sansthan; subsequently, the tradition continues. For the Bombay Brahmans, it was a Hinduized inclusive reformist answer to the traditional colonial structure that prevailed. Gradually, the Saibaba Sansthan's Hinduized stance has subtly replicated the caste-based social, cultural, and economic structure of society in general and Hindu society in particular. Caste–class inferiority is not only spatial but also normative – the alterity of the subaltern is replicated in the organizational culture with privileges endowed on the bourgeoisie. Simultaneously, there is a representation of the Hinduized version of Saibaba phenomenon through the work of the apostles – Dasganu, Nanasaheb Chandorkar, and Hemadpant – and a continuity of that experience is communicated through time and history. This 'representationality' makes the mimetic world of the Saibaba phenomenon figurative. The fourth level of hegemony is ontological; three stages of 'being' and existence have been prescribed: sattwic (the pure and sublime state endowed to a privileged few), rajasic (the state of enchantment with material desires), and the tamasic (or the state of subservience and decline).

Brahmakumaris' normative-ideational stance owing to its very edifice of distinction between soul consciousness and body consciousness betrays hegemonic overtones. Furthermore, the exclusivity in its world-rejecting avatar adds to the dominant tone. In terms of Chinmaya Mission perspectives, the shades of hegemony are visualized through the social hierarchy, patriarchy, and micropolitics of purity–pollution and chastity–contamination schisms camouflaged under the garb of 'oneness' of the Advaita tenets. With claims to universal access and attainment of Chinmaya Mission socialization (as they are world-accommodating in terms of anyone willing to become a member or join the Vedanta course, monastic training is permitted), there are continuing but subtle Sanskritization endeavours through emphasis on traditional scriptures.

In the philosophical repertoire of Sri Aurobindo Society, hegemony gets unveiled through the concept of supramental manifestation entailing binary oppositions between human existence, and mind and the Supermind. Effectively, this promotes socio-existential negations of current realities – the evolutionary quest focusing primarily on futuristic trends. This quest is further coloured by the social collage which is writ with antagonisms and contradictions upon which ideals of integral yoga are imposed. Hence, hegemony gets permeated wherein the locus shifts from the 'realpolitik' to the 'utopian'.

For Vivekananda Kendra, shades of hegemony are visualized in the claims of universalism of Vedanta philosophy as overriding extant ecumenical, Judaic, Islamic, and Buddhist tenets. The fourfold Yoga path and sanatana dharma have subtle underpinnings of Brahminization, Sanskritization, and other traditional hierarchies. The other component includes forms of Brahminical patriarchy, such as constructions of femininity and glorification of motherhood. Originating from a discarding of Buddhistic thought (which permitted women in the ascetic fold), the sole accepted model of feminine behaviour is where women followed their 'sthreedharma' (historically Swami Vivekananda considered Sarada Devi, Sister Nivedita, Sister Christine, and Mrs. Sara Bull as spiritual exemplars who followed the paths of 'masters', thereby confining them to patriarchal religion and negating their own personal political spheres; gender inclusivity and equality in Vivekananda Kendra is essentially within the patriarchal fulcrum).

Shades of cultural hegemony in Amritanandamayi Mission are evident through the proclamations of sanatana dharma as the face of harmonious integration. In the lecture 'Cultivating Strength and Vitality', delivered at the inauguration of the Vivekananda Foundation International Centre at New Delhi by Mata Amritanandamayi, the core is that texts in the sanatana dharma explain the vastness of truth and knowledge; the whole creation is looked at as a manifestation of the divine consciousness and

Vedanta as the very foundation of India's all-embracing vision with regards to religion. Although there are claims of oneness and equity, a clear demarcation is made between the seekers and the sought, that is, the Absolute. These binary prescriptions about social existence in Amritanandamayi Mission's repertoire are instrumental in establishing the notions in the realm of the institutional 'other' pertaining to society, law, and polity.

For the Art of Living foundation, hegemony is displayed when, packaged in a modernist and scientific frame, Sri Sri emerges virtually as a cultural translator of Vedic thought (akin to that genre of socio-religious reform that is engaged in glorification of the extant traditional order). Furthermore, syncretism and interfaith harmony are discussed within a conversion-oriented frame, attempting to depict congruence and parallels in Art of Living perspectival leanings and those of other faiths globally. A sense of aporia sets in with a simultaneous lack of religious specificity and subtle drawings from Vedic tenets and an emphatic assertion of absolute ethical categorical imperatives of evangelical leanings of love and service.

Communal strands

Communal overtones in the HIFMs do imply exclusionary modes and constructions of 'othering'. The distinction here is that the 'other' is not diametrically opposed but different/uninitiated into the fold. Reactionary modes do not entail overt antagonism/violence but a sort of mental distancing.

For the Ramakrishna Mission, nuances of communalism are visualized in the process of identity creation as followers of Ramakrishna–Vivekananda ideals (and hence, the Ramakrishna religion), differentiated from the 'other', which is sometimes Hinduism in general, or the 'totally other', meaning different religions. The monastic order creates a life-world with specific codes, mores, and norms-forms similar to sectarian manifestations (the male monastics wear ochre robes and the women have ochre or white garments draped in a particular fashion). For householder devotees an austere and exclusivist adherence to the Ramakrishna–Vivekananda ideals through personal involvements of reading Ramakrishna literature and practicing Vedantic ideals is the norm. This devotionalism and following Vedantic ideals become arenas for communitas and connect as a precursor to communalist politics. Essentially, communal overtones are subtle, limited to an otherness assertion and do not catapult onto violence.

Swaminarayan Sansthan's clear sectarian stance is a precursor to the communal 'othering' of non-adherents wherein there is not exactly antagonism but an individualization and exclusivity of sorts. BAPS members feel the sense of 'difference' with other sects, faiths, and schisms leading to an individualized (Swaminarayan Sansthan-oriented) outlook on macro social issues, fissures in the religious landscape, and an increasing tendency towards privatizing faith in terms of norms of beliefs. For Saibaba Sansthan, nuances of communalism are visualized in the process of identity creation as Sai adherents are differentiated from the 'other' (or non-Saibaba Sansthan members). They create a life-world with specified codes, mores, and norms-forms similar to sectarian manifestations (for instance, the priests in the Samadhi mandir wear saffron robes and the sevaks wear red army attire akin to the courtly mannerisms of Maratha kings, also spearheading the tradition of attributing Hindu royalty status to Saibaba).

Brahmakumaris, in their exclusivist form, project themselves as a reformist and emancipating faith orientation of the soul-conscious bourgeoisie. The 'other' in these scheme of things is the 'body conscious' *lumpen proletariat* resulting in their objectification and subsequent marginalization. Communal and Hindu nationalist tones in Chinmaya Mission are seen in terms of re-inscription of the Sankara's inclusive victory tour into a new trajectory – one element of which is the progressive development from few to all – and from a religion of the elite to a spiritual ideal for all Indians – a radical revelation of 'essential oneness' despite any appearance of diversity. The Hindu narrative is thus said to possess a universal resonance and intrinsic power of recognition beyond culture, circumstances, or historical era. In Sri Aurobindo Society, exclusivity is derived through the quest of Integral Yoga, and that is seen as the bedrock of commune development. Those who are 'on the path' are considered to be superior compared to the 'others' who are yet to embark on this journey.

In Vivekananda Kendra, the 'other' is the evangelical subject whose missionary object interferes with the Vivekananda Kendra mission of outreach. Hence, the communal sense enters when the 'spread' of spiritual knowledge by Vivekananda Kendra to aggregate the (supposedly scattered) Indian nation is placed in juxtaposition to evangelical proselytization.

In Amritanandamayi Mission, practices, mores, and the Hinduized fulcrum of operations reveal further subtleties. These include the institutionalized study of Vedic texts and scriptures, Hinduized devotional music, and veneration to versions of deities in the Hindu pantheon as characteristic of Amritanandamayi Mission adherents. Socialization of these norms and forms leads to a concretization of 'identities' of Amritanandamayi Mission adherents defined and constructed vis-à-vis the 'other' that is not Amma disciple and/or not familiar with 'Hindu sanatana dharma'. Amritanandamayi Mission-adherents' identities emerge from a dialectic between the individual and the Amma charisma which gets institutionalized through a familism of sorts (in general, entire families are devotees of Amma and participate in different activities at Amritanandamayi Mission); through the Amma icon, religion gets implicated in the individual and collective follower identities. The 'other' then acquires a counter-ontological status of three forms: (a) those who have not attained the plane of spiritual transcendence by following the prescribed path, with whom there is a sense of psychic and spiritual distance maintained (the novice adherents); (b) those who are more recipients than adherents, and hence an object of compassion rather than camaraderie (the beneficiaries); and (c) those who have not been engulfed in any manner in the Amritanandamayi Mission fold (the uninitiated) and are thus the radical other. From the psychoanalytic lens, this 'radical other' forms the purport of existence of the Amritanandamayi Mission adherent emissary – initiation and later co-option being the goal. Akin to Sudhir Kakkar's propositions on communal identities, Amritanandamayi Mission followers also form repositories of unconscious images of the 'other' (an 'other' who has not been enveloped in the Amma embrace) which brings in an increase in the sense of well-being in the narcissistic realm.

With respect to Art of Living, communalism is subtly pervasive, with discussions on SK&P and SSY as desiderate, both essentially based on systems of Yoga and Vedic tenets. There is a certain 'construction' through four types of theological connections which consist of historical derivation, structural isomorphism, self-referential knowledge, and paradigmaticity.[2] SK&P and Sri Sri Yoga are believed to be historically derived from ancient postulates; there is a structural consolidation of the same which is reproduced over time. This forms a paradigm of ethnocentrism which feeds into the communal discourse.

Aspects of Hindu nationalism

The ideational strands of these HIFMs, albeit internationalist in scope and plan, have specific nationalist underpinnings that ominously foreshadow the Hindutva doctrine and probably signify a socio-spiritual Darwinism of sorts. The whole exercise of Hindu nationalism of HIFMs is geared towards a fascist agenda of transforming the 'different', that is, non-adherent/non-theist into 'others' as foes. It is effectively camouflaged by sanatana dharma as a doctrinally non-confrontational pan-Hindu dictum (Zavos, 2001).[3] There have been, as Basu and Bannerjee (2006) have proposed in the context of Hindu nationalism in the nineteenth-century Bengal, hyper-masculinized imaginings of revolutionary nationhood – (particularly seen in the context of Ramakrishna Mission and Vivekananda Kendra directly and Chinmaya Mission and Sri Aurobindo Society indirectly).[4] Hinduized national construction is rooted in the wider heritage of the exclusivist masculine language of imperialism, despite the supposed radical opposition of the Occident and the empire.

---

2 See Vries and Sullivan (2007) for a further discussion on Foucault's theological connections. Contemporary theology is proposed to be derived historically, situated structurally, based on believers/followers' reference system of self and, hence, leading to a kind of paradigm of belief systems of a particular nature.

3 Zavos's (2001) essay on socioreligious reform and Hindu revivalism in the late-nineteenth-century India refers consistently to the idea of sanatana dharma as an indicator of 'orthodox' resistance to change in the context of a modernizing religion. His article questions this presentation of sanatana dharma as an unmediated reactionary force. It argues that sanatana dharma as orthodoxy in fact emerged as an influential feature of the modernization process, most particularly in the development of a doctrinally non-confrontational, pan-Hindu identity.

4 Basu and Bannerjee (2006) propose that Bengali elites drew on traits of hegemonic masculinity utilized by the British colonial rulers to justify their presence and embarked on a cultural quest for manhood and political virility. This narrative of indigenous masculinity (represented as warrior monk and Hindu soldier – illustrating thereby the dynamic dance between the gendered metaphors used to imagine the liberated nation. Another reference could be Ashis Nandy's *The Intimate Enemy*.

In the aim to evolve a unique perspectival base, HIFMs have engaged with a legacy of exclusion – forming imaginary, real, and virtual boundaries through the realpolitik of discourse. In a constructivist sense, there are power dynamics embedded in the understandings projected by HIFMs on faith and nation. The Hindu faith-oriented and governed language of difference is used as a way to legitimize the dominance of HIFMs and marginalize the 'others'. The competing versions of Hindu nationalisms projected through history by HIFMs have also garnered sociopolitical support.

In Ramakrishna Mission, Hindu nationalism is packaged through the syntax and semantics of Advaita and Vaishnava Bhakti – a result of the composite discourse created by Ramakrishna Mission's ideational stance with an enduring set of practices including ritual communication and pilgrimage. For Ramakrishna Mission adherents, the pilgrimage to the Dakshineshwar Kali temple is virtually canonical; the other important shrines being Belur Math and the maths at Baranagore, Alambazaar, and Jayrambati.

In Swaminarayan Sansthan, Hindu nationalism is evident through the projection of the Swaminarayan faith as a transcendent representation of Hindu sanatana dharma. The nationalist flavour for Swaminarayan Sansthan is the link between family values as prescribed by Swaminarayan Sansthan and the exalted vision of nation reconstruction. It is a classical one based on theistic naturalism – the idea that nationality is derived directly from God and depends on the patriotism of the nobility, church, and masses (Hayes, 1931): in the Swaminarayan Sansthan context, the variation being sadhus, the sect, and the householder adherents. Historically, owing to its nineteenth-century origins and leanings towards Hindu revivalism in the colonial era, the version of nationalism that Swaminarayan Sansthan harboured was an ideological reaction to colonial domination (read notions of Westernization for the Swaminarayan Sansthan context). What Swaminarayan Sansthan has claimed to tackle is the spiritual domain is imagining the nation to have material and spiritual dimensions, and the efforts of the sampradaya were about 'readying' society (read followers) towards this so that the material domain can be tackled. The spiritual sphere for Swaminarayan Sansthan is represented by the sampradaya faith, sect social structure, and adherent families. To quote an office bearer of the women's wing,

> At the sampradaya, we believe that by following the Swaminarayan principle of ghar satsang, good family values are inculcated. When at the family level good ideals are followed, then automatically at the societal and national levels goodness will flow. Then there will be peace and harmony. But Swaminarayan Sansthan firmly believes that the starting point is the family and the home. Swaminarayan Sansthan is a spiritual organization. It aims at tackling all issues from the spiritual lens – even national development and reconstruction. For that we believe that the starting point is the individual and family. We see where we have influence – within our faith and adherent families. So we start from there – when good ideals are instilled at that level, Westernization influences get diminished and automatically patriotic ideals and worship of our nation, Mother India, develops. (Ahmedabad, March 2012)

Saibaba Sansthan re-enforces the basic organizational belief as the 'sanatana dharma' (a secularization idiom embedded in Hindu logic of equality). Furthermore, it reiterates a certain glorification of the 'Hindu Bharat'. This thesis is transcended to a trans-bordered cultural semiosis where 'Hindu culture, Bharatiya culture, and world culture' are declared synonymous. In Saibaba Sansthan, these aspects are evident in the rhetoric of sanatana dharma and Hindu Bharat, which is a result of the composite discourse created by the Saibaba Sansthan ideational stance with an enduring set of practices including ritual communication and pilgrimage. Shirdi has gradually attained the status of a 'modern' pilgrim centre, particularly after the announced proclamations of Baba's trans-conscious activities after his physical departure, when Shirdi was seen as a sanctum sanctorum of emancipation from sins. Furthermore, the historical rechristening of Saibaba, the Sufi pir (saint) by training, to an avatar or embodiment of the Puranic deity Dattatreya can also be viewed as a Hinduized Maharashtrian catapulting of the Sufi mystic stance onto a nationalist discourse of syncretic assimilation. The Saibaba charm has managed the accommodative heuristics of syndicated Hinduism and inclusion-seeking Islamic identities.

For Brahmakumaris, in its assimilative and world-affirming form, Hindu nationalism is unveiled in two modes – the first being the proclaimed universalism of the essentially 'Hindu' terminological base through the translocal marketing of Raja Yoga as a universal salvation good. The second is evident in its firm contention of the 'oneness' of the Absolute (as the Incorporeal Shiv Baba). Furthermore, as per their world tree theory 'other' faiths (such as Judaism, Christianity, Islam, and sects and cults that have emerged in the historically degenerated 'copper age') are considered only dissensions and schisms that would eventually be overcome through the New Age, post the current confluence age. The role Brahmakumaris and Raja Yogic liberation and salvation army plays is that of averting the apocalypse – by asserting and exhorting the hoi polloi to re-ascertain their belief in the Absolute Incorporeal as prescribed by Brahmakumaris as also adhering to the Raja Yoga proforma. The Hindu nationalist stance in Brahmakumaris is through the base of 'Raja Yoga' and 'Adi Sanatana Dharma'.

Historically, Swami Chinmayananda has been viewed in connection with the rise of Hindutva in India and the co-founding of the Vishwa Hindu Parishad in 1964 (Bhatt, 2001). The complex and ambivalent relationship of Chinmaya Mission and the broader Hindutva movement can be tracked – Swami Chinmayananda explicitly affirmed a form of cultural nationalism in his public preaching and teaching, both in India and abroad. He portrayed Chinmaya Mission as carrying forward the victory tour of Adi Sankara. Furthermore, Swami Chinmayananda attributed the 'national disintegration' witnessed in India to a lack of attention to its spiritual heritage and, as Sax (2000) has proposed, he strongly argued for the 'dig vijaya' ideal (Adi Sankara's victory tour) of unity through territorial conquest and incorporation (of non-Hindus to Hinduism). The continuing mission and historic legacy of Sankara is modified and unfolded explicitly in social and institutional terms (Locklin & Lauwers, 2009).

Hindu nationalism automatically flows – at one level through a historic RSS connection, and another level, its continuing form which assumes the following faces. Hindu ideals form the basis of socialism or ethical socialism, which in turn prove to be the vanguard and political utopia of national unity and peace. There is also a transformation of pure Vedanta into a political stance of national cohesiveness and peace. Finally, there is a mimesis – Chinmaya Mission with its metaphysical-social-political-spatial paraphernalia and formulations is posited as a replica of national harmony and peace. The master-crafting of Vedanta and Hindu philosophy is in a manner in which it fits into the scheme and frame of the 'secular'. This entails oneness at the metaphysical level; inclusiveness and world accommodation at the social level; penchant for and exhortation of universal political values of equity, justice, and peace at the political level; and the geographical construction of local/translocal/global centres and Sandeepanys (retreat and monastic training centres) at the socio-spatial level. This is compounded with ascetic and householder training and initiations in multiple languages, answering to the linguistic-political division of the national polity and simultaneously representing the postcolonial Hindu revivalism at the translocal/global levels by exporting 'Hindu' and 'Indological' heritage to the materialism-prone 'West' – the quintessential occidental 'other'.

In Sri Aurobindo Society, the arguments of Hindu nationalism dominate and are derived from the historical orientations of Sri Aurobindo and his writings. From 1893 to 1934, Sri Aurobindo pronounced his stand on nationalism by initially publishing ten articles in the *Indu Prakash* of Bombay on 'India and the British Parliament'. In a series titled 'New Lamps for the Old' published in nine instalments, he portrayed a severe take on the moderate stand of the Congress. In a pamphlet titled *Bhawani Mandir* published shortly before August 1905, the idea of the temple of Bhawani and of an order of political sanyasins was floated, further inspired by his brother Barindra. From 1906 to 1908, in *Bande Mataram*, a newspaper founded by Bipin Chandra Pal and edited by Sri Aurobindo from November 1906, he emphasized on the need for defensive resistance, the doctrine of passive resistance, and the double policy of defensive resistance and self-development. After his release from jail in 1909, on charges pertaining to the Alipore Bomb trial case, Sri Aurobindo started two journals - *Karmayogin* in English and *Dharma* in Bengali, where he proposed his ideas on nationalism, doctrine of sacrifice to the nation, and nationalism as sanatana dharma. On the Hindu Mahasabha, he proposed that it meant that the Hindu was awakening to the need of unity and cohesion; for the Muslim League he interpreted that the Mohammedan was awakening to the need for change, the growth of aspiration in the world around him but, however, not yet to the broad ideas modern life demanded. This was a subtle critique on the divisive politics of Jinnah and an assertion of Hindu nationalism as the way forward (Sri Aurobindo

Ashram Trust, 1965). The most popular nationalist dialogue during that time was the Uttarpara speech delivered by Sri Aurobindo in 30 May 1909 on the behest of the Uttarpara Dharma Rakshini Sabha wherein he emphasized that nationalism was not a politics but a sanatana dharma. The Hindu nation is born with the sanatana dharma, with which it moves and grows. When the sanatana dharma declines, the nation also declines (Ghosh, 1919). Furthermore, Sri Aurobindo maintained that the nation was a mighty Shakti (power) and is composed of the *Shakti* of the millions of people in India, thereby bestowing a motherhood status to the political boundaries of the nation. He discussed the nation as a living unit; however, a temporary one until a greater living unit could be found.

In Vivekananda Kendra Hindu nationalism is visualized in (a) 'Hindu' scriptural exegesis as educational agencies of 'Indian' life (Nivedita, 1988, 4e, considered *Ramayana* and *Mahabharata* as playing that role: most tales of Hindu mythology considered as having cradle socialization values), (b) 'Hindu' sociopolitical tenets as apocryphal gospels (Nivedita 1988, 4e, equated *Puranas* to apocryphal gospels), and (c) the Swami Vivekananda version of 'Hindu' and 'Hinduism' as an oriental ammunition to safeguard from occident – a symbol and metaphor for scientism, materialism, and binaries. As per a *karyakarta*,

> What Swami Vivekananda had said in 1893 in Chicago holds true even now. He had said that India has a spiritual wealth and that is the heritage of Indian culture. Vedanta has the capacity to prove to be a universal religion. What he brought back from there is a collective and world perspective on Hindu thought which, when re-employed in the Indian context, ensures national growth and development. At Vivekananda Kendra Eknathji did precisely that – used the polished version of Hindu thought which had the clear vision of demarcation from Western thought to build an organization that engages in developing a cadre for national regeneration. That tradition continues till date. (Kanyakumari, April 2011)

Vivekananda Kendra Hindu nationalism thus derives from Swami Vivekananda. Commencing with the postulate of the educative role of India to the West in the sphere of value, religion, and spirituality as per the 1893 Chicago address, the insertion of 'religion' as a keynote to the national life of India became integral. Using the ideational support of nationalists, the contenders (in the Hindu frame) were perceived to spearhead the freedom struggle as also challenge the material science of the West (Parameswaran, 2004). Both Swami Vivekananda and Eknath Ranade used two domains to assert this contention: karma yoga as the practical philosophy symbolizing a spiritual activism of sorts and youth as the salvation army. Hindu nationalism in practice for Vivekananda Kendra utilizes the central theme of Bharat Mata historically. Hindu ethos of one manifested as many, and universal sacralization, made the inclusive approach of Hindutva simultaneously spiritual, universal, and nationalistic. The focus is quasi militant, conquering the extant spiritual passivity/inertia and establishing a vitality deriving from the glorious past of the Hindu *punya bhoomi* (sacred land; Vivekananda Kendra Prakashan, 1963) since historicity.

Hence, what Vivekananda Kendra continues to capitalize on is the new idiom in the discourse of Swami Vivekananda which appropriated the conservative and popular elements of Hinduism. This re-ushered a modernity into the cultural space of the colonized world (which was brought in earlier by movements such as the Brahmo Samaj, but which showed signs of weakening with pressures from conservative Hindus). According to Basu (2002), Swami Vivekananda's neo-Hinduism was an attempt to reconstruct the unity, history, morals, and destiny of this national self. Thus, some of the nuances of nationalism which Vivekananda Kendra has suitably imbibed through the Eknathji dialect (of RSS roots) are (a) the continued addressal of the nationalist problematic of the way to make Hindu religion compatible with universal values, (b) a philosophy of self-mastery through ascetic practices as one of the mainstays, and (c) sublimating the sensuous through an appeal to divine love experienced limitlessly for the larger community and the nation. In a Machiavellian sense, the energies of love, devotion, and attachment are to be reactivated towards larger social objects; in the case of the Kendra, it means service to the nation or national reconstruction. One of the mainstays of the *karyakarta* (*jeevan vratis* and *seva vratis*) training in Vivekananda Kendra is the emphasis on liberating the lower self to dedicate oneself to the service of the nation (Parameswaran, 2007).

Amritanandamayi Mission's version of Hindu nationalism places credence on Hindu symbolism and discussions on Indian cultural heritage as essentially Hindu. As per a monastic order member,

> Amma tells us that our job is to maintain and preserve Hindu culture – all that is Indian. With that approach we must work for our ancient scriptures and the Dharmashastras as they have all things that are required to lead a good and righteous life. The range is from sublime to this-worldly – they talk about higher things like *atman* [Soul] and Brahman [supreme soul] and worldly and tangible things like how to lead a life, importance of service, and other things. All these things are translated for us in a simple manner by Amma, and Amritanandamayi Mission is an embodiment of those very ideals which we follow. (Amritapuri, December 2011)

The sense of 'imagined community' of Amritanandamayi Mission adherents and the either/or logic that inadvertently, albeit subtly, accompanies it further feeds into a 'liminal' sense of religious/Hindu nationalism. It is liminal as there are no overt expressions owing to the equity–secularization endorsement. Amritanandamayi Mission on the national and global scenario is posited as a representation of the Orient – claims to nationhood/territoriality then naturally mature as essentially Hindu, with Amma as the face of the organization. Furthermore, she is the ambassador of the spiritual culture over which Hindu nationalism has sovereignty (as spirituality is considered the epitome of Indian culture).

In Art of Living, elements of Hindu nationalism are unearthed through Sudarshan Kriya as a metaphor of Art of Living; the assertions are essentially Vedic Hindu propositions under the garb of ancient wisdom and Sri Sri Yoga, with *sadhana* and *seva* as positional norms. With SK&P and SSY as representations of 'ancient wisdom', this forges a configuration of nationalism based on the 'high culture' of Art of Living, building into one nuance of Hindu nationalism. Apart from these 'primordial attachments', institutionalized devotionalism of Art of Living further intensified by media and virtual communication is also an element of the Hindu nationalist discursive field.

Hindu nationalism in HIFMs thus echoes a sense of belonging or membership to the Hindu commune. It has a genealogical meaning for HIFMs, as it enables roots-searching and attestation of traditions. Furthermore, it facilitates positioning in political engagements. Taking forward Sartori's (2003) argument that it can be viewed as a fetishistic expression of the logic of Hindu ideology to the mediating logic that structures capitalist society, some further propositions can be made. HIFMs' ideals and nationalism share a sort of common symbolic order. At both ends the 'nation-state' is the discursive field. From the semiological point of view, there are certain homologies: familism, patriarchical submissions, and spirit–matter/corporeal–incorporeal binaries. There is a natural clash with general acknowledged features of democracy as a sense of chauvinism prevails.

Somewhere, there are elements of representative politics, but there is a difference vis-à-vis historical version of Hindu nationalism. In terms of HIFMs, the Hindu nationalisms are ideological fragmentations preventing a seamless unity, so each HIFMs' version is like a single piece that forms part of a bigger mosaic: they all converge at the normative level to form the dominant collage. Deriving from Peter van der Veer's communalism–nationalism distinctions, HIFMs' face of Hindu nationalism is fairly moderate – accepting cultural pluralism and equality among different communes within the nation (Zavos, 1999), yet protruding its own lens pragmatically. The nation is constructed along with cultural configurations, and discursive frameworks are determined, based on the HIFM-designed Hindu faith developed from snippets of a distant sociocultural past. Teleologically, there is disenchantment with the current political rubric, and ideology comes as utopia within the state apparatus. Drawing from the primordialist-instrumentalist versions of Hindu nationalism as proposed by Christopher Jaffrelot, it can be said that HIFMs' version Hindu nationalism is instrumental (but not necessarily cynical) as it is constructed by re-interpretation of themes from the established traditions of Hinduism through the HIFM's ideological lenses. It is also a cultural strategy to preserve and defend Brahminical hegemony by the ideationally driven HIFMs. Schematic images and mental frameworks of the ideal Hindu social order are constructed to rationalize this as well as to modulate, defend, and make autonomous politics possible.

The fact remains that in this 'imagined community' in the Andersonian sense, HIFMs cannot tease out the varied Hindu philosophical thoughts, practices, and rituals. Hence, we cannot talk of a singular Hindu nationalism, but 'nationalisms' as they precipitate from Ramakrishna–Vivekananda teachings, and concepts propounded by Sri Aurobindo, Swaminarayan, Brahmakumaris, Chinmayananda, and other contemporary gurus. Epigraphs from the Hindu past have been used but modified in myriad ways, juxtaposing the 'other' and emptying them of their credibility. The key hagiographical-autobiographical-biographical works can serve to be texts which in the sense of Benedict Anderson's 'nation as a print community' can provide faith nationalist readings. The general central theme is divinizing the charismatic guru and their generous inclusion of the disavowed 'other'.

The charismatic gurus occupy a familiar-familial space, which draws adherents into the Hindutva fold. Further transnational affiliations are sought and promoted while espousing rhetoric of insularity, cultural pride/parochialism, and self-sufficiency. Drawing from Zavos's (2010) analysis, it can be said that HIFM's intentionality is seen in multilocal diasporic contexts where the Hindutva effect is fuelled. There is a kind of consciousness effect, which develops in the imagined connections through which HIFMs (and the associates) create mental pictures of a Hindu nation culturally organized along 'oneness' philosophy. Among the range which crafts the imagined connections there is a strong construction of the Hindu nation/homeland/rashtra/bhoomi, transported later in a multilocal discursive space, since all HIFMs have a translocal presence.

Camouflage: Secularization flavours and syncretic components

The secularization trend in HIFMs can be said to be, drawing from Pitulac and Nastuta (2007), a social filtering and incipient identification with macro-social processes. The announced premise is a response to modernity, and secularist claims of HIFMs institutionalize democratism and manifest integralism in the public space. At another level, secularization promotes a combination of pure and practical reason and legitimizes the return of the spirit or the 'religious' under the aegis of the secular state (Yildirim, 2010). It is not a strictly classical definition of secularization based on the axiom of religious decline or for that matter watertight sacred–profane compartments, differentiation, and privatization rhetoric. The peculiarity that emerges for the HIFMs is that there is a clear faith assertion alongside the modes of knowledge and sensibilities of modernity. Akin to Ronald Ingelhart and Pippa Norris' theory, existential insecurities are tackled and, simultaneously, faith supply–demand complex is tackled as well, thereby negating the classical dictums of secularization. This means that in a secular scheme of things and modernity frame, religious decline creates insecurities, a situation in which HIFMs intervene with their faith package. This package is such that it contains faith capital and monopoly of the cultural good of salvation and its management. The dimensions are so determined that they fit in seamlessly into the secular-modernity canon, with 'New Age faith goods' having high demand and correspondingly high supply from the HIFM end. From their mythical fund, the sacred is regained and communicated differently. Although there may be cultural-political context variations, the above-mentioned logic holds regardless of them.

Syncretism of HIFMs has a historico-graphical meaning as there are varied tendencies and inclinations for faith mergers. Furthermore, there exists a thin dividing line between the syncretic and the plural, as the latter comes into picture with spirituality gaining a regal entry in the faith discourse including aspects of meaning, moral compassion, and social connections having relevance across the spectrum of initiatives. HIFMs then join the pluralist produce through their salvation goods that embody and transform faith taxonomies at individual as well as communal levels.

Sri Aurobindo Society and Brahmakumaris have distinctive secular components and syncretic peculiarities. In other HIFMs, these aspects overlap under the garb of integration, harmony, and tolerance. In Ramakrishna Mission, shades of secularization and syncretism arise from the core Vedantic contentions of unity and oneness, which trigger components of cultural reciprocation and synthesis, particularly of local cultures, where there is an institutional presence. The underpinning behind the same is the celebrated 'harmony of religions' maxim of Sri Ramakrishna. However, the detour here is that alongside the episteme of syncretism, there is no reassertion of new cultures and identities as forms and modes of dissent from the hegemonic mainstream. Rather, there is a sociocultural co-option of sorts with the symbolic and concrete positions of Oneness. There has been a systematic shift from the mysticism of

Sri Ramakrishna, to a reinstatement of 'postcolonial', a reassertion of the Hindu stance (with Ramakrishna's tryst with the Brahmo Samaj), Swami Vivekananda's orientalist resurgence of neo-Hinduism,[5] and Vedantic ideals (with the ecumenical overtones of missionary work). The linguistification is essentially 'Hindu' – secularism and syncretism being synthetic addendums.

With respect to Swaminarayan Sansthan, although historically literature testimonies exist testifying for the incorporation by Lord Swaminarayan of non-Hindus into the sampradaya (Viveksagardas, 1977; Dave, 2000), the version of secularization–syncretism integration platform that persists in the contemporary times is that of tolerance. Shades of secularization and syncretism arise from the core contention of unity and oneness of Saibaba Sansthan, which trigger components of cultural reciprocation and synthesis, the underpinning behind the same being social tolerance. A different version of secularization and syncretism persists in Brahmakumaris' assimilative and proselytization frame, drawing solely on the fundamental tenet of 'accommodation', from the original etymology. At the first level, there is a dogmatic distinction between Brahmakumaris' stance and 'other' and subsequent acceptance of the dissonance between what they believe and what others outside Brahmakumaris believe. At the second level, Brahmakumaris posit their beliefs as objectively true, not by aligning to 'Hindu traditional metaphor', but by making reference to adherents' personal experiences, scientific rationalism, and other forms of culturally accepted academic discourse. In the words of a Brahmakumari,

> We are as a spiritual community tolerant of other faiths and spiritual beliefs. We hold and stick to our beliefs and philosophies and others also can do so. But those who come to Brahmakumaris realize the truth in what we are saying because they are open to the experiences. Brahmakumaris is not orthodox; it is a spiritual organization and that is evident

5 Particular reference needs to be made of Swami Vivekananda's efforts. Despite the imbrications in the colonial process and the unavoidable transformations in the social and ideological constructions through his voyages, Vedanta and Indic ideals were used to resist the typification and subjectification of indigenous people as passive objects in the 'Occident precipitated Orientalist discourse' (Basu, 2002).

> in its work on the local, as well as global, platforms. We do not advocate rituals and dogma; rather ours is a very scientific, transpersonal, and transcendental discourse. Raja Yoga is scientific and that has been proved by the studies. It has a systematic physiological, psychic, and spiritual impact and that is not drawn from only one particular religion. We have our own postulates just like probably what Dalai Lama does or the Transcendental Meditation technique which is quite popular abroad. Raja Yoga has the good points of all and is truly secular in its intent and spirit. It is open to all, irrespective of caste, creed, race, and nationality, and, like a true philosophy of emancipation, it has accommodated itself to the demands of the contemporary age. The main problem of the Iron Age is stress, and Raja Yoga is the correct formula to eliminate stress and lead a Godly lifestyle. There is nothing ritualistic about it. (Abu, June 2011)

The third form of syncretism in Brahmakumaris is the thesis of 'relativism' – all spiritual understanding is relative and, hence, a matter of personal faith. Thus, contrary to its original world tree thesis when all other faiths manifested in the Copper Age and were representations and manifestations of schism, disjuncture, and debilitating difference from the 'pure' religion of the Golden Age and associated monism; in the world-affirmation phase, 'relativism' is another face of its syncretic stance. This is evident from the following excerpt from discussions with a Brahmakumari:

> In the current world, no religion is inferior or superior. They all come from that one supreme God and are only variations in terms of belief systems and practices. Raja Yoga of Brahmakumaris is also a prescription of Godly life from Shiv Baba. But unlike other religions and belief systems there are no variations and modifications – the direct word of God is placed before all in the unadulterated form. That is why Raja Yoga is Godly knowledge and religion. When others get oriented, then they too realize the point that Brahmakumaris tries to make. We don't try to convert anyone – we just make people realize the truth in what we are saying. (Mumbai, June 2012)

Chinmaya Mission, with a keen take on Hinduism and Hindu culture as well as nation-building, has a thin crust of secularization-syncretism determined from the vantage point of Vedanta as a universal philosophy. Historically religious nationalism, or Hindu nationalism, has formed the subtle edifice of Sri Aurobindo Society; later on those being catapulted onto secularization and syncretism. Secularization endeavours are evident in the sanitized version of the conceptual basket – transcendence, supramental manifestation, divine life, and Supermind being the elements of the secularist collage. Within it, syncretic claims are evident through claims of universality and harmony. With respect to Vivekananda Kendra, the sole flavour of secularization and syncretism is the epistemological claim to universalism, In Amritanandamayi Mission, the secular face is predominant in terms of the beneficiary outreach of 'all castes, creed, and ethnic leanings', and syncretism is a sister concern with emphasis on 'harmonious integration of all religions'. Pertaining to Art of Living, shades of secularization and syncretism are evident in the interfaith harmony proposition – the micropolitics emerging when 'Yoga' is manufactured as secular and a universally exchangeable salvation good.

The consolidation and the episteme of praxis

From a practical point of view, in the HIFMs there is a coagulum; communalism, Hindu nationalism, secularization, and syncretism coagulate to form an epistemic praxis. With respect to Ramakrishna Mission, the episteme is akin to 'liminality'; there are contact zones of synthesis and in-between structures of consciousness oscillating between communal 'othering' and secular and syncretic tolerance. In Swaminarayan Sansthan, the sect politics has intertwined with nationalism to form newer fixations and categories of hierarchy.[6] In Saibaba Sansthan, there

6 Post the Yagnapurushdas schisms, the sect has been dominated by Patidars, Thakkars, Kathis, and Rajputs, and class dynamics have been further intensified within the sect social structure by the diaspora commune. Hence, the original schism in the name of the tailor-mahant Pragji Bhagat intending to subsume all followers from the traditional lower caste into the sampradaya (with reformist attitudes and the agenda of proselytization and sect expansion) has over the years assumed newer fixations and categories of hierarchy.

is an exhortation of ethical lineages which are comparable,[7] placed in interlocutory relationship with one another. This then leads to the origin of transcendence, translating into metaphors of tolerance, equity, and theistically emanated social justice.[8] Brahmakumaris' coagulum comprises of two aspects: New Ageification and relativism. Raja yoga, world tree theory, *murlis*, and the Adi Sanatana Dharma combine to give a New Age feel. Relativism is used as an astute strategy for alliance and allegiance building, with the motto that can be defined as the 'delivery of a reasonable message that fits into universal, acceptable, and rational scheme of things and yet simultaneously forwards the basic postulates of Brahmakumaris like "first among equals," as well as building camaraderie and allying translocally'.

The coagulum of Chinmaya Mission emerges as the Body–Mind–Intellect (BMI) chart.[9] The BMI chart, according to Locklin and Lauwers (2009), renders the Advaita message into an accessible, universal, and systematic form, beyond the limitations of its original Sanskrit and Hindu idiom – and it can travel. The Sri Aurobindo Society's face, as explained by Sanyal and Roy (2007), is that of Indian renaissance through the reception of the European contact, the reaction and partial assimilation of European influence, and the stage of new creation further gaining impetus by national education as a means to national consciousness. In Vivekananda Kendra it is the philosophy of spiritualism (or Hindu spiritualism) and search for man's forgotten soul as a metaphor for discovery of Bharat Mata or motherland (spirit of collective self or nation described as an extension of the individual self).[10] The coagulum with respect to Amritanandamayi

7 Sufi and Hindu ethics are compared continuously to demonstrate a comparison, with *Allah Malik* and *Sabka Malik Ek* epithets as well as Shraddha–Saburi tenets providing the necessary components.

8 Furthermore, through the historical references made by Saibaba on the life of Chokhamela, his assertions of Hindu–Muslim tolerance, a vision of universality grounded not only in the belief of oneness of God but also in the intuition of oneness of human nature provides pluralistic shades to the Saibaba Sansthan repertoire.

9 What was Chinmayananda's unique addition to the repertoire was the scientific interpretation (the BMI format) whence worldly material objects along with scientific enquiry force individuals to remain limited by the conditionings of the body, mind, and intellect. The Vedanta knowledge is the key to transcending this limiting state to experience the divinity within.

10 The Hindu past is reconstructed in order to demonstrate the universality of Hindu ideals and practices in history: nationalism to Swami Vivekananda was an act of self-

Mission is the emergence of Amma as the forerunner of packaging Indian spirituality and its hermeneutics in a universalist carton. In a translocal sense,[11] the stance is reformist and bourgeois, with transnationalism having solidified the 'Hindu' edifice on which Amritanandamayi Mission is based. With respect to Art of Living the characteristic components are SK&P, SSY, and the New Age dictum – guided by spiritualizing the secular (SK&P lends a spiritual angle to breath and breath control which is universally applicable) and secularizing the spiritual (SSY is looked at as a translocal salvation good, derived nevertheless from the 'ancient wisdom' of Vedas).

---

revelation, of going back to the origin of the Hindu self, and a Hinduism rising to self-consciousness. What Vivekananda Kendra capitalizes on is Swami Vivekananda's reversion to an ancient mode of Hindu religiosity (lost through historicity and re-found in the cultural treasure trove) eulogized sufficiently to form a postulate of universal enlightenment. Furthermore, as per Basu (2002), Swami Vivekananda's link between religion and nationalism is related to a deeper antinomy of a link between Hinduism and rationalism through a relationship of non-contradiction.

11 On the international platform, pilgrimage to Amritapuri, international migration (as per the statistics, around one-third of the Amritapuri residents are foreign nationals), and media images of the hugging saint Mata Amritanandamayi, as also international entourages of Amma and her monastic disciples, have lent a transnational experience to Amritanandamayi Mission.

7

Transformational Actors: Private and Public Agendas

Social transformation visions emerge from the main HIFM ideational stances and essentially reveal a 'sociology of hope' derived from faith, beckoning a divine fiat for change. For all HIFMs the order-power proposes both, transcendental and life-course-enhancing influences for the followers and associates. This is a sort of 'quest orientation', and the self is an important component of the discourse. Existential-social implications for followers are about creation of structures and meaning systems as also a cultural habitus. Social support and faith–well-being links are proposed. As actors in social transformation, HIFMs re-create genres and propose osmosis effects. Genre re-creation is in terms of insertion of the faith episteme into civic culture. Apart from the same, complementarity, demystification of superiority of 'secular' services, and collaboration/partnerships are also the genres. Osmosis is a sort of permeation of faith into the secular–profane fabric, which could be of the nature of faith–permeation, faith–centeredness, faith–affiliation, faith–groundedness, and faith–secular partnerships. This is taking into consideration the tangible expressive ways in which faith manifests in action/programmes. As transformational actors, HIFMs provide institutional forms and strategies of action. What then emerges is a sort of metamorphosis of HIFM ideals onto the third sector (more popularly known as the voluntary sector).

HIFMs' visions of social transformation

For HIFMs, their social transformation visions' core emanates from the charismatic guru and the main ideational/epistemic stance. There are meta dimensions and micro forms, with meta dimensions used as techniques, components, variants, and formulations that explicate and exemplify the social transformation core. Micro form or specialities of transformation are sectarian/community beliefs peculiar to certain HIFMs, such as 'ideal of familism or world family' of the Swaminarayan Sanstha, Brahmakumaris' Raja Yoga, Sri Aurobindo Society's Integral Yoga, and Art of Living's Sudarshan Kriya.

For Ramakrishna Mission, it is a movement from self-consciousness to God consciousness; the knowledge of the self essentially requiring a self-purification through selfless action (Adiswarananda, 2006). For Swaminarayan Sanstha, the core pathway to transformation (both personal and social) is the worship of Akshar Brahman, abiding by prescribed moral laws and incantations of the Swaminarayan Mantra. In the words of an office bearer,

> In one question-and-answer session, Pramukh Swami Maharaj has proposed that the future will be good if one worships Lord Swaminarayan and Gunatitanand Swami and obeys their commands. Also, moral and spiritual living means, according to Pramukh Swami, a residence in the Satyuga. Finally, reciting the Swaminarayan mantra always (which is 'Jai Swaminarayan') is the key to change, as it has cosmic influences. (Ahmedabad, June 2011)

Saibaba Sansthan purports the Archimedean standpoint of social transformation as connection with Saibaba – as the Absolute incarnate on this material world. The subservience under Saibaba's inclusive and all-encompassing scheme is perceived as the ideal way forward. To quote a Sansthan office bearer,

> When we come under the grace of Saibaba it is the most appropriate way as he alone prescribes the ideal way forward. His benevolent stance of unity is what is required in today's world and that is the change or transformation that we need. (Shirdi, February 2012)

For Brahmakumaris, the world drama wheel provides the organizational vision of social transformation. As per a Brahmakumari,

> The world of today is Ravan Rajya. The Brahmakumaris are the Siva Sakti Pandava Sena (the liberation army) who will bring about change. (Abu, March 2011)

For Chinmaya Mission, the summum bonum of the social transformation is the repackaging of the metaphysical consignment of Vedanta into a social philosophy, in particular, socialism. The belief then matures into the concept of 'Hindu socialism', which stems from the recognition of the supreme divinity that is the core of all. The universe is believed to comprise multiple expressions of the infinite factor and, hence, the need to live a life of 'mutual love, consideration, and charity'. Success of the notion of 'community' is contingent on this notion of oneness – striving for progress and welfare of society as a whole (Central Chinmaya Mission Trust, 1987a). This version of socialism is a departure from the scientific version of socialism towards moral and ethical versions, proposing that through the ethical lens socialism can be viewed to have desirable values like all ethical precepts that have universal validity. As per a member of the monastic order,

> It is this vision of oneness that is the harbinger of social change. At Chinmaya Mission we believe that in Hinduism rest all the ideals for a just and equitable society, as Vedanta contains the very sublime message of unity and all beings as manifestation of Godhead. This philosophy then becomes the essence of socialist thought. (Mumbai, September 2011)

Sri Aurobindo Society's core vision of social transformation comprises vision of divinity in all, divine life upon the earth, integral yoga as the future psychology, and the supramental realization as a hologram and metaphor for future evolution. The core of social transformation for Vivekananda Kendra is a reinstatement of Vedanta as a future religion as it is believed to be universal in its appeal and content (Advaita Ashrama, 1999c, 12e). Furthermore, Vedanta spiritualism is believed to be the world saviour vis-a-vis Western materialism as it creates an inclusive perennial religious worldview. In the words of a *karyakarta*,

> Empathy for others, identification with the larger community, and absence of a sense of discrimination were all inculcated and developed through Vivekananda's twin precepts of Bhakti and Advaita. Following Vivekananda's ideals, at Vivekananda Kendra we firmly believe that Vedantic spiritualism is inclusive and a source of all knowledge – right from metaphysics, to the discoveries of science, mythology, Gnosticism, and agnosticism; all can be fitted in with that understanding. Hence, Vedanta is considered as the appropriate way forward. (Kanyakumari, April 2011)

Amritanandamayi Mission's vision of social transformation is governed by utopian tenets of equity, justice, rights, and peace (MAM Trust, 2010). For Art of Living, the understanding of 'oneness' and 'equity' becomes the cornerstone of social transformation as they are perceived as the ethical way forward (Sri Sri Publications Trust, 2010c).

The meta dimensions and micro forms of social transformation

For Ramakrishna Mission, there are three meta dimensions: (a) human freedom as the ultimate goal that can be attained through knowledge of individual self and the Absolute Self, (b) the recognition of pluralism of thought and the coexisting juxtapositions of renunciation and service, and (c) the ultimate goal of transcendence and salvation of all beings. With respect to human freedom it means moving beyond imposed patronages towards higher goals, pluralism of thought is the accepted maxim of harmony of religions, and coexisting juxtapositions is a spiritual ministration that incorporates the transcendent and the real simultaneously (Adiswarananda, 2006). Hence, spiritual endeavours and service coexist, and this forms the raison d'être of social transformation, the ultimate goal of which is salvation. In a certain sense the social transformation vision of Ramakrishna Mission has a Nietzschean[1] feel – the desideratum of salvation and divinity of all existence providing the necessary parallels.

Swaminarayan Sanstha's vision of social transformation has an agenda chalked out within its contemporary frame that qualifies as meta dimensions and includes (a) harnessing youth potential by engaging them in the higher socio-spiritual care endeavour of Swaminarayan Sanstha; (b) collective sectarian philanthropy as 'giving in the service of God', which would, in the utilitarian sense, ensure the greatest good; (c) teleological ethics with Swaminarayan as the vantage point – qualified as purificatory ideals of compassion and character-building at the individual level, then catapulted onto the societal level; and (d) the culture of 'giving' as a symbol and metaphor of Swaminarayanization and divinity. Ascetics, or the sadhus and parshads of the Swaminarayan Sanstha fold, serve as proximate determinants of social transformation operationalized from an individual position initially. As per an office bearer,

> The main change in society comes from doing good to others, good thoughts, and keeping good company such as that of sadhus. Just as we cannot get diamonds from a hawker, similarly true knowledge of change cannot be obtained from anyone. Swaminarayan Sanstha sadhus can provide that. The joy one does not find in money and power is by doing good. Change in society can come if we associate with a bonafide satpurush (virtuous person) and engage in satsang. (Ahmedabad, March 2012)

With respect to Saibaba Sansthan, two blends of transformative attitudes are visualized, which qualify as meta dimensions: (a) faith-oriented consecration towards Saibaba and (b) pluralist vision which builds on the core syncretic stance of Saibaba.[2] Saibaba Sansthan's

---

1 Particularly the dimension of the 'superman' being able to rise above the restrictions of ordinary morality – the salvation rhetoric of Ramakrishna Mission is similar to the transcendence of the superman.

2 In terms of the first one, the tint is spiritual – akin to transcendentalism and transpersonalism. Parallels can also be sought in the scholastic theology within the Sufi

pluralism pre-empts a distinction between divine-in-itself (the *Allah Malik* dictum of Saibaba) versus the divine as humanly experienced. As the divine-in-itself is one (*Sabka Malik Ek*), pluralism (i.e., the fact that divine is experienced by followers differently) gains ground in the Saibaba Sansthan's transformative scheme of things.

The meta dimensions of social transformation vision of Brahmakumaris are characterized by three epistemic components: (a) the inevitable apocalypse, (b) the liminality of the confluence age and its accompanying praxis of Raja Yoga, and (b) the prophetic New Age advent facilitated by the incorporeal visionary, Brahma Baba. Here, 'New Age' is qualified by mental orientations of beings as soul incarnates of the Absolute, and, hence, the prerogative of those beings is to move towards a utopia of peace and harmony. This is substantiated by Brahmakumaris as follows:

> When there is degeneration in moral and spiritual values, the climax is reached. Then, God descends into the body of the old man who he names Brahma and through him he imparts Godly knowledge; teaches Raja Yoga which helps to inculcate divine qualities in human beings. This transformation of human beings then brings about the golden age again. Those who do not divinize themselves suffer destruction and also punishment of their evil acts. The purushottama sangamyuga, that is, the auspicious age, enables traversing from hell to heaven through the ladder of Raja Yoga. In this ladder, soul consciousness is the first step, second is the knowledge of God, the third is the faith in that knowledge, and finally the remaining steps are about purposeful remembrance of God. (Abu, March 2011)

realms and Jewish kabbalistic cosmology. As an ontological postulate, the pluralist hypothesis rationally promotes the postulation of a divine noumenal reality, named Saibaba, underlying and unifying the diverse phenomenal religions through a common ultimate referent (for their differential conceptions of the Real). Methodologically, there is a proposing of a 'revisionist' conception of, and approach to, religious diversity, involving the notion that the same soteriological process of human transformation takes place within the contexts of the differential religions and cultural traditions (the basic contention of Saibaba that Ram and Rahim are one). Then, the following methodological assumption is adopted: basic religious conviction that religious experience and thought mediate real contact with the higher reality, namely, Saibaba – also called 'in-principled veridicality' of religious experience and thought.

For Chinmaya Mission, social transformation is derived from personal transformation, the backbone of which is Vedanta. The firm contention is in the multifacetedness of Vedantic tenets to effect change and herald a corresponding ethically sound social milieu. For Sri Aurobindo Society, the core also comprises the following meta dimensions: (a) divinity in all, (b) divine life upon the earth, (c) integral yoga, and (d) supramental realization. Divinity in all emerges from the proposition of the beings as manifestations and attributes of the Absolute (Sri Aurobindo Ashram, 1993). Divine life upon the earth is understood as the descent of the supermind – bringing down of the divine consciousness into all parts of the being, which can happen through a synthesis of yoga. The major component of this descent is the human mind, to which Sri Aurobindo's philosophy gives major credence, and, thus, the entire vision is essentially idealistic. In Sri Aurobindo's words, and as explained and exemplified by a sadhak in the regular discourse sessions,

> A divine life upon earth – the ideal we have placed before us can only come about by a spiritual change of our whole being and a radical and a fundamental change, an evolution or revolution of our nature. The embodied being upon earth would have to rise out of the domination over it . . . into the greater consciousness and greater power of the being and the larger and freer life of spirit. (Pondicherry, August 2011)

Integral yoga as future psychology distinguishes between four elements that make up the totality of man's being – the conscious, subconscious, subliminal, and the superconscient (Dalal, 2007). In terms of supramental realization as a hologram and metaphor for future evolution, the position is that it transcends religion and occultism and endeavours to bring about an active change.

Meta dimension for Vivekananda Kendra is characterized by Vedantic socialism[3] with Advaita Vedanta as the base, entailing a realization of

3 What has been cardinal to both Marxian and Vedantic thoughts is the elimination of the feeling of alienation and attainment of self-realization. Where Marxian socialism has a materialistic substratum, the Vedantic version has a spiritualist base. Vedantic socialism proposes a climate of change through an arousal of spirituality and the practical interpretation endowed to the 'Hindu' concept of Vedanta. Traditional socialism,

the man as essentially divine and manifestation of that divinity as a way to overcome alienation. Amritanandamayi Mission's meta dimensions of transformational vision are derived from the core of human dignity, justice, rights, and peace. With respect to human dignity, parallels can be drawn to the Aristotelian/Marxian conception that the human being is a social and political being who finds fulfilment in relationships with others. Amritanandamayi Mission essentially favours a deontological conception of justice with benevolent sentiments and welfare state conceptions as *a priori*. About rights and peace, discourses of Amritanandamayi Mission have ideals of the 'human' as the component of the Absolute, reproducing norms of spirituality into human rights language and texts and transcendental arguments for the universality of peace and rights in ways that make possible, in good conscience, an awareness of the stretches of human and social suffering and its emancipatory quest (MAM Trust, 2010). Alignments are also seen with the Gandhian praxis of reconstruction and action. To quote a monastic disciple at Amritapuri,

> What Amritanandamayi Mission proposes as the vehicle of social transformation is 'saswata dharma', and as the Mahatma has proposed for our nation – 'punarnirman' and 'karma yoga'. All this happens from the Amritapuri Ashram which is not merely a cluster of inanimate buildings, temples, and trees, but the very embodiment of Sadguru's grace. Through the social and spiritual activities undertaken by the ashram, Amma is in fact leading us in accordance with ideas of justice, equity, and rights, all of which are ideal forums for applying karma yoga attitude. This then leads to the restructuring of the spiritual DNA of not only the individual but the society as a whole. (Amritapuri, December 2011)

Social transformation for Art of Living Foundation has twin formulations: collective quest for perfection and pure knowledge that facilitates the expansion of consciousness. The first aspect is the dissertation on perfection, which is in turn of three kinds: in action or

according to Vivekananda, would retain the proletarianization of the masses Vedantic socialism would naturally alleviate (Parameswaran, 1987).

work, in speech, and in feelings and intention. Dispassion (*vairagya*), discretion (*anasuya*), and spiritual practice (*sadhana*) facilitate this perfection (Vyakti Vikas Kendra, 2005a). Pure knowledge becomes then the knowledge of consciousness which is beyond time and space – the understanding of 'oneness' and 'equity' then become the cornerstones of social transformation as that feeds into the ethical desideratum. In a discourse compilation titled Punarnava (meaning transformation and rejuvenation; Sri Sri Publications Trust, 2009), the following excerpt from Sri Sri's talks corroborates the aforementioned:

> Pure knowledge is that knowledge which should lead you to that beautiful point of 'I don't know.' The purpose of knowledge is wonder. The completion of knowledge leads you to amazement and wonder. It makes you aware of this existence. Consciousness is beyond time and space, it is all just vibrations. The essence of life is to experience me not just in the body, but 'me' expanded in 'everybody'. Enlightenment is that state of being mature and unshakeable in any circumstance – come what may nothing robs the smile from your heart. All that exists in this universe belongs to me and that is enlightenment. It is not identifying with limited boundaries and feelings. The whole evolution of man is from being somebody to being nobody and from being nobody to everybody. Enlightenment is a rare combination of innocence and intelligence – it is the core of our Being. This body belongs to the earth, and the mind belongs to the unseen Big Mind in the universe, which is responsible for all three – growth, maintenance, and dissolution. When you become hollow and empty you experience the presence of the Big Mind. Awareness nurtures the intellect, Belongingness nurtures the heart, and Commitment nurtures life, which together bring direction to our lives; transformation is by observing this ABC of life. (Sri Sri Publications Trust, 2009, pp. 1–8, 27).

Micro forms refer to certain specificities of transformational visions peculiar to certain HIFMs. Four HIFMs under study (Swaminarayan Sanstha, Brahmakumaris, Sri Aurobindo Society, and Art of Living) have micro forms which qualify as signature statements of social transformation vision. With respect to Swaminarayan Sanstha, the micro forms are (a) subjectification of the 'other' who is in need of 'joy, goodness and progress', and the Swaminarayan Sanstha followers are believed to have the ability to provide and fulfil these needs and (b) the penetrating ideal of 'familism' – sentiments of 'world family'. The penetrating ideal of 'familism' – sentiments of 'world family' (Vasudhaiva Kutumbakam) is propounded with propositions of theistic equality of all. The affirmation and internalization of this ideal of 'familism' by Swaminarayan Sanstha followers is believed to be instrumental in transformation.

For Brahmakumaris, the Raja Yoga technique is perceived to be the raison d'être of transformation techniques which is further elucidated by a Brahmakumari:

> Raja yoga is the only means for social change and the coming of the golden age once again. This is because it is based on soul consciousness and God consciousness. The mind comprises different layers and to keep that state of mind eternally happy the consciousness must be changed – the 'I' orientation must move to soul and God orientation. It is only Raja Yoga which can do this and hence facilitate the movement from the crime age to the divine age. (Abu, March 2011)

With respect to Sri Aurobindo Society, the transpersonal psychology of integral yoga and the tenet of supramental realization comprise the micro forms. In terms of supramental realization, there are three phases which categorically invite transformation: 'psychic', referring to intellect and emotion; 'spiritual', referring to ideation and spirit; and 'supramental', referring to the supermind (which happens with the descent of the supramental or the divine being which reconciles opposites and promotes a oneness of consciousness. This is the operational version of Sri Aurobindo Society for universality (Saint-Hillaire, 1963). In Art of Living, Sudarshan Kriya is the signature micro form which is inherently perceived to be ameliorative.

This transformation quest, drawing from Trompf's (2000) cross-cultural analysis of millenarian beliefs and change in the history of religions entails (a) a sociology of hope of a specifiable faith kind as a supra-human fiat is beckoned; (b) final resolution and cosmic salvation in which a divine comfort is sought within the anxieties of temporal existence anchored through the HIFMs; and (c) a meta-technological engagement[4] referring to the fact that the transformation envisaged by HIFMs is in line with divine techniques and that followers need to engage with it sufficiently to operationalize the same. Furthermore, there is a utopian restructuring through negative dialectics typically borne out of a consciousness of unacceptance of the extant, and a quest for that which has 'not yet evolved, is supra-rational and attainable only through spiritual rigour' – a task towards which HIFMs are essentially geared. There is a historical re-visioning of an innovative kind – a bricolage of text, HIFM teachings context, and the discursive social space – the level-playing field.

Life course-transforming implications for followers: Views of HIFMs' order–power structure

For all HIFMs, the order-power proclaimed transcendental life course implications for followers, adherents, and associates – transcendence was defined in terms of alleviation and establishing connections with the Absolute. Existential-social implications are also proposed by HIFM order-power in terms of cultivating a cultural habitus, faith-based social capital, and enhancing the quality of life in practical ways, but from the lens of faith.

Transcendental implications

The Ramakrishna Mission order-power proposed a mystic elevation and transcendence through the Advaita tenet. To quote a senior Swami,

> The Advaita philosophy as experienced by Sri Ramakrishna and subsequently developed by Swami Vivekananda provides at once an inexplicable mystic growth and a transcendence or an upwards movement towards existential developments

4 This term has been adapted from William Tremmel's terminology by Trompf (2000), referring to the fact that things are done with techniques appropriate to Gods that will make them work on behalf of humans. Meta-technological operations assure participants that textually or prophetically disclosed promises of the divine are true and that 'the followers' require engagement with the spirit order to actualize those promises.

which are intellectual in nature – a studied development of the mental faculties and cognitive abilities happens. (Belur Math, May 2011)

For their own self, the experience of Swaminarayan Sanstha sadhus-parshads is a transcendental allegiance with Godhead, as 'becoming one with the Pragat Brahmarup'. What keeps the ascetics going is the strong spirit of surrender and internalization of sect-based institutionalization, and for parshads (the new recruits) it is the 'spiritual wealth' and a romance of life dedicated to the service of the Lord. Unlike the Advaita conception of the unseen – God as a higher power and Absolute soul with attributes – the contention of Swaminarayan philosophy has mass appeal in that it is held that the God as Lord Swaminarayan is seen, tangible, has a human form, continues to be embodied in the spiritual heads, and offers moral/ethical precepts which give definitive normative-ideational base to existence. For the followers, the perceived transcendental implications are alignment and rendezvous with the Godhead himself (a rare prospect not available to the hoi polloi) and opportunities for salvation that transcend gender.

In terms of Saibaba Sansthan, the transcendental implications are that of divine realization through Baba's teachings. Transcendence is the quest and attainment of the seemingly ephemeral and transpsychic. Owing to these transcendence feelings a relationship of obligation is established with Saibaba, which devotees call the Rinanubandh (obligatory) relationship. To quote an office bearer,

Being a part of this organization, in itself leads to growth. One is able to experience the divine because of that. In a world full of conflict and difficult choices, Baba's teachings provide a light and hope for understanding and realizing the divine. There is guidance from within and hence, the miracle of inner transformation happens with association with Saibaba Sansthan. We are in a constant state of indebtedness to Baba, because it is because of him that we exist. He is the source of all our joys and sorrows – he is our friend, philosopher, and guide. We are able to seek answers to questions such as what is life and what is the secret of permanent happiness. (Shirdi, February 2011)

Transcendentalism, soul consciousness, and God communion are the life-course implications of association and involvement with

Brahmakumaris. In particular, the virtues of Raja Yoga are elaborately extolled. To quote a Brahmakumari,

> Raja yoga meditation changes a person's internal physiological response to the environment or circumstances, thereby adapting more behavioural responses to life's pressures. It provides physiological and psychological rest necessary for the body to replace chemical resources replaced by fight-or-flight responses, excessive fear, anger, and chronic distress. Through Raja Yoga one is connecting with God. By tuning in with the supreme, all suppressed dissatisfactions are dissolved and one feels free, light, and satisfied. Raja Yoga essentially promotes natural well-being; tuning in mind to God increases will power, deep experience of peace, love and purity, as the original attributes of the soul results in a natural aversion of therapy, and creates a real and inwardly felt emotion of repulsion towards an unhealthy habits. (Abu, July 2011)

Furthermore, some in-house publications also discuss the health efficacy of Raja Yoga in scientific terms (PBIV, no date). One of the assimilative strategies of Brahmakumaris is the 'transplantation of divinity/soul/special "being" qualification' onto individuals who come in contact with their network. This essentially operates through the extension of the interpretation of the 'world tree' thesis and, in particular, the 'transcendental souls' therein who would survive the apocalypse. The prophecy is that '16108' would be the number of Brahmakumaris in the end (i.e., those who finally emerge survivor victors post the catastrophe), who would then herald the 'New Age'. Those who come in connect with the magical '16108' (either in this life, or in the past, or in the future lives, as there are believed to be 84 births all across the time span of 5000 years), either in real or clairvoyant terms, are the 'fortunate' souls. So, willy-nilly all currents followers, ordinary users, or the serious searchers are 'fortunate', transplanted with the divine status. In the words of a Brahmakumari at Abu headquarters,

> Those who come in contact with us in one way or the other are the divine souls ... those who will remain in the coming

> satyuga (golden age). In the current confluence age, they have had the fortune of the Godly knowledge because of their good deeds in the past lives. It is only action that determines birth . . . the main effect is that once they recognize their true selves, the souls . . . the divinity embedded in them, they adapt to the right life that is necessary for spiritual growth. (Abu, July 2011)

Hence, as a life-course implication, the advanced version of soul consciousness (which also functions as a proselytization strategy) is the transplantation of divinity – the germination of which is through the popular 'world tree–world cycle' thesis.

For Chinmaya Mission, the transcendental implications perceived are the grace of Chinmayananda deified and venerated post the transcendental and transpersonal experiences of audiences of the historical discourses or *jnana yagnas*. The second transcendental implication entails the initiation into 'true Hinduism' (Chinmaya Mission institutionally being a vanguard of Hinduism and Chinmayananda's unabashed claim of 'introducing Hinduism to Hindus') as a universal spiritual-ethical-moral apparatus endowing ontological security. For the more serious followers, the addendum to the above is the 'supreme understanding of Advaita philosophy as true knowledge' (Tejomayananda, 1995, p. 46). This contrivance bestows the sincere Chinmaya Mission seekers with a salvation good of unquantifiable use value and high-end cultural exchange value (particularly in the trade-off relationship between occidental materialism and orientalist spiritualism). In the words of a swami,

> For the sincere seekers, they are exposed to the very deep understanding of Advaita Vedanta. This benefits them in terms of priceless soul knowledge. In terms of their social role, this knowledge is useful in spreading the real knowledge of our cultural heritage and replacing timeless spiritual values in this world of materialism. (Mumbai, February 2011)

Transcendental experiences, divine light attainment, sense of communion with the agenda of the Supreme, and rendezvous visions have been some of the life-course experiences described by the Sri Aurobindo

Society sadhaks. The attainment of 'divine life' is the very concept of a sense of Presence of the Mother which the sadhaks experience (Mehta, 2003). Rendezvous visions are described as 'the potent touch of the grace of Sri Aurobindo and the Mother'. To quote a sadhak,

> In association with Sri Aurobindo Society one feels that life is a field of manifestation of the divine consciousness. Things that are difficult at the material level become possible with the grace of the divine Mother. That is when we feel the upward upliftment which is transcendental. One need not know, or even accept, the human form of the Mother; still if one is deeply or sincerely pining for the divine mother, he is sure to get the response – the divine light. The whole body must be made up of the 'heart' and become the 'heart' itself, then alone she can fill the body with Her presence and divine light constantly. Through this prayer to the personal divine, the Mother makes us feel that one has participated in the divine's action plan. She embodies love and grace and knows what is good for every being on this earth. She is aware of the pathways laid down for humankind in general and will work out the scheme for all accordingly. We always say that 'let thy will be done and not mine' – which means that we surrender to the Mother and allow her will to work in our material being. For she alone knows what is best for us. (Pondicherry, August 2012)

In terms of transcendental life-course implications, the order and power of Vivekananda Kendra extol virtues of Yoga, the package practiced and delivered at Vivekananda Kendra. Furthermore, the yoga–Vedanta dyad as an individual good is perceived to have self-reproducing and exalting capacities. In the words of a *karyakarta,*

> The main thing has been the four texts on Yoga as written by Vivekananda. His Raja yoga explains the unity of the 'being' and the cosmos through the control of the mind. Karma yoga reveals oneness through work without material desires. Bhakti yoga looks at the reverence to the divine, and Jnana yoga proposes the ethics of 'not I, but thou'. All these are the core

> to existence and development of human being and humankind in general. (Kanyakumari, April 2011)

For Amritanandamayi Mission the transcendental implications are that of the Integrated Amrita Meditation (IAM) meditation technique and the 'embrace' which is characteristic of Amma. In terms of the IAM technique, the focus is on breath control and meditation on a concrete object (distinguishing thereby between the subject and the object), with the purport to enhance concentration and thereby consecration. Transpersonalism is operationalized in the characteristic Amma 'embrace', implying for the followers a sense of well-being. This is an illuminative epistemology of sorts, which proposes a theory of knowledge by physical presence of Amma – the charismatic teacher. Social memories are created of this embrace as a pre-sentient intuitive phenomenon that is believed to have therapeutic properties.

For Art of Living, the transcendental self–world connections are facilitated, through the pillars of sadhana, satsang, and seva. Furthermore, the Sudarshan Kriya technique is firmly believed to provide the pathway to transcendence.

Existential-social implications

For Ramakrishna Mission existential-social implications entail a congruence of terrestrial and supramental phenomena through the service ethos of divinity in man. In the words of a swami,

> Sri Ramakrishna's main teaching was 'siva jnane jiva seva', meaning service to beings by seeing the potential of divinity in them. This is very important because through this we are at once able to be in this world and realize the divine. The service ethos of Ramakrishna Mission is very unique. We see the potential of Godhead in all and our service principles are guided through that. So even when we are working at the brass tacks of life, we are continuously having our personal trysts and realizations of divinity. This is a very important teaching of the divinity not being out there but very much here. The higher philosophical explanation is that when 'this' and 'that' merge – divinity comes alive. That is what exactly happens through our seva. (Belur Math, May 2011)

For the Swaminarayan Sanstha followers, the existential-social implications are perceived by the order-power as vistas of upward mobility in the sect's social structure (swaminarayanization) by abiding by ritual prescriptions, sect culture, and participating in all activities that lead to self-enhancement for followers coupled with life-skills development. Particularly, with respect to the component of self-enhancement and life-skills development, the group work culture in Swaminarayan Sanstha has visualized a paradigm shift from a pure purpose of religio-spiritual teaching orientation and cadre development to a laissez faire package incorporating aspects of general knowledge and leisure games. This shift from ritualism to liberalism has been in response to the diaspora influences and urbanism of Swaminarayan Sanstha (headquarters shifted from native Bochasan to urban Shahibaug, Ahmedabad). Hence, instead of sole discourses on the Swaminarayan faith and its tenets, there are also activities for life-skills development, arenas for vocational skill development, and practical training sessions. For beneficiaries of the several social projects, the implications perceived are fulfilment of material needs through an exalted mission like Swaminarayan Sanstha, arenas for rendezvous with the sect, connection with members of the sadhu–parshad fold and other Swaminarayan Sanstha senior devotees, and the opportunity to align to Swaminarayanism as a continuing tradition. In the words of a woman office bearer,

> Our beneficiaries of various projects are very fortunate. At one level, Swaminarayan Sanstha sadhus and volunteers take care of their material needs. Especially in remote villages where we have our projects, the people benefit from the vicharan activities of our sadhus. People get to connect with them and eventually they also have the chance to join the Swaminarayan fold. (Ahmedabad, March 2011)

For Saibaba Sansthan, it entails 'enhancement' which is connected to the aspects of growth and personal gains of tangible and intangible nature. For the 'instrumental' and 'eclectic' users (see Walliss, 2007), Brahmakumaris provide an arena for provision of spiritual solace – the quintessential 'soup for the spiritually parched soul'. Raja Yoga is viewed as the core mechanism through which divine virtues are cultivated. These divine virtues then enable God communion and a transcendental movement from sheer body consciousness. With respect to Chinmaya Mission, there are realist practical implications perceived and emphasized, such as concrete influences of the ethereal Vedantic knowledge on followers' lifestyles and mentalities, which include rising above and transcending negativities and thoughts, dissolution of fear, and introspective capabilities. To quote a senior swami posted at Ellayapalle ashram,

> All Chinmaya Mission followers are advised to look within and silently search – this is possible through the art of slowing down. One should create no opinion about what one perceives, but create space, let others have their opinion, and choose one's own thoughts carefully. One should rise above negative thoughts, delay negative reactions, build relationships without expectations, and avoid publicizing negative attitudes. Fear should be dissolved by meditation in solitude and understanding the transitory nature of things. There is also a need to rise above thoughts by avoiding compulsive thinking, recognizing source of thoughts, and cultivate mindfulness. Through the power of silence, the deep recesses of the mind are reached and followers can then conquer the mind by practice and dispassion. (Ellayapalle, October 2011)

In Sri Aurobindo Society, the efficacy of integral yoga is described from a consciousness-oriented integral psychology lens. Thus, integral yoga is believed to have life-changing and existential-social implications for followers. The transformation is through change of consciousness. There are also studies describing the efficacy of integral yoga from a consciousness-oriented integral psychology lens. Some of the interpretations about integral yoga include: integral yoga is a reversal of consciousness, it is integral psychology concerned with the exploration and understanding of the totality of human phenomena, it is also psycho-cosmology with the primacy of consciousness, it is integral psychotherapy based on existential Vedanta, and it is a yogic method that facilitates transformation of oneself to be in communion with the universal consciousness.[5]

---

5 Dalal's (2001) proposition is that yoga in general, and integral yoga in particular, leads to a reversal of consciousness – a complete turnover of consciousness that takes place

For Vivekananda Kendra, the Vedanta–yoga dyad is converted as a durable lifestyle translating into existential ethics of frugality, cosmocentrism, and preference for alternative technologies. Three other perceived existential-social implications for Vivekananda Kendra associates include (a) amity with Indian (read Hindu) culture/cultural heritage, (b) renewing links with antiquity, and (c) safe-depositing cultural capital for posterity to help followers from the general public emancipate from impending moral avalanche. In the words of a *karyakarta*,

> Yogic lifestyle promotes restricted consumption, control of the mind and senses, and living in harmony with nature. Surya

at each radical transition in the evolutionary ascent of consciousness: the emergence of life from matter, the emergence of mind from life, and the evolution of overmind into supermind. Sherazi (2001) discusses that integral psychology is a psychological system concerned with exploring and understanding the totality of human phenomena. It is a framework that not only addresses the behavioural, affective, and cognitive domains of the human experience within a singular system but is also concerned with the relationships between the above-mentioned domains in the context of human spiritual development. It is a system that, at its breath dimension, covers the entire body–mind–psyche–spirit spectrum, whereas at its depth dimension it encompasses the previously explored unconscious and the conscious dimensions of the psyche as well as the supra-conscious dimension traditionally excluded from psychological inquiry. Integral yoga as parallel to integral psychology has principle tenets as wholeness of personality, different levels of consciousness, importance of all phases and areas of experience, need for personal integration and the concept of integral self-realization, doctrines of transformation and motivation, and the method of integral experientialism. Within it, the metaphors of personal integration are the reconciliation of opposites; a shift from state of fragmentation to state of wholeness; the unification of mind, body, and the spirit; and a journey from unconsciousness to self-consciousness to super-consciousness. Shraddhavan (2001) describes Sri Aurobindo's psycho-cosmology as a paradigm wherein exists a complementary relationship between involution and evolution, which implies that evolution has a purpose, and each individuality is a projection, a partial expression of some divine consequences which in the involution become ego. In describing integral yoga as parallel to integral psychotherapy, Cortright (2001) has described it as an exploration of is-ness which, when we have a spiritual aspiration, allows us to penetrate more deeply within in our journey to awaken to the psychic being and *atman*. It is a movement that begins with the existential surface of our empirical self and ends with the essential spiritual experience of our central being. In this way integral psychotherapy can be thought of as existential Vedanta – a psycho-spiritual practice that involves exploring our lived experience so that our physical, vital, and mental self is the most coherent, vibrant, and fit vehicle for our inner being; more purified and, therefore, more capable of a wholehearted surrender; more calm and, therefore, able to hold the peace from above and within; and more integrated and unified and so more capable of a single-minded aspiration for the Mother and for the Divine.

> Namaskar, mantra meditation, and use of Ayurveda/nature cure methods are all aspects that Vivekananda Kendra followers abide by. Those who come in contact with Vivekananda Kendra get to understand the real Indian/Hindu cultural heritage. The emphasis that we lay on reading and understanding the scriptures and the multilingual translations that are available do precisely that. We even hold Gita chanting competitions for schools through which, right from a young age, students learn the richness of our scriptural content. This connection brings links with the ancient heritage – something which tends to get forgotten in the routines of life. This knowledge can then also be preserved and transmitted to the next generation so that there is no moral degradation. Several material aspects attract people today, especially the younger generation. But to rise above them and do higher things in life, we need anchor points. Vivekananda Kendra has managed to preserve a trend of spiritual knowledge which is actually over a hundred years old. The main thing is now to translate it to the next generation for their spiritual and moral upliftment. (Kanyakumari, April 2011)

A link is envisaged between the individual associate, the Kendra, and its vision of national reconstruction. To quote a *jeevan vrati*:

> Vivekananda Kendra develops individuals through yoga and that is the correct path to national development. For, when all individuals adopt the yogic lifestyle then the nation is bound to develop, as true values are instilled through that. Vivekananda Kendra associates are engaged in self-transcendence . . . that automatically builds into a larger face of change. The very formulation of Vivekananda Kendra is such that its ideals naturally have a larger significance. When a smaller group adheres to them, the effect flows. (Kanyakumari, April 2011)

Association with Amritanandamayi Mission is seen as (a) enabling the strengthening of the followers' faith and roots with Amma's faith culture, (b) as a source of activity engagement and providing a spiritually productive leisure-time activity, (c) as enabling the propagation of the teachings of Amma, and (d) as promoting an understanding of a perspective to altruism and work/service inspired by faith. In the words of a Swami at Amritapuri,

> Those who align and associate themselves with Amritanandamayi Mission naturally get geared towards understanding our ancient scriptures better. That is because Amma's teachings are based on them. Then they are better in tune with their faith allegiances. Even small children who come to Amritanandamayi Mission regularly can recite significant portions from difficult scriptures. That is the effect of Amritanandamayi Mission. They become rooted in the ancient traditions. Amritanandamayi Mission followers get to enrich themselves, grow spiritually, and use their spare time in a productive manner. Instead of wasting it in material and futile pursuits, at Amritanandamayi Mission they are exposed to the richness of our Indian spiritual heritage, get re-energized, and also find spiritual solace in the work that they do. Amritanandamayi Mission followers get the unique chance to spread the divine words of Amma which are true words of wisdom. She epitomizes truth, light, and the timeless path. She is the embodiment of love and service which forms the base of all the humanitarian activities that this organization undertakes. The greatest miracles that take place in her presence occur in the hearts of those who come to her – the gentle and gradual awakening of love, compassion, and selflessness. All disciples of Amma get to understand and imbibe the true meaning of philanthropy, service, and altruism which comes from her teachings. (Amritapuri, December 2011)

Art of Living teachers say that association with Sri Sri and his ideas means having (a) dexterity in social adaptability and personal transcendence, (b) rendezvous with the 'art' of living based on Vedic values, and (c) Sudarshan Kriya as a powerful tool for health and well-being. In the words of a senior Art of Living teacher,

> Association with Art of Living either as a volunteer or as a beneficiary allows a person to adapt positively with one's environment and also be more in touch with the higher power – a feeling that one is aspiring for the right things in life and not getting immersed in its impermeabilities. Art of Living teaches us ways to improve our lives and live life to the fullest and in the best possible manner – adjusting to contemporary demands and yet keeping our roots alive. Some of the core things are to understanding life's impermanence, making meditation a part of life, prayer as a vital tool, focus on self-enhancement and improvement continuously keeping in mind one's limitations, counting your blessings, undertaking seva both in a planned and spontaneous manner, lifelong quest to learn, and aspiration to attain the divine. All this is explained by reference of the ancient texts. That way one is in touch with traditions and yet one is able to see their relevance in today's world. (Mumbai, May 2012)

Sudarshan Kriya and Pranayama are looked at as having life-changing implications with carefully planned course outlines and curriculum.[6] Furthermore, the Art of Living teacher said:

---

6 Apart from verbal testimonials there is a body of systematic scientific literature examining the efficacy of SK&P procedure for health and well-being: Bhatia, M., Kumar, A., Kumar, N., Pandey, R.M., and Kochupillai, V. (2003) Electrophysiologic Evaluation of Sudarshan Kriya: An ECG, BAER and P300 study. *Indian Journal of Physiological Pharmacology, 47*, 157–163; Brazier, A., Mulkins, A., and Verhoef, M. (2006) Evaluating a Yogic Breathing and Meditation Intervention for Individuals Living with HIV/AIDS. *American Journal of Health Promotion, 20*, 192–195; Brown, R.P., et al. (2005) Sudarshan Kriya Yogic Breathing in the Treatment of Stress. Anxiety and Depression: Part 1 – Neurophysiologic Model. *Journal of Alternative and Complementary Medicine, 11*(1), 189–201; Brown, R.P., et al. (2005) Sudarshan Kriya Yogic Breathing in the Treatment of Stress, Anxiety and Depression: Part II – Clinical Applications and Guidelines. *Journal of Alternative and Complementary Medicine, 11*(4), 711–717; Descilo, T., Vedamurthachar, A., Gerbarg, P.L., Nagaraja, D., Gangadhar, B.N., Damodaran, B., et al. (2009). Effects of a Yoga Breath Intervention Alone and in Combination with an Exposure Therapy for Post-traumatic Stress Disorder and Depression in Survivors of the 2004 South-East Asian Tsunami. *Acta Psychiatria Scandinavia*, 1–12; Janakiramaiah, N., Gangadhar, B.N., Naga Venkatesa Murthy, P.J. (1998) Therapeutic Effects of Sudarshan Kriya Yoga (SKY) in Dysthymic Disorder. *NIMHANS Journal, 16*(1), 21–28; Janakiramaiah, N., Gangadhar, B.N., Naga Venkatesa Murthy, P.J. Harish, M.G., Subbakrishna, D.K., and Vedamurthachar, A. (2000) Anti-Depressant Efficacy of Sudarshan Kriya Yoga in Melancholia: A Randomised Comparison with Electroconclusive Therapy (ECT) and Imipramine. *Journal of Affective Disorders,*

> SK&P facilitates everything for a person – it gives support, enables relationship building and maintenance, coping with changing roles, stress and anxiety, provides a pathway to transcendence, and most importantly, allows one to be in harmony with self and others through dispassion and detachment. (Mumbai, May 2012)

Hence, HIFMs order-power claim a mothering of spiritual maturation for the followers through the association. This is then labelled as a *valued state of consciousness*, socially constructed by HIFMs as mystical visions or non-material visualizations and mindfulness. There are also indications of God consciousness and spiritual openness/quest orientation as perceived to be derived from the association. Furthermore, this transcendence is not agreement with doctrines/dogma but an intrinsic orientation towards belief in, and reliance on, a higher power as defined by the guru or a prescribed technique which then influences followers' well-being.

Drawing from Guthrie and Stickley[7] (2008), it can be said that association with HIFMs is then supposed to result in an altered state of consciousness for followers through experiences/enlightenment. That is the reason, for the followers, the perceived implications are at once existential-social and transcendental. Parallels can also be drawn to Heinz Kohut's self-psychology[8] – particularly notions of self–object and transmuting internalizations. Akin to Kohut, the transcendence specified by the HIFM order-power comprises three self–object experiences of

---

57(1–3), 255–259; Kochupillai, V., Kumar. P., Singh. D., Agarwal, D., Bharadwaj, N., Bhutani, M., and Das, S.N. (2005) Effects of Rhythmic Breathing (Sudarshan Kriya and Pranayam) on Immune Functions and Tobacco Addiction. *Annals of New York Academy of Science, 1056*, 242–252; Vedamurthachar, A., Janakiramaiah, N., Hegde, J.M., Shetty, D.K., Subbakrishna, D.K., Sureshbabu, S.V., and Gangadhar, B.N. (2006) Antidepressant Efficacy and Hormonal Effects of Sudarshan Kriya Yoga in Alcohol-dependent Individuals. *Journal of Affective Disorder, 94*(1–3), 249–253; Gangadhar, B., Janakiramaiah, N., Sudarshan, B., and Shetty, K.T. (1999) *Stress-related Biochemical Effects of Sudarshan Kriya Yoga in Depressed Patients*. Bangalore, India: NIMHANS..

7 Guthrie and Stickley (2008) have undertaken a qualitative study based on a small group of clergy in the UK exploring their views and perceptions on the relationship between spiritual experience and mental distress.

8 The important goal of Kohutian self-psychology (Heinz Kohut) is to look at updating individual's spiritual internalizations by bringing them in conscious contact with individual's changing experiences of reality (Amarasingam, 2009).

idealizing, mirroring, and twinship (like non-duality; Amarasingam, 2009) – the object in the case of HIFMs being the guru or teacher who is essentially charismatic. These experiences then become necessary for a cohesive sense self of the followers, the sine qua non of HIFM associateship. Transcendence implies that the self–object relationship experiences are not emotionally driven or compulsively dependent but are characterized by freedom and mature, transmuting internalization. Herein an individual/associate is perceived to possess a chance to participate with the supra-ordinate self's scheme.

Drawing from Carr[9] (2000) and Black (2000), it can also be said that the perceived existential-social implications lend an external and internal validation to individual's faith – through the social function of faith and the idea of personal wholeness. The range of perceived existential-social implications for associates by the HIFM order-power demonstrate traditional orthodox views, psychologistic/positive psychology explanations, and organic/transcendental/mystical visions. The idea is that HIFM engagement leads to enhanced exceptional experiences, including transpersonal trust, social support, and sense of support. Regular practice of meditation and associating with an HIFM to provide seva has stress-annihilating impact aiding cognitive and psychological processes. Life environments are believed to be influenced by HIFM faith modelling,[10] which, akin to the social cognitive theory, is a kind of social learning process influenced both by availability of suitable behavioural models (the guru in this case) and by intra-individual factors, such as motivation and self-perception. There is also an inimitable link between faith and well-being. As per the paradigms of Indian psychotherapy as described by Hoecke[11] (2006), existential-social perceived implications present the

9 Carr (2000) has used object relations theory, especially the concept of transitional object, to link religious thinking and psychoanalysis.

10 This is parallel to the philosophy of the Spiritual Modelling Inventory of Life Environments (SMILE) measure of perceptions of spiritual models, defined as prominent people who have functioned as exemplars of spiritual qualities such as compassion, self-control, and faith.

11 Hoecke (2006) has described three paradigms in Indian psychotherapy: the Bhagavad Gita paradigm, which guides the individual to larger macrocosmic domains instead of exploring the edges of individuality; the guru–chela paradigm, which focuses on authority, context, and morality instead of normality; and the *abhyasa* paradigm, which accentuates the interpersonal dimensions of the therapeutic relationship.

struggle of beingness and HIFM association as transcendental. Certain shifts take place through this – from general value orientation to HIFM authority orientation, from individual choice to follower/associateship drive, and from absolute morals to definitions of transcendence as determined by HIFM ideals.

HIFMs as actors in social transformation: Re-creating genres and osmosis

HIFMs have relationships with other bodies such as civil society, state, and translocal bodies in terms of re-creating genres through the faith–service link and osmosis. They have demonstrated an apparent exchange, a consortium of collaborative and consociational relationships with them.

Creating/re-creating genres of Hindu-inspired service

Ramakrishna Mission creates a genre of Hindu-inspired service in the following ways: (a) the movement posits a pioneer brand of Hindu religiosity/spiritually oriented social service owing to its historical existence and involvement in an array of social initiatives, (b) it depicts a genus of amalgam of this world and the higher world (particularly the apophthegm of 'atmano mokshartham jagat hitaya cha', that is, a simultaneous self-transcendence and social orientation), and (c) it develops an 'indigenized and Hinduized' version of ecclesiastical and ecumenical ideals of love and service through congregational endeavours. Evangelical influences are prominent through history, which also builds into its very name as the 'Mission'.

With respect to Swaminarayan Sanstha, genre creation/re-creation is visualized through the formation of a religio-spiritual panopticon-like structure creating realms of spiritual-social discursivity. What is established is Swaminarayan Sanstha as a historical formulation of the Kathiawad social-geographical context and a more transcendent variation of the qualified dualist Vaishnavite theology. The 'social' emerges from this very stance – the simultaneous portrayal of historical social leanings of the founder and his apostles, and the 'social' as a package deal of the contemporary assimilative stance. Swaminarayan Sanstha now takes pride in maintaining its sectarian exclusivity but simultaneously maintains with alleys and tributaries of 'social outreach' through its social service projects.

In Saibaba Sansthan, two dimensions emerge: one is the creation of the faith-based organizational habitus on the edifice of the social memory of Saibaba, and the other is the temple–institution–service nexus. To quote discussion with a Sansthan office bearer,

> The Saibaba phenomenon is so vast that it has a spread throughout and our service activities only strengthen the local base. We have created a devotee brand loyale (devotees whose *ishta devata* – sole deity or Godhead is Sai) among those who reside here in the nearby areas. This has actually generated a human resource base for the organization based on the logic of altruism. . . . Those who stay in other places and have the means have started their own small *mandals*, *sanghas*, and *sansthans* at their own levels to replicate the model of Saibaba Sansthan. The capital they begin with is Sai grace, and the rest all just follows. So, along with devotional and ritual activities, they also undertake social service initiatives at their local levels. (Shirdi, February 2012)

In terms of the temple–institution–service nexus, what Saibaba Sansthan creates is a genre of faith-based social service institutions where tradition and modernity coincide. There is a traditional temple in the form of the Samadhi Mandir with an elaborate darshan iconography as the core source of revenue. The institution is the registered trust functioning as an organization, and the revenue generated is utilized through this trust, which functions as a lynchpin between the much-venerated temple structure and the 'society' (this refers to the devotee–beneficiary group which forms the raison d'être of Saibaba Sansthan's social service compass).

Brahmakumaris' millenarian legacy creates its own genre, which then percolates into the agenda of spirituality-propelled 'change' and transformation. The 'problematics' of the present age are presented which then are supposed to herald the inevitable apocalypse. The advent of the 'New Age' has to be facilitated in that scheme of things by a contention 'beyond rationality, reason, and exacting science', which is currently held as a reserve with Brahmakumaris. In sync with the 'New Age' parlance, 'apocalypse' is presented as the antagonisms and contradictions in the current scheme of social issues which cannot be disputed (such as war, natural calamities, corruption). Change is presented through projecting Brahmakumaris' social service efforts as ideal/exemplary, complementing/supplementing state efforts (the seva–governmentality argument). The genre that Brahmakumaris like to fit in is that of a 'spiritually attuned organization with social leanings'.

The genre of Chinmaya Mission is that of an organization rekindling Hindu ideals and reaching out to society simultaneously through service projects. As a faith-based movement relying on Hindu ideals, Chinmaya Mission re-creates genres for other organizations projecting the universal and inclusive nature of Hinduism, which combines at once the proliferation of Hindu thought and secular social service. Other organizations are allied organizations and sister concerns, secular funding bodies, state, Hindu revivalist/renunciant organizations with whom Chinmayananda had historical connections (Divine Life Society, Anandashram, Shankaracharya Maths), and contemporary religio-spiritual organizations (such as Vivekananda Kendra, Divine Life Society) with whom there is an aspect of camaraderie and lateral collaboration (in the form of participation in commemorations and conventions).

Sri Aurobindo Society creates a genre of combining transcendence and tangibility being reified in the practical action of social service projects. There is a translation of traditional Vedic tenets into a post 'modern' and post 'colonial' frame of reference which is shown as the hallmark of 'universality' and 'harmony'. Then, there is a 'cultural transportation and catapulting' from faith in the classical sense to spirituality in the contemporary sense. So, the original works of Sri Aurobindo on interpretations of Vedas, Upanishads, and the Gita, then take the form of abstract terminologies and conceptualizations of supramental manifestation and integral yoga. Effectively then these postulates shift focus from the ephemeral and abstract to that of a hybrid position on 'practicalities of life' and 'integral living'.

In terms of the genre re-creation, Vivekananda Kendra posits to other stakeholders, as a 'postmodern' version of a Hindu missionary who can be, at once, secular in intent and outreach. The 'postmodern' turn arises from the recognition of the public face of religion akin to liberation theology. There is a pragmatic operationalization of divine teleology; discourses move beyond conventional theology to express the 'political image of religion' (Jennings, 1985; Vries & Sullivan, 2007). In this quest for the political face of faith, there is a level of fuzziness in the sacred–secular dichotomy which reveals a genre of militia mores: coexistence of the transcendent and immanent/antinomian with equal prudence. For instance, the loyalty to Hindu scriptural study is equivalent to the level of loyalty in secular partnerships in service projects to fulfil goals and needs. Functional norms are moulded with ease to abide by state/secular funding prescriptions, making operations fuzzy. This fuzziness is in itself a mirage, as patterns of faith–secular spasmodic interplay are not always predictable. To quote a *karyakarta*,

> The Kendra has managed to maintain Swamiji's dream and carry it through the ages. We have preserved the Hindu scripture heritage, culture, and knowledge and are able to also modify it to suit the modern-day requirement. This is particularly evident in our natural resources and rural development projects where we make use of age-old indigenous ethics, knowledge, and technology but deliver it in a manner to suit modern-day requirements. That is the model that we present to all our partners, funders, and collaborators. Also, when partners and funders require us to modify certain terms and conditions when we ask for funding, we do so. We may not make drastic changes, but when we are clear that we want social change, some modifications are also necessary from our part. (Kanyakumari, April 2011)

With the range, nature, and focus of Amritanandamayi Mission's work, the members of the order believe that genres are re-created in terms of demonstrating a faith-based habitus employing ethics of unconditional love and compassion, orientation towards people-centeredness (combining both Amma's followers and novice adherents), and Amma's 'maternalism'; that is, the guru's embrace and expansive agency is seen as facilitating social service. In the words of a swami,

> All the social service done under the aegis of Amritanandamayi Mission is a model. It has its own league. We combine professional service delivery but also render it with Amma's

> touch, and all beneficiaries get double benefits when they also get Amma's embrace. (Amritapuri, December 2011)

In terms of re-creating genres, Art of Living, through its social leanings, proposes to establish a faith-based development trajectory – an organizational profile with a twofold self–society orientation. This is further operationalized through repackaging traditional wisdom in modern parlance. As per an Art of Living teacher,

> We show what it means to be a social and politically conscious spiritual movement. Most of Art of Living ideas are about the eternal question of self. Who am I? – This is the main question. Especially in the world of multiple attractions and acute consumption, we forget ourselves, our core in the process. What organizations like Art of Living do is to enable us to get in touch with our inner selves. (Mumbai, May 2012)

Osmosis within and outside: What does it mean for HIFMs and their social mandates?

Positing sacred as the organizing principle and service as the lever, there is an osmosis effect in Ramakrishna Mission. Organizational ideational norms create a Hindu collegiality. There is a collocation of Hindu philosophical tenets and practical spirituality along with a sense of an already extant culture of 'social service sentiments' or 'seva' as embedded within it. This projects the Ramakrishna Mission service model as distinctive. To quote a monastic member,

> What we do is not just charitable work; it is *jiva seva* with the *siva jnane* mandate. We do service with the sense of divinity in all beings. That way there is a detour of tradition, and we create our own form of social service inspired by Ramakrishna–Vivekananda ideals. (Belur Math, May 2011)

In Swaminarayan Sanstha, the osmosis effect is seen through the BAPS sect-based habitus creation and perpetuation of moral imperatives proposed by 'God' himself (Lord Swaminarayan, the founder). Social service and sociality is then the linking pin – a component of God connection eventually moving into sect consecration. As per an office bearer,

> One of the main aspects of Swaminarayan Sanstha service activities is that, apart from fulfilling the basic needs of people, we are also able to generate attachments and loyalties to the Swaminarayan way of thinking and living. For other organizations, this is like a model because in ordinary social service activities, there is a sense of detachment. People take/avail of the services and then move on. Here, they get attracted to the very ethos, the very philosophy with which we function, our morals, ideals, the anchor that we provide, the rootedness with traditions, and a 'we' feeling that comes with being fellow Swaminarayan followers. (Ahmedabad, March 2011)

Tangible social service has an osmosis effect within and outside the Saibaba Sansthan. A sense of collegiality for Saibaba Sansthan exists with the state apparatus, since as a pilgrim centre, and as one of the biggest sources of revenue through individual/devotee donations, it is an important source of revenue for the Maharashtra government. Saibaba phenomenon is reasonably dominant in constituting and reproducing a particular form of society based on asymmetrical exchange[12] – apart from the traditional market-driven economy and polity-driven state structures. Positing Saibaba as the charismatic organizing principle beyond boundaries and social service of the Sansthan as the lever, the osmosis effect then leads to a routinization – eventually only those aspects are institutionalized which have elective affinity with the followers of Saibaba or at least those who accept his authority. As per a Sansthan office bearer,

> Although Saibaba Sansthan does not formally collaborate, it nevertheless establishes a compatriot relationship with the state, other organizations, and bodies which it encounters

12 Here one can also talk about Neubert's (2008) notion of dépense, that is, the expenditure, which is made by people, driven by faith, without any expectations in return. This defies the traditional rational-choice models in economics, which propose that people spend when the return from the expenditure is equivalent.

> in the work process. If not similar, at least there has to be compatibility in ideas and ideologies and a basic belief in Baba. (Mumbai, June 2012)

Osmosis in the Brahmakumaris is of the two forms which retains their uniqueness and, at the same time, draws devotees. First, they have developed and maintained communes of followers despite their offbeat philosophy and invented traditions. Second, they oscillate comfortably between exclusive norms and assimilative/accommodative ideals. This keeps their distinctiveness intact and at the same time draws more followers into their fold through their range of tailor-made programmes comparable to 'modern' training sessions, albeit with a 'New Age' philosophical flavour.

Chinmaya Mission projects itself as a vanguard of Hinduism, true knowledge, and 'Indian' (Hindu) culture. They claim their stance to be pure and superior, and osmosis is through a process of selective routinization – eventually only those aspects are institutionalized/imbibed from outside and within where the 'scripture/tradition' superiority/authority of Chinmaya Mission is maintained. To quote a member of the order,

> Chinmaya Mission is pure in its ideologies – we associate with likeminded organizations on issues and things as and when required. That is the openness of Chinmaya Mission to external influences. We collaborate when our ideas and approach is accepted; long-term collaborations are generally dependent on that. Agencies such as NORAD and similar other organizations have accepted our ideology as the appropriate way forward and are willing to understand and accept our worldview. Those kinds of relationships are sustainable. (Mumbai, May 2012)

In Sri Aurobindo Society, the osmosis effect is seen in terms of development of a virtual and literal community of recipients of the Divine Grace of the Mother. There is thus a selective routinization or bridging – within and outside; in keeping with the catholicity in functioning and administrative rigour, coalition (even for social service projects) is sought primarily in those aspects that fall in line with the larger mandate of Sri

Aurobindo Society. Otherwise, the communitas sense is primarily at the nonfigurative consciousness level. To quote a sadhak,

> All the people who are in direct and indirect connection with Sri Aurobindo Society become one large commune as they are all under the fold and protective grace of the Mother. The divine grace binds us, but administratively we have to keep a distance. Yes, there are influences – both ways, but exclusivity is also important. We collaborate when from both ends there is compatibility without excessive compromise. (Pondicherry, August 2011)

In Vivekananda Kendra, with respect to other organizations, the osmosis effect takes two forms: (a) an ethnocentricity originating from the Vivekananda allure transferred through historicity and (b) a historiographic construction of 'Hindu' and 'Hindu allies' imagined commune on the Vivekananda edifice. As a vanguard of Vivekananda's Advaita Vedanta and 'man making [*sic*] nation building' mission, As a vanguard of Vivekananda's Advaita Vedanta and 'man making [*sic*] nation building' mission, Vivekananda Kendra perceives its moral superiority vis-à-vis other organizations and society at large. From the Vivekananda Kendra lens, all perceived associations with 'significant other' bodies is in the Hindu spirit – the associations either made with those to self (Hindu) or allied to self (supporting Vivekananda/Vivekananda Kendra/Hindu stance). To quote a *karyakarta*,

> Vivekananda Kendra has managed to maintain Swamiji's dream and carry it through the ages. We have preserved the Hindu scripture heritage, culture, and knowledge, and are able to also modify it to suit the modern-day requirement. This is particularly evident in our natural resources and rural development projects where we make use of age-old indigenous ethics, knowledge, and technology but deliver it in a manner to suit modern-day requirements. That is the model that we present to all our partners, funders, and collaborators. Most of our associates support our ideology, believe in it, and see the relevance of it in today's world. (Kanyakumari, April 2011)

In Amritanandamayi Mission, osmosis is through the creation of a transbordered imagined community of Amma's followers as spiritual aspirants and recipients of her iconic embrace. There is a transactional relationship for the followers between obtaining Amma's love and performing service; hence, service to Amma is equated to service to humankind.[13] To quote a swami,

> Serving Amma's children is like service Amma herself. And Amma is so magnanimous that everybody is her children. So when we serve society, we serve Amma. (Amritapuri, December 2011)

In Art of Living, osmosis is visualized through (a) spiritual communitas among the followers, (b) a habitus of 'other-worldly-and-yet-this-worldly' alliances, (c) spiritualizing of the cognitive domains of the followers, and (d) brand establishment of 'social' orientations of contemporary faith. On spiritual communitas as an osmosis effect, in a senior Art of Living office bearer's words,

> What is formed in Art of Living is a community where people are not always actually connected but they are still forming a commune at the psychic level. (Udayapura, April 2012)

A habitus of 'other-worldly-yet-this-worldly' allegiances refers to the simultaneous quest among the followers for self-transcendence and social transformation through service engagements. Spiritualizing of the cognitive domains of the followers is by giving them a 'salvation good' in the form of Sudarshan Kriya. This popular Kriya is believed to combine the package of devotion, silence, inwardness, love, and service, giving the followers both an inward orientation and an outward social sensitivity. Eventually, there is a brand establishment of the Art of Living Foundation's spirituality, which is not just abstract but concrete since it talks about the unseen and unknowable through the very tangible and material (love and service). For Art of Living, *seva* as a tangible and material component is a prescribed pathway to the ethereal aspiration of transcendence.

---

13 See Copeman and Ikegame (2012) for a discussion on the equivalence of *guru seva* and *manav seva*.

Genre re-creation is in terms of varied proformas of coalescing, apparently juxtaposed, notions of 'transcendental' and 'social', inserting the 'exclusive' faith episteme into the 'inclusive' and profane discourse of development. In a way, the HIFM genre re-creation implies ways in which faith shapes civic culture. Drawing from Til and Ross's (2001) historical mapping of philanthropy–voluntary service and the emergent themes, HIFM genre re-creation elaborates a story of (a) 'antecedent and complement', referring to linking of voluntarism vision with faith-oriented values of meaning and service; (b) 'apostasy' in terms of demystifying the notions of superiority of secular service, particularly with its bridging claims; and (c) 'auxiliary and alternative', in terms of connecting with third-sector realities through partnerships and collaborations through which tangible realities are shared.

Finally there is osmosis, which refers to an 'impressionist permeation' within and outside. Drawing from Sider and Unruh (2004), it can be said that the forms of osmosis are of the nature of faith–permeation, faith–centeredness, faith–affiliation, faith–groundedness, and faith–secular partnerships. This is taking into consideration the tangible expressive ways in which faith manifests in action/programmes. Some questions on HIFMs' osmosis effects pertain to the nature of visible faith expression and multiple levels of osmosis in the faith–secular continuum, sometimes even of a counterintuitive nature. Further looking into the osmosis process to decode how the faith factor figures and whether it is intended/unintended is a matter of further deliberation.

Assertions in the realms of the third sector: HIFMs as transformational actors

For the third-sector/voluntary initiatives, HIFMs take on different institutional forms and devise strategies of action through which they metamorphose themselves into transformational actors.

Demonstrating institutional forms

The institutional forms are (a) faith-oriented frame of reference, (b) sectarian faith-based initiatives, (c) juxtaposed coexistence of re-traditionalization and reflexivity, (d) institutional model of transforming world-rejecting philosophies into world-accommodating ideology of praxis, and (e) postcolonial, postmodern faith–social nexus. Ramakrishna Mission, Saibaba Sansthan, and Art of Living represent a faith-oriented frame of reference as an institutional form. As per a swami at Ramakrishna Mission,

> Through our service work, we can show other NGOs what spiritual organizations like us can do for society . . . we are an example of how spiritual organizations like ours not only talk about abstract philosophical things but also demonstrate in terms of action. (Belur Math, May 2011)

To quote a teacher from the Art of Living Foundation,

> Our work combines spirituality and service. We base all the seva on spirituality. This can be a model for development. (Mumbai, May 2012)

A Saibaba Sansthan office bearer said:

> Through the donations that we get and the work that we do, it only shows the power of faith in Saibaba. We contribute to state revenues. That also goes into development work. (Shirdi, February 2011)

Swaminarayan Sanstha posits itself as a sectarian faith-based initiative in the civil society and social realms, engaging in collaboration with the establishment by supplementing its efforts through the wealth of the adherent–volunteer support base at its disposal. Swaminarayan Sanstha posits as an intermediate sphere between the household and the state, with the object of promoting a democratic sociopolitical culture with the sect's moral philosophy at its base. Hence, this portrays that democracy as an ideal depends not only on the state but also on groups outside and within the Indian context; the sect-based stance of Swaminarayan Sanstha is one such sphere. It promotes the possibility of concerted action and civility towards its adherent base and civil society at large (even through the interests and perspectives of the latter group differs).

For third-sector/voluntary initiatives, Brahmakumaris are an institutional metaphor for the juxtaposed coexistence of 're-traditionalization' and 'reflexivity' (Walliss, 2007) – epistemes through which 'social' needs are met. Through apparent projections of 'autonomy' and 'choice' (in its instrumental form as signifiers of reflexivity), routinization, codes, and mores are reinforced.

Chinmaya Mission is an institutional model of transformation of the metaphysical world-rejecting Vedanta, to a praxis-oriented world-affirming/accommodating contrivance with an universalist appeal and 'modern' sociopolitical ideals of equity, fraternity, and liberty. Furthermore, it posits as a faith movement capitalizing on the religious capital in terms of value systems which are instrumental in nation-building. With respect to Sri Aurobindo Society, there is a postcolonial reinstatement of an institutional form, a typology of an institutional actor whose core is cosmic consciousness deriving from notions of theistic existentialism. Vivekananda Kendra, at the ideational level, is a form of faith movement aligning to neo-Vedanta. It disconnects the ritual in favour of a more radical action on the man's part – a form of spiritual action where the self of man has to be directed to renounce society and the material world in order to serve it. Amritanandamayi Mission projects an institutional form with a clear faith–social nexus drawing from Amma's allure.

Faith-based institutional forms stand in sharp distinction to the institutional theories of secularization (Carp, 2011), giving place to faith in the public sphere. It can be said that the attempts are to transplant faith into the social structure, divesting, or in a way deprogramming, *a priori* notions of the private role of faith and cultivating sensibilities in favour of HIFMs.

Strategies of action

There are strategies of action that demonstrate differential faith-oriented sacral modes of functioning as also a sacred public/private partnership (see Ikegame, 2012a). In Ramakrishna Mission, Saibaba Sansthan, and Art of Living, the strategies of action demonstrate a postcolonial flavour, the starting point being the belief that cultural hegemony of the occident still persists in different forms; complete cultural and social autonomy has not been attained. Furthermore, the postcolonial angle comes with attempting to undercut thematically and formally the discourses that support colonization: myths of power, race classifications, and imagery of subordination. This is done typically through a glorification of the classical orient which brings in narratives of social development and modes of cultural analysis that are discounted by the 'Western' approaches. A senior swami at Ramakrishna Mission said:

> What big organizations like WHO and UN do for the country still has a Western angle to it. We have to show through our work that we also have the capacity and the resources to bring change. Ramakrishna Mission has a wealth of spiritual resource owing to the Ramakrishna heritage. As a pioneer organization in this direction, we now have the responsibility to transfer this spiritual resource into a social change tool – using the strengths in Indian culture. (Belur Math, May 2011)

Despite operating within the same legal and political frameworks of secular civil society, Swaminarayan Sanstha operations are guided by sectarian notions. It discounts the purely 'reasoned' origin of values and notions of public and collective good, the starting point being the practical philosophies as embedded in Shikshapatri and Vachanamrutam – a duty-oriented language characterized by obligations towards Lord Swaminarayan and spiritual successors and the sect in general. Simultaneously, there is also a belief in transformation and a concern for justice.

With respect to Brahmakumaris, in the social intervention realms, three levels of strategies of action are seen: (a) tangible service, (b) buffet of 'spiritual remembrance' (vis-à-vis spiritual amnesia) designed to appeal to different palates (depending on health interventions, peace initiatives, or correctional settings work), and (c) the eventual presentation of Raja Yoga as the undisputed gourmet delight (for instance, in the prison setting, the entry point is understanding tangible needs through the officials. This is followed by the first contact course whereby the felt needs and stress/violence-triggering factors/vulnerabilities of the inmates are understood by Brahmakumari members. The subsequent courses are of instrumental nature and then there is the final presentation of the 'true knowledge' open and accessible to those who have 'arrived'. The basic course ends with an exhortation to participant-inmates to align with advanced courses which they are privileged to have a passport to by having undergone the basics; Pandya, 2013b).

In Chinmaya Mission, akin to neoclassical theism, there are theistic elements of contingency, becoming, and variability without diluting the theological components of the constancy and necessity of Vedanta. Furthermore, in its contemporary form it has modified its original RSS–VHP supportive stance to further assert its identity as a faith movement with 'noble' ideals albeit 'pure Vedantic ideologies'. This is done through a critique of 'world negation', renunciation, extant social structure, and stratification. Chinmaya Mission has identified of theological sources on universal love and compassion and reclaiming them as critical texts (such as the Narada Bhakti Sutra which talks of divine love) as one strategy to project the Mission's social service operations as inclusive and universal. Finally, the strategic focus is on developing a pragmatic spirituality which emerges from moral categories of praxis such as nonviolence and peace.

In Sri Aurobindo Society, issues of imbalance of the cosmic order and disharmony are considered as *a priori,* sources of which may be colonization of the lifeworld and distortion of worldviews. Strategic action entails that through spirituality catalogues, the effort should be to reinstate harmonized worldviews and transcend to larger macro-cosmic domains with metaphors of equity, transcendence, and reverence for life. The eventual outcome is defined as cosmic transcendence and synergies of being and becoming (Saint-Hillaire, 1963).

Vivekananda Kendra as a faith movement uses religion as a political ideology, and its philosophy of empowerment takes the form of a religious discourse. There is a belief in the divine inevitability of the rise of the subaltern through 'man making [*sic*] and nation building' along with 'spiritually oriented service'. For the same, the 'Arise Awake' clarion call is used in a liberation theology way. Vivekananda Kendra's urgency lies in making the metaphysics of Advaita and the Hindu idiom 'social' so as to correct the anachronistic presence of modernity in a society which has its own inclusive and universalist culture. To quote a *karyakarta,*

> At Vivekananda Kendra, although our main focus is revival of Advaita as a universal thought, we connect with the larger society – even people who are the most vulnerable for whom at present such philosophies may not have meaning, for eventually through this powerful philosophy they will also rise towards Godhead. We believe that for nationalist action to become

> meaningful, it should have the idea of social and economic liberation. With Vedanta as the base, both the purposes of national appeal and indigenous cultural rootedness are served. Further, this stand does not separate but puts up a stand where the Hindu religion is in a dialogue with Western rationalism. (Kanyakumari, April 2011)

However, Vivekananda Kendra's organizational critique of development/modernity is not romantic, albeit realist and interventionist in intent, with the contention that in a society under domination, liberation can come through a form of rigorous social service that is advocated as the ultimate spiritual act. Finally, this 'Arise, Awake' apophthegm and 'spiritually oriented service' epithet are utilized to mould an intensely political simmering sectarian saffronized proposition (Eknathji's founding of Vivekananda Kendra was in several ways lending an acceptable faith movement shape to an unfinished RSS dream) into a metaphysically oriented spiritual organization reified by sublime service notions.

In Amritanandamayi Mission, there is an emphasis on the macro role of religiosity- and spirituality-inspired humanitarian activities as a pragmatic operationalization of Amma's divine teleology. As per a monastic order member,

> Amritanandamayi Mission is a demo to the world about what a faith-based spiritual organization can do for society. In particular, it is a form of non-profit with a clear ideological base rooted in our traditions. (Amritapuri, December 2011)

Strategies of action encompass the recognition of HIFMs' political role in the framework of a pluralist–corporatist dichotomy. This is compounded by the perceived HIFMs' salience in discourses on civil society and development and their partnering in the political agenda of faith-fuelled identity politics. HIFMs' strategies of action somewhere can also be seen to promote a revitalization of public religion – beyond simple moral-spiritual regulation of the private space. Hence, there is a multi-tier engagement with public policy, sociopolitical processes, and direct intervention, deploying faith as a socio-political and socio-cultural construct. Strategic drawing on elaborate spiritual-moral values represents an important adjunct to the secular development discourse. Intense transnational networks coupled with embeddedness in political contests and governance processes hone these strategies further. Probably, what also emerges is a faith-governed entrepreneurship supported by a historical precedent, institutionalization, search for legitimacy, and leadership influences.

Some aspects of strategic management are also visualized, which according to Miller's (2002) analysis of religious organizations in the context of US, can be analysed well from the resource-based and institutional perspectives. HIFMs have unique spiritual products and collective production of faith, which distinguish them from other organizations. Furthermore, they operate through intangibles such as brand image, epithets, and apophthegms. These serve to be the operational resources on which strategies of action are designed, simultaneously managing tensions between tradition and innovation. Such resources are promoted by HIFMs in order that the ideational core is preserved while simultaneously stimulating innovation in action (for instance, practical Vedanta, Raja Yoga, Integral Yoga, SK&P and SSY, as well as the IAM techniques all have a Hindu philosophical base and are core resources for programmatic action for HIFMs). This is also a sort of contextualization in which traditional beliefs are re-enacted while sustaining ongoing innovation in action. The gains from tradition are supernatural compensators, and innovation in action means projecting HIFMs' contemporary relevance/ legitimization. Tradition also becomes a resource for competitive advantage for the HIFMs; impetus is further gained through alliance-building in programmes, with tradition as the advantageous fulcrum of negotiations. Institutionally, for all HIFMs, a sense of 'strictness' governs the modus operandi. The determinants of strictness are monastic-ascetic and follower demographics and preferences – HIFMs elicit from them high levels of commitment and resources as a form of premium pricing. This strictness in a way also guides HIFMs' performance. HIFMs have also gone beyond traditional 'religious economies' literature in terms of looking at state-establishment as exogenous determinants of action. Rather, their programmatic engagements signify that they seek to build alliances of the nature of economies of scale with varied network patterns that prove beneficial in the long run. This then promotes accommodation (which sometimes give a secular–profane feel) and organizational renewal.

Metamorphoses: Transformational acts

The discourse on HIFMs' role in social transformation eventually projects metamorphoses as concretization of newer genus and unconscious assimilation of HIFM ideas into domains of secular and profane and vice versa. Metamorphoses of newer genus and transposing HIFMs' ideals onto the secular–profane plane can be said to be a kind of transitional-transformational collateral while ensuring continuity within the social fabric. Giving a faith twist to popular ideals and inserting faith in perceived vacuums are the norms of penetration of Hindu nationalism. Drawing from Collins (2002) it can be said that HIFMs have a sort of implicit tendency to articulate their ideational presence in several spheres in order to promote consciously and/or unconsciously their organizational identity, posited in consonance with the social canvass.

Several forms of metamorphoses qualify in HIFMs as transformational acts. In Ramakrishna Mission, there is a certain faith-based institutional isomorphism that has set in. With the pioneering missionary efforts of Ramakrishna Mission, a genre of faith-oriented spiritual service initiative emerges. The larger claim is that of 'Indianness' in the initiatives vis-à-vis the 'Western' – Ramakrishna Mission as metaphorically linked to 'Indian' with its overarching mandate of Vedanta and *seva*. The words of a senior swami at the headquarters corroborate this:

> We demonstrate an Indian touch to the voluntary sector – our ideals are deeply rooted in Indian thought, and so Ramakrishna Mission can be seen as a model of social initiatives rooted in Indian ideals. (Belur Math, May 2011)

With philosophical and religio-spiritual renditions as the base, Swaminarayan Sanstha institutionally catapults this to aspects of social existence and consciousness by remapping subjectivities (self is viewed as 'beingness' in the larger realm of existence which is taken cognisance of). What it engages in appears to be a transcendental dialect ('what ought to be' from the Swaminarayan Sanstha religio-spiritual lens), thereby engaging in several ways in a critique of modern reason.

In Saibaba Sansthan, there is a glorification of the classical orient, which brings in narratives of social development and modes of cultural analysis that are discounted by the 'Western' approaches. To quote a Sansthan office bearer,

> Right from Baba's times the focus has been on the indigenous and the Indian. Though Baba did not physically live to see the end of the British rule in our country, he was always of the opinion that these British forces are outsiders and they will ultimately have to leave. He gave great importance to indigenous systems of beliefs and practices and that continues till today. Saibaba Sansthan in all its work, whether spiritual, charitable, or service, believes in an Indian approach rooted in traditions. (Shirdi, February 2011)

In Brahmakumaris, two components are seen: (a) persistence of tradition as a source of moral and identity-conferring authority and (b) the manner in which such persistence becomes a site of personal reflexivity and bricolage (Walliss, 2007). The peculiarity is that Brahmakumaris' *Weltanschauung*, or worldview, is based on the founder's vision of the end of this corrupt world and the emergence of the New Age that is totally unlike the present. Thus, while it may act as a social conscience on one level, wanting to share its values for a better world, this better world is in no way connected to this world, except perhaps in its nullification. For the third sector, Brahmakumaris are a classic case of a 'utopian sect' in the field of social service, in an almost shadow–light interplay of proselytization and world accommodation. Interestingly, the outcome is not either/or which essentially adds to the ambivalence.

Chinmaya Mission movement stands for some metaphysical/philosophical postulates, demonstrating a 'philosophy in praxis' for a third sector, which include: (a) Vedanta of Adi Shankaracharya as giving a universal formula for action and (b) Chinmayananda-Tejomayananda as vanguards of an organic wholeness in worldviews that seeps into social spaces thereby enabling a 'modelling' of grounded non-state action.

Transcending orient–occident binaries, the eventual institutional shape of Sri Aurobindo Society signifies: (a) shifting from theological/communion with God notions, to more surreal and transcendental notions of spirituality, simultaneously constructing personal meanings of spirituality; (b) moving from duality-oriented beliefs to non-duality orientations; (c) reinstating unconditional love and forgiveness, altruism, detachment, disengagement, and positive coping; and (d) developing among the followers a propensity for spiritual experiences. Drawing from traditional Indic faith tenets, and with spiritual experiences as the core, what emerges is a faith-based institutional form, the essence of which is collective existential transcendence. The focus on the collective then lends the 'social' face to Sri Aurobindo Society and promotes its transformational vision.

There is also an unconscious assimilation of HIFMs' ideas into domains of the secular and the profane, and vice versa, as seen in Vivekananda Kendra, Amritanandamayi Mission, and Art of Living in the following forms. To further emphasize the Hindu and the indigenous, Vivekananda Kendra supports recognition of an eco-theological, spiritual worldview akin to the Gaia hypothesis, recognizing trajectories of development and modes of existence other than Enlightenment science and rationality. This equation of 'Indic-back to roots-alternative and in tune with nature-worldview sacralization' is the core to Vivekananda Kendra's assertion in the third sector. Two purposes are served through it: (a) projection of the organizational ideology of Advaita as the source of all 'ancient scientific heritage' and (b) ironing the creases in the philosophical-sociological question of the tradition–modernity relationship. Vivekananda Kendra's notion of totality as proposed by Advaita provides insights into the logic of history successfully emanating out of the universalization rhetoric – that the tradition of Hinduism is the source of all modernity.

In Amritanandamayi Mission, what is constructed then is a grammar of 'political theology' – the contextual-classical, attempting to relate classical Hindu theological tradition to the contemporary situation. Hence, in its functionality Amritanandamayi Mission pre-empts an 'ethics of toleration' and 'moral notions of justice'. Some tenets are common with liberation theology, particularly the emphasis on orthopraxis positing a dialectical relationship between theology and praxis. Amritanandamayi Mission is visualized as an institution that makes sociocultural freedom possible, the starting point being harmonious integration of all faiths, and a beneficiary outreach that transcends caste, creed, and religion. It is, in a sense, an orientalist institutional answer on the edifice of Hindu sentiments catapulted onto universalist overtones to the question of modernity's terse assertions of relegating faith to the private realm alone. In Art of Living, the postcolonial angle comes attempting to undercut thematically and formally the discourses that support colonization and glorifying the 'orient' as designed by Sri Sri.

The HIFM metamorphoses stories, although plotted separately, into an overarching narrative, as a representation in the expression of 'nouveau contemporary Hinduized norm'; in other words, it is a sort of re-homecoming of the Hindu nationalist narrative, to draw from Steiner (2011), a manifestation of the 'soft power' of HIFMs. This becomes a macro-level explanatory construct of their public presence and forms of dialogic-discursive mode of functioning, seeping into the national sociopolitical fabric.

8

Actors in Social Transformation: Deliberating on a Model

From the analogous/derivative discussions, a model of Hindu-Inspired Faith-Based Social Transformation (henceforth, the HIFBST model) has been developed. HIFBST model proposes a redeeming intervention of faith through the divine qualities of the charismatic gurus. Traditionally, faith is understood through the interpretation of the meaning of transcendence. In the HIFBST model, few other components are added: (a) existential-empirical issues of the human followers vis-à-vis the ultimate Being; (b) human existence signifying 'what is not yet' and, hence, the quest for transcendence; and (c) faith in dialectical relationships with plurality, alterity, and difference (non-faith, secular, modern). Of particular relevance here is the faith culture, language, and the linguistic transmission of the faith experience, thereby considering faith-constitutive lingo as primordial. Transcendence is then grasped through difference, that is, binaries of transcendence and reification, ephemeral and ethereal, and communitas and externalization. With this 'faith' becomes critical. In built in this structure is the language of hope, transformation, and possibly freedom.

The focus is on conceptions of God rather than concept, a non-metaphysical realism of sorts wherein exist multiple realities. Some of the building blocks of faith include notions of ultimacy, revelation, identity, imagination, critical assertion, dialectic systematic theorizing, and symbolic interpretations guiding faith practices. Faith is expressed through language games. Furthermore, there are traces of constructivism, and faith becomes a mode of existence of the mortal humans, emerging from the factual lives of individuals examining the existential insecurities and searching for modes of transcendence. In the HIFBST model, faith attempts to question the doxastic ideal, that is, the traditional picture of ideally formed beliefs or objective knowledge, in favour of subjectivity.

Overarching philosophy

The central concept is that of faith, which is not diametrically opposed to reason yet possesses traces of philosophical faith. This is because it is not solely transcendence, which is emphasized but faith expression plays the primary role in concrete human actuality. There is both a demand for moral faith and a fundamental need for tradition-faith as having an important standing as a human phenomenon. Consciousness is naturalized, spiritualized, and it becomes an object of reflection.

Collectively, what is also proposed is a theory of value,[1] derived integrally from faith with a focus on worldview cultivation and providing an account of the meaning of human life. Since the worldview is not unilinear, it is subjective or, more specifically, incorporates 'critical subjectivism'. This means that the 'subjects' for whom the worldviews are crafted are logical beings who act on 'values', thereby lending meanings to them. Worldviews in turn gain meaning only when subjects are positively anchored in them and the grounds that the HIFBST model adopts for the same is the domain of values. Here, rather than purely theoretical values practicalities are privileged.

Rather than practical cognitive interests, there are emancipatory cognitive interests akin to the theologies of liberation. The invariance that exists between the charismatic figure and the current sociohistorical issues/realities are praxeologically aimed to be surpassed in the interest of transformation/liberation. Faith is understood as critically oriented,

1 Theory of value is discussed at length by neo-Kantian Heinrich Rickert, whose work influenced Heidegger in philosophy, Weber and Simmel in sociology, and Troeltsch in theology (Crowe, 2010).

methodically interlocking knowledge and interest, that is, generating a theological knowledge that is interested in its own liberation through the liberation of sociohistorical misery. Finally, transcendence is not merely an ephemeral term but is transformative in social terms.

The prominence is given to the HIFM-constructed meaning of the social world comprising consciousness, action, culture, and systems. The struggle is to dissolve the antinomy between 'communicative action' and 'faith-inspired epistemocentrism', that is, commune creation and the perpetual coming to terms with the primacy of transcendent reality advocated by all HIFMs.

HIFBST model: Ontology

The model ontology means how the agency of associates/followers is understood by the HIFMs. In HIFBST model, ontologically it can be said that there is a notion of 'relative agency' – follower subjects are at once perceived 'free' through transcendence and 'bounded' by HIFM norms. The paradox is intensified by the binary logic of self-other, ownness-alienation, and consciousness-body. The adherent–subject agency is both, a subject and an instrumentality through which HIFMs realize their ideals. HIFM associateship also entails that several identities might be brought into consonance in terms of a shared habitus. There are elements of transpersonal development through the prominence of a non-dualistic vision,[2] thereby proposing ontological attitudes of simultaneous freedom and responsibility.

There is in the HIFMs a charismatic kind of guru fetishism as the starting point representative of all socio-philosophical-transcendental desirables. Using the inwardness argument,[3] the sacral nature-divinization of this charisma is accepted unequivocally. It is like an absolute telos, which facilitates the subjective reflection for the followers by enabling them to focus on an existential possibility (provided by the HIFM) that becomes a real possibility for them. For instance, an existential possibility

2 Todres (2000) has also drawn parallels to the thoughts of Husserl, Heidegger, and Merleau Ponty on the non-dualistic vision in which human beings participate in development and non-development.

3 According to Kierkegaard, faith is the appropriation in passionate inwardness of an objective uncertainty – the inwardness argument (De Nys, 2002).

is spiritual gains/transcendence; what makes it real for the followers is the HIFM epithet varieties, which include Raja Yoga, Sudarshan Kriya, Integral Yoga, Vedanta, and IAM technique among others. To the mastery of this charismatic guru, the believer/follower is ontologically subjectivated (using Judith Butler's term). We can also see here the ambivalence of the spiritual power's productive and repressive aspect. The ontological argument is that the power of faith can be really understood when it is reified in the followers' practicalities of prayer experience and worship. The follower 'self', in turn, is not condensed but becomes dispersed and multi-vocal, influenced by late modernity/postmodernity. This self is reinstalled in the world/HIFM world wherein it becomes the ultimate hermeneutic authority, incorporating within it the powers of authority, decision, adventure, judgement in choosing from the HIFMs' repertoire. Loyalties are then reflexive-relational, determined by multiple factors such as originality, charisma power, embodiment legitimacy, and, more important, perceived personal gains.

HIFBST model: Epistemology and component constitution

Model epistemology has some critical components that can be described as charisma, historiography, genealogy and trajectory, faith narrative, sociality, parochialism-hegemony, macrosocial cartography, and distinctiveness-difference-otherness.

Charisma

Charisma proposes an epistemological dependency on the guru (as opposed to epistemological individualism). The accompaniments of charisma include a belief in the divine revelation and obedience, referring to the free submission of will to the charismatic authority. This intellectual-emotive submission is due to the charismatic guru being perceived as the paragon of truth that is created in the image and likeness of the Godhead. The argument for the existence of the charismatic persona as the embodiment is projected as the proof, demanding nothing other than itself.[4] There is

---

4 This is derived from theologian Anselm's proposed ontological argument in his Proslogion, written 1077–1078, wherein the existence of God is a proof demanding nothing other than itself (Simpson, 2003).

simultaneously the creation of 'two worlds' – the transcendental world of charisma and the material world of the institution operationalized by followers.

Historiography

Historiography has its complexities with the base being that of Hindu texts and scriptures. But, more important, the 'real' sources are hagiographies, biographies, autobiographies, and works by apostles, which, although dated, are believed by the HIFMs to be the main sources for revealing the historical truth and factuality. There is surely a mix of communal and personal in this storytelling and, to some degree, a filtering process, re-enactment, creative interpretations, and imaginations. These narratives may have in themselves changed over time. This peculiarity of HIFMs, something that we need to acknowledge, is that this historiography reveals some logics (particularly the embodiment chronicles and devotion sentiments) we may not easily understand. HIFBST model historiography thus demands that hermeneutic sensitivity which eventually impinges upon truth, knowledge, fact, event, and agency.

Genealogy and trajectory

HIFMs' genealogy accompanies historical memories[5] and establishes a theological pedagogy that is interested in the making of transcendence. Theoretically the invariance that exists between the charisma's vision and the real sociohistorical conditions is praxeologically aimed to be overcome through branching/proliferation – metaphorically understood as 'spreading/sharing' good messages/visions with society at large. This happens through the dialectics of praxis, bridging faith and action. The action is directed towards liberation and 'emancipatory cognitive interests'. The key is the development of intentional consciousness, the flourishing of the psychology of spirituality as a common human behaviour in an essentially pluralistic society. The other dimension is the virtual expansion of HIFMs, which in the model can be looked at as a shift from place to space. This, in MacMillen's (2011) terms, is a phenomenon of capitalist modernity when the traditional 'centre' evaporates into

---

5 This is opposed to Nietzschean active forgetfulness and Derrida's forgetting as a synonym for the disjointedness of time (Abeysekara, 2006).

'space' – a form of 'techgnosis'. The sustained internet/virtual presence and related expansions of HIFMs is representative of this gnosticism inherent in so-called modernity.[6] Essentially, the trajectory follows (to some extent) patterns of rituals, beliefs, and social organizations.[7] There is a certain thematization according to which the global diffusion occurs[8] – HIFMs engage in matters that are both internal and external.

Faith narrative

HIFBST model's faith narrative is 'beyond enlightenment', modified suitably by the founder/ charismatic guru in tune with sociopolitical realities and to create/maintain public memories. Some aspects, which are characteristic in the HIFBST faith narrative, are configuring written discourses, that is, the word of the guru, and reinterpreting texts entailing a critical reading of a tradition. Thus, there are simultaneous processes of distanciation, that is, preserving tradition–text autonomy and appropriation, that is, making it one's own – a process that all HIFM agents undertake.[9] Normative and canonical status is attributed

6 According to MacMillen (2011), virtual pilgrimage is a great example of two cultural phenomena: (a) an increasing individualization and compartmentalization of the notion of place into space and the increasing abstraction (removal of the body) and alienation of religion into the cognitive away from the sensuous experiencing human and (b) the growing profusion of 'art' in a mechanical age of reproduction, where 'reality' is dispensed into dimensionless visual, spatial forms that do not provide interpretive distance or presence of craft as found in older forms of representation (see also Goldman, 2006).

7 Although it is argued that Durkheim's work is not applicable to faith in modern societies, in his 1969 article titled 'Individualism and the Intellectuals' he has proposed some hypotheses, which can be connected. One postulate is the structural correspondence between social organization and religious beliefs and rituals. That is, sacralization is linked to commonly held societal beliefs. The second postulate is the representational aspects of religion – the symbolic and metaphoric expressions of the individual's relationship with the society and segments engendered by collective life. The third postulate is functional in terms of the microscopic and macroscopic role of faith in ordering human lives and thereby social lives.

8 Robert Wuthnow has also compared this to the transnational division of labour, but the analysis has been critiqued on account of its excessive focus on economy (Robertson & Chirico, 1985).

9 Paul Ricoeur has described this process of rescuing the meaning of the text from the estrangement of distanciation and placing it in the proximity of ownness as 'pharmakon'. Reading as pharmakon encompasses the dialectic between understanding and explanation generated by the text–reader encounter. Understanding refers to the process by which the reader, in directing themselves towards the intentional unity of discourse, grasps as a whole its chain of partial meanings. At first, understanding is a naive grasping of the

to the repertoire of traditional Hindu texts, which are continuously decontextualized and re-contextualized.

Sociality

HIFBST model proposes that HIFMs are agents of sociopolitical legitimation for the associates: a demarcation of the sacred space and interaction with the community that provides patronage and maintains it. In that sense, the identity 'Hindu' gets consolidated through cultural artefacts, performances, precepts, and practices laid down by HIFMs. There is a communal creation of faith meanings through ritual language and discursive strategies, which get ingrained in the follower psyche. Furthermore, what is also transported is the valency of 'Hindu' values for various aspects of social existence, such as economics.

There is the creation of the commune locally, and the wider milieu is created by linkages through the metaphor of pilgrimages. Furthermore, the HIFM normative powers determine associateship, which operates even in a liberal, anti-authoritarian scheme of things owing to the focus on 'self'.[10] Moreover, the HIFM alignments are active and symbolic of reflexive role enactment by the associates. The strategies generally forwarded entail intrinsic-ness appeal, interactionist approach, and persuasion. The entire quest is towards endowing meaning to personal and social existence believed to be unavailable in the utilitarian scheme of things. Premium is placed on interpersonality which accounts more fully for life-history-and-life-world-relatedness of faith.[11]

---

meaning of the text as a whole, an act akin to a guess. But by the next stage, it becomes a sophisticated mode of comprehension supported by explanatory procedures. The two phases of understanding are bridged by the process of explanation, which unfolds the range of propositions and meanings of the discourse by giving analytic attention to the structure of the text. Explanation, in turn, opens the way for appropriation (Cartagenas, 2010).

10 See Repstad (2003) for an analysis of memberships in Norwegian conservative groups in a liberal, anti-authoritarian scenario. The analysis challenges certain aspects of rational-choice theory proposing that strict profiled organizations may tend to have the greatest success.

11 Some inspiration has been derived from Fowler's (2001) Faith Development Theory developed at the Harvard Divinity School around 1981. In the project examining Identity and Faith, Fowler looked at structural aspects with which to trace faith journeys. Taken together they give an operational depiction of faith as complex, central, and centring constituent of selfhood. These were forms of logic (derived from Piaget), perspective-

Parochialism-hegemony

Parochialism-hegemony in the episteme is a mimesis of the past, and drawing from Rene Girard, there is a teleology of cognitive violence embedded in the dynamic of imitation. New-ageification, which all HIFMs aspire and claim to move towards, prompts the questioning of traditional hierarchies, thereby giving space for newer conflicts, which are not puritan but hybrid. Hence, in the HIFBST model parochialism is naturalized through bonding/communitas metaphor and hegemonies are surreal/subtle. Othering happens at two levels: at one level, with those whose differences can easily be overlooked where there are elements of co-option and tolerance. At another level, the others with whom there is little affinity and conflict of interests there are elements of indifference and/or subtle contempt.

Hegemony issues are more so, with issues of interculturality somewhere bearing traces of the double-voicedness of the colonial discourse. There are, at once, claims to inclusion on one hand and exclusivity on the other. Exclusivity (bordering on ethnocentrism) happens due to the propensity to align to pan-cultural identity markers, which, in the case of HIFMs, is 'Hindu'. Hegemony is subtly institutionalized when Hindu discourse is attributed the quality of 'science' and, hence, a logical way forward. This is very often done by locating all material nature within the framework of divine consciousness, as also endowing matter with consciousness and agency, with little spaces for epistemic generosity.

---

taking (derived from Selman), form of moral judgment (derived from Kohlberg), bounds of social awareness, locus of authority, form of world coherence, and symbolic function. In his latter developments on the work, Fowler has proposed that faith and development of faith have a triadic structure. There is the self, there are the primal and significant others in the self's relational matrix, and there is the third centre of relational engagement – the ultimate Other, or the centre(s) of value and power in one's life structure. The study of the self in faith development perspective, therefore, according to him, must attend to the process of the increasingly self-aware construction of that relational matrix and of its change over time. One element has been that Fowler's theory has mixed the cognitive-developmental and psychodynamic paradigms (McDargh, 2001). Later Streib (2005) has suggested for a revision in the theory to account not only for structural diversity but also for narrative and content diversity. He suggests the inclusion of content-analytical and narrative-analytical procedures into faith development research.

Macrosocial cartogram

HIFBST model at the macro level is attributed with the task of changing/ challenging boundaries. This boundary construction and subsequent negotiations of faith identity in locations such as local, regional, and nation-state, from the HIFM lens, determines the macro cartography.[12] There are clear influences of the state and market and, therefore, tinges of the political. In the post-secular scheme of things, civic practices and social projects become central to the formation of a politics of common good. Faith posits as a defining force within culture and in a postmodern world. The macro is also about decentring and critique of faith in the social realms as also identity negotiations across time and space. It is an assertion of Taylor's notions of social imaginaries[13] – conditions of belief/ faith prevent their forgetting in a secularity/secularized scheme.

Further globalization adds another complexity in terms of blurring 'real' boundaries and categorizations. So, the HIFM trajectories also sometimes reveal contradictory tendencies of modern/anti-modern and secularizing/ de-secular. This also means being responsive to environmental realities of privatization and pluralism with the accompanying elements of market and commodification. In particular, the relativization thesis permits the coexistence of contradictions rather than an either/or situation. Probably that is why in the macro scenario HIFMs continue to thrive, resisting antagonistic pressures at times, as they provide for the human need of supernatural compensators.

The HIFBST model depicts some macro social motifs, which propose the socioeconomic potential of the HIFMs – manifest or latent. A core among them is the liberatory and detraditionalization axis[14] and faith

---

12 See Barker (2006) for a detailed analysis of religious identities and boundaries.

13 Lyon (2010) has proposed that Charles Taylor's notion of social imaginaries takes us beyond the mere Kantian assertions about the gulf between 'religion' and 'reason'. It allows scholars to stand back and to grasp the significance of emotion and embodiment that lie behind the abstract and the cerebral that too frequently mars social science analyses, including especially those of 'religion'. Second, Taylor's emphasis on social practices leads him to lean explicitly not merely towards Catholicism but in particular to Ivan Illich's understanding of the church as a 'way of living together' as opposed to an organizational code of rules. Third, the social imaginary informing his theory and theory assessment is one that cares deeply about relationality and about making space for the Other.

14 See also Dorien's (2006) work on liberation theology. He organizes the discussions in the forms of spiritual personality, visions of liberation, theology and modern doubt, new

interactions in the public square.[15] Traces of political theology are seen in the HIFBST model, with HIFMs as actors shifting their ethical and political subjectivities from metaphysical to post-metaphysical conditions. This means that there is a shift from a mode of existence, which is more discreet and autonomous towards one which is more engaged. Rather than an imaginary ethical vacuum, there are forms of proactive ethical systems – social projects and social service endeavours enabling that engagement further.

Distinctiveness-difference-otherness

The distinctiveness comes with the efforts to reinsert the faith paradigm in the macro development discourses. This is more so from the 'culture' vantage point, with a focus on the emergence of a civic culture that recognizes faith, particularly in response to the need for greater social cohesion in the individualistic late modern age. This comes with the affirmative recognition of faith in the development discourse. The idea is to provide alternatives to modern epistemology through gnosis[16] or different ways of looking at postcolonial futures. Where in the mainstream episteme the response is to logic, in the HIFBST model the response is to a transcendent reality.

Difference comes with the syntactic and semantic category of 'newness' – in understandings, views on self, mimicry of family (HIFMs believe followers to be bound by norms of family), and societal/cosmological

---

metaphysics and divine reality, rethinking traditions, and a renaissance of sorts.

15 Matthews (2007) has, in his book, explained this by using the Augustinian theological argument wherein all transactions and relationships, including pluralism, are God-determined.

16 Paranjape (2009) has used the concept 'border gnosis' as knowledge from a subaltern perspective or knowledge conceived from the exterior borders of the modern/colonial world system. Border gnoseology is a discourse about colonial knowledge, which is conceived at the conflictive intersection of the knowledge produced from the perspective of modern colonialisms (rhetoric, philosophy, science) and knowledge produced from the perspective of colonial modernities in Asia, Africa, and the Americas/Caribbean. Border gnoseology is a critical reflection on knowledge production from both the interior borders of the modern/colonial world system (imperial conflicts, hegemonic languages, directionality of translations, etc.) and its external borders (imperial conflicts with cultures being colonized as well as the subsequent stages of independence and decolonization).

transformation towards a predetermined (sometimes millenarian) transcendental goal. Otherness is a distancing of sorts arising from identity, commune, memory, and imaginations.

HIFBST model: Ethics

As transcendence is one of the core elements, discourse ethics prevail, developed through the constructed and transcendental powers vested in HIFMs. God discourses occupy the centre stage. Simultaneously, there is recognition of plurality, multiplicity, disjuncture, and difference. Ethics provide moral grounds derived from HIFM doctrines and are essentially consequential.[17] This means that a certain criterion of goodness is laid down and conscience is oriented towards that visible, intelligible good. These moral acts then facilitate the development of faith through consent to HIFMs scheme of things (including worldviews, stances) and thereby assent towards the divine.[18]

Connections are sought between pure faith, notions of love, and hope through the transformation quests. This actually brings together considerations of the general/public good and the absolute/right. What prevails is the notion of 'economy of the gift', that is, a dialectical understanding of the relationship between the human and the divine[19] and the resulting dialectical moral relationship between the self and the other.[20] This moves into the relationship between the good and the right, because what is prominent in the postmodern HIFM scheme of things are the ethics of human transformation in relation to the divine.

The good and the right both presuppose and transform each other. Out of faith in humanity's ultimate teleological goodness arises the deontological obligation to love one another; out of this deontological obligation of love arises, in turn, a critical teleological hope for humanity's

17 Consequentialism is a perspective in ethics according to which a fact is good as long as it has good consequences (Narita, 2009).

18 Derived from Barad's (1986) analysis of Thomas Aquinas's assent–consent distinction in defining acts of faith and moral conduct.

19 This understanding of dialectics is not Hegelian (Adamut, 2008) but signifies the relationship between the self-understanding of beings which is perceived to be complacent and the radical critique provided by God's transcendent perspective.

20 This is derived from Wall's (2001) analysis of Paul Ricoeur's theological ethics.

ultimate reconciliation. Hence, there is a circular exchange relationship between the elements in the economy of faith, love, and hope. The 'gift' concept exists because the good and right concepts are given by the charismatic guru.

Essentially there is a kind of pilgrimage ethic – or ethics of the ways that describe the journey to social transformation through HIFM affirmative interventions. This hermeneutics of hope, which is at once kergymatic[21] and correlational,[22] enables, according to HIFMs, the annihilation of the perceived evil/problematic conditions in human society.

The other side to the HIFBST's ethical repertoire is the prevalence of Hindu utilitarianism, which has an embedded violence in it due to the logic of equivalence. Whereas in economics utilitarianism may signify reciprocity and maximization, the 'greatest good' logic may also entail greater marginalization, owing to its essential totalitarianism. As the public sphere is not neutral, common good notions are writ with a constitutive impurity, materiality, and ultimate undecidability of action. In this the philosophical foundations of rights/justice-related issues face some dangers. As the general ethical basket of the HIFBST model is in an extra-state location, that is, they are non-state actors essentially, there is in some ways a claim made to an exclusive access to the metaphysical foundations for welfare/rights/justice (outside state norms/prescriptions). However, in terms of actual realization, the positions range between that of partner, mediator, or barrier (to the state). Hence, there are both enabling and destabilizing elements in terms of HIFMS' ethical assertions in the public sphere. In that sense, they are cultural citizens with personalized ideas, images, and texts on morals/ethics.

Moving further, although the HIFBST model has firm ethical foundations, the substantive claims cannot extend beyond certain boundaries of HIFMs' own context. Only certain formal principles such as equity and equality have rational validity. In that sense, the moral claims of rightness, which are inclusive and universalizable, maintain priority

21 Kergymatic hermeneutics have been proposed by twentieth-century Anglo-European philosopher Karl Barth, who looks at interpretations as frozen in time-space signified as the 'strange world of the Bible'.

22 Correlational hermeneutics have been proposed by Paul Tillich, which propose that meanings are shaped by the ultimate questions raised in our particular historical situation.

over the 'actual good'. Pragmatic and dialogic shades are, thus, prominent rather than puritan ethical proceduralism.

The praxis lens: Norms, exchange, and performance

In the HIFBST model, praxis norms are subjectivity driven, particularly in terms of looking at and building on faith experiences. These faith experiences are inherently diverse with inbuilt elements of fine-tuning traditions. Through these experiences, commitment is generated.[23] Further aspects of consciousness, transgression, and transcendence are facilitated by the HIFMs utilizing an array of metaphors. Practice is an exchange between the individual self and the HIFM culture, warranting an emotional commitment. Certain memetic aspects are visualized in the interplay between HIFM culture and the follower self – viewed as a construct built on the edifice of HIFM culture. The performative elements are of two levels: individual and institutional. Individual-level performative elements entail transcendence quests, which subvert secular materialism.[24] These are further compounded as HIFMs incorporate technological forms, discursive protocols, and market values of globalizing media infrastructure. At the institutional level, the faith ties of the agency influence structure and social service to various degrees. The ties could be that of ideational resource, traditional authority modified suitably by the charisma, and cultural capital formation/consolidation. This cultural

23 Howell (1997) has undertaken a study of experiences generated through Brahmakumari association in Australia. The theoretical stance adopted has been that of ontological neutrality that allows experience to be construed as encompassing not only the qualia of experience but also the operations (in the broadest sense, inclusive of practices, set, and setting) with which those qualia are associated. Adoption of this position avoids cultural, social, and physiological reductionism as well as subscription to the particular belief system studied. At the same time, its adoption positively directs research towards empirical study of the interrelations of all systems associated with the 'breaking through' of ecstatic experiences into everyday life and their impact on organizations.

24 See Nash (2006) for an analysis of fasting; see Wardell and Engebretson (2006) for a taxonomy on understanding the spiritual in health/healing, in terms of circumstances, manifestations, and interpretation. Circumstances included the aspects of setting, situation, and timing. Manifestation incorporated the modes of awareness and the phenomena of the experience. Components of interpretation included personal meaning and congruence with social norms. Hatcher (2007) has discussed the Hindu quest to balance the material and the spiritual.

capital or habitus encompasses view of self, cosmos, and the faith metaphor.

What it therefore means is to acknowledge the faith dimension in the lives of associates/adherents/believers/beneficiaries, particularly well-being links and social tangibles,[25] synergies between social transformation and some faith understandings, working in or with HIFMs as a part of social transformation horizon,[26] and accompanying skillset development in practice so as to capitalize on distinctiveness–difference aspects and minimize otherness factors.[27]

Model applications

The applications of the HIFBST model are evident through (a) the macro/societal-level implication of faith in terms of premiums and antagonisms-contradictions, (b) the perceived links between social transformation and faith understandings, (c) working in (and with) HIFMs as a part of social

25 These are parallel to characteristics of the reflexive traditions as discussed by Walliss (2000) drawing from Mellor. He has problematized the notion of 'tradition' presented in the recent sociological analysis of Anthony Giddens in relation to reflexivity and late modernity. Three broad areas of critique are highlighted and discussed: the view of tradition as simultaneously static and reflexive, the view that within the 'post-traditional' world tradition survives and flourishes, and the view that tradition and reflexivity are historically mutually exclusive phenomena. Furthermore, HIFMs provide their associates with cultural artefacts akin to anime/animation (Park, 2005) to which they express their loyalties. See also Clanton and Gunter (2011) for a pragmatic, non-metaphysical, naturalistic understanding of God in the lives of believers, based on the philosophy of Chicago school pragmatist Edward Scribner Ames of the early part of the twentieth century, who was influenced by William James and John Dewey. See also Hodge and Boddie (2007) for a study on links between personal spiritual characteristics and conceptualizations on religion and spirituality.

26 See also Knepper (2003) for a contemporary argument on faith-based interventions in crime prevention. He proposes that if faith 'works', then the government should support faith-based initiatives because in doing so it is not endorsing religion but science. Drawing on the ideas of Karl Popper, Michael Polanyi, and others, the essay reviews the argument within the framework of the philosophy of social science. The discussion reviews such concepts of falsification, structural causality, objectivity, and evidence-based policymaking to affirm the place of both faith and science in public life. See also Cnaan, Boddie, and Danzig (2005) for a discussion on inclusion of faith, organized religion, and faith-based social service agencies in social work curriculum. Dave and Sahoo (2006) have considered the linkages between social work, spirituality, and the diaspora through the social service activities of the Sathya Sai Baba movement.

27 Crisp (2011) has proposed interesting views on incorporation of religion in the social work curriculum in the Australian context.

transformation and the skill set required for the same, and (d) episteme and praxis implications.

At the macro level, there are premiums in terms of religiosity–spirituality gradations and ethics geared towards the *seva* epithet inspired by theistic existentialism. The antagonisms-contradictions arise due to the embedded cultural hegemonies and Hindu nationalism, which permeate the social compass.

Social transformation theory is realist and critical realist[28] in nature. Hence, categorically there has been a journey from religious volitional philanthropy to scientific systematization of institutional-residual welfare, to then incorporate psychodynamics, systems perspective, and radical insertions/assertions. Historically, there are four distinct paradigms: functionalism (fixing), interpretivism (meaning search), radical humanism (consciousness-raising), and radical structuralism (revolution). Within functionalism are located the systems theory, psychoanalysis, and behavioural work. Within interpretivism is client-centred and interactionist social work. Radical humanism relates to the raising of consciousness, which aims to tackle alienation from a fourfold stance: reification of society (Georg Lukas), notion of ideological hegemony (Antonio Gramsci), idea of the one-dimensional man (Marcuse), and pathology of communication (Habermas). Consciousness-raising is through radical practice and feminist work. Based on a materialist view of the world, radical structuralists operate on norms of conflict, aim at redistribution of wealth and power through the method of socialist welfare work, and Marxist practice.[29]

28 According to the critical-realist philosophy of Roy Bhaskar, it is logical and scientific to draw on theories that rely on transcendental arguments. A transcendental argument is one that starts with an agreed description of an event and then goes on to ask what mechanisms might exist for that event to be possible. The mechanisms in question might not be open to empirical observation but are nevertheless real and influential. Moreover, they can be subjected to critical, investigative inquiry. Thus, it is perfectly permissible to hypothesize that the mechanism of attachment is fundamental to human experience even though it is not a physical entity that we can see under a microscope. It is real because we can measure its *effects*. It follows, therefore, that if we can hypothesize about the presence and nature of these mechanisms and subsequently test their existence, we have the basis of a scientific method, albeit one that differs from the traditional form of positivistic investigation (Houston, 2005).

29 See Howe (1987).

In all of the above, the destination has been 'change' – modifications, assertions, mainstreaming, inclusion-integration, harmony, self-referential dynamics, and autopoeisis, celebrating difference-disjuncture, and reinstating nouveau ideational-normative patterns.

Faith understandings also posit transcendence as the core operating on the theo-socio-ontological imagination of hope and transformation. Although HIFM mechanisms of transformation may be differential – Vedantic nondualism, swaminarayanism, Sai epithet, millenarianism and Raja Yoga, Adi Shankaracharya's Vedanta and BMI, Integral Yoga, Hindu transnationalism, IAM technique and Sudarshan Kriya – there is one thread that runs across all of them – 'transcendence'. This transcendence entails negation of the contemporary in quest for the not-yet-there – precipitated by the Absolute Being (crafted differentially based on HIFM derivatives).

Hence, in the critical-realist sense transcendence is agreed upon and mechanisms are derived for attaining the same making it possible. These mechanisms are in turn open for empirical investigations in an experiential way, only to further affirm their efficacy. Hence, the transformative quest as also the accompanying social ethics (teleological-deontological) have certain parallels in both the logic of social transformation and that of HIFMs' sociality. That is the common ground to work with.

While working in HIFMs is probably boundaried by adherence obligations, working with HIFMs requires a mutual worldview and epistemological generosity. Nuances of secularization-syncretism, which HIFMs claim to demonstrate through harmony–integration rhetoric are steps towards that. Pitching-in and synchronization is probably what is required.

In working with individuals/groups/communes, at the micro level, an active cognisance of faith as a source of granting life's meaning/space for reflection for those who believe is crucial. This would mean providing a window to the same in the background data and using the same as an anchor point in designing interventions. Furthermore, looking at transcendence as an important mircosociological imagination of hope/transformation is important. Value systems form an important lynchpin of intervention, which in the sense of the HIFM microcosm are derivatives of that faith. Framing the individual/group/commune situation to reveal these dimensions is also the core. However, this creation of space/

reframing needs to leave adequate room for dissent/defection, since if adherence/alignment is volitional and the accompanying room for discussion on the same is natural then the opposite may also hold. That is, leaving room for people to move on, as also a sense of permission to not talk about this aspect, is of equal relevance.

In working with HIFMs, a cognitive generosity and practical work with organizations whose aims, values, and structures have arisen from a philosophical value basis other than secular work is the need. This may mean interacting with the order-power, associates-adherents, and possibly collaboration as non-state actors. Furthermore, this entails utilizing the affirmative epistemic-exclusive elements for innovative outreach and minimizing/erasing the antagonistic aspects.

Episteme implication is the affirmative recognition of the Hindu faith-based social, sociality, and social service ideas. This would effectively mean an incorporation of, and generosity towards, those worldviews, discourses on 'being', social ethics, and visions of social transformation. Practice implications mean consideration of HIFMs as potential sites of, and for, intervention and trainings thereof. Tackling with value-based antagonisms-contradictions and skillset development are the crucial accompaniments. The exercise may entail at once a self-reflexivity in terms of one's own faith belief system and HIFM stance and active engagements with HIFM worldviews.

References

Abeysekara, A. (2006). Desecularizing secularism. *Culture and Religion, 7*(3), 205–243.

Adamut, A. (2008). Ethics and religion in Hegel or on how reason speaks differently than it thinks. *Journal for the Study of Religions and Ideologies, 10*(28), 176–198.

Adiswarananda, Swami. (2006). Ramakrishna Mission–Its gospel of service. In Swami Lokeswarananda et al. (eds), *The story of Ramakrishna Mission: Swami Vivekananda's vision and fulfilment* (pp. 922–929). Kolkata: Advaita Ashrama.

Advaita Ashrama. (1996). *Spiritual talks by the first disciples of Sri Ramakrishna.* Kolkata: Author.

Advaita Ashrama. (1997a). *The complete works of Swami Vivekananda* (Vol. 3, 17th ed.). Kolkata: Author.

Advaita Ashrama. (1997b). *The complete works of Swami Vivekananda* (Vol. 5, 17th ed.). Kolkata: Author.

Advaita Ashrama. (1998a). *The complete works of Swami Vivekananda* (Vol. 4, 14th ed.). Kolkata: Author.

Advaita Ashrama. (1998b). *The complete works of Swami Vivekananda* (Vol. 7, 13th ed.). Kolkata: Author.

Advaita Ashrama. (1999a). *The complete works of Swami Vivekananda* (Vol. 2, 19th ed.). Kolkata: Author.

Advaita Ashrama. (1999c). *The complete works of Swami Vivekananda* (Vol. 8, 12th ed.). Kolkata: Author.

Advaita Ashrama. (2000a). *Letters of Swami Vivekananda* (11th ed.). Kolkata: Author.

Aksharjivandas, Sadhu. (1997). *Pure devotion.* Ahmedabad: Swaminarayan Aksharpith.

Alain, G. (2000). *Auroville: A dream takes shape.* Pondicherry: All India Press.

Alan & Tim. (1998). *The Auroville handbook* (compiled). Auroville: Auroville Communications Centre.

Allahyari, R.A. (2000). *Visions of charity: Volunteer workers and moral community.* Berkeley: University of California Press.

Amarasingam, A. (2009). New age spirituality, quantum mysticism and self-psychology: Changing ourselves from the inside out. *Mental Health, Religion & Culture, 12*(3), 277–287.

Amritaswarupananda, Puri. (1988). *Mata Amritanandamayi: A biography.* Amritapuri: Mata Amritanandamayi Mission Trust.

Amrutvijaydas, Sadhu. (1998). *Pathways to peace.* Ahmedabad: Swaminarayan Aksharpith.

Amrutvijaydas, Sadhu. (2007). *100 years of BAPS: Foundation–formation–fruition.* Ahmedabad: Swaminarayan Aksharpith.

Appadurai, A., & Breckenridge, C.A. (2004). The South Indian temple: Authority, honour and redistribution. In T.N. Madan (ed.), *India's religions* (pp. 73–92). Oxford: Oxford University Press.

Appadurai, A. (1996). *Modernity at large: Cultural dimensions of globalization.* Minneapolis: University of Minnesota Press.

Appleton, N. (2011). In the footsteps of the Buddha? Women and the Bodhisattva Path in Theravada Buddhism. *Journal of Feminist Studies in Religion, 27*(1), 33–51.

Arif, Y. (2008). Religion and rehabilitation: Humanitarian biopolitics, city spaces and acts of religion. *International Journal of Urban and Regional Research, 32*(3), 671–689.

Ashcraft, M.W. (2005). Field notes: A history of the study of new religious movements. *Nova Religio: The Journal of Alternative and Emergent Religions, 9*(1), 93–105.

Ashenden, S., & Owen, D. (1999). *Foucault contra Habermas: Recasting the dialogue between genealogy and critical theory.* London: Sage.

Babb, L.A. (1986). *Redemptive encounters: Three modern styles in the Hindu tradition.* Berkeley: University of California Press.

Bacchetta, P. (1999). Militant Hindu nationalist women reimagine themselves: Notes on mechanisms of expansion/adjustment. *Journal of Women's History, 10*(4), 125–147.

Bahuguna, R.P. (2009). Beyond theological differences: Sant–Vaisnava interaction in Medieval India. *Indian Historical Review, 36*(1), 55–79.

Ballard, R., Thandi, S., & Singh, P. (1996). Panth, Kismet, Dharm te Qaum: Continuity and change in four dimensions of Punjabi religion. In P. Singh & S. Thandi (eds), *Globalisation and the religion: Explorations of Punjabi identity* (pp. 7–37). Coventry: Coventry University Press.

Barad, J. (1986). Aquinas on faith and the consent/assent distinction. *Journal of the History of Philosophy, 24*(3), 311–321.

Barker, E. (2006). We've got to draw the line somewhere: An exploration of boundaries that define locations of religious identity. *Social Compass, 53*(2), 201–213.

Barlingay, S.S. (1998). *Reunderstanding Indian philosophy*. Delhi: D.K. Printworld.

Barrett, R. (2008). *Aghor medicine: Pollution, death, and healing in northern India*. Berkeley: University of California Press.

Basu, A. (1999). Women's activism and the vicissitudes of Hindu nationalism. *Journal of Women's History, 10*(4), 104–124.

Basu, S. (2002). *Religious revivalism as nationalist discourse: Swami Vivekananda and new Hinduism in nineteenth-century Bengal*. Delhi: Oxford University Press.

Basu, S., & Banerjee, S. (2006). The quest for manhood: Masculine Hinduism and nation in Bengal. *Comparative Studies of South Asia, Africa and the Middle East, 26*(3), 476–490.

Bauman, C. (2012). Sathya Sai Baba: At home abroad in Midwestern America. In J. Zavos, P. Kanungo, D. Reddy, M. Warrier, & R. Williams (eds), *Researching public Hinduisms* (pp. 128–139). London: Sage.

Baxi, U. (2006). *The future of human rights*. Delhi: Oxford University Press.

Beckerlegge, G. (1995). *A study of continuity within the Ramakrishna Mission with reference to the practice of seva, service to humanity*. Unpublished PhD thesis. Lancaster, UK: University of Lancaster.

Beckerlegge, G. (1998). Swami Vivekananda and *seva*: Taking social service seriously. In W. Radice (ed.), *Swami Vivekananda and the modernisation of Hinduism* (pp. 158–193). Delhi: Oxford University Press.

Beckerlegge, G. (2000a). Swami Akhandananda's *seva vrata* (vow of service) and the earliest expression of service to humanity in the Ramakrishna Math and Mission. In A. Copley (ed.), *Gurus and their followers* (pp. 22–47). Delhi: Oxford University Press.

Beckerlegge, G. (2000b). *The Ramakrishna Mission: The making of a modern Hindu movement*. Delhi: Oxford University Press.

Beckerlegge, G. (2003). Saffron and *seva*: The Rashtriya Swayam*sevak* Sangh's appropriation of Swami Vivekananda. In A. Copley (ed.), *Hinduism in public and private* (pp. 31–65). Delhi: Oxford University Press.

Beckerlegge, G. (2004). Iconographic representations of renunciation and activism in the Ramakrishna Math and Mission and the Rashtriya Swayamsevak Sangh. *Journal of Contemporary Religion, 19*(1), 47–66.

Beckerlegge, G. (2006). *Swami Vivekananda's legacy of service: A study of the Ramakrishna Math and Mission*. New Delhi: Oxford University Press.

Beckerlegge, G. (2007). Responding to conflict: A test of the limits of neo-Vedåntic social activism in the Ramakrishna Math and Mission? *International Journal of Hindu Studies, 11*(1), 1–25.

Beckerlegge, G. (2008). Swami Vivekånanda's iconic presence and conventions of nineteenth-century photographic portraiture. *International Journal of Hindu Studies, 12*(1), 1–40.

Beckerlegge, G. (2010). An ordinary organisation run by ordinary people: A study of leadership in Vivekananda Kendra. *Contemporary South Asia, 18*(1), 71–88.

Bellin, E. (2008). Faith in politics: New trends in the study of religion and politics. *World Politics, 60*(2), 315–347.

Beltz, J. (2003). Bhima Bhoi: The making of a modern saint. In A. Copley (ed.), *Hinduism in public and private* (pp. 230–253). Delhi: Oxford University Press.

Belur Math. (2009). *Ramakrishna Museum* (3rd reprint). Belur Math: Ramakrishna Math and Ramakrishna Mission.

Berger, J. (2003). Religious non-governmental organisations: An exploratory analysis. *Voluntas, 14*(1), 15–39.

Bhajananda, Swami. (2006). *Selfless work: Its basis, methods and fulfilment.* Belur Math: Ramakrishna Mission Vivekananda University.

Bharucha, R. (2003). Muslims and others: Anecdotes, fragments and uncertainties of evidence. *Economic and Political Weekly,* 4238–4250.

Bhatt, C. (2001). *Hindu nationalism: Origins, ideologies and modern myths.* Oxford: Berg.

Bhattacharya, R. (2003). The nautee in the 'second city of the empire'. *Indian Economic and Social History Review, 40*(2), 191–235.

Bhavani & Elia. (1999). *Environmental consciousness: Compiled from the writings of Sri Aurobindo and the Mother* (compiled). Pondicherry: Sri Aurobindo Ashram Trust.

Bhawuk, D.P.S. (2010). Methodology for building psychological models from scriptures: Contribution of Indian psychology to indigenous and universal psychologies. *Psychology and Developing Societies, 22*(1), 49–93.

Bhide, N.R. (2003). *Eknathji – Mission personified.* Chennai: Vivekananda Kendra Prakashan Trust.

Bhuteshananda, Swami. (2006). Sri Ramakrishna – The prophet of the New Age. In Swami Lokeswarananda et al. (eds), *The story of Ramakrishna Mission: Swami Vivekananda's vision and fulfilment* (pp. 25–37). Kolkata: Advaita Ashrama.

Biebricher, T. (2011). Faith-based initiatives and the challenges of governance. *Public Administration, 89*(3), 1001–1014.

Black, D.M. (2000). The functioning of religions from a modern psychoanalytic perspective. *Mental Health, Religion & Culture, 3*(1), 13–26.

Blanke, S. (2004). Civic foreign policy: Human rights, faith-based groups and U.S.–Salvadoran relations in the 1970s. *The Americas, 61*(2), 217–244.

Bolter, J.D., & Grusin, R. (1999). *Remediation: Understanding new media.* Cambridge, MA: MIT Press.

Bowman, W. (2004). Confidence in charitable institutions and volunteering. *Nonprofit and Voluntary Sector Quarterly, 33*(2), 247–270.

Bradley, T. (2009). A call for clarification and critical analysis of the work of Faith-Based Development Organisations (FBDOs). *Progress in Development Studies, 9*(2), 101–114.

Bradley, T. (2011). The politicisation of mothering in Hindu Missions. *Politics, Religion & Ideology, 12*(2), 161–177.

Brajranjan, M. (2005). *Debrahminising history: Dominance and resistance in Indian society*. Delhi: Manohar Publications.

Bratosin, S., & Ionescu, M.A. (2009). Church, religion and belief: Paradigms for understanding the political phenomenon in post-communist Romania. *Journal for the study of Religions and Ideologies, 8*(24), 1–18.

Brooks, C.K. (1989). *The Hare Krishnas in India*. Princeton, NJ: Princeton University Press.

Brown, L. (2007). Performance, status and hybridity in a Pakistani red-light district: The cultural production of the courtesan. *Sexualities, 10*(4), 409–423.

Brown, M.C. (2010). The design arguments in classical Hindu thought. *International Journal of Hindu Studies, 12*(2), 103–151.

Bunn, C., & Wood, M. (2012). Cultured responses: The production of social capital in faith-based organisations. *Current Sociology, 60*(5), 636–652.

Burghart, R. (ed.). (1987). *Hinduism in Great Britain: Religion in an alien cultural milieu*. London: Tavistock.

Campbell, D., & Glunt, E. (2006). Assessing the effectiveness of faith-based programs: A local network perspective. In S.C. Boddie & R.A. Cnaan (eds), *Faith-based social services: Measures, assessments and effectiveness* (pp. 241–259). Binghamton, NY: Haworth Pastoral Press.

Carp, R. (2011). Religion in the public sphere: Is there a common European Model? *Journal for the Study of Religions and Ideologies, 10*(28), 84–107.

Carr, W. (2000). Some reflections on spirituality, religion and mental health. *Mental Health, Religion & Culture, 3*(1), 1–12.

Carroll, M.M. (2001). Conceptual models of spirituality. In E.R. Canda & E.D. Smith (eds), *Transpersonal perspectives on spirituality in social work* (pp. 5–21). London: Haworth Press.

Cartagenas, A.L. (2010). The social teachings of the church in light of Paul Ricoeur's interpretation theory: Implications for the critical reading of a 'tradition'. *The Heythrop Journal, 51*(1), 636–657.

Casanova, J. (1994). *Public religion in the modern world*. Chicago: University of Chicago Press.

Casolari, M. (2002). Role of Benares in constructing political Hindu identity. *Economic & Political Weekly*, 1413–1420.

Central Chinmaya Mission Trust (CCMT). (1987a). *Hinduism at a glance*. Mumbai: Author.

Central Chinmaya Mission Trust (CCMT). (1989b). *Vedanta in action*. Mumbai: Author.

Central Chinmaya Mission Trust (CCMT). (1990a). *We must . . . talks by Swami Chinmayananda*. Mumbai: Author.

Central Chinmaya Mission Trust (CCMT). (1991a). *Harmony and beauty in man and his world*. Mumbai: Author.

Central Chinmaya Mission Trust (CCMT). (1991b). *The choice is yours: Ethics in Vedanta*. Mumbai: Author.

Central Chinmaya Mission Trust (CCMT). (2003). *Swami Chinmayananda's address on religion and human values*. Mumbai: Author.

Central Chinmaya Mission Trust (CCMT). (2007). *Advice to householders*. Mumbai: Author.

Chakrabarti, M. (1989). *Gandhian mysticism*. Delhi: Atlantic Publishers and Distributors.

Chakrabarti, R. (2004). An enchanting sea scape: Through the epigraphic lens. *Studies in History, 20*(2), 305–315.

Chakravarthi, R. (2001). Saving the self? Classical Hindu theories of consciousness and contemporary physicalism. *Philosophy East and West, 51*(3), 378–392.

Chandra, S. (2009). Social and attitudinal change in medieval India: Thirteenth-seventeenth century. *Indian Historical Review, 36*(1), 23–35.

Chapman, R., & Lowndes, V. (2008). Faith in governance? The potential and the pitfalls of involving faith groups in urban governance. *Planning Practice and Research, 23*(1), 57–75.

Chaubey, A.S. (2003). Technology and culture among the iron workers of Bihar during the seventeenth and eighteenth centuries. *The Medieval History Journal, 6*(1), 75–109.

Chaudhari, B. (1981). *The Bakreshwar Temple: A study of continuity and change*. New Delhi: Inter India Publications.

Chaves, M. (1993a). Denominations as dual structures: An organisational analysis. *Sociology of Religion, 54*(2), 147–169.

Chaves, M. (1993b). Intra-organisational power and internal secularisation in protestant denominations. *American Journal of Sociology, 99*(1), 148 - 163.

Chaves, M. (1994). Secularisation and declining religious authority. *Social Forces, 12*(3), 749–774.

Chinmayananda, Swami. (1976). *A manual of self-unfoldment*. Mumbai: Central Chinmaya Mission Trust.

Chinmayananda, Swami. (1980). *Meditation and life*. Mumbai: Central Chinmaya Mission Trust.

Chinmayananda, Swami. (1990). *The art of living*. Mumbai: Central Chinmaya Mission Trust.

Chinmayananda, Swami. (1991). *The pursuit of happiness*. Mumbai: Central Chinmaya Mission Trust.

Chodorow, N. (1978). *The reproduction of mothering*. Berkeley: University of California Press.

Ciotti, M. (2007). Ethnohistories behind local and global bazaars: Chronicles of a Chamar weaving community in the Benares Region. *Contributions to Indian Sociology, 41*(3), 321–354.

Clanton, J.C., & Gunter, J. (2011). Edward Scribner Ames, pragmatism, and religious naturalism: A critical assessment. *The Heythrop Journal, 52*(1), 1–16.

Clarke, G. (2006). Faith matters: Faith-based organisations, civil society and international development. *Journal of International Development, 18*(4), 835–848.

Cloke, P., Williams, A., & Thomas, S. (2011). *Faith-based organisations and social exclusion in the United Kingdom*. Leuven, Belgium: Acco.

Clothey, F.W. (1983). Pilgrim centres in the Tamil cults of Murugan. In F.W. Clothey (ed.), *Rhythm and intent* (pp. 145–152). Chennai: Blackie & Sons.

Cnaan, R.A. (1997). *Social and community involvement of religious congregations housed in historic religious properties: Findings from a six-city study*. Philadelphia: University of Pennsylvania School of Social Work.

Cnaan, R.A., Boddie, S.C., & Danzig, R.A. (2005). Teaching about organized religion in social work. *Journal of Religion & Spirituality in Social Work: Social Thought, 24*(1–2), 93–110.

Cohen, L. (2004). Operability: Surgery at the margin of the state. In V. Das & D. Poole (eds), *Anthropology in the margins of the state* (pp. 85–102). Santa Fe, NM: School of American Research Press.

Cohen, L. (2011). Accusations of illiteracy and the medicine of the organ. *Social Research, 78*, 123–142.

Cohen, L. (2012). The gay guru: Fallibility, unworldliness, and the scene of instruction. In J. Copeman & A. Ikegame (eds), *The guru in South Asia* (pp. 82–96). London: Routledge.

Cojocaru, D., Cojocaru, S., & Sandu, A. (2011). The role of religion in the system of social and medical services in post-communism Romania. *Journal for the Study of Religions and Ideologies, 10*(28), 65–83.

Coleman, S. (2004). The charismatic gift. *Journal of the Royal Anthropological Society, 10*(1), 421–442.

Collins, P.J. (2002). Habitus and the storied self: Religious faith and practice as a dynamic means of consolidating identities. *Culture and Religion, 3*(2), 147–161.

Colpe, C. (1977). Syncretism and secularization: Complementary and antithetical trends in new religious movements? *History of Religions, 17*(2), 158–176.

Constable, P. (2000). Sitting on the school verandah: The ideology and practice of 'untouchable' educational protest in late nineteenth century western India. *Indian Economic and Social History Review, 37*(4), 383–422.

Cook, C. (1997). Faith-based health needs assessment: Implications for empowerment of the faith community. *Journal of Health Care for the Poor and Underserved, 8*(3), 300–310.

Copeman, J. (2006). Cadaver donation as ascetic practice in India. *Social Analysis, 50*(1), 103–126.

Copeman, J. (2009). *Veins of devotion: Blood donation and religious experience in North India*. New Brunswick, NJ: Rutgers University Press.

Copeman, J., & Ikegame, A. (2012). Guru logics. *HAU: Journal of Ethnographic Theory, 2*(1), 289–336.

Copley, A. (2000). *Gurus and their followers*. Delhi: Oxford University Press.

Copley, A. (2003). Introduction: Debating Indian nationalism and Hindu religious belief. In A. Copley (ed.), *Hinduism in public and private* (pp. 1–30). Delhi: Oxford University Press.

Copley, A. (ed.). (2003). *Hinduism in public and private.* Delhi: Oxford University Press.

Cortright, B. (2001). Integral psychology as existential Vedanta. In M. Cornelissen (ed.), *Consciousness and its Transformation: Papers presented at the Second International Conference on Integral Psychology.* Pondicherry: Sri Aurobindo International Centre for Education and Sri Aurobindo Ashram, pp. 65–79.

Crisp, B.R. (2011). If a holistic approach to social work requires acknowledgement of religion, what does this mean for social work education? *Social Work Education, 30*(6), 663–674.

Crnic, A. (2009). Cult versus church religiosity: Comparative study of Hare Krishna Devotees and Catholics in Slovenia. *Social Compass, 56*(1), 117–135.

Crowe, B. (2010). Fichte, Eberhard and the psychology of religion. *Harvard Theological Review, 104*(1), 93–110.

Dalal, A.S. (2007). *Sri Aurobindo and the future psychology*. Puducherry: Sri Aurobindo International Centre for Education.

Dalal, A.S. (ed.). (2001). *A greater psychology: An introduction to the psychological thought of Sri Aurobindo.* Pondicherry: Sri Aurobindo Ashram Publications Department.

Dalmia, V., & Steitencron, H. Von. (1995). *Representing Hinduism*. New Delhi: Sage.

Dalmiya, V. (2000). Loving paradoxes: A feminist reclamation of the Goddess Kali. *Hypatia, 15*(1), 125–150.

Dalmiya, V. (2009). The metaphysics of ethical love: Comparing practical Vedanta and feminist ethics. *Sophia, 48*(1), 221–235.

Das, T.K., & Datta Ray, I. (2008). Monopolistic competitive market in religion: A case study of Hindu temples. *Applied Economics Letters, 15*(1), 69–72.

Datta, B.N. (1954). *Swami Vivekananda: Patriot-prophet*. Kolkata: Navbharat Publishers.

Dave S., & Sahoo, A.K. (2006). Social work, spirituality, and diasporic communities. *Journal of Religion & Spirituality in Social Work: Social Thought, 24*(4), 75–88.

Dave, H.T. (2000). *Life and philosophy of Lord Swaminarayan: 1781–1830*. Ahmedabad: Swaminarayan Aksharpith.

De Nys, M.J. (2002). Faith, self-transcendence and reflection. *International Journal for Philosophy of Religion, 51*(1), 121–138.

Delphy, C. (1970). The main enemy. *Partisans, 5*(4), 45–56.

DeNapoli, A. (2010). Crossing over the ocean of existence: Performing mysticism and exerting power by female sadhus in Rajasthan. *Journal of Hindu Studies, 3*(3), 298–336.

Dhar, S. (2006). Ramakrishna Mission and the total uplift of humanity—An overview of Ramakrishna Mission's contributions. In Swami Lokeswarananda et al. (eds), *The story of Ramakrishna Mission: Swami Vivekananda's vision and fulfilment* (pp. 855–868). Kolkata: Advaita Ashrama.

Diesel, A. (2002). Tales of women's suffering: Draupadi and other Amman goddesses as role models for women. *Journal of Contemporary Religion, 17*(1), 5–20.

Dinham, A. (2008). Commentary: From faith in the city to faithful cities: The 'third way', the Church of England and Urban Regeneration. *Urban Studies, 45*(10), 2163–2174.

Dinham, A., & Lowndes, V. (2008). Religion, resources and representation: Three narratives of faith-engagement in British Urban Governance. *Urban Affairs Review, 43*(6), 817–845.

Divatia, S.C. (1993). *Idealistic thought in Indian philosophy*. Delhi: D.K. Printworld.

Dorrien, G. (2006). *The making of American liberal theology: Crisis, irony, and postmodernity, 1950–2005*. Louisville, KY: Westminster John Knox Press.

Dowsett, N.J., & Jayaswal, S. (1975). *Dimensions of spiritual education*. Pondicherry: Sri Aurobindo Society.

Dube, S.C. (1965). The study of complex cultures. In T.K.N. Unnithan, I. Deva, & Y. Singh (eds), *Towards a sociology of culture in India* (pp. 34–56). New Delhi: Prentice Hall.

Dutta, A. (2005). Sahmat 1989–2004: Liberal art practice against the liberalised public sphere. *Cultural Dynamics, 17*(2), 193–226.

Dutta, R. (2010). Pilgrimage as a religious process: Some reflections on the identities of the Srivaisnavas of South India. *Indian Historical Review, 37*(1), 17–38.

Ebaugh, H.R., Pipes, P.F., Chafetz, J.S., & Daniels, M. (2003). Where's the religion? Distinguishing faith-based from secular social service agencies. *Journal for the Scientific Study of Religion, 42*(3), 411–426.

Eikenberry, A.M. (2007). Philanthropy, voluntary association and giving beyond state: Giving circles and challenges of democracy. *Administration and Society, 39*(7), 857–882.

Emir, R. (1994). *Undoing – returning to simplicity*. Mumbai: CCMT.

Faubion, J.D. (2010). From the ethical to themitical (and back): Groundwork for an anthropology of ethics. In M. Lambek (ed.), *Ordinary ethics: Anthropology, language, and action*. New York: Fordham University Press.

Ferguson, K., Wu, M., Qiaobing, Sprujit-Metz, D., & Dyrness, G. (2007). Outcomes in faith-based social services: Are we evaluating faith accurately? *Research on Social Work Practice, 17*(2), 264–276.

Fischer-Tine, H. (2003). Inventing a national past: The case of Ramadev's Bharatvars ks Itihaas (1910–1914). In A. Copley (ed.), *Hinduism in public and private* (pp. 110–142). Delhi: Oxford University Press.

Flanagan, K. (2008). Sociology into theology: The unacceptable leap. *Theory, Culture and Society, 25*(7&8), 236–261.

Fowler, J.W. (2001). Faith development theory and the postmodern challenges. *International Journal for the Psychology of Religion, 11*(3), 159–172.

Freitag, S. (2002). The realm of the visual: Agency and modern civil society. *Contributions to Indian Sociology, 36*(1&2), 365–397.

Fridolfsson, C., Elander, I., Granberg, M., & Amma, E. (2009). FBOs and social exclusion in Sweden. In D. Dierckx, J. Vranken, & W. Kerstens (eds), *Faith-based organisations and social exclusion in European cities: National context reports* (pp. 161–195). Leuven, Belgium: Acco.

Friedrichs, J., & Klockner, J. (2009). FBOs and social action in Germany. In D. Dierckx, J. Vranken, & W. Kerstens (eds), *Faith-based organisations and social exclusion in European cities: National context reports* (pp. 69–135). Leuven, Belgium: Acco.

Fuller, C.J. (1992). *The camphor flame: Popular Hinduism and society in India*. Princeton, NJ: Princeton University Press.

Fuller, J.D. (2003). Remembering the tradition: Bhaktivinoda Thakura's Sajjanatosani and the construction of a middle class Vaisnava Sampradaya in nineteenth century Bengal. In A. Copley (ed.), *Hinduism in public and private* (pp. 173–210). Delhi: Oxford University Press.

Gandhi, K. (1965). *Social philosophy of Sri Aurobindo and the new age*. Pondicherry: Sri Aurobindo Ashram Publications Trust.

Ghosh, S. (2006). Brahmavadin – Its role in documenting the earliest philanthropic activities of the Ramakrishna Mission. In Swami Lokeswarananda et al. (eds), *The story of Ramakrishna Mission: Swami Vivekananda's vision and fulfilment* (pp. 823–831). Kolkata: Advaita Ashrama.

Ghosh, Sri Aurobindo. (1919). *Uttarpara speech*. Pondicherry: Sri Aurobindo Ashram Publications Department.

Ghosh, Sri Aurobindo. (1962). *The human cycle – the human unity – war and self-determination*. Pondicherry: Sri Aurobindo Ashram Publications Department.

Goldman, M.S. (2006). Cults, new religions, and the spiritual landscape: A review of four collections. *Journal for the Scientific Study of Religion, 45*(1), 87–96.

Govekar, P.L., & Govekar, M.A. (2002). Using economic theory and research to better understand volunteer behavior. *Nonprofit Management and Leadership, 13*, 33–48.

Grau, A. (2007). Political activism and South Asian dance: The case of Mallika Sarabhai. *South Asia Research, 27*(1), 43–55.

Greene, T., & Hudson, H.H. (trans.). (1960). *Religion within the limits of reason alone by Immanuel Kant*. New York: Harper Torchbooks.

Grieve, G.P. (2003). Symbol, idol and mūrti: Hindu god-images and the politics of mediation. *Culture, Theory and Critique, 44*(1), 57–72.

Gronbjerg, K.A. (1993). *Understanding non-profit funding: Mapping revenues in social service and community development organisations*. San Francisco, CA: Jossey Bass.

Gronbjerg, K.A., & Nelson, S. (1998). Mapping small religious non-profit organisations: An Illinois profile. *Nonprofit and Voluntary Sector Quarterly, 27*(1), 13–31.

Grube, J., & Piliavin, J.A. (2000). Role identity, organisational experiences, and volunteer experiences. *Personality and Social Psychology Bulletin, 26*, 1108–1120.

Guerrlero, S. (2000). L'ISKCON an Bresil: la transformation occidentale d'une religion vedique et l' incorporation de ses caracteristiques culturelles a la societe locale. *Social Compass, 47*(2), 241–251.

Gupta, D. (2009). *The caged phoenix: Can India fly?* New Delhi: Viking.

Gupta, K.P. (1973). Religious evolution and social change in India: A study of the Ramakrishna Movement. *Contributions to Indian Sociology, 8*(1), 26–50.

Guthrie, T., & Stickley, T. (2008). Spiritual experience and mental distress: A clergy perspective. *Mental Health, Religion and Culture, 11*(4), 387–402.

Guzy, L. (2003). Mahima Dharma ascetics: A case study on popular asceticism and its patronage structure in rural Orissa. In A. Copley (ed.), *Hinduism in public and private* (pp. 211–229). Delhi: Oxford University Press.

Göcmen, I. (2013). The role of faith-based organisations in social welfare systems: A comparison of France, Germany, Sweden, and the United Kingdom. *Nonprofit and Voluntary Sector Quarterly, 42*(3), 495–516.

Harden, M.G. (2006). Towards a faith-based program theory: A reconceptualization of program theory. *Nonprofit and Voluntary Sector Quarterly, 30*(4), 481–504.

Hardgrove, A. (2002). Merchant houses as spectacles of modernity in Rajasthan and Tamil Nadu. *Contributions to Indian Sociology, 36*(1–2), 323–364.

Harris, M., Hutchison, R., & Cairns, B. (2005). Community-wide planning for faith-based service provision: Practical, policy and conceptual challenges. *Nonprofit and Voluntary Sector Quarterly, 34*(1), 88–109.

Hassija, J.C. BK. (1981). *Adi Dev*. Mount Abu: Prajapita Brahmakumari Ishwariya Vishwavidyalaya.

Hassija, J.C. BK. (1994). *The nature of consciousness in the light of Raja Yoga, Gita and some other disciplines.* Paper Presented at the IV International Symposium on Science and Consciousness at Uxmal, Yucatan, Mexico. Mount Abu: Prajapita Brahmakumari Ishwariya Vishwavidyalaya.

Hassija, J.C. BK. (1996). *One week course for attainment of complete purity, peace and prosperity*. Mount Abu: Prajapita Brahmakumari Ishwariya Vishwavidyalaya.

Hassija, J.C. BK. (2006). *The true essence of Srimad Bhagwad Geeta*. Mount Abu: Prajapita Brahmakumari Ishwariya Vishwavidyalaya.

Hatcher, B. (2007). Bourgeoise Vedanta: The colonial roots of middle class Hinduism. *Journal of the American Academy of Religion, 75*(2), 298–323.

Heehs, P. (2003). The centre of the religious life of the world: Spiritual universalism and cultural nationalism in the works of Sri Aurobindo. In A. Copley (ed.), *Hinduism in public and private* (pp. 66–83). Delhi: Oxford University Press.

Hefferan, T. (2007). Finding faith in development: Religious non-governmental organisations (NGOs) in Argentina and Zimbabwe. *Anthropological Quarterly, 80*(3), 887–896.

Heilman, S.C., & Witztum, E. (2000). All in faith: Religion as the idiom and means of coping with distress. *Mental Health, Religion & Culture, 3*(2), 115–124.

Hejduk, R. (2010). Step into liquid: Rites, transcendence and transgression in the modern construction of the social sacred. *Culture and Religion, 11*(3), 277–293.

Hester, R.D. (2002). Spirituality and faith-based organisations: Their role in substance abuse treatment. *Administration and Policy in Mental Health, 30*(2), 173–178.

Hodge, D.R., & Boddie, S.C. (2007). Social workers' personal spiritual characteristics and their conceptualizations of spirituality and religion. *Journal of Religion & Spirituality in Social Work: Social Thought, 26*(1), 53–70.

Hodges, S. (2005). Revolutionary family life and the self-respect movement in Tamil Nadu, South India, 1926–49. *Contributions to Indian Sociology, 39*(2), 251–277.

Hodgkinson, V.A., & Weitzman, M.S. (1993). *From belief to commitment: The community service activities and finances of religious congregations in the United States.* Washington, DC: Independent Sector.

Hoecke, G Van. (2006). Paradigms in Indian psychotherapy: Applicability in a western approach. *Mental Health, Religion and Culture, 9*(2), 119–125.

Houston, S. (2005). Philosophy, theory and method in social work: Challenging empiricisms' claims to evidence-based practice. *Journal of Social Work, 5*(1), 7–20.

Howe, D. (1987). *An introduction to social work theory: Making sense of practice.* Saint Louis, MO: Wildwood Press.

Howell, J.D. (1997). ASC induction techniques, spiritual experiences, and commitment to new religious movements. *Sociological Analysis, 58*(2), 141–164.

Howell, J.D. (2005). Muslims, the New Age and marginal religions in Indonesia: Changing means of religious pluralism. *Social Compass, 52*(4), 473–493.

Huff, J. (2010). Operationalising opportunities and creating publics in Salvadorian Churches: Findings from an ethnographic process evaluation. *NAPA Bulletin, 33*(1), 105–125.

Huffer, A. (2010). Female immigration as a catalyst for ritual practice: A social history of Hinduism in the United States. *The Journal of Hindu Studies, 2*(2), 189–215.

Hula, R., Jackson-Elmoore, C., & Reese, L. (2007). Mixing god's work and the public business: A framework for the analysis of faith-based service delivery. *Review of Policy Research, 24*(1), 67–89.

Ikegame, A. (2010). Why do backward castes need their own gurus? The social and political significance of new caste-based monasteries in Karnataka. *Contemporary South Asia, 18*(1), 57–70.

Ikegame, A. (2012a). The governing guru: Hindu mathas in liberalising India. In J. Copeman & A. Ikegame (eds), *The guru in South Asia* (pp. 22–43). London, UK: Routledge.

Ikegame, A. (2012b). *Princely India re-imagined: A historical anthropology of Mysore from 1799 to the present*. London: Routledge.

Infield, L. (trans.). (1963). *Poverty and charity, in Kant's lectures on ethics*. New York: Harper and Row.

Isaac, J.C. (2003). Faith-based initiatives: A civil society approach. *The Good Society, 12*(1), 1–10.

Ishwarananda, Swami. (2002). *Conscious living*. Mumbai: Central Chinmaya Mission Trust.

Ishwarananda, Swami. (2004). *Silent search*. Mumbai: Central Chinmaya Mission Trust.

Ishwarchandradas, Sadhu. (1979). *Satsang reader Part 3*. Ahmedabad: Swaminarayan Aksharpith.

Jackson, R., & Nesbitt, E. (1993). *Hindu children in Britain*. Stoke on Trent, UK: Trentham.

Jaffrelot, C. (1993). *The Hindu nationalist movement and Indian politics: 1925–1990s*. London: Oxford University Press.

Jain, K. (2002). More than meets the eye: The circulation of images and the embodiment of value. *Contributions to Indian Sociology, 36*(1&2), 33–70.

Jamoul, L., & Wills, J. (2008). Faith in politics. *Urban Studies, 45*(10), 2035–2056.

Jayasree, G.S. (2006). The ways of faith: Zenana Mission in Trivandrum, 1864–1964. *Economic and Political Weekly*, April 29, 1669–1674.

Jennings, T.W. (1985). *Beyond theism: A grammar of god language*. New York: Oxford University Press.

Jnaneshwardas, Sadhu., & Mukundcharandas, Sadhu. (2001). *Hindu rites and rituals*. Ahmedabad: Swaminarayan Aksharpith.

Johnston, D., & Sampson, C. (eds). (1994). *Religion, the missing dimension of statecraft*. New York: Oxford University Press.

Jones, K.W. (1989). *Socio-religious reform movements in British India*. Cambridge: Cambridge University Press.

Jones, M.S. (2006). Culture as religion and religion as culture in the philosophy of Lucia Blaga. *Journal for the Study of Religions and Ideologies, 5*(24), 66–87.

Joshi, K., & Artaud, Y. (1974). *Exploration in education: Two essays*. Auroville: Auropublications Trust.

Juergensmeyer, M. (1991). *Radhasaomi reality: The logic of modern faith*. Princeton, NJ: Princeton Press.

Kanungo, P. (2012). Fusing the ideals of the math with the ideology of the Sangh? Vivekananda Kendra, ecumenical Hinduism and Hindu nationalism. In J. Zavos, P. Kanungo, D. Reddy, M. Warrier, & R. Williams (eds), *Researching public Hinduisms* (pp. 221–239). London: Sage.

Kaplan, S. (2009). Grasping at ontological straws: Overcoming reductionism in the Advaita Vedanta—Neuroscience dialogue. *Journal of the American Academy of Religion, 77*(2), 238–274.

Kaplan, S.A., Calman, N.S., Golub, M., Ruddock, C., & Billings, J. (2006). The role of faith-based institutions in addressing health disparities: A case study of an initiative in the Southwest Bronx. *Journal of Health Care for the Poor and Underserved, 17*(2), 9–19.

Kapp, K.W. (1963). *Hindu culture, economic development and economic planning in India.* Bombay: Asia Publishing House.

Kasturi, M. (2010). All gifting is sacred. *Indian Economic and Social History Review, 47*(1), 107–139.

Kennedy, M.T. (1925). *The Chaitanya movement.* Calcutta: Associates Press.

Kennedy, S.S., & Bielefeld, W. (2002). *Charitable choice: First results from three states.* Indianapolis, IN: Center for Urban Policy and the Environment.

Kennedy, S.S., & Bielefeld, W. (2006). *Charitable choice at work: Evaluating faith-based job programs in the States.* Washington, DC: Georgetown University Press.

Khandelwal, M. (2004). *Women in ochre robes: Gendering Hindu renunciation.* New York: SUNY Press.

Khandelwal, M. (2012). The cosmopolitan guru: Spiritual tourism and ashrams in Rishikesh. In J. Copeman & A. Ikegame (eds), *The guru in South Asia* (pp. 121–33). London: Routledge.

Khandelwal, M., Hausner, S.L., Gold, A.G., & Hanssen, K. (2006). The true river Ganges: Tara's begging practices. In M. Khandelwal, S.L. Hausner, & G.A. Grodzins (eds), *Women's renunciation in South Asia: Nuns, yoginis, saints, and singers* (pp. 95–124). New York: Palgrave Macmillan.

Kher, V.B. (2001). *Sai Baba: His divine glimpses.* New Delhi: Sterling Publishers.

Kim H. (2008). Managing deterritorialisation, sustaining belief: The Bochasanwasi Shree Akshar Purrushottam Swaminarayan Sanstha as case study and ethnographic foil. In G.W. Armin & M. Warburg (eds), *New religions and globalisation: Empirical, theoretical and methodological perspectives* (pp. 225–243). Aarhus, Denmark: Aarhus University Press.

Kim, H. (2010). Public engagement and personal desires: BAPS Swaminarayan temples and their contribution to the discourses on religion. *International Journal of Hindu Studies, 13*(3), 357–90.

Kline, N. (2010). Disparate powers and disparate resources: Collaboration between faith-based and activist organisations in Central Florida farmworkers. *NAPA Bulletin, 33*(1), 126–142.

Knepper, P. (2003). Faith, public policy, and the limits of social science. *Criminological Journal, 2*(2), 331–352.

Knott, K. (1986). *Hinduism in Leeds: A study of religious practice in Indian Hindu community and related groups: Monograph series community religions project.* Leeds, UK: University of Leeds.

Knott, K. (2000). In every town and village: Adaptive strategies in the communication of Krishna Consciousness in the UK – The first 30 years. *Social Compass, 47*(2), 153–167.

Kochuyt, T. (2009). God, gifts and poor people: On charity in Islam. *Social Compass, 56*(1), 98–116.

Kocsis, N. (2004). Krishna in heroes square: Devotees of Krishna and national identity in post-communist Hungary. *Journal of Contemporary Religion, 19*(3), 329–335.

Kohls, N., Walach, H., & Wirtz, M. (2009). The relationship between spiritual experiences, transpersonal trust, social support, and sense of coherence and mental distress – A comparison of spiritually practising and non-practising samples. *Mental Health, Religion and Culture, 12*(1), 1–23.

Kopf, D. (1979). *The Brahmo Samaj and the shaping of the modern Indian mind.* Princeton, NJ: Princeton University Press.

Kripal, J.J. (2004). Comparative mystics: Scholars as gnostic diplomats. *Common Knowledge, 10*(3), 485–517.

Kulkarni, D. (1998). *Ahead to nature.* Chennai: Vivekananda Kendra Prakashan Trust.

Kurien, P.A. (2006). Multiculturalism and 'American' religion: The case of Hindu Indian Americans. *Social Forces, 85*(2), 723–741.

Kvasmy, L., & Lee, R. (2010). The paradoxical consequences of the White House faith-based and community initiatives for Black churches. *New Media and Society, 12*(4), 619–636.

Lakshmi Kumari, M. (1991). *Sadhana of service – Compilation of talks by Eknath Ranade.* Chennai: Vivekananda Kendra Prakashan Trust.

Lal, V. (1999). The politics of history on the Internet: Cyber diasporic Hinduism and the North American Hindu Diaspora. *Diaspora, 8*(2), 137–172.

Lam, P. (2006). Religion and civic culture: A cross-national study of voluntary association membership. *Journal for the Scientific Study of Religion, 45*(2), 177–193.

Lockhart, W.H. (2005). Building bridges and bonds: Generating social capital in secular and faith-based poverty-to-work programs. *Sociology of Religion, 66*(1), 45–60.

Locklin, R., & Lauwers, J. (2009). Rewriting the sacred geography of Advaita: Swami Chinmayananda and Sankara Dig Vijaya. *Journal of Hindu Studies, 2*(3), 179–208.

Lövheim, M. (2011). Mediatisation of religion: A critical appraisal. *Culture and Religion, 12*(2), 153–166.

Lucas, P.C. (2004). New religious movements and the 'acids' of postmodernity. *Nova Religio: The Journal of Alternative and Emergent Religions, 8*(2), 28–47.

Lyon, D. (2010). Being post-secular in the social sciences: Taylor's social imaginaries. *New Blackfriars, 2*(2), 648–664.

Lysenko, V., & Hulin, M. (2007). *Classical Indian philosophy re-interpreted*. Delhi: Decent Books.

MacMillen, S. (2011). The virtual pilgrimage: The disappearing body from place to space. *Journal of Religion and Society, 13*(1), 1–19.

Madan, T.N. (ed.). (2004). *India's religions*. Delhi: Oxford University Press.

Madsen, F. (2000). Asrama, yukta vairagya et structure d'organisation de l'ISKCON. *Social Compass, 47*(2), 187–204.

Majumdar, R.C. (1965). *Swami Vivekananda: A historical review*. Calcutta: General Printers Publishers.

Mallapragada, M. (2010). Desktop deities: Hindu temples, online cultures and the politics of remediation. *South Asian Popular Culture, 8*(2), 109–121.

Marcos, S. (2009). Mesoamerican women's indigenous spirituality decolonising religious beliefs. *Journal of Feminist Studies in Religion, 25*(2), 25–45.

Mastromattei, R., & Rigopoulos, A. (eds). (1999). *Shamanic cosmos*. Delhi: D.K. Printworld.

Matthews, C. (2007). *A theology of public life*. Cambridge: Cambridge University Press.

Mayaram, S. (2004). Hindu and Islamic transnational religious movements. *Economic and Political Weekly*, January 3, 80–88.

McDargh, J. (2001). Faith development theory and the postmodern problem of foundations. *International Journal for the Psychology of Religion, 11*(3), 185–199.

McKean, L. (1996). *Divine enterprise: Gurus and the Hindu nationalist movement*. Chicago: University of Chicago Press.

Mclain, K. (2012). Praying for peace and amity: The Shri Shirdi Sai Heritage Foundation Trust. In J. Zavos, P. Kanungo, D. Reddy, M. Warrier, & R. Williams (eds), *Researching public Hinduisms* (pp. 182–193). London: Sage.

McMillin, S.E. (2011). Faith-based social services: From communitarian to individualistic values. *Zygon, 46*(2), 482–490.

Meduri, A. (ed.). (2005). *Rukmini Devi Arundale (1904–1986): A visionary architect of Indian culture and the performing arts*. New Delhi: Motilal Banarasidass.

Mehta, R.B. (2008). The missionary sanyasi and the burden of the colonized: The reluctant alliance between religion and nation in the writings of Swami Vivekananda (1863–1902). *Comparative Studies of South Asia, Africa and the Middle East, 28*(2), 310–325.

Mihut, L. (2011). Lobbying – A political communication tool for churches and religious organisations. *Journal for the Study of Religions and Ideologies, 10*(29), 64–86.

Miller, K.D. (2002). Competitive strategies of religious organisations. *Strategic Management Journal, 23*(5), 435–456.

Mishra, V. (1962). *Hinduism and economic growth*. Bombay: Oxford University Press.

Montagne-Villette, S., Hardill, I., & Lebeau, B. (2011). Faith-based voluntary action: A case study of a French charity. *Social Policy & Society, 10*, 405–415.

Morearty, J. (1975). *The two-edged word: The treacherousness of symbolic transformation: Rammohan Roy, Debendranath, Vivekananda and 'The Indian Golden Age'*. Studies in Bengal, Papers Presented at the 7th Annual Bengal Studies Conference, University of Minnesota, Minneapolis. Ann Arbor, MI: Asian Studies Centre.

Muir, S. (2007). The good of new age goods. *Culture and Religion, 8*(3), 233–253.

Mukherjee, J.K. (1990). *From man human to man divine*. Pondicherry: Sri Aurobindo International Centre of Education.

Mukhopadhyay, K.K. (1995). Volunteerism and volunteers in welfare and development: Some observations. *Indian Journal of Social Work, 56*(1), 73–92.

Mukhyananda, Swami. (1998). *Vedanta the science of integral reality vis-à-vis modern science*. Chennai: Vivekananda Kendra Prakashan Trust.

Mukta, P. (2000). The public face of Hindu nationalism. *Ethnic and Racial Studies, 23*(3), 442–466.

Mumukshananda, Swami. (1997). *Religion and its practice*. Calcutta: Advaita Ashrama.

Murray, M. (1980). Seeking the master: A guide to the ashrams of India. London: Neville Spearman.

Naidu, T.S. (1984). *A cultural study of a sacred complex: A case study of Tirumala Tirupati Devasthanam*. Mysore, India: University of Mysore.

Naidu, T.S. (1985). Pilgrims and pilgrimage: A case study of Tirumala Tirupati Devasthanam. In M. Jha (ed.), *Dimensions of pilgrimage* (pp. 167–183). New Delhi: Inter India.

Narayan, B. (2008). De-marginalisation and history: Dalit re-invention of the past. *South Asia Research, 28*(2), 169–184.

Naregal, V. (2000). Language and power in pre-colonial western India: Textual hierarchies, literate audiences and colonial philology. *Indian Economic and Social History Review, 37*(3), 259–294.

Narita, I. (2009). Paradoxes of consequentialism. *Journal for the Study of Religions and Ideologies, 8*(23), 36–47.

Nash, J. (2006). Mutant spiritualities in a secular age: The fasting body and the hunger for pure immanence. *Journal of Religion and Health, 45*(3), 310–327.

Neiheisel, J., Djupe, P.A., & Sokhey, A.E. (2009). Veni, vedi, disseri: Churches and the promise of democratic deliberation. *American Politics Research, 37*(4), 614–643.

Neubert, F. (2008). Indicating commitment: The notion of dépense in the study of religion and ritual. *Journal of Classical Sociology, 8*(2), 306–320.

Nivedita. (1988). *Cradle tales of Hinduism* (4th ed.). Calcutta: Advaita Ashrama.

Nussbaum, M. (2006). *Frontiers of justice: Disability, nationality, species membership*. Delhi: Oxford University Press.

Nye, M. (1995). *A place for our gods*. Richmond, UK: Curzon Press.

O'Hanlon, R. (2007). Cultural pluralism, empire and the state in Early Modern South Asia – A review essay. *Indian Economic and Social History Review, 44*(3), 363–381.

O'Shea, J. (2007). *At home in the world: Bharatanaytam on the global stage*. Middletown, CT: Wesleyan University Press.

O'Toole, T. (2003). Secularising the sacred cow: The relationship between religious reform and Hindu nationalism. In A. Copley (ed.), *Hinduism in public and private* (pp. 84–109). Delhi: Oxford University Press.

Oomen, T.K. (2004). *Nation, civil society and social movements*. New Delhi: Sage.

Orye, L. (2004). Globalisation, society and religion: From mono-metastructural theory to metatheoretical reflexivity. *Culture and Religion, 5*(3), 383–400.

Pace, E. (2006). Salvation goods, the gift economy and charismatic concern. *Social Compass, 53*(1), 49–64.

Palmer, S.J. (1988). Charisma and abdication: A study of the leadership of Bhagwan Shree Rajneesh. *Sociological Analysis, 49*(2), 119–135.

Pandya, S.P. (2012). All for faith: Profiles, engagement chronicles, and perceived implications of adherents to Indic faith-based organisations. *SAGE Open*, October–December 2012, 1–17.

Pandya, S.P. (2013a). Beneficiaries of social initiatives of Indic faith-based organisations: Profiles, service experiences, and implications. *SAGE Open*, April–June 2013, 1–13.

Pandya, S.P. (2013b). The 'social' face of the Brahmakumaris in India: Contemporary perspectives and praxis nuances. *Fieldwork in Religion, 8*(1), 50–73.

Paramanandadas, Sadhu. (1998). *Searching questions, fulfilling answers: Pramukh Swami Maharaj in interview* (compiled). Ahmedabad: Swaminarayan Aksharpith.

Parameswaran, P. (1987). *Marx and Vivekananda*. Chennai: Vivekananda Kendra Prakashan Trust.

Parameswaran, P. (2000). *The story of Vivekananda Rock memorial as told by Shri Eknathji Ranade*. Chennai: Vivekananda Kendra Prakashan Trust.

Parameswaran, P. (2004). *Karma Yoga as discussed by Swami Dayananda Saraswati*. Chennai: Vivekananda Kendra Prakashan Trust.

Parameswaran, P. (ed.). (2007). *Sri Guruji: A living example of spiritual nationalism. Vivekananda Kendra Patrika half-yearly publication*. Chennai: Vivekananda Kendra Prakashan Trust.

Paranjape, M. (2009). The third eye and two ways of (un)knowing: Gnosis, alternative modernities, and postcolonial futures. In P. Bilimoria & A.B. Irvine (eds), *Postcolonial philosophy of religion* (pp. 55–67). London: Springer Science + Business Media B.V.

Park, C. (2005). Religion as a meaning-making framework in coping with life stress. *Journal of Social Issues, 61*(4), 707–729.

Paul Chaudhary, D. (1971). *Voluntary social welfare in India*. New Delhi: Sterling Publishers.

Pedziwiatr, K. (2007). Creating new discursive arenas and influencing the policies of the state: The case of the Muslim Council of Britain. *Social Compass, 54*(2), 267–280.

Penumakka, Moses P.P. (2006). Luther and Sankara: Two ways of salvation in the Indian context. *Dialog: A Journal of Theology, 45*(3), 252–262.

Percy, M. (2000). The church in the market place: Advertising and religion in a secular age. *Journal of Contemporary Religion, 15*(1), 97–119.

Percy, M. (2005). Adventure and atrophy in a charismatic movement: Returning to the 'Toronto blessing'. *Journal of Contemporary Religion, 20*(1), 71–90.

Perlmutter, F. (1968). The effect of public funds on voluntary sectarian services. *Journal of Jewish communal Service, 45*, 312–321.

Peterson, S.M. (2009). Rational choice, religion, and the marketplace: Where does Adam Smith fit in? *Journal for the Scientific Study of Religion*, 48(1), 185–192.

Pillai, S.J. (2007). *Imperial conversations, Indo-Britons and the architecture of South India*. New Delhi: Yoda Press.

Pimpley, P.N., & Sharma, S.K. (1983). Arya Samaj and the untouchables of Punjab. *Punjab Journal of Politics, 7*(2), 45–57.

Pinney, C. (2002). A secret of their own country or how Indian nationalism made itself irrefutable. *Contributions to Indian Sociology, 36*(1&2), 113–150.

Pipes, P.F., & Ebaugh, H.R. (2002). Faith-based coalitions, social service and government funding. *Sociology of Religion, 63*(1), 49–68.

Pitulac, T., & Nastuta, S. (2007). Choosing to be stigmatized: Rational calculus in religious conversion. *Journal for Studies in Religion and Ideology, 6*(16), 80–97.

Prajapita Brahmakumari Ishwariya Vishwavidyalaya (PBIV). (1983). *Just a moment*. Mount Abu: Author.

Prajapita Brahmakumari Ishwariya Vishwavidyalaya (PBIV). (1996a). *Raja Yoga – New beginnings*. Mount Abu: Author.

Prajapita Brahmakumari Ishwariya Vishwavidyalaya (PBIV). (1996b). *Practical meditation*. Mount Abu: Author.

Prajapita Brahmakumari Ishwariya Vishwavidyalaya (PBIV). (1998). *The spiritual powers of the soul*. Mount Abu: Author.

Prajapita Brahmakumari Ishwariya Vishwavidyalaya (PBIV). (1999). *Report of the International Conference on Spiritual Wisdom for Changing Times – February 5–8, 1999*. Mount Abu: Author.

Prajapita Brahmakumari Ishwariya Vishwavidyalaya (PBIV). (2011). J. Watumull Global Hospital and Research Centre. *Jnanamrut, 46*(10), 36–40.

Prajapita Brahmakumari Ishwariya Vishwavidyalaya (PBIV). (no date) *Landmarks in the history of Prajapita Brahmakumari Ishwariya Vishwavidyalaya*. Mount Abu: Author.

Raghavachar, S.S. (1986). *New epoch of Vedanta: Ramakrishna-Vivekananda*. Bangalore: Sri Ramakrishna Ashrama.

Rajan, R.S. (2000). Introduction: Feminism and the politics of resistance. *Indian Journal of Gender Studies, 7*(2), 153–165.

Ramakrishnan, C. (2006). Ramakrishna Mission's pioneering work as a voluntary organisation: Introductory remarks on Ramakrishna Mission's contributions.

In Swami Lokeswarananda et al. (eds), *The story of Ramakrishna Mission: Swami Vivekananda's vision and fulfilment* (pp. 564–571). Kolkata: Advaita Ashrama.

Ramakrishnanda Puri. (2003). *Racing along razor's edge: Discourses on spirituality.* Amritapuri: Mata Amritanandamayi Mission Trust.

Ramaswamy, V. (1997). *Walking naked: Women, society and spirituality in South India.* Shimla, India: Indian Institute of Advanced Studies.

Ramsay, T., Manderson, L., & Smith, W. (2010). Changing a mountain into a mustard seed: Spiritual practices and responses to disaster among New York Brahma Kumaris. *Journal of Contemporary Religion, 25*(1), 89–105.

Ranade, P. (1953). *Gautami Ganga Godavari: Shree Godavari Upasani Maharaj (Mataji) yanche samagra charitra. Bhag 1 ani Bhag 2.* Sakori: Shree Upasani Kanyakumaristhana.

Ranganathananda, Swami. (2006). Swami Vivekananda – The architect of global unity. In Swami Lokeswarananda et al. (eds), *The story of Ramakrishna Mission: Swami Vivekananda's vision and fulfilment* (pp. 61–90). Kolkata: Advaita Ashrama.

Rao, M.S.A. (2004). Religion and economic development. In R. Robinson (ed.), *Sociology of religion in India* (pp. 147–184). New Delhi: Sage.

Redden, G. (2005). The new age: Towards a market model. *Journal of Contemporary Religion, 20*(2), 231–246.

Reddy, D., & Zavos, J. (2010). Temple publics: Religious institutions and the construction of contemporary Hindu Communities. *International Journal of Hindu Studies, 13*(3), 241–260.

Reese, L.A. (2004). A matter of faith: Urban congregations and economic development. *Economic Development Quarterly, 18*(1), 50–66.

Reichley, J. (2001). Faith in politics. *Journal of Policy History, 13*(1), 157–180.

Reinert, D.F., & Bloomingdale, J.R. (2000). Spiritual experience, religious orientation, and self-reported behavior. *International Journal for the Psychology of Religion, 10*(3), 173–180.

Repstad, P. (2003). The powerlessness of religious power in a pluralist society. *Social Compass, 50*(2), 161–173.

Rigopoulos, A. (1993). *The life and teachings of Sai Baba of Shirdi.* Delhi: Sri Satguru Publications.

Rigopoulus, A. (1998). *Dattatreya: The immortal guru, yogin and avatara.* Delhi: Sri Satguru Publications.

Robertson, R., & Chirico, J. (1985). Humanity, globalization, and worldwide religious resurgence: A theoretical exploration. *Sociological Analysis, 46*(3), 219–242.

Robinson, R. (ed.). (2004). *Sociology of religion in India.* New Delhi: Sage.

Rochford, E.B. (1989). Factionalism, group defection, and schism in the Hare Krishna Movement. *Journal for the Scientific Study of Religion, 28*(2), 162–179.

Rodney, S., & Parameswaran, A. (2008). Hare Krishnas in Singapore: Agency, state, and Hinduism. *Sojourn: Journal of Social Issues in Southeast Asia, 23*(1), 63–85.

Rotberg, R.I. (2012). Charisma, leadership and historiography. *Journal of Interdisciplinary History, 42*(3), 419–428.

Roy Wallis, R. (1984). *The elementary forms of the new religious life*. London: Routledge and Kegan Paul.

Roy, B.K. (1970). *Socio-political view of Vedanta*. New Delhi: People's Publishing House.

Roy, S. (2006). Ramakrishna Mission and the advancement of Indian women. In Swami Lokeswarananda et al. (eds), *The story of Ramakrishna Mission: Swami Vivekananda's vision and fulfilment* (pp. 686–694). Kolkata: Advaita Ashrama.

Royo, A.L. (2003). Classicism, post-classicism and Ranjabati Sircar's work: Redefining terms in Indian contemporary dance discourse. *South Asia Research, 23*(2), 153–169.

Rustau, H. (2003). The Hindu woman's right to sanyasa: Religious movement and the gender question: The Sri Sarada Math and the Ramakrishna Sarada Mission. In A. Copley (ed.), *Hinduism in public and private* (pp. 143–172). Delhi: Oxford University Press.

Saha, S. (2007). The movement of Bhakti along a north-west axis: Tracing the history of the Pustimarg between the sixteenth and nineteenth centuries. *International Journal of Hindu Studies, 11*(3), 299–318.

Saint-Hilare, P.B. (1963). *Sri Aurobindo - The future evolution of man: The divine life upon earth* (compiled). Pondicherry: Sri Aurobindo Ashram Publications Department.

Salamon, L.M. (1994). The rise of non-profit sector. *Foreign Affairs, 67*(4), 718–740.

Sanctis, S. (1927). *Religious conversion: A bio-psychological study*. London : Kegan Paul.

Sangha, D., & Sahoo, A.K. (2006). Social work, spirituality, and diasporic communities. *Journal of Religion & Spirituality in Social Work: Social Thought, 24*(4), 75–88.

Sanyal, I., & Roy, K. (2007). *Sri Aurobindo and his contemporary thinkers*. Delhi: D.K. Printworld.

Sapp, C.L. (2011). Obama's interfaith service challenge: A call for a new theology of service in American higher education. *Dialog: A Journal of Theology, 50*(3), 280–288.

Saran, A.K. (1969). Hinduism in contemporary India. *Convergence, 3*(1), 3–10.

Saraswati, B. (2000). Sociology of religions. In M.S. Gore (ed.), *Third survey of research in sociology and anthropology* (pp. 165–93). Delhi: ICSSR.

Sartori, A. (2003). The categorical logic of a colonial nationalism: Swadeshi Bengal, 1904–1908. *Comparative Studies of South Asia, Africa and the Middle East, 23*(1 & 2), 271–285.

Satpathy, C.B. (2001). *Shirdi Sai Baba and other perfect masters*. New Delhi: Sterling Publishers.

Sax, W.S. (2000). Conquering the quarters: Religion and politics in Hinduism. *International Journal of Hindu Studies, 4*(1), 39–60.

Scheifinger, H. (2009). The Jagannath temple and online darshan. *Journal of Contemporary Religion, 24*(3), 277–290.

Schjoedt, U., Stødkilde-Jørgensen, H., Geertz, A.W., Lund, T.E., & Roepstorff, A. (2011). The power of charisma – Perceived charisma inhibits the frontal executive network of believers in intercessory prayer. *SCAN, 6*(1), 119–127.

Schrader-Frechette, K.S., & McCoy, E.D. (1993). *Method in ecology*. Cambridge: Cambridge University Press.

Sears, T.I. (2009). Fortified mahals and fortress mosques: The transformation and reuse of Hindu monastic sites in the thirteenth and fourteenth centuries. *Archives of Asian Art, 59*(1), 7–31.

Sen, A. (2010). Architecture and world making: Production of sacred space in San Francisco's Vedanta temple. *South Asian History and Culture, 2*(1), 76–102.

Sen, S. (1998). Religion, relief, rehabilitation: Landmarks in the development of voluntary organisations in India. *Humanscape, 5*(5), 27–30.

Sethi, M. (2002). Avenging angels and nurturing mothers: Women in Hindu nationalism. *Economic and Political Weekly*, April 20, 1545–1552.

Shah, A.M. (2006). Sects and Hindu social structure. *Contributions to Indian Sociology, 40*(2), 209–248.

Sherazi, B. (2001). Integral psychology: Metaphors and processes of personal integration. In M. Cornelissen (ed.), *Consciousness and its transformation: Papers presented at the Second International Conference on Integral Psychology* (pp. 29–53) Pondicherry: Sri Aurobindo International Centre for Education and Sri Aurobindo Ashram.

Shraddhavan. (2001). Savitri: A key to Sri Aurobindo's psycho-cosmology. In M. Cornelissen (ed.), *Consciousness and its transformation: Papers presented at the Second International Conference on Integral Psychology* (pp. 54–64). Pondicherry: Sri Aurobindo International Centre for Education and Sri Aurobindo Ashram.

Sider, R.J., & Unruh, H.R. (2004). Typology of religious characteristics of social service and educational organisations and programs. *Nonprofit and Voluntary Sector Quarterly, 33*(1), 109–134.

Simpson, J. (2003). Faith and hermeneutics: Pragmatism versus pragmatism. *Journal of Medieval and Early Modern Studies, 33*(2), 215–239.

Singer, M. (1956). Religion and social change in India – Max Weber Phase 3. *Economic Development and Cultural Change, 14*, 13–28.

Singh, L. (2007). Retrieving voices from the margins: The courtesan and the nation's narrative. *Indian Journal of Gender Studies, 14*(1), 93–116.

Singh, Y. (1973). *Modernisation of Indian tradition: A systematic study of social change*. Delhi: Thompson Press.

Singleton, J. (2010). Malignant faith and cognitive restructuring: Realism in Adam Bede. *Victorian Literature and Culture, 39*(2), 239–260.

Smarananda, Swami. (2006). The motto of the Ramakrishna Mission – 'Atmano moksartham jagat hitaya cha'. In Swami Lokeswarananda et al. (eds), *The story of Ramakrishna Mission: Swami Vivekananda's vision and fulfilment* (pp. 917–921). Kolkata: Advaita Ashrama.

Smith, S.R., & Lipsky, M. (1993). *Non-profits for hire: The welfare state in the age of contracting*. Cambridge, MA: Harvard University Press.

Snell, R. (2005). Introduction: The study of pre-modern Hindi literature. *South Asia Research, 25*(1), 5–11.

Spivak, G.C. (2001). Moving devi. *Cultural Critique, 47*(Winter), 120–163.

Squarcini, F. (2000). In search of identity within the Hare Krishna Movement: Memory oblivion and thought style. *Social Compass, 47*(2), 253–271.

Squarcini, F. (2002). 'Power of mysticism; and 'mysticism of power': Understanding the socio-political history of a neo Hindu movement. *Social Compass, 49*(3), 343–364.

Sri Aurobindo Ashram. (1956). *Sri Aurobindo and the Mother on education*. Pondicherry: Sri Aurobindo Ashram Publications Department.

Sri Aurobindo Ashram Archives and Research Library. (1993). *The Integral Yoga: Sri Aurobindo's teaching and method of practice*. Pondicherry: Sri Aurobindo Ashram Publications Department.

Sri Aurobindo Ashram Trust. (1965). *Sri Aurobindo – On nationalism*. Pondicherry: Sri Aurobindo Ashram Publications Department.

Sri Aurobindo Society. (1978). *On women: Compilation from the writings of Sri Aurobindo and the Mother*. Pondicherry: Author.

Sri Aurobindo Society. (1994). *The teachings of Sri Aurobindo and the one aim of his yoga*. Pondicherry: Author.

Sri Aurobindo Society. (1997). *An introduction to true spirituality*. Pondicherry: Author.

Sri Aurobindo Society. (1998b). *The divine grace. Words of Sri Aurobindo and the Mother*. Pondicherry: Author.

Sri Aurobindo Society. (1999a). *Flowers: The smile of the divine*. Pondicherry: Author.

Sri Aurobindo Society. (1999b). *Mystery of life: Words of Sri Aurobindo and the Mother*. Pondicherry: Author.

Sri Aurobindo Society. (2010). *Towards tomorrow: An introductory booklet*. Puducherry: Author.

Sri Sri Publications Trust. (2003). *Narada Bhakthi Sutras – The aphorisms of love: A discourse by H.H. Sri Sri Ravi Shankar*. Bangalore: Author.

Sri Sri Publications Trust. (2005). *Secrets of relationships: Talks by H.H. Sri Sri Ravi Shankar*. Bangalore: Author.

Sri Sri Publications Trust. (2006). *Power of love: Talks by H.H. Sri Sri Ravi Shankar*. Bangalore: Author.

Sri Sri Publications Trust. (2007a). *Spirituality: Talks by H.H. Sri Sri Ravi Shankar*. Bangalore: Author.

Sri Sri Publications Trust. (2007b). *Mind matters: Talks by H.H. Sri Sri Ravi Shankar*. Bangalore: Author.

Sri Sri Publications Trust. (2008a). *Wisdom for the new millennium: Excerpts from talks by H.H. Sri Sri Ravi Shankar*. Bangalore: Author.

Sri Sri Publications Trust. (2009). *Punarnava – new again: Talks by H.H. Sri Sri Ravi Shankar*. Bangalore: Author.

Sri Sri Publications Trust. (2010a). *Ayurveda and breath: A discourse by H.H. Sri Sri Ravi Shankar*. Bangalore: Author.

Sri Sri Publications Trust. (2010b). *Waves of emotions: Talks by H.H. Sri Sri Ravi Shankar*. Bangalore: Author.

Sri Sri Publications Trust. (2010c). *An intimate note to the sincere seeker: Daily knowledge sutras*. Bangalore: Author.

Srinivas S. (2008). *In the presence of Sai Baba: Body, city, and memory in a global religious movement*. Leiden, the Netherlands: Brill Academic Publishers.

Srinivas, M.N. (1966). *Social change in modern India*. Berkeley: University of California Press.

Srinivas, S. (1999a). Sai Baba: The double utilisation of written and oral traditions in a modern South Asian religious movement. *Diogenes, 47*(3), 88–99.

Srinivas, S. (1999b). The brahmin and the fakir: Suburban religiosity in the cult of Shirdi Sai baba. *Journal of Contemporary Religion, 14*(2), 245–261.

Srinivas, S. (2008). *In the presence of Sai Baba: Body, city and memory in a global religious movement*. London; Leiden Brill.

Srinivas, T. (2010a). Building faith: Religious pluralism, pedagogical urbanism, and governance in the Sathya Sai Sacred City. *International Journal of Hindu Studies, 13*(3), 301–36.

Srinivas, T. (2010b). *Winged faith: Rethinking globalization and religious pluralism through the Sathya Sai movement*. New York: Columbia University Press.

Srinivas, T. (2012). Relics of faith: Fleshly desires, ascetic disciplines and devotional affect in the transnational Sathya Sai Movement. In B. Turner (ed.), *Routledge handbook of body studies* (pp. 121–143). London: Routledge.

Srinivasan, M.S. (2010). Social service, philanthropy and spirituality. *Sri Aurobindo's Action, 11*(4), 23–34.

Stark, W. (1964). *The routinisation of charisma: A consideration of Catholicism*. Lecture delivered at the meeting of the Metropolitan New York Chapter of the American Catholic Sociological Society, October 1964.

Stein, B. (1960). The economic functions of a medieval South Indian Temple. *Journal of Asian Studies, 19*(2), 163–176.

Steiner, S. (2011). Religious soft power as accountability mechanism for power in world politics: The Interfaith Leaders' Summit(s). *Sage Open*, 1–16.

Stolz, J. (2006). Salvation goods and religious markets: Integrating rational choice and Weberian perspectives. *Social Compass, 53*(1), 13–32.

Streib, H. (2001). Faith development theory revisited: The religious styles perspective. *International Journal for the Psychology of Religion, 11*(3), 143–158.

Streib, H. (2005). Theory: Faith development research revisited: Accounting for diversity in structure, content, and narrativity of faith. *International Journal for the Psychology of Religion, 15*(2), 99–121.

Stritt, S.B. (2008). Estimating the value of the social services provided by faith-based organisations in the United States. *Nonprofit and Voluntary Sector Quarterly, 37*(4), 730–742.

Sullivan, B.M. (1975). *The place of the spiritual master: A study of the International Society of Krishna Consciousness*. MA Thesis, Trinity University, San Antonio, TX.

Sullivan, B.M. (2000). Theology and ecology at the birthplace of Krsna. In L. Nelson (ed.), *Purifying the earthly body of god: Religion and ecology in Hindu India* (pp. 56–78). Delhi: D.K. Printworld.

Sunderasan, V. (2000). Conflicting hagiographies and history: The place of Śaṅkaravijaya texts in Advaita tradition. *International Journal of Hindu Studies, 4*(2), 109–184.

Sutherland, S., Holden, L., Clarke, P., & Hardy, F. (eds). (1988). *The world's religions*. London: Routledge.

Sutton, M.Y., & Parks, C.P. (2011). HIV/AIDS prevention, faith, and spirituality among Black/African American and Latino communities in the United States: Strengthening scientific faith-based efforts to shift the course of the epidemic and reduce HIV-related health disparities. *Journal of Religion and Health*, published online 2011, Springer Media + Business Science, LLC.

Swatos, W.H., Jr. (1981). The disenchantment of charisma: A Weberian assessment of revolution in a rationalised world. *Sociological Analysis, 42*(2), 119–136.

Swayamprakashdas, Sadhu. (ed.). (2008). *Swaminarayan bliss – Swaminarayan Sanstha centenary celebrations*. Special Issue – January-February 31(1–2). Ahmedabad: Swaminarayan Aksharpith.

Tapasyananda, Swami. (1995). *Ramakrishna Math and Mission*. Madras: Sri Ramakrishna Math.

Tarde, G. (1903). *The laws of imitation* (trans. E.C. Parsons). New York: Henry Holt.

Tathagatananada, Swami. (2010). *Celebrating Sri Ramakrishna: Essays for the 175th birth anniversary of Sri Ramakrishna*. New York: Vedanta Society.

Taylor, D. (1987). Charismatic authority in the Sathya Sai Baba Movement In R. Burghart (ed.), *Hinduism in Great Britain: The perpetuation of religion in an alien cultural milieu* (pp. 182–199). London: Tavistock.

Taylor, M. (2008). What enables canonical literature to function as 'True'? The case of the Hindu Puranas. *International Journal of Hindu Studies, 12*(3), 309–328.

Tejomayananada, Swami. (1998). *Manah Sodhanam*. Mumbai: Central Chinmaya Mission Trust.

Tejomayananda, Swami. (1995). *Jnanasarah – The essence of knowledge*. Mumbai: Central Chinmaya Mission Trust.

Tejomayananda, Swami. (1997). *Dhyanaswarupam*. Mumbai: Central Chinmaya Mission Trust.

Tejomayananda, Swami. (2001). *Towards greater success*. Mumbai: Central Chinmaya Mission Trust.

Thapan, A.R. (2005). *The Penguin Swami Chinmayananda reader*. New Delhi: Penguin Books.

Thomas, S., & Jaisinghani, B. (2012). HC dissolves Shirdi Temple Trust, *Times of India*, Wednesday, March 14.

Til, J. Van & Ross, S.W. (2001). Looking backward: Twentieth-century themes in charity, voluntarism, and the third sector. *Nonprofit and Voluntary Sector Quarterly*, *30*(1), 112–129.

Tilson, D.J., & Venkateswaran, A. (2006). Toward a covenantal model of public relations: Hindu faith communities and devotional–promotional communication. *Journal of Media and Religion*, *5*(2), 111–133.

Todres, L.A. (2000). Embracing ambiguity: Transpersonal development and the phenomenological tradition. *Journal of Religion and Health*, *39*(3), 227–238.

Trivedi, M. (1999). Tradition and transition: The performing arts in medieval North India. *The Medieval History Journal*, 2(1), 73–109.

Trompf, G.W. (2000). Millenarism: History, sociology, and cross-cultural analysis. *The Journal of Religious History*, *24*(1), 103–124.

Turner, H. (1987). *The structure of sociological theory*. Jaipur, Rajasthan, India: Rawat Publications.

Tweed, T.A. (2006). *Crossing and dwelling: A theory of religion*. Cambridge, MA: Harvard University Press.

Twombly, E.C. (2002). Religious versus secular human service organisations: Implications for public policy. *Social Science Quarterly*, *83*(4), 947–961.

Tyagananda, Swami. (2006). Ramakrishna Mission – A spiritual organisation. In Swami Atmapriyananda (compiled and edited) *Ramakrishna Mission: A saga of service for a hundred years and more* (pp. 195–202). Belur Math: Ramakrishna Mission.

Unruh, H., & Sider, R. (2001). *Religious elements of faith-based social service programs: Types and integrative strategies*. Annual meeting of the Society for the Scientific Study of Religion, Columbus, OH.

Upadhyay, S.B. (2002). Representing the underdogs: Dalits in the literature of Premchand. *Studies in History*, *18*(1), 51–79.

Vaidyanathan, B., Smith, C., & Hill, J.P. (2011). Religion and charitable financial giving to religious and secular causes: Does political ideology matter? *Journal for the Scientific Study of Religion*, *50*(3), 450–469.

Valpey, K. (2010). Found in translation: Revisiting the Bhagavad-gītā in the twenty-first century – A review article. *The Journal of Hindu Studies*, 2(2), 258–269.

van der Veer, P. (2002). Transnational religion: Hindu and Muslim movements. *Global Networks*, 2, 95–109.

van der Veer, P. (2007). Global breathing: Religious utopias in India and China. *Anthropological Theory*, *7*(3), 315–328.

Vanderwoerd, J.R. (2004). How faith-based social service organisations manage secular pressures associated with government funding. *Nonprofit Management and Leadership*, *14*(3), 237–262.

Vasudeo, G. (1998). *This sacred earth*. Kanyakumari: Vivekananda Kendra–NARDEP.

Venugopal, C.N. (2004). Foreword. In R. Robinson (ed.), *Sociology of religion in India* (pp. ii–viii). New Delhi: Sage.

Vertovec, S. (1997). Three meanings of 'Diaspora', exemplified among South Asian religions. *Diaspora*, *6*(3), 277–299.

Vertovec S. (2000). *The Hindu diaspora: Comparative patterns*. London: Routledge.

Vijay. (1978). *Seeds of light* (compiled). Pondicherry: Sri Aurobindo Society.

Vijay. (1984). *Light. Endless light* (compiled). Pondicherry: Sri Aurobindo Society.

Vijay (ed.). (1981). *Whispers of nature*. Pondicherry: Sri Aurobindo Society.

Vivekananda Kendra Prakashan. (1963). *Swami Vivekananda's rousing call to the Hindu nation: Compiled by Eknathji Ranade*. Chennai: Vivekananda Kendra Prakashan Trust.

Vivekananda Kendra Prakashan. (1992). *Impact of Swami Vivekananda on society and the individuals*. Chennai: Vivekananda Kendra Prakashan.

Vivekananda, Swami. (1985). *Shiksha* (26th ed.). Nagpur, Maharashtra, India: Ramakrishna Math.

Viveksagardas, Sadhu. (1977). *Kishore Satsang Pravesh*. Ahmedabad: Swaminarayan Aksharpith.

Vries, H. de & Sullivan, E. (2007). *Political theologies: Public religions in a post-secular world*. Delhi: Social Science Press and Orient Longman Private Ltd.

Vyakti Vikas Kendra. (2005a). *Source of life: A compilation of talks by H.H. Sri Sri Ravi Shankar*. Bangalore: Author.

Vyakti Vikas Kendra. (2005b). *Spirit of inquiry: Talks by H.H. Sri Sri Ravi Shankar*. Bangalore: Sri Sri Publications Trust.

Vyakti Vikas Kendra. (2006a). *The space within: Talks on meditation by H.H. Sri Sri Ravi Shankar*. Bangalore: Author.

Vyakti Vikas Kendra. (2006b). *Buddha – The manifestation of silence*. Bangalore: Author.

Wagner, A. (2008). Religion and civil society: A critical reappraisal of America's civic engagement debate. *Nonprofit and Voluntary Sector Quarterly*, *37*(4), 626–645.

Wall, J. (2001). The economy of the gift: Paul Ricoeur's significance for theological ethics. *Journal of Religious Ethics*, *29*(2), 235–260.

Walliss, J. (2001). The problem of tradition in the work of Anthony Giddens. *Culture and Religion*, *2*(1), 81–98.

Walliss, J. (2007). *The Brahmakumaris as a reflexive tradition: Responding to late modernity*. Delhi: Motilal Banarasidass.

Walters, S. (2006). Ramakrishna Movement and a new orientation to family life. In Swami Lokeswarananda et al. (eds), *The story of Ramakrishna Mission: Swami Vivekananda's vision and fulfilment* (pp. 703–710). Kolkata: Advaita Ashrama.

Wardell, D.W., & Engebretson, J.C. (2006). Taxonomy of spiritual experiences. *Journal of Religion and Health, 45*(2), 215–233.

Warren, M. (2004). *Unravelling the enigma: Shirdi Sai Baba in the light of Sufism*. New Delhi: Sterling Publishers.

Warren, M.R. (2009). Community organizing in Britain: The political engagement of faith-based social capital. *City and Community, 8*(2), 99–127.

Warrier, M. (2003). The *Seva* ethic and the spirit of institution building in the Mata Amritanandamayi Mission. In A. Copley (ed.), *Hinduism in public and private* (pp. 254–289). Delhi: Oxford University Press.

Warrier, M. (2006). Modernity and its imbalances: Constructing modern selfhood in the Mata Amritanandamayi Mission, *Religion, 36*(4), 179–195.

Webb, B., Bopp, M., & Fallon, E.A. (2011). A qualitative study of faith leaders' perceptions of health and wellness. *Journal of Religion and Health,* Springer Science+Business Media LLC, 2011.

Weisbrod, B.A. (1998). Institutional form and organisational behavior. In W.W. Powell & E.S. Clemens (eds), *Private action and the public good* (pp. 69–84). New Haven, CT: Yale University Press.

White, L.J. (1992). The Sai Baba movement: Approaches in the study of Indian saints. *The Journal of Asian Studies, 31*(4), 863–878.

Williams, R.B. (1984/2001). *A new face of Hinduism: The Swaminarayan religion* (1e, 2e Revised). Cambridge: Cambridge University Press.

Williamson, L. (2010). Transcendent in America: Hindu-Inspired Meditation Movements as new religion. *Journal of Hindu Studies, 3*(3), 381–384.

Wills, J., Datta, K., Evans, Y., Herbert, J., May, J., & McIlwaine, C. (2009). Religion at work: The role of faith-based organisations in the London living wage campaign, Cambridge Journal of Regions. *Economy and Society, 2*(3), 443–461.

Wilson, C.E. (2008). Faith-based motivation and leader development: International service experiences as catalyst for moral development and cultural intelligence. *Culture and Religion, 9*(3), 287–300.

Wilson, E. (2011). Much to be proud of, much to be done: Faith-based organisations and the politics of asylum in Australia. *Journal of Refugee Studies, 24*(3), 548–564.

Winchester, D. (2008). Embodying the faith: Religious practice and the making of a Muslim moral habitus. *Social Forces, 86*(4), 1753–1780.

Wood, M. (2010). Jalaram Bapa: The public expression of regional vernacular tradition among Gujarati Hindus in the UK. *Journal of Hindu Studies, 3*(3), 238–257.

Wuthnow, R. (2000). How religious groups promote forgiving: A national study. *Journal for the Scientific Study of Religion, 39*, 125–139.

Yildirim, E. (2010). Return of the spirit and demise of politics. *Journal for the Study of Religions and Ideologies, 9*(27), 107–131.

York, M. (2001). New age commodification and appropriation of spirituality. *Journal of Contemporary Religion, 16*(3), 361–372.

Zaidman, N. (1997). When the deities are asleep: Processes of change in an American Hare Krishna temple. *Journal of Contemporary Religion,* 12(3), 335–352.

Zaidman, N. (2000). The integration of Indian immigrants to temples run by North Americans. *Social Compass, 47*(2), 205–219.

Zaidman, N. (2003). Commercialisation of religious objects: A comparison between traditional and new age religions. *Social Compass, 50*(3), 345–360.

Zaidman, N. (2007). New age products in local and global contexts. *Culture and Religion, 8*(3), 255–270.

Zavos, J. (1999). Searching for Hindu nationalism in Modern Indian history: Analysis of some early ideological developments. *Economic and Political Weekly,* August 7, 2269–2276.

Zavos, J. (2000). *The emergence of Hindu nationalism in India.* Delhi: Oxford University Press.

Zavos, J. (2001). Defending Hindu tradition: *Sanatana dharma* as a symbol of orthodoxy in colonial India. *Religion, 31*(2), 109–123.

Zavos, J. (2010). Situating Hindu nationalism in the UK: Vishwa Hindu Parishad and the development of British Hindu identity. *Commonwealth & Comparative Politics, 48*(1), 2–22.

Zavos, J. (2012). Public Hinduisms: An introduction. In J. Zavos, P. Kanungo, D. Reddy, M. Warrier, & R. Williams (eds), *Researching public Hinduisms* (pp. 2–29). London: Sage.

Index

Abeysekara, A. 239
Adamut, A. 245
Adiswarananda, Swami 106, 120, 131, 192, 194
Advaita Ashrama 40, 56, 105, 115, 124, 194
Agency v, vii, 5, 7–8, 13, 15, 18, 21, 59, 61, 66, 71, 77, 86, 114, 155, 218, 237, 242, 247
Aksharjivandas, Sadhu 121
Alain, G. 135
Alan and Tim 135
Allahyari, R. A. 16
Amarasingam, A. 213, 214
Amritaswarupananda, Puri 45, 116, 137
Amrutvijaydas, Sadhu 119, 121, 132
Appadurai, A. 13
Appadurai, A., & Breckenridge, C. A. 6
Appleton, N. 60
application questions 103
Arif, Y. 24, 165
armies of compassion 165
Art of Living 13, 26, 29, 39, 45, 47, 58–59, 62, 70–71, 77–78, 84–85, 90, 95, 99, 102, 105, 107, 116, 119, 125–126, 139, 146, 154, 158–159, 161, 163, 171, 173, 181, 187, 189, 192, 194, 198–200, 206, 211–212, 219, 223, 225–226, 233
Ascription 72–75, 77
Ashcraft, M. W. 47
Ashenden, S. & Owen, D. 70
Assimilative v–vi, 12, 14, 66, 80, 100, 104, 159, 167, 176, 185, 203, 215, 221

Babb, L. A. 10, 18
Bacchetta, P. 24
Bahuguna, R. P. 7
Barad, J. 245
Barker, E. 245
Barlingay, S. S. 6
Barrett, R. 17–18
Basu, A. 24
Basu, S. 76, 180, 185, 189
Basu, S., & Banerjee, S. 17, 174
Bauman, C. 12
Baxi, U. 8
Beckerlegge, G. 2, 3, 10, 12–13, 15, 22–24, 61, 87, 126
Bellin, E. 21, 44, 77
Belur Math 27, 36, 40, 99, 120, 162, 175, 202, 206, 219, 225, 227, 231
Berger, J. 1
Bhajananda, Swami 118

Bhakti
  Bhakti movement 7
  Bhakti studies 7
Bharucha, R. 24
Bhatt, C. 177
Bhattacharya, R. 7
Bhavani & Elia 113
Bhawuk, D. P. S. 6
Bhide, N. R. 44
Bhuteshananda, Swami 50
Biebricher, T. 142
Black, D. M. 214
Blanke, S. 21, 72
Bochasanwasi Shree Akshar Purushottam Swaminarayan Sanstha (BAPS) 26
body consciousness 13, 52, 97, 106, 110, 111, 118, 123, 132, 145, 160, 169, 208
Body-Mind-Intellect Chart (BMI chart) 53, 164, 188
Bolter, J. D. & Grusin, R. 87
Bourdieu 155–156
Bowman, W. 11
Bradley, T. 14, 24, 165,
Brahmakumaris 10, 12, 26, 28–29, 36, 41–43, 46, 52, 66–68, 70, 74, 81–82, 88–89, 94, 97, 100–101, 104, 106, 110, 119, 122, 130, 133, 144, 148, 152, 157, 159–160, 162–163, 167, 169, 172, 176–177, 183–186, 188, 192–193, 196, 199–200, 203, 207, 216–217, 221, 225, 227, 232.
Brajranjan, M. 7
brand building 21, 65, 69, 78–80, 82
brand creations vi, 14, 59
Bratosin, S. & Ionescu, M.A. 24
Brooks, C. K. 10
Brown, L. 6
Brown, M. C. 48
Bunn, C., & Wood, M. 5
Burghart, R. 12
Campbell, D., & Glunt, E. 4
Carp, R. 25, 226,
Carr, W. 214
Carroll, M.M. 147
Cartagenas, A. L. 241
Casolari, M. 17
Cause collaborators 20, 39–40, 45
Central Chinmaya Mission Trust 44, 193
Chakrabarti, M. 8
Chakrabarti, R. 7
Chakravarthi, R. 14, 48
Chandra, S. 7
Chapman, R., & Lowndes, V. 4
charisma
  charisma domination 33
  charisma engagements 20
Charismatic gift 34, 143
  charismatization 33
Charitable Choice Reform 1
Chaubey, A. S. 7
Chaudhari, B. 6
Chaves, M. 4
Chinmaya Mission 12, 26–28, 29, 36, 43–44, 46, 53, 54, 59, 68–70, 75, 82, 89, 94, 97, 101, 104, 106, 111, 119, 123, 134, 145, 149, 158–160, 163, 169–170, 172, 174, 177, 187–188, 193, 197, 204, 208, 217, 221, 226, 228, 232
Chinmayananda, Swami 2, 36–37, 43–44, 53–54, 68–69, 75, 101, 106, 123, 134, 149, 158, 177, 183, 188, 204, 217, 232
choice 21, 77, 90, 110, 135, 142, 202, 215, 220, 226
Ciotti, M. 7
civil society v, viii, 1–5, 9, 16, 19, 21–24, 30–31, 65, 69, 72, 77, 87–88, 90, 105, 143, 156, 164, 215, 225, 227, 229

Civil Society xi, 21, 65, 67, 69, 71, 79, 81, 83, 85, 87, 89, 91
Clanton, J. C. & Gunter, J. 248
Clarke, G. 25
Cloke, P., Williams, A., & Thomas, S. 5
Clothey, F. W. 6
Clubbiness 11, 15
Cnaan, R. A. 4, 248
Cnaan, R. A., Boddie, S. C., & Danzig, R. A. 4, 248
Cohen, L. 18
Cojocaru, D., Cojocaru, S., & Sandu, A. 117
Coleman, S. 34, 143
Collins, P. J. 231
colonial vii, 8–9, 14, 17, 22, 26, 36, 40, 72–73, 95, 117–118, 169, 174, 175, 185, 217, 242, 244
colonial nativist continuum 117
colonization of lifeworld 115
Colpe, C. 25
commodification 21, 65, 79–84, 86, 243
communalism 24, 171–173, 182, 187
communicatio idiomatum 127
Communicative action 107, 237
Communicative rationality 70
communitarian notions 164
community development 126, 164
Constable, P. 7
Contact zones 70, 187
contingency 21, 77, 228
Cook, The Reverend Ces' 23
Copeman, J. 13, 18
Copeman, J. & Ikegame, A. 16–18, 223
Copley, A. 3, 19
Correlational 246
Cortright, B. 209
Covenantal model of public relations 91
Crisp, B. R. 248
Critical subjectivism 236
Crnic, A. 9, 20
Crowe, B. 22, 236
cultural habitus 25, 83, 191, 201

Dada Lekhraj 28, 36, 41–43, 52, 74, 157
Dalal, A.S. 55, 197, 208
Dalmiya, V. 22, 34, 103
dana 6, 9, 15, 123, 144, 148, 158, 159
Das, T. K. & Datta Ray, I. 85
Dave S. & Sahoo, A.K. 248
Dave, H.T. 41, 185
De Nys, M. J. 237
Delphy, C. 110
DeNapoli, A. 8
Desktop spiritual cultures 87
deterritorialized global culture 130
development literature 4, 8, 16
development literature and economic development 8, 136,
development literature, Hindu ideals and economic development 8
Dhar, S. 120
Diaspora consciousness 71
Diesel, A. 34
Difference vi, 7, 14, 17, 22, 40, 42, 46, 52, 74, 102, 112, 114, 125, 149, 162, 168, 172, 175, 182, 186, 235, 242, 245
Digitality 87
Dinham, A. 4
Dinham, A., & Lowndes, V. 4
disaster relief and rehab operations 77, 138
Discourse ethics 245
Distinctiveness 93, 221, 244
Divatia, S. C. 6
doctrinarism 144, 149, 151, 154
Doers of service 15

Dowsett, N. J. & Jayaswal, S. 112
Dube, S. C. 8
Dutta, A. 7

Ebaugh, H. R., Pipes, P.F., Chafetz, J.S., & Daniels, M. 23–24
ecology 93, 112–116, 136
Education
 educational services 137
Eikenberry, A. M. 143
Eknath Ranade 28, 39, 44, 56, 98, 124–125, 136, 154, 180
Emancipatory cognitive interests 236, 239
Embodiment testimonies 34
Emir, R. 101
Emplacing 165
environmental initiatives 138
ethical subjectivity 103
exchange 110, 122, 127, 130, 141, 143, 156, 187, 204, 215, 220, 246–247
existential-social 25, 191, 201, 206–209, 213–214
experiential realism 127
extrinsic religiosity 143

faith iii, v, vii, viii, xi, 1–2, 4–5, 8–14, 16, 17–26
faith active in love 155
faith movements iii, v, xi, 2, 65
Faith narrative 117, 238, 240
faith-based organisations 85
 faith-based social service 4, 12, 30, 216, 248
faith-coded biopolitics 24, 165
Faith-inspired epistemocentrism 237
Faith-oriented frame of reference 224–225
Familism 118, 173, 182, 192, 200
Faubion, J. D. 18
Female sadhus 7
Ferguson, K., Wu, M., Qiaobing, Sprujit-Metz, D. & Dyrness, G. 4
Field Work vii, 29, 30
Flanagan, K. 155
Fowler, J. W. 241–242
framework questions 103
Freitag, S. 7
Fridolfsson, C., Elander, I., Granberg, M., & Amma, E. 4
Friedrichs, J., & Klockner, J. 4

Gandhi, K. 73, 105, 115, 132, 136, 198
Genealogy 154, 164, 238–239
Genesis 20, 26, 35–36, 38–40, 46–47, 129, 131, 133, 135, 137, 139
Genres 31, 191, 215, 217–219
Ghosh, S. 94, 131, 179
Ghosh, Sri Aurobindo 28, 38, 75
Global political economy 21, 65, 68–71, 78
Global spiritual marketplace 86
Glocalization 86–87
Goldman, M. S. 240
Govekar, P. L., & Govekar, M. A. 16
Grau, A. 6
Greene, T. & Hudson, H.H. 125
Grieve, G. P. 34
Gronbjerg, K. A. 4
Gronbjerg, K. A., & Nelson, S. 4
Grube, J., & Piliavin, J. A. 16
Guerrlero, S 9, 20
Gupta, D. 10, 12, 16, 18, 36
Gupta, K. P. 20
guru i, iii, v–viii, xi, 1–10
guru agency xi, 33, 35, 37, 39, 41, 43, 45, 47, 49, 51, 53, 55, 57, 59, 61, 63
Guru fetishism 237
Guthrie, T. & Stickley, T. 213
Göcmen, I. 5

Habermas vi, 13, 22, 70, 249

Habitus 25, 66, 83, 155, 156, 191, 201, 216, 218, 219, 223, 237, 248
Hannah Arendt 22
Harden, M. G. 19
Hardgrove, A. 7
Hare Krishna Movement 9, 15
Harris, M., Hutchison, R., & Cairns, B. 4
Hassija, J. C. BK. 52, 106, 111, 119, 122, 133
Hatcher, B. 14, 22, 95, 247
Health 4, 10, 16, 26, 67–68, 77, 89–90, 93, 108, 110–112, 116
Heehs, P. 3
Hefferan, T. 23
Hegemony v–vi, xi, 1, 3, 5, 7, 9, 11, 13, 15, 17, 19, 21, 23–25, 27, 29–31, 80, 102, 109, 162–163, 165
Heilman, S.C. & Witztum, E. 25
Heinz Kohut 213
Hejduk, R. 47
Hermeneutics of hope 246
Hester, R. D. 23
HIFBST model 31, 32, 239–248
Hindu ideology vii, 17, 182
Hindu Inspired Faith Movements v, 2
Hindu Mahasabha 2, 9, 178
Hindu nationalism vi, xi, 2, 17, 24, 30, 31, 167, 174, 176–185, 187, 189, 249
    Hindu nationalism primordialist-instrumentalist version, 182
Hindu Sabha vii, 2, 17
Hindu utilitarianism 246
Hindu-inspired faith-based social service 12
Hindutva vi–vii, 3, 5, 17, 24, 75, 174, 177, 180, 183
Historicity 27, 51, 71, 82, 96, 180, 189, 222
Historiography 126, 164, 238–239
Hodge, D.R. & Boddie, S.C. 248
Hodges, S. 6
Hoecke, G Van. 15, 214
Hologram 8, 35, 46, 77, 84, 161, 194, 197
hospice and healthcare services 138
Houston, S. 249
Howe D. 249
Howell, J.D. 12, 20, 67, 247
Hula, R., Jackson-Elmoore, C., & Reese, L. 142

Ikegame, A. 16–19, 142, 223, 226
Imagined community 117, 143, 181, 183, 223
imago dei 155
Impressionism 87
Impure altruism 11, 15
incarnational theology 155
Indian psychotherapy 15, 214
Infield, L. 125
inner transformation 15, 22, 112, 126–127, 202
Institutional forms 25, 191, 224, 226
Institutionalised devotionalism 181
Institutionalization 20, 39, 79–80, 84, 202, 230
Integral Yoga 55, 59, 71, 82, 93, 105, 149–150, 158, 161, 163–164, 170, 172, 192–193, 197, 200, 208–209, 217, 230, 238, 250
Intergated Amrita Meditation technique 58–59
International expansion 62, 133
Intertextuality 48
Isaac, J. C. 23
Ishwarananda, Swami 54, 111, 123
Ishwarchandradas, Sadhu 73
ISKCON 9, 63

Jackson R. and Nesbitt E. 12
Jaffrelot, C. 182
Jain, K. 7

Jamoul, L., & Wills, J. 8, 22
Jennings, T.W. 218
Jnaneshwardas, Sadhu & Mukundcharandas, Sadhu 121
Johnston, D. & Sampson, C. 1
Jones, K. W. 9
Joshi, K. & Artaud, Y. 112

Kanungo, P. 12
Kaplan, S. 23
Kaplan, S. A., Calman, N.S., Golub, M., Ruddock, C. & Billings, J. 23
Kapp, K. W. 8
Kasturi, M. 9, 15, 21
Kennedy, M. T. 9
Kennedy, S. S., & Bielefeld, W. 4, 24, 165
Kergymatic 246
Khandelwal, M. 8, 15
Khandelwal, M., Hausner, S. L., Gold, A. G., & Hanssen, K. 8, 15
Kher, V.B. 27, 101, 110
Kim H. 12, 61
Kline, N. 23
Knepper, P. 248
Knott, K. 12
Kochuyt, T. 23
Kocsis, N. 63
Kohls, N., Walach, H. & Wirtz, M. 25
Kripal, J. J. 34
Kulkarni, D. 115, 136
Kurien, P. A. 21
Kvasmy, L., & Lee, R. 4

Lakshmi Kumari, M. 125
Lal, V. 86
Lam, P. 25
legacy of exclusion 175
legal system 23, 107, 142
Liberation theology 217, 228, 233, 243
Liminal 181, 187, 196
lived religion 141, 156
livelihood 26, 77, 108, 116, 130, 133, 137–139, 141
Lockhart, W. H. 24
Locklin, R. & Lauwers, J. 11–12, 20, 68–69, 177, 188,
love 11, 14, 46, 52–53, 55, 57–59, 70, 86, 97, 99, 100–101, 103, 105, 112, 116, 120, 123, 126, 137, 146, 151, 155, 158, 161, 171, 180, 203, 205, 211, 215, 218, 223, 228, 232, 245, 246
Lucas, P. C. 60
Lyon, D. 243
Lysenko, V., & Hulin, M. 6

MacMillen, S. 239–240
Macro social cartography 238
Madan, T.N. 2
Madsen, F. 9, 20
Mallapragada, M. 87
Marcos, S. 22
Market 11–12, 21, 24, 30–31, 59, 65, 72, 77, 78, 80, 81–87, 139, 141, 143, 159, 177, 220, 243, 247
Market model logic 85
Mastromattei, R. & Rigopoulos, A. 6
Mata Amirtanandamayi Mission 26
Matthews, C. 244
Max Weber 33
Mayaram, S. 21
McDargh, J. 242
McKean, L. 13, 159
Mclain, K. 12
McMillin, S. E. 164
Media 86–86, 142, 181, 189, 247
Mediatization of religion 86
Meduri, A. 6
Mehta, R. B. 17, 205
Memory 20, 24, 28, 30, 31, 136, 156–159, 161, 163–164, 216, 245
Meta dimensions of social transformation 196

Metamorphoses 231, 234
Micro forms of social transformation 194
Middle class 11, 43, 60
Mihut, L. 25
Millenarian 10, 42, 43, 52, 67, 75, 200, 216, 245, 250
Miller, K. D. 230
Mishra, V. 8
missionary consciousness 130
mnemonics 164
Montagne-Villette, S., Hardill, I., & Lebeau, B. 4
moral considerability 22, 103
moral weight 22, 103
Morearty, J. 20
Muir, S. 86
Mukherjee, J. K. 101
Mukhyananda, Swami 56
Mukta, P. 15
Multiculturalism 62
Mumukshananda, Swami 132
Murray, M. 23

Narayan, B. 7
Naregal, V. 7
Narita, I. 245
Nash, J. 247
Nation-state 21, 182, 243
Nationalisms 72, 175, 182–183
Neiheisel, J., R., D., Paul, A., & Sokhey, A. E. 4
Neoclassical theism 228
Network capital flows 87
Neubert, F. 9, 220
New Age
    New Age market theorizations 21, 85
New media conceptualisations 87
New-Ageification 159, 242
Nivedita 179
normative-ideatioal frame 79–80, 160, 169, 202
Nussbaum, M. 8
Nye, M. 12

O'Hanlon, R. 7
O'Shea, J. 6
O'Toole, T. 3
Oblivion vii, 5, 17, 18, 24, 30, 31, 156–159, 161, 164
Online prescence 21, 86
organisational memory 156–158
Oriental 72, 83, 102, 161, 163, 179
Orthodox v, vi, 7, 9, 12, 13, 174, 185, 214
Orye, L. 62
Osmosis 25, 31, 39, 191, 215, 219–224
Otherness 172, 238, 244, 245, 248

Pace, E. 86
Palmer, S. J. 33
Pandya, S. P. 15, 16, 27, 60, 227
Paramanandadas, Sadhu 121
Parameswaran, P. 21, 44, 107, 119, 153, 180, 198
Paranjape, M. 14, 48, 244
Park, C. 23, 248
Parochialism-hegemony 238, 242
Peace vii, 5–6, 13, 18, 46, 51–52, 57–58, 67, 70, 73, 82–85, 90, 106, 119, 121, 133, 140, 148, 164, 176–178, 194, 196, 198, 203, 209, 227–228
Pedziwiatr, K. 78
Penumakka, Moses P.P. 127
Percy, M. 20–21, 85
Perlmutter, F. 4
Peterson, S. M. 85
Philanthropy 6, 11, 15, 18, 23–24, 26, 80, 100, 104, 121–122, 141, 143–144, 158, 164, 195, 211, 224, 249

Philosophy vii, 10, 17, 36–37, 41–42, 48, 54, 56, 85, 94, 98, 104–105, 118, 125, 127, 144–145, 150, 152, 158, 162–163, 170, 178, 180, 183, 186–188, 193, 197, 201–202, 204, 214, 220–221, 225, 228, 232, 236, 244, 248, 249
Pilgrimage ethic 246
Pillai, S. J. 6
Pimpley, P. N., & Sharma, S. K. 9
Pinney, C. 24
Pipes, P. F. & Ebaugh, H.R. 23
Pitulac, T. & Nastuta, S. 183
Pluralist-corporatist dichotomy 229
Political capital 19, 22
Political theology 8, 233, 244
Post modern v–vi 5, 8, 13, 26, 29, 34, 59–60, 158, 217, 243, 245
Postcolonial vi, 26, 28, 118, 158, 163, 178, 185, 225–226, 233, 244
Practical cognitive interests 236
Practical spirituality 11, 51, 161, 219
Prajapita Brahmakumari Ishwariya Vishwavidyalaya (Brahmakumaris) 26, 46
Pramukh Swami 41, 50, 79, 121, 132, 133, 144, 156, 157, 160, 192
Prarthana Samaj 8
Praxis viii, 5, 8, 20, 24, 26–27, 32, 49, 53–54, 60, 94–95, 99–101, 135, 149, 160, 162–163, 165, 187, 196, 198, 225–226, 228, 232–233, 239, 247, 249
Prescription 31, 50, 66, 72–75, 77, 99, 109, 144, 147, 156, 171, 186, 207, 218, 246
Prescriptivism 144, 146–150, 155
Primordial attachments 181
Proliferation v, xi, 2, 5, 11, 21, 33–35, 39, 47, 52, 59, 60, 71, 139, 217, 239
public memory 28, 156–158
public sphere v, 8, 22, 72, 78, 94, 226, 246
Pure altruism 11

Radhasaomi 10
Raghavachar, S.S. 50
Raja Yoga 27, 43, 52, 59, 67–68, 70–71, 75, 81–82, 89, 97, 100–101, 119, 122, 123, 133–134, 148, 157, 159–160, 164, 177, 186, 188, 192, 196, 200, 203, 205, 207, 227, 230, 238, 250
Rajan, R. S. 7
Ramakrishna Mission 2, 10, 12, 14, 26–27, 29, 35, 39–40, 44–46, 49, 61, 65–66, 69–72, 78, 87, 94–95, 99, 104, 106–108, 118, 120, 131, 144, 147, 156, 158–159, 162, 167–168, 171, 174–175, 184, 187, 192, 194–195, 201, 206, 215, 219, 225–227, 231
Ramakrishnan, C. 50, 108
Ramakrishnanda Puri 57, 146
Ramaswamy, V. 7
Ramsay, T., Manderson, L. & Smith, W. 130
Ranade, P. 169
Ranganathananda, Swami 50, 125
Rao, M. S. A. 8
re-inventing government argument 143
Recipients of service 127
Redden, G. 21, 85
Reddy, D. & Zavos, J. 94
Reese, L. A. 4
Reichley, J. 24
Reinert, D. F. & Bloomingdale, J.R. 25
Relative agency 237
Religio-spiritual capital creation 87
Religious actors 86
Remediation 87
Repstad, P. 241

residential institutions for vulnerable groups 134, 138
Rigopoulos, A. 6, 148
Robertson, R. & Chirico, J. 86, 240
Robinson, R. (Ed.). 8
Rochford, E. B. 15
Rodney, S. & Parameswaran, A. 21
Rotberg, R. I. 20
Routinization 20, 47, 65, 78–80, 82–84, 161, 220–221, 226
Roy Wallis. R. 33, 43
Roy, B.K. 150, 188
Roy, S. 50
Royo, A. L. 6
Rustau, H. 3, 20

Sacral 29, 48, 158, 226, 237
Sacred 6, 8, 11, 14, 16, 23, 27–28, 47–48, 61, 80, 87, 104, 115–116, 129, 141, 152, 180, 183–184, 214, 219, 226
Sacred-secular dichotomy 218
Saha, S. 14
Sai Baba devotionalism 27
Saint-Hilare, P.B. 107, 200, 228
salvation good 21, 25, 56, 78–86, 177, 184, 187, 189, 204, 223
Sanatana dharma 9, 13, 17, 58, 162, 170, 173–179, 188
Sanatana Dharma Sabha 9
Sanctis, S. 1
Sangha, D., & Sahoo, A. K. 4
Sanyal, I & Roy, K 150, 188
Sapp, C. L. 155
Saran, A.K. 20
Saraswati, B. 8
Sartori, A. 17, 182
Sathya Sai Baba 10–11, 18, 248
Satpathy, C.B. 27
Sax W. S. 177
Scheifinger, H 86
Schjoedt, U., Stødkilde-Jørgensen, H., Geertz, A.W., Lund, T.E. & Roepstorff, A. 33
Schrader-Frechette & McCoy, E.D. 25
Sears, T. I. 25
Sectarian faith-based initiaties 224–225
Sectarianism 80
Secular vi, vii, 4, 12, 13, 17–19, 22–23, 25, 30, 66, 78, 90, 118, 127, 134, 141–142, 158–161, 163–164, 178, 183–184, 186–187, 189–191, 217–218, 224, 227, 230–231, 233, 235, 243, 247, 251
Secularisation flavours 183
Self 3, 25, 34, 52–53, 57–58, 94, 103, 111
Self-object 213–214
Self-psychology 213
    self-transcenence 57, 70
    service ideals vi, 14
    service strategies 15
Sethi, M. 168
Seva
    seva governmentalities v
    seva performativity 12
Shah, A. M. 13
Sherazi, B. 209
Shraddhavan 209
Shree Saibaba Sansthan Trust 26, 36, 66, 74
Sider, R. J. & Unruh, H.R. 19, 224
Simpson, J. 238
Singer, M. 8
Singh, L. 6
Singh, Y. 8
Singleton, J. 20
Smarananda, Swami 118
Smith, S. R., & Lipsky, M. 4
social action vii, 5, 7, 18, 30, 86, 118, 164
Social capital viii, 1, 19, 21–22, 24, 65, 88, 90, 129, 130, 142, 144, 161, 201
social citizenship 164

social consciousness 22, 31, 91, 93–94, 103–105, 109
social ethics 21, 51, 93, 99, 100–104, 160, 250–251
social issues 4, 21, 22, 23, 30, 31, 93, 106, 107, 108, 110, 111, 112, 114, 116, 118, 172, 217
Social metaphor 35, 46
social problems 106–108, 115–116
social sectors of development 130
social stratification 21, 93, 95, 97–99, 107
social transformation iii, v, vii, xi, 1, 5, 19, 25, 31, 32, 34, 47, 70, 145, 191–200, 215, 223, 231, 235, 246, 248, 249–251
Sociality v, vi, xi, 1, 5, 19, 21, 30, 31, 144, 153, 156, 164, 219, 238, 241, 250–251
Society v–viii, xi, 1–10, 14, 16, 17, 19, 21–24, 26, 28–30, 31, 37–39, 43–46, 55–56, 59
sociology of faith vii, 5
Sociology of hope 25, 191, 200
soul consciousness 13, 110, 111, 123, 144, 145, 160, 169, 196, 200, 202, 204
spiritual practice 35, 57, 79, 90, 125, 146, 199, 209
spiritual teachings 22, 126
Spiritual-material cultures 91
Spirituality vi–vii, 6, 11, 13, 26, 34–35, 44–45, 47, 51–52, 56, 58, 67–68, 83–85, 101, 105–106, 114, 118, 126, 133–135, 143–147, 151, 153–154, 160–161, 179, 181, 184, 189, 197–198, 216–217, 223–225
Spivak, G. C. 34
Squarcini, F. 9, 20
Sri Aurobindo Ashram 2, 29, 38, 150, 197
Sri Aurobindo Ashram Archives and Research Library 150
Sri Aurobindo Ashram Trust 38, 76
Sri Aurobindo Ghosh 28
Sri Aurobindo Society 26, 28–29, 37–39, 44, 46–47, 55, 59, 69–70, 71, 75, 82–83, 89 94, 98, 101, 104, 106, 112, 113, 119, 123, 135, 145, 149–150, 152, 158–159, 161, 163, 167, 170, 172, 174, 178, 184, 187–188, 192–193, 197, 199–200, 205, 208, 217–221, 222, 226, 228, 232–233.
Sri Ramakrishna Paramahansa 27
Sri Sarada Devi 50, 61, 83
Sri Sri Publications Trust 58–59, 106, 116–117, 119, 126, 146, 194, 199
Sri Ravishankar 16, 29
Srinivas S. 11, 13, 15, 18, 20, 22, 61–62, 123
Srinivas, T. 15, 18
Srinivasan, M.S. 15, 18, 61, 123
Stark, W. 20
state
State/establishment 65, 72, 77, 78, 230
state/establishment exchange 72
Stein, B. 8
Steiner, S. 234
Stolz, J. 24
Streib, H. 242
Stritt, S. B. 143
Styles 10, 72, 156, 204
subaltern approach 7
Sudarshan Kriya & Pranayama 45, 70, 212, 213
Sunderasan, V. 14, 20
Sutton, M. Y. & Parks, C.P. 23
Swami Akhandananda 131
Swami Chinamyananda 28
Swami Vivekananda 2, 27–28, 35–36, 39–40, 44, 47, 55–56, 61, 69–70, 76, 83, 98, 102–103, 114–115, 124, 131, 136, 153–154, 170, 179–180, 185, 188–189, 201

Swatos, W. H. Jr. 20
Swayamprakashdas, Sadhu 106, 133
Symbolic devotional world 61
Syncretic components 183
syncretic metaphysical
ritualization 80, 81

Tathagatananada, Swami 50
Taylor, D. 117
Taylor, M. 48
Teachings vi, xi, 14, 20, 22, 28, 30, 33, 43, 45, 48, 49–53, 55, 57–60, 79-81, 84, 90, 100, 102, 110, 126, 142, 151, 157–159, 162–165, 183, 201–202, 211
Tejomayanananda, Swami 53
temple studies 6
Thapan, A. R. 37, 43, 46
The Mother 28, 37, 39, 44–45, 50, 55, 82, 90, 135, 138, 158, 161, 205, 209, 221–222
theological justifications 6
Theory of value 236
Third sector 25, 30–31, 192, 224–225, 232–233
Thomas, S. & Jaisinghani, B. 5, 74
Til, J. Van & Ross, S.W. 25
Tilson, D. J. & Venkateswaran, A. 90
Todres, L. A. 237
Traditional tenets 3, 20, 27, 48
Trajectory 47, 172, 219, 238–240
Transcendence 12, 14, 20, 22, 43, 48, 75, 79–80, 85, 91, 95, 96, 99, 104, 110, 120, 151–152, 173, 187–188, 194–195, 201–202, 206, 211, 213–215, 217, 223, 228, 233, 235–239, 245, 247, 250
Transformational actors 30, 191, 224
Transformational acts 231
Transmuting internalizations 213
Trivedi, M. 6
Trompf, G.W. 25, 200, 201
Tweed, T. A. 68
Twombly, E. C. 24
Tyagananda, Swami 104

Unruh, H., & Sider, R. 19
Upadhyay, S. B. 7

Vaidyanathan, B., Smith, C., & Hill, J.P. 23
Valpey, K. 14, 48
van der Veer, P. 17, 20, 182
Vanderwoerd, J. R. 4
Vasudeo, G. 115, 136
Vedanta 2, 10, 14–15, 28, 36–37, 47, 50, 53–56, 58, 68–69, 71, 82, 87, 89, 93–95, 101–102, 106, 111, 113, 115, 119, 120, 123, 129, 131, 145, 149, 150, 153–154, 160–164, 168, 170–171, 177–179, 185, 187–188, 193–194, 197, 204–205, 209, 222, 226, 228–232, 238, 250
Vedanta missionary work 131
Venugopal, C. N. 2
Vertovec, S. 12, 21, 71
Vijay 113, 119
Virtuality
visions on society 22, 31, 94
Vivekananda Kendra 12, 26, 28–29, 35, 39, 44, 59, 61, 69–70, 76, 78, 83, 90, 94, 98, 102, 105, 107, 114–115, 119, 124–125, 136–137, 146, 150, 153–154, 158–159, 161, 163–164, 170, 172–174, 179–180, 187–189, 194, 197, 205, 209–210, 217, 222, 226, 228, 229, 233
Vivekananda Kendra Prakashan 115, 180
Vivekananda, Swami 2, 27–28, 35–36, 39–40, 44, 47, 55–56, 61, 69–70, 76, 83, 98, 102–103, 114–115,

124, 131, 136, 153–154, 170, 179–180, 185, 188–189, 201
Viveksagardas, Sadhu 185
Volition 30-31, 144, 146
Volunteerism 16, 159
Vries, H. de & Sullivan, E. 174, 218
Vyakti Vikas Kendra 58, 146, 199

Wagner, A. 19, 22
Wall, J. 245, 248
Walliss, J. 11–13, 42, 67, 97, 152, 157, 207, 226, 232, 248
Walters, S. 50
Wardell, D. W. & Engebretson, J.C. 247
Warren, M. 12, 27, 51, 81, 122, 168
Warren, M. R. 23
Warrier, M. 2, 3, 10, 13, 15, 22, 24, 159
Webb, B., Bopp, M., & Fallon, E.A. 25
Weisbrod, B. A. 19, 23
Williams R.B. 12
Williamson, L. 20
Wills, J., Datta, K., Evans, Y., Herbert, J., May, J. & McIlwaine, C. 8, 22, 23
Wilson, C. E. 62, 144
Wilson, E. 144
Winchester, D. 156
Wood, M. 5
World accommodation 133, 178, 232
World rejection 46, 68, 81
World tree and world cycle 157
Worldview 6, 15, 54, 95, 101, 104, 106, 115, 142, 194, 221, 228, 232–233, 236, 245, 250–251
Wuthnow, R. 4, 16, 240
Yildirim, E. 183
Yoga 27–28, 38, 55–56, 59, 71, 82, 83, 85, 93, 102, 105, 112–113, 118–119, 123–124, 130, 149, 153–154, 158, 161, 163, 170, 172–173, 187, 192–193, 197, 200, 205, 208–210, 212, 217, 230, 238, 250
York, M. 86

Zaidman, N. 20, 63, 86

956 r
09/12/17